BEN HECHT

BEN HECHT

THE MAN BEHIND THE LEGEND

◆

WILLIAM MacADAMS

CHARLES SCRIBNER'S SONS
New York

Excerpts from *A Child of the Century* by Ben Hecht, copyright © 1954, 1982 Ben Hecht Estate. Reprinted by permission of Donald I. Fine, Inc.
The quotes from Stuart Sherman, which appear on pages 54–55, 60–61, are reprinted with permission of Charles Scribner's Sons, an imprint of Macmillan Publishing Company, from *Critical Woodcuts* by Stuart Sherman. Copyright © 1926 by Charles Scribner's Sons, renewed by Mrs. Ruth Sherman.
The quote from Josef Von Sternberg's autobiography, which apears on page 104, is reprinted with permision of Macmillan Publishing Company from *Fun in a Chinese Laundry* by Josef Von Sternberg. Copyright © 1926 by Josef Von Sternberg, renewed 1965.

Charles Scribner's Sons
Macmillan Publishing Company
866 Third Avenue, New York, NY 10022
Collier Macmillan Canada, Inc.

Library of Congress Cataloging-in-Publication Data
MacAdams, William.
  Ben Hecht : the man behind the legend / William MacAdams.
    p.   cm.
  Filmography: p.
  Bibliography: p.
  Includes index.
  ISBN 0-684-18980-1
  1. Hecht, Ben, 1893–1964—Biography.   2. Authors, American—20th century—Biography.   I. Title.
PS3515.E18Z75 1990
818'.5209–dc19   [B]   88-19046   CIP

Macmillan books are available at special discounts for bulk purchases for sales promotions, premiums, fund-raising, or educational use. For details, contact:

Special Sales Director
Macmillan Publishing Company
866 Third Avenue
New York, NY 10022

10 9 8 7 6 5 4 3 2 1

Printed in the United States of America

For Gertrude Stout,
Lynn Walcutt,
and Paul Nelson

CONTENTS

Contents

ACKNOWLEDGMENTS

With sincerest thanks for their help: John Coleman-Holmes, C. T. Fuller, Rose Caylor Hecht, Will Fowler, Howard Hawks, John Ford, Lee Garmes, Nicholas Ray, Henry Hathaway, Otto Preminger, Frank Tashlin, Don Siegel, John Lee Mahin, Peter Hecht, Charles Lederer, Groucho Marx, King Vidor, Rouben Mamoulian, Allan Dwan, William Wellman, Donald Ogden Stewart, Ella Winter, Robert Florey, Howard Dietz, Lucinda Ballard, Rosalind Russell, Robert Parrish, Gordon Douglas, George Abbott, Hugh Gray, Harry Hansen, Thomas Quinn Curtis, George Oppenheimer, Ian McLellan Hunter, Ring Lardner Jr., Eleazer Lipsky, Jack O'Brien, Ken McCormack, Edward Schreiber, Emmet Lavery, Bob Samuels, Abram Ginnes, Edward Bernds, Lydia Schiller, William K. Everson, Helen Hayes MacArthur, Thomas Augustus Gallagher, Ephraim Katz, Joëlle Scheiber, Elizabeth Anne McAdams, Lucy Pritchett, Vincent and Bessie McAdams, Mary Sullivan, Connie and Allen Weiss, Lee Gongwer, Edward T. Chase, Fifi Oscard, Kevin McShane, Charles Flowers, Jerry Hoff, Jerry Kutter, Joseph McAdams, Henri Langlois, Diana Haskell of the Newberry Library, George Whitman and Shakespeare & Company, Jerry Berns and "21," Jay Handy, Geoff Brown and the British Film Institute, Sam Flores, the Berg Collection of the New York Public Library, the Museum of Modern Art, the American Library (Paris), Harvard Library, the Library of Congress, the Research Library of the University of California, the Library of the Academy of Motion Picture Arts and Sciences, the Benjamin Franklin Library (Paris), La Bibliothèque des Hautes Etudes Cinématographiques, La Bibliothèque Nationale, La Musée de la Ville de Paris, and the British Museum.

INTRODUCTION

Ben Hecht wrote almost half the entertaining movies produced in Hollywood, Pauline Kael opined in an essay published during the sixties. An exaggeration of course but one that lent support to a growing enthusiasm for Hecht: I knew that when I finally managed to get myself to New York, he was the person I most wanted to meet. But one snow-bright April afternoon, driving to Oxford, Ohio, I heard on the radio that he had died of a heart attack in his Manhattan duplex early that morning. I felt as if someone close to me had died, that a large part of the excitement of life and literature had been denied me forever.

In my early teens, an obsession with stories in the form of books and movies had led me to a copy of Hecht's fanciful autobiography, *A Child of the Century*, in a local bookstore. Reading it not only fueled my youthful romanticism but made me aware for the first time that there were authors who actually wrote movies as well as novels. So I not only continued to seek out any and all of Hecht's books I could find, but began to look for his name in the credits of old films on television as well as in the new movies I saw at the local picture palace. Several years later, having become immersed in movie history, I wanted to read a book about Hecht's scriptwriting to see how far-reaching his influence had been on the shaping of the American cinema—since he had worked for virtually every major American director. There was no such book. In fact, there wasn't even a published list of the scripts he had written. Although it seemed as if almost every book having to do with American movies, theatre, journalism, literature, or with the formation of the state of Israel made mention of Hecht, no one had chronicled his forty-year affair with the movies. Hecht himself in *A Child of the Century* wrote only a few pages about Hollywood, not once mentioning that he had directed seven pictures as well as having worked on the scripts of well over a hundred.

Thus, I began a quest that led me back in time to Chicago during the teens and twenties, to New York and Hollywood from the twenties to the sixties, from the East coast to the West and back again, to London and Paris.

Having decided to write a book on Hecht, I began with the obvious—the film study centers at the Museum of Modern Art and Lincoln Center. Then, with a mass of notes, books, and photocopies filed away, I was ready to start talking to people, the most important of whom was Rose Hecht, Ben's wife since the mid-twenties. I dropped a line to Helen Hayes (wife of Charles MacArthur, Hecht's best friend and frequent collaborator) in Nyack, New York, where both the Hechts and the MacArthurs had lived, and was informed of Rose's New York City address. When Rose heard someone wanted to write Ben's biography she was delighted, the two of us spending many hours in her and Ben's small, museumlike duplex on West Sixty-seventh Street. While I listened and took notes, Rose ranged freely over her more than forty years together with Hecht. An extremely strong-willed, highly opinionated lady full of mysterious hatreds, Rose never stuck to a subject for more than a few minutes, any question of mine leading her to the beginnings of an answer that splintered into tangents, which in turn led to more tangents. After several weeks of this, I decided what I must do was go to Hollywood and interview everybody I could find who would talk with me about Hecht. Then I would arrange all my information coherently and chronologically, meet with Rose again, and go through Ben's life from her perspective. Unfortunately, this was not to be.

Upon my return to New York, Rose was in virtual seclusion, no longer talking to anyone but close friends, her "last joy in life" snatched away. The Hechts' only daughter, Jenny, who had been an actress with the Living Theater, had returned to the United States with her boyfriend and fellow actor after the Living Theater broke up in Europe. In Los Angeles, she played in a low-budget biker movie, *The Jesus Trip* (1971), and shortly thereafter was found dead in her downtown hotel room, the result of suicide or, as Ben's friend Lee Garmes believed, an accidental overdose.

The interviews with Rose in New York, which I thought would be the beginning of many, turned out to be the only ones I would ever conduct with her. My last encounter with Rose, a few years before her death in 1978, was the result of two letters I wrote her. The first requested another interview, which she declined. In a brief note, she expressed her approval of what I was saying about Ben, but confessed she was ill and considering going into the hospital, and consequently couldn't see me.

My second letter contained a list of questions that were plaguing me about Hecht, which she could answer by letter, at her leisure. Her response, which closed the books on our odd relationship, was a one-page, handwritten vituperation, in which she accused me of dishonestly gaining the confidence of Lee and Ruth Garmes by telling them that she had sent me. I told Lee Garmes I was writing a biography of Ben Hecht and he was more than willing to be of assistance; I never met Ruth Garmes. Rose went on to accuse me of publishing a pamphlet crediting Hecht with work on the script of *Rope*, a picture she claimed was possibly the worst ever made, one that Hecht had had nothing to do with. I produced no pamphlet, and it was Rose herself who first alerted me to Hecht's behind-the-scenes tightening of the *Rope* script, since confirmed by Donald Spoto in *The Dark Side of Genius: The Life of Alfred Hitchcock*.

Over the years not one of the many people I interviewed expressed much fondness for Rose, their reactions running from outright dislike to Howard Hawks's amused tolerance. Nevertheless, despite her turning on me, the most profound feeling I was left with, and continue to feel to this day, is awe. Not for her intelligence, which was penetrating, or for her talent, evident more in her scores of letters to and copious notes about Hecht than in her published works or screenplays. I remain awed by the depth of her love for Ben Hecht, the inspiration that informed it, but especially by the relentless tenacity and duration of that love. In one of our talks, she pled, "I hope that those who care for his works will share his opinion that life with me was not wasted." I, for one, share it, and envy Ben his Rose.

Before Rose isolated herself, I did get to Los Angeles, where I spent six months digging into Ben's past. The other day, looking through the tapes I made there, I was startled to see that in one two-week period I had interviewed Lee Garmes, Don Siegel, Henry Hathaway, Lewis Milestone, John Ford, and Howard Hawks. Along with D. W. Griffith (and, some would contend, Orson Welles), Hawks and Ford are unquestionably the greatest native-born movie directors America has yet produced. Hawks had worked directly with Hecht on many scripts, and Ford, I thought then, had only filmed Hecht's lightning rewrite of *Hurricane*, which he had done at Sam Goldwyn's request, not Ford's. Thus, it was essential I speak with Hawks and of little or no consequence to my book whether or not I got to Ford (except for my own admiration for and curiosity about the legendary curmudgeon of American movies). I didn't even know if John Ford and Ben Hecht had ever met, and if they had it seemed unlikely that they would have become intimates.

Experience was teaching me that Hecht, even more than most Hollywood writers, had had little contact with the men who translated his words into pictures. For instance, since more than one reliable source had confirmed that Hecht and Gene Fowler had rewritten the script of *Queen Christina* for David O. Selznick, I had contacted Rouben Mamoulian, the picture's director, to ask if he would talk with me about it, and was invited to his Beverly Hills home. When I arrived—ushered into a study the size of a movie set—and once again explained my purpose, Mamoulian informed me that Hecht hadn't written a word of the *Queen Christina* script and that was all he knew about Hecht. End of interview. Why couldn't he have told me that over the phone? And why was he so positive Hecht hadn't worked on the picture, knowing as he did that virtually every script produced under the Hollywood factory system was reworked by any number of staff writers?

Another experience along the same lines I had early on in Hollywood was even more comical—and frustrating. I had written Sam Goldwyn for an interview since he and Hecht had long been associated with one another but I found he was ill and was seeing no one. His wife Frances, however, granted me an interview at the studio. Upon my arrival, a secretary in an outer office showed me into a large room, which turned out to be Mrs. Goldwyn's secretary's office. After a short wait, I made it to the inner sanctum where former starlet Frances Goldwyn, attired in an electric-pink pantsuit, greeted me cordially. She took her place behind an oversized desk while I set up my portable tape recorder, ready for a flood of memories. She waited patiently till the machine was assembled to tell me that she had met Ben a few times at parties, never knew him well, and couldn't think of another thing to tell me. I was in and out of her office in less than five minutes.

One of the many strokes of good luck I had in Los Angeles was to meet a member of the Directors Guild, sympathetic to my project, who took me to the guild offices and looked up the unlisted phone numbers of every director I wanted to interview. When I said I wanted Ford's number, he said forget it, Ford wouldn't talk, hadn't talked to interviewers for years. After I'd got the fifteen or so numbers I needed, I asked him again to get me Ford's number, figuring all Ford could do was say no and if I didn't try I'd always regret it. He looked it up, advising me to talk to Ford's daughter Barbara first, explain what I wanted, and let her tell it to Ford before I talked with him.

Later that week, I phoned. Barbara Ford answered and was more than willing to plead my case. I waited while she went to tell her father who was calling. A few minutes later, John Ford was on the other end of the line. Since he was partially deaf, I shouted out what Barbara had just told him. He and Ben had been "very good friends," he said and there were several interesting anecdotes he could tell me. He suggested we get together the following week, I should phone again to set up a day.

Next time when I called—after reminding Barbara who I was, retelling Ford what I wanted—he was not so sympathetic, telling me he had "a lot of projects and work" and that "There's not a hell of a lot I can tell you about Ben." Call again next week. I did. Same routine. I call the fourth week:

FORD: Good afternoon, Mr. MacAdams.

MACADAMS: Mr. Ford, I called up to bother you again.

FORD: Yeah.

MACADAMS: It's about Ben Hecht . . .

FORD: About what?

MACADAMS: About Ben Hecht . . .

FORD: I wish to hell there was something I could tell you about him, but I don't know any anecdotes . . .

MACADAMS: But you told me you did have an anecdote or two . . .

FORD: Yeah, but thinking them over they were pretty dull. I think we'd better call it off. I couldn't give you a comprehensive paragraph or two on Ben Hecht, I didn't know him that well.

MACADAMS: How about telling me that one dull anecdote?

FORD: Well, I suppose . . . when do you want to see me?

MacAdams: Any time is fine with me.

Ford: I'll be in my office tomorrow afternoon. You know where that is? Well, neither do . . . yes I do. Two thirty-one Beverly Drive. In the afternoon sometime, make it two o'clock.

I drove from my apartment in Hollywood to Beverly Hills, arriving twenty minutes early. Plenty of time. But I couldn't find the address Ford had given me. I parked, searched the block, but no such number existed. Five minutes till the appointed time. The only thing to do was call his house, but there aren't pay phones on every streetcorner in downtown Beverly Hills. I rushed back to my car and found a phone some ten blocks away. I called, Barbara answered. I told her I couldn't find 231 Beverly Drive. I must have taken the number down wrong, she said; I'd transposed two of the numbers. (Later I checked the tape of my last conversation with Ford, and found I had not got the number wrong. He had. Or had he?) In a sweat—I was now keeping John Ford waiting—I tore back to 321 Beverly Drive, parked, located the building, dashed to his office, composed myself, and walked in—fifteen minutes late. Ford was not there. Twenty minutes later he arrived, dressed in rumpled clothes and a naval commander's khaki ballcap.

He shuffled over to me, waited while I shouted out who I was, then invited me into his office, a simple room with filing cabinets, an oil painting of himself in his admiral's uniform, and watercolors of Harry Carey lining the walls. He sat behind his desk at one end of the room while I unpacked my tape recorder, plugged it in, assembled the mike and stand, positioned it on a corner of the desk, and switched on.

"What's that?" he inquired.

"A tape recorder . . ."

"You can't use it." I switched it off and began to disassemble it, asking if he minded if I took notes.

After a long pause, during which he watched me repack the recorder, he relented: "Okay, go ahead, use it. You can misquote me more accurately that way."

My initiation over, he talked freely for the next hour, revealing Hecht's contribution to the script of *Stagecoach*, unbeknownst to anyone but himself, Hecht, and Walter Wanger. Saint Cinema had smiled, my persistence rewarded with the hitherto unrecorded story of Hecht's uncredited "laying out" of one of the classic Westerns of all time.

While still in his early teens, Tag Gallagher—author of the excellent critical study, *John Ford: The Man and His Films*—wrote a fan letter full of boyish enthusiasm for one of Ford's Westerns and received a personal reply. When as a young man he wrote Ford again, asking perceptive questions about another of his pictures, the only answer was silence. Howard Hawks, on the other hand, was perhaps a little too willing to grant interviews, frequently overlooking the facts to reshape history to conform to the contours of his own legend. He often told how upon first meeting some other famous man, they "went out and got drunk together." Although hardly famous, I felt I was participating in the myth the day I spent with him at his Palm Springs home, the two of us putting away a bottle of Scotch. He regaled me with oft-told stories about Clark Gable, Ernest Hemingway, William Faulkner (a few days earlier he'd found an unpublished Faulkner short story in his basement!), Harpo Marx, the movie he wanted to make with Steve McQueen and Clint Eastwood, the racing cars he and his son were building. On the subject of Hecht, though, he was candid, scrupulously honest, and full of admiration for Hecht's "genius" as a writer, drinker, and womanizer. Hawks's warmth, courtesy, and wonderful stories made it one of the best days of my life. Although there wasn't one sterling anecdote that shone so bright as Ford's, Hawks contributed a wealth of information and opinion about his work and friendship with Hecht, from *Underworld* in 1926— which Hawks collaborated on with Hecht before Josef von Sternberg was assigned to the picture—to their last collaboration, *Monkey Business*, in 1952.

My biggest disappointment was Alfred Hitchcock's refusal to see me. Then, I thought it was perhaps distaste for Rose Hecht that kept him silent. But in the light of the many recent and startling revelations about Hitchcock, it's probable that he wouldn't have confided anything to me that didn't add to his own reputation. Anything he might have told me concerning Hecht's work for him would have been suspect, but I still regret the loss of his point of view on Hecht the man.

The other larger-than-life figure who wouldn't talk was Orson Welles. I wanted to ask him about his *Journey into Fear*, which Hecht had written unaided by credited "screenwriter" Joseph Cotten, a fact that Welles always kept quiet about. When Welles tried to buy Herman Mankiewicz's screen credit for *Citizen Kane* for fifty thousand dollars, Hecht advised Mank to "take the money and screw Welles" by claiming credit anyway. For *Journey into Fear* Hecht took the money but didn't give a damn about the credit, an attitude incomprehensible to Hitchcock and Welles. In comparison, Hawks looks the arbiter of Absolute Truth.

Hawks and Ford were hardly the only moviemakers I interviewed in

Los Angeles, but along with master cinematographer Lee Garmes and Gene Fowler's son Will, they were the most fascinating and informative. During my six months on the West Coast, I collected pieces of the Hecht jigsaw from scores of movie people, almost all of whom went out of their way to be helpful (Don Siegel screened a difficult-to-see Hecht for me at Universal; in Paris several years later, Henri Langlois screened another).

Although I amassed more raw material from my Hollywood sojourn than from any other source, it was just the end of the beginning of my on-again off-again search to put order and sense into the telling of Hecht's life. Over the next half a dozen years I continued to seek out anyone who knew Hecht. I sat with the almost-ninety-year-old literary critic Harry Hansen in his New York office while he gleefully discussed Hecht and other compatriots from the Chicago Literary Renaissance, all of whom were "pushing up daisies." From the blind side of the banquette at Fouquet's, I listened as biographer Thomas Quinn Curtis told me of the play Hecht and Erich von Stroheim almost wrote together. (Curtis was also the catalyst, presumably unintentional, of an embarrassing moment. Since Hecht had adapted *The Hunchback of Notre Dame* for the Hakim brothers in the fifties, Curtis suggested I contact Raphael Hakim, living in Paris in one of the first-class hotels. When I phoned and asked for him, the concierge informed me that Monsieur Hakim had died earlier that week.)

Screenwriter Donald Ogden Stewart invited me to spend the afternoon at his London home (once owned by a prime minister), which he shared with his wife Ella Winter, the former Mrs. Lincoln Steffens. The amiable Stewart—proof that a communist could be rich yet suffer no qualms of conscience—talked mainly about himself, the old Hollywood, Ernest Hemingway's modeling Bill Gorton in *The Sun Also Rises* on him, and a little bit about Hecht. No fault of Stewart's that he didn't know more, since Hecht wasn't the type, no matter how much money he made, to socialize with the left-wing playboys of the thirties. Frank Tashlin, over lunch, told me he had recently driven down to Hecht's Oceanside house and even though this wooden castle on the beach seemed smaller than he remembered, Hecht had only grown larger for him over the twenty years since they had worked together. (I was not to realize until seven months later—when I read his obituary in *The New York Times*—that our talk was the last interview he granted.)

I culled Hecht anecdotes from Otto Preminger, screenwriter Ian McLellan Hunter, Doubleday editor Ken McCormack, scriptwriter and publisher George Oppenheimer, from correspondence with Hecht's younger brother Peter, from the Hechts' long-time chauffeur (still living in Nyack), and from others too numerous to mention. Shards of information were dislodged from the British Museum, the Bibliothèque Nationale, the Berg Collection, the Newberry Library (the repository of the papers and manuscripts of the Chicago Literary Renaissance writers), Harvard Library, Leland Hayward's papers, the Lillie Library, and many others.

At long last I feel satisfied that I have done my utmost to tell Hecht's story as fully and completely as possible, in spite of suggestions that I make the book "more gossipy," which I have never entertained. Sensation has never been the goal, only accuracy and truth presented as fluidly and entertainingly as possible. Others have complained that I should interject myself more in the book, be critical, analytical, apply the new film criticism, Claude Lévi-Strauss, structural anthropology, hermeneutics, semiotics, to Hecht's works. Not only would that kind of analysis require a score of stupefyingly dull volumes, it would be so antithetical to Hecht's life and work that every time someone brought the subject up, I was sure I could hear Hecht having a good laugh somewhere.

—WILLIAM MACADAMS
Woodstock, New York

1

PREVIEW

Of the score of writers I had come to know in Hollywood . . . Ben Hecht seemed the personification of the writer at the top of his game, the top of his world, not gnawing at and doubting himself as great writers were said to do, but with every word and every gesture indicating the animal pleasure he took in writing well. . . . I forgave Hecht his cheek and brassiness. Possibly because I had been exposed to so many Hollywood blowhards, I preferred people who talked and walked quietly and let their words speak for them. But damn it, Ben Hecht had done it, he had taken the giant step upward that almost every newspaperman dreams of and only one in a thousand manages to accomplish.

—Budd Schulberg
Moving Pictures: *Memories of a Hollywood Prince*

He was thirty-three years old and broke again. Although he'd been an ace crime reporter in gangland Chicago, had published seven novels and seen two of his plays produced on Broadway, he and his new wife Rose were penniless. A few months earlier, he'd made a small fortune writing publicity for a Florida real-estate tycoon during the last days of the boom there, but getting a divorce from his first wife and moving to Manhattan's Beekman Place had eaten up all the cash and he was once again faced with the problem of how to make money as a writer.

When Ben Hecht was a young reporter in Chicago, he'd been asked by Theodore Dreiser to collaborate on a new venture: the writing and production of motion pictures, which Dreiser assured him were going to replace literature. Hecht had turned Dreiser down, convinced movies were a tawdry, passing fancy. But now, in 1926, Harold Ross's new magazine *The New Yorker* was reporting that "the producing corporations have gobbled up all our literary talent with frantic insistence, and set it to work upon epics for the screen. They have collared every young fellow in New York who displayed a ray of craft or intelligence and bundled him off to Hollywood. . . . They have even mentioned the word Art."

Hecht's new friend David Selznick had recently left New York to go to work for MGM as a script reader, sharing a house with his brother Myron and film director Lewis Milestone, whom Hecht had met in Florida. Another friend, Herman J. Mankiewicz (who would later write *Citizen Kane*), had gone to Hollywood in July 1926 to write titles for silent pictures. In November, he wired Hecht: "Will you accept three hundred per week to work for Paramount Pictures? All expenses paid. The three hundred is peanuts. Millions are to be grabbed out here and your only competition is idiots. Don't let this get around." Hecht was in Los Angeles before the month was out.

One of many writers, directors, and actors rushing to Hollywood from New York and the capitals of Europe, Hecht knew full well what awaited him: lots of money and little intellectual challenge. Nevertheless he would be competing with some of the top literary talent in America: by the early thirties, William Faulkner, George S. Kaufman, John O'Hara, Dorothy Parker, Maxwell Anderson, and Ring Lardner were pocketing big checks for scripts. Knowing he could write for Eastern publishers as well as for Hollywood—while the literary establishment maintained that scriptwriting was a prostitution of one's talent, that the huge movie salaries removed the incentive to write books and plays—Hecht was determined to beat the literati at the movie game by becoming the highest-paid, most successful screenwriter in history.

The first step was *Underworld*. Hecht rejected the formula plot Paramount assigned him for his first picture but, not knowing what to write to replace it, he consulted Mankiewicz. Mank pontificated, "In a novel a hero can lay ten girls and marry a virgin for a finish. In a movie this is not allowed. The hero, as well as the heroine, has to be a virgin. The villain can lay anybody he wants, have as much fun as he wants cheating and stealing, getting rich and whipping the servants. But you have to shoot him in the end." So Hecht broke the rules. He dispensed with a hero entirely, and wrote the first gangster film, *Underworld*, basing it on both Chicago hoodlum Tommy O'Conner and Al Capone.

With *Underworld*, Hecht transformed what had passed for tough-guy movies up to that time, movies with villains in turtleneck sweaters and cloth caps, hangovers from the dime novels popular at the turn of the century. Hecht dressed his protagonist Bull Weed in a business suit, put a bulge under his left arm and an itch to the forefinger of his right hand, and spun out a street saga more realistic than anything thus far written for the American screen.

Although *Underworld* was a ground-breaking film, Hecht was dissatisfied with it because it was silent. This meant he was a writer without a voice, able to turn all the plots he wanted but for characters who could never speak. Fortunately, he had arrived in Hollywood at the moment when movies were about to open their mouths, and he was to make them talk better than anyone. Howard Hughes, who began in the film business at the same time as Hecht, gave him the chance. In 1930, Hecht and Howard Hawks collaborated on *Scarface* for Hughes's Caddo Company and created one of the first masterpieces of the sound era.

At that point, film itself was so new that the craftsmanship necessary for feature-length narrative had only recently been mastered (D. W. Griffith's *The Birth of a Nation* had been made only a decade and a half before). Then, seemingly overnight, sound-on-film and amplification technology forced the entire art of the cinema to be reevaluated. New answers had to be found both by writers and directors. Writers had to develop full-length scripts with dialogue and not just outline plots and write titles. In one stroke, almost everything silent directors had learned about camera movement was, at least temporarily, negated. A cumbersome sound booth enveloped the camera—to keep the whirr of the motor from being recorded—and nailed it in one spot. Ernst Lubitsch and Rouben Mamoulian are the two directors generally credited with making the most fluid films before cameras were blimped and released from the confines of the sound booth, simply because they shot action sequences silent. Howard Hawks was another pioneer, as *Scarface* makes clear. Hawks also used the sound booth only to record dialogue, otherwise shooting his action scenes silent—as in the brilliant three-and-a-half-minute tracking shot that opens the film, which legend has it ran eleven minutes and was the longest single take in a movie up to that time, just slightly longer than a ten-minute take in Mary Pickford's *Coquette*. But without Hecht's script, a virtual textbook for the writing of sound films, there would have been no *Scarface*.

In 1929, Hecht won the first Academy Award for a screen story (*Underworld*). In 1934, he was nominated for his script of *Viva Villa!*, then the following year he won a second Oscar for *The Scoundrel*, which he both wrote and directed. By the end of the thirties, he was a legend—in Hollywood, in newsrooms all over the country, and in literary and theatrical circles (his and Charles MacArthur's *The Front Page* had been a smash hit on Broadway in 1928). In 1939, at his peak, ten films on which he'd worked were released, among them *Gone With the Wind* (for David Selznick), *Stagecoach* (for John Ford), *His Girl Friday* (for Howard Hawks), *Gunga Din* (for George Stevens), and *Wuthering Heights* (for William Wyler). He had accomplished his goal to become the highest-paid scriptwriter in Hollywood, had perfected two film genres (the gangster film and the screwball comedy), and was the envy of every struggling screenwriter, including the newly arrived F. Scott Fitzgerald.

Born during the Mauve Decade, dead at the age of seventy in 1964, Hecht left behind novels, short stories, essays, poetry, plays, musicals, biographies, an autobiography, memoirs, letters, reportage, newspaper columns, eulogies, song lyrics, a children's book, film, book and music criticism, two literary magazines, and a late-night TV talk show. But Ben Hecht will be best remembered because he was the most influential writer in the history of American movies, creating a new and exciting language for the screen at the same time that such writers as Dashiell Hammett and Ernest Hemingway were busy revitalizing the novel.

2

PREMATURE CHILD OF THE CENTURY

There are only two kinds of newspapermen—those who try to write poetry and those who try to drink themselves to death. Fortunately for the world, only one of them succeeds.

—Ben Hecht
Erik Dorn

The story drifted around Hollywood for years that Ben Hecht had been born in a toilet. "Born perversely . . . out of this natal perversity," he wrote in an autobiographical sketch during the twenties. Seeing himself as a storyteller, Hecht fictionalized everything he ever wrote about himself, including his own birth—it was a cousin born prematurely in a toilet.

His parents, Joseph Hecht and Sarah Swernofski, had emigrated from Minsk in southern Russia in 1878 to the Lower East Side of New York, where they were married in 1892. Benjamin was born the following year, on February 28th. He attended the Broome Street school briefly, met the great actors of the Yiddish theatre at his Aunt Lubi's, studied the violin, and several times a week was allowed to go to a music hall or vaudeville show. Six years after Ben was born, Joseph Hecht, unable to rise above the position of cloth cutter in the garment district, moved the family—which now included another son, Peter—to Chicago.

Peter remembered an incident that took place there that produced Ben's first piece of writing: "Mother, Ben, and I, when Ben was eight, were passengers on an open streetcar, typical of the time in 1901. As we were traveling through a street intersection a runaway horse came at the car and hurled itself through the car, a hoof striking the man in the seat ahead of us and killing him. Ben observed this scene with interest, he listened to the passengers, the ambulance people, and the police. He asked questions and listened. After reaching our apartment, Ben locked himself in our bedroom and spent hours writing and rewriting his version of the bloody mess—the commotion, fainting, et cetera. This as far as I know was Ben's first effort as a journalist."

In 1903 the Hecht family relocated in nearby Racine, Wisconsin, on the banks of Lake Michigan, where Joseph began manufacturing a line of women's fashions he had designed. Joseph spent most of his time on the road pushing his line while Sarah managed Paris Fashions, their downtown Racine outlet. Hecht, left to his own devices, took photographs with a box camera, put on shadowgraph and magic shows, and built an eighteen-foot sailboat on which he and his friends sailed to neighboring towns up and down the coast of Lake Michigan. For three summers their landlady's son, a trapeze artist and "human fly," taught Ben and Peter how to perform a routine on a trapeze he had rigged up in the barn behind the house. Then during the summer of 1908, Ben and Peter went on the road with a circus and performed their act as the Youngest Daredevils in America.

During high school, Ben worked in the Racine shop after school, taught himself to type on his mother's machine, continued to study the violin, and read voraciously, consuming Horatio Alger, Dick Merriwell, Nat the Naturalist, and Sherlock Holmes. Joseph, although he believed in the value of education and fancied himself an educated man, read very little and never really mastered the English language. But, for Ben's thirteenth birthday, Joseph presented him with the most influential gift of his early years—four wooden packing crates containing leather-bound sets of Shakespeare, Dickens, and Twain, a fifty-two-volume world history, and a set of the world's famous orations. After devouring the 167 books from his father, Hecht went on to digest large helpings of Bret Harte, Richard Harding Davis, Poe, Dumas, Balzac, Gorki, Gogol, Maupassant, and Thackeray. Finding school dull in comparison to his own reading, he didn't waste much time on it, copying his themes out of newspapers for his English teacher, Miss Church. He put his energy into extracurricular activities, played football, ran on the track team, wrote class plays, and was a cheerleader. What was left of his spare time he spent playing in an orchestra in a Racine saloon, going to vaudeville shows, and writing rhyming advertisements for his high-school yearbook, in which his first published work appeared—

> *In Hades on the Brimstone*
> *Burning, sizzling by the ton*
> *There are many men a-popping*
> *For the sins that they have done.*
> *The sins they have committed,*
> *My friends, are not a few—*
> *And the greatest of them all is*
> *They forgot to buy from Pugh!*

When Hecht graduated from high school in 1910, he moved in with his Aunt Chasha and Uncle Harris in Chicago. His parents had given him enough money to live on while he decided what he wanted to pursue in life, but there was never any doubt in the young man's mind: he was going to be a writer. One evening at the home of Emanuel Moyses, another uncle's business partner, he was asked what his ambitions were. When Hecht confided his plans, Moyses told him he might be able to help. A few days later, Moyses contacted Hecht to tell him he had arranged an interview with John Eastman, the publisher of the *Chicago Daily Journal.*

When they met, Eastman liked the garrulous, intelligent young man, hired him, then introduced him to managing editor Martin Hutchins. Hutchins, having little time for another of Eastman's discoveries, turned Hecht over to Ballard Dunne, the city editor. Dunne passed him on to his assistant Eddie Mahoney, who told Hecht to report at six the following morning, July the 4th. When Hecht balked about working on a holiday, Mahoney instructed: "There are no holidays in the dreadful profession you have chosen."

Chicago in 1910 was the capital of the Midwest, a raw sprawling city making its living from steel mills, slaughterhouses, and scandal sheets. With a population of 2½ million, it was the home of the Swift and the Armour meat-packing empires, Marshall Field's great department store (where the customer was always right), and the burgeoning University of Chicago. It was a city two hundred miles square with four thousand miles of streets that had sprung up without planning. The great influx of Eastern European refugees at the end of the century had created scores of ramshackle districts where Greek cafés mingled with Yiddish theatres and German beer halls.

Cities were isolated in those years, people rarely straying from their own hometown. Chicago was culturally isolated. Publishing was centered in Boston—soon to be challenged by New York—while the movie business was moving out of New York to relocate in California. Chicago didn't have exclusive rights to any part of the culture industry, but in those early years Hecht didn't mind. Although he was to live a good part of his life in New York and Los Angeles, he would never have another affair with a city like he was to have with Chicago.

Hecht's first job on the *Journal* was as a picture chaser, an extinct type of newspaperman whose sole justification lay in his ability to beg, borrow, or most often steal photos of recently murdered, raped, divorced, or otherwise newsworthy people. Hecht's Aunt Chasha sewed large pockets in the lining of his coat to conceal his newly acquired burglar tools as well as stolen photographs. Hecht's friend Charles Samuels recalled that Hecht "clambered up fire escapes, crawled through windows and transoms, posing when detected as everything from a gas meter inspector to an undertaker's assistant. In a short while he was recognized as the most adept and audacious picture thief in Chicago. He seldom failed to return from his missions with photographs snatched from the walls, bureau drawers, mantlepieces of the homes of killers, brides jilted at the altar, suicides, eloping couples, and accident victims." Once Hecht was chased all the way to the *Journal* by an irate woman with a gun. Another time, city editor Dunne reprimanded him for stealing a four-by-four-foot oil painting of a murder victim—the only likeness he could find—but rewarded his zeal with a raise.

Scooping all the other papers in town, Hecht reached the peak of his picture-chasing career a year and a half after he began. A double suicide involving a seventeen-year-old girl and a minister was inflaming the public, but no paper could get a photo of the girl because her mother refused to talk to the press. Hecht waited outside her house for ten hours one winter day till all the reporters and other picture chasers had given up, then he climbed to the roof and capped the chimney with boards. When the girl's mother burst from the smoke-filled house, Hecht slipped into the living room and snatched a photo. As a result of this derring-do, Walter Howey, editor of William Randolph Hearst's *Chicago Examiner*, tried to lure him over to his paper, but Hecht loyally remained with the *Journal*. Money had not yet begun to matter.

On another occasion, Mahoney sent him out to get a picture of an old man who had been strangled. "We want those pictures," Mahoney told him. "Don't come back without them." Hecht arrived at the old man's house and found the door locked, but quickly gained entry with a skeleton key. He could hear the family and the police conferring in the kitchen, so he sneaked into the parlor where the old man's body was stretched out on an ironing board propped up by two chairs. Above the body were three oil paintings that Hecht was unhooking when the ironing board, which he was standing on, collapsed, dumping him, the body, and the paintings on the floor. Disentangling himself, he fled with the oils. He glanced behind him as he ran, expecting to see the police and the outraged family in pursuit, but was surprised to see neither. His lone pursuer was P. Aloysius Tribaum, a rival picture chaser.

"Stories of the manner in which Russian noblemen riding through the woods in their sleighs had been pursued by packs of wolves and how they had held these ravenous ones off by throwing pieces of clothing to them, obviously inspired my action. For as I saw the fateful Tribaum gaining on me, handicapped as I was by my burden, I deliberately dropped one of them—that of the son it turned out later. And Tribaum, picking it up a few moments later found himself outdistanced for the rest of the way into the *Journal* office."

Eventually, Hecht felt it time to try something new. Mahoney gave him the chance when he sent him out to get an interview as well as a photo of a woman whose husband was suing her for divorce for sleeping with a regiment. Accepting everything she told him, Hecht returned to the office and began writing a Victorian sob story about the lady's maligned virtue. Sports editor Sherman Duffy, peering over Hecht's shoulder at the story he was tapping out, advised, "Don't be a horse's ass. Read Rabelais. There's a man who knew women for what they are. Gila monsters. Puff adders. I suggest you study the blue nosed Mandrill in the zoo, a monkey that sports an ass like a rainbow. Which is a damn' fine definition of a woman, if I do say so myself. As my friend Gene Field wrote in his ditty 'The French Crisis,' there is only one honest feature to the female." Duffy quoted: " 'Here's to her orifice of sin—that lets her liquefactions out and other factions in.' " Hecht tore up his story.

Since Hecht usually had his picture chasing done by ten every morning, Mahoney began sending him out to look for news stories, with the proviso that he not believe everything that he was told. As yet Hecht didn't know the ways and means of getting a story. He didn't know desk sergeants, lawyers, criminals, courthouses, police stations, morgues, and all the other places a reporter goes looking. Still smarting from his first attempt, he was unsure exactly how to ascertain the facts. Undaunted, he simply made them up.

Mahoney was so impressed with what he thought was his cub reporter's nose for news that he assigned a photographer to accompany Hecht on his daily forays. The photographer, Gene Cour, was delighted with Hecht's novel news-gathering methods. They spent months creating hoaxes and scooping all the other dailies. Cour induced a police captain to pose gun in hand on the deck of a police boat, while unbeknownst to the captain Hecht had positioned himself in front of the tug in a row boat. The *Journal's* headline the next day read POLICE PURSUE RIVER PIRATES. Their tale of a runaway streetcar was denied by the transit company but it thrilled readers.

The height of their hoaxing came with the invention of the Great Chicago Earthquake. Hecht had been reading a book on geophysics, and decided to put his newfound knowledge to use. He and Cour stole out early one morning and dug a trench in Lincoln Park to simulate an earthquake fissure, then Cour photographed it. The picture appeared the following day, along with photos of Hecht's landlady standing in her kitchen beside pieces of broken crockery. Experts denied the story, but Hecht had scored another coup.

He was only too aware that he could create news with impunity, but he hadn't yet learned not to tamper with his publisher's image. One day he filed a heartrending story about an impoverished Bulgarian princess slinging hash on Wabash Avenue, and chose a well-known prostitute to pose for the photo of the princess. Unfortunately for Hecht, John Eastman's friends laughed him out of his club the following afternoon for being hornswoggled into printing a whore's picture on his paper's front page. Eastman, who had "a bellow that could shake windows," returned to the office and would have sacked Hecht on the spot but for Duffy's intervention. Duffy counseled Hecht to disappear for a week, assuring him everything would be all right when he came back.

The first commercial radio station didn't begin broadcasting until 1920, so the teens was the last decade when the newspaper was the fastest, most effective means of presenting news. The news story was different in those years too. Who, what, when, where, and how were still uppermost in importance, but whereas newspaper pieces today are more or less straightforward reports of events, in the teens a journalist had to set a scene like a novelist or playwright, introduce his characters, and develop his plot in a format as tight as that of a short short story. In those years, a reporter wasn't a college journalism graduate who had been hired by a newspaper to turn out a uniform product, but generally a cynical, whoring, hard-drinking adventurer who was writing poetry or a novel between the stories he was banging out on his tall office Underwood. Hecht said the press rooms of the day were peopled with "drunks, scholars, poets, fighters and dusty egoists" and that if any of that vanished breed existed today, they would be found "lurking in slum pool halls, desert huts or juvenile detention homes."

Sherman Reilly Duffy could have been the prototype for yesterday's newspaperman. He haunted brothels and bars, talked endlessly with other writers and reporters passing through Chicago on their way to and from foreign exploits, caroused with boxers and baseball players, and knew the whole seedy underground of big-money sports, crooked politicians, cops, madams, and shady businessmen. "Socially," Duffy quipped, "a journalist fits in somewhere between a whore and a bartender but spiritually he stands beside Galileo. He knows the world is round."

Duffy was as much of an intellectual as it was possible to be without affecting a pince-nez and a British accent. He was fluent in French, Latin, and Spanish, could quote passages from the classics, was a Phi Beta Kappa member, an expert horticulturist, and knew as much about literature as a college professor but chose newspaper reporting as the most interesting life-style available to him. He was the first older, seasoned reporter to take an interest in Hecht, who learned Chicago's "thirty-two feet of intestines" quickly from the streetwise veteran. Duffy, in turn, was delighted to teach him.

Duffy whipped Hecht's reportage into shape and convinced managing editor Hutchins to promote him to full-time reporter, if only conditionally. Skeptical, Hutchins agreed and Hecht began writing the news as he saw it. During the next two years—the second half of his career at the *Journal*—Hecht became an ace reporter, covering the Dayton flood of 1913 in the company of then-famous newsman Christian Dane Hagerty; the public funeral services held in 1914 for the marines killed during the occupation of Veracruz, for which he received his first byline; the formation of Teddy Roosevelt's Bull Moose Party; innumerable trials, with famous lawyers Clarence Darrow and Edgar Lee Masters and others, involving witness buying, jury bribing, and police graft.

Because he had interviewed Wilhelm Stekel—author of early studies of sadomasochism—Hecht became the local room's lunacy expert, entitling him to cover the story of the man who murdered his wife and made her skull into a tobacco jar; the surgeon who unnecessarily removed hundreds of women's uteruses; the newly married man who tied his wife to a chair in a downtown hotel and whipped her with a cat-o'-nine-tails; the mortuary worker who died as a result of eating part of a corpse's leg.

For Hecht it was all entertainment.[1]* "He covered multiple murders," Charles Samuels said, "with the same high spirits with which he wrote about Vaudeville shows and circuses." Of the scores of murderers Hecht wrote about, interviewed, and played cards with, he saw half a dozen executed in the Cook County jail. One man put on make-up before he was led to the scaffold and died shrieking like a chorus girl. Another sang "Dear Old Pal of Mine" while he waited for the trap door to be sprung. Witness with Hecht:

* Chapter notes are to be found at the back of the book.

A hanged man dies in a few seconds if his neck is broken by the drop. If his neck isn't broken, due to the incorrect adjustment of the noose, he chokes to death. This takes from eight to fourteen minutes. While he hangs choking, the white-covered body begins to spin slowly. The white-hooded head tilts to one side and a stretch of purpled neck becomes visible. Then the rope begins to vibrate and hum like a hive of bees. After this the white robe begins to expand and deflate as if it were being blown up by a leaky bicycle pump. Following the turning, spinning, humming, and pumping up of the white robe comes the climax of the hanging. This is the throat of the hanging man letting out a last strangled cry or moan of life.

3

SHOVELING ADJECTIVES: THE CHICAGO LITERARY RENAISSANCE

I wouldn't sell my chances on a bet.

—BEN HECHT (1910)

Would that our writing had been as fine as our lunches.

—BEN HECHT

Chicago had had a literary community stretching back as far as the Mauve Nineties, when newspaperman George Ade wrote his Artie stories for the *Record*, Gene Field turned out verses six days a week for the *News*, and critic and novelist Henry Fuller wrote the first novel about modern city life, *The Cliff-Dwellers* (1893). Also living and working in Chicago at that time were novelist and University of Chicago professor Robert Herrick and early proponent of fictional realism, Hamlin Garland. None of these men wrote lasting works during this period, but they set the scene for the coming of the Chicago Literary Renaissance in the sense that they created a loose community of artists and writers rebelling against societal convention. These older writers held fast through the first decade of the next century, but by the second had begun to disperse. Garland had moved to New York and Herrick was living in Maine. Where the older generation had been interested in liberation from social injustice, from the smothering ethic of "business for business's sake," the upcoming younger group, dissatisfied with the halfway measures of novelistic social protest, decided that liberation had to be personal, individual, anarchic.

Literary critic Burton Rascoe marked the beginning of the Renaissance with Francis Hackett's creation in 1909 of the *Friday Literary Review*, an eight-page book section published in the *Post*. In 1912, Maurice Browne, a London stage director bent on bringing modern plays from Britain and the Continent to America, opened the first little theatre in the United States. This type of theatre, partway between an amateur and a professional company, was to become increasingly popular throughout the country. The same year, Harriet Monroe began the first American magazine devoted solely to poetry, *Poetry: A Magazine of Verse*, in which she published Vachel Lindsay, Hart Crane, T. S. Eliot, Carl Sandburg, and Ezra Pound, some of them for the first time. Thus the three fronts of the new liberation were established—newspaper book pages, alternative theatre, and the literary magazine.

Although Hecht admired Francis Hackett, he didn't write for the *Friday Literary Review*, since he was still a picture chaser when Hackett quit in 1911 and twenty-four-year-old Floyd Dell became the new editor. Hecht was acquainted with Dell because they both worked in the newspaper world, but despite Hecht's fascination with literature he wasn't interested in writing for a rival paper. He was absorbed in becoming the *Journal*'s star reporter.

By 1914, though, he had become the number one reporter on the *Journal* and was ripe for something new, journalism fast becoming too limited for a young man with so much ambition. Literature was what he wanted to write. In the back room of his parents' apartment (his family had moved back to Chicago when Joseph's business failed), he had been scribbling short sketches and poetry influenced by the Imagist poets. The first anthology of their work had been published in 1912, edited by Ezra Pound, but Hecht took his direction from Harriet Monroe's *Poetry*, which had begun the same year with Pound serving as foreign editor. In 1913 Hecht submitted some of his city sketches but they were rejected, his writing filled "with grotesque and incoherent strings of adjectives which often sent the editors who read them into surprised bursts of laughter."

The same year he met Kenneth Sawyer Goodman, a Princeton graduate with a degree in theatre who aspired to be a dramatist. The son of a lumber millionaire, Goodman had left-wing tendencies and planned to open a theatre in a Maxwell Street slum, free admission for the people. Until that was possible he had decided to produce plays at Jane Addams's Hull House, where Francis Hackett had once lived and Floyd Dell had taught English to immigrants. Goodman and Hecht began collaborating and turned out half a dozen innocuous dramas during the spring and summer, the best of which, *The Wonder Hat*, Hecht described as "a Little Theatre caramel which I helped write in the days of my adolescence." These early one-act romances had very little of Hecht in them and none of the spirit of the Chicago Renaissance, but they marked the beginning of Hecht's writing career outside reportage.

Early in 1914, Hecht also met *Daily News* writer Margery Curry, who invited him to one of her Friday-night literary gatherings. Six months before, she had separated from her husband, Floyd Dell, who in October of 1913 had resigned the editorship of the *Friday Literary Review* to become editor of *The Masses*. Margery lived at Fifty-seventh Street and Stony Island in one of the corrugated midway buildings—left over from the World's Fair of 1893—which attracted writers and painters because of the cheap rents and the nearness of the University of Chicago. This little bohemia was the social center of the Renaissance and Floyd's and Margery's studios (Margery's had formerly been occupied by Thorstein Veblen) served as its focal point. When Dell left for New York, the sharpness of the focus began to blur, partially because the social director was gone, but also because his successor at the *Friday Literary Review*, Llewellyn Jones, had toned down Dell's audacious book reveiwing. Also, *Poetry* was excluding the local talent and only publishing well-known Imagists, primarily Europeans and expatriate American writers; Maurice Browne's Little Theatre, supported by wealthy Chicagoans, was presenting new but exclusively European plays. What had once seemed new and vital had begun to pale.

In February of 1914, at one of Margery's literary evenings, Hecht met the as-yet-unpublished Sherwood Anderson, who was renting a room on Fifty-seventh Street but spent most of his time at Margery's. The gathering was not the usual Friday-night open house, however, but a party to celebrate the beginning of a new magazine destined to become the voice of the Renaissance—as *Poetry* had never been—and an influence on world literature. A beautiful icy blonde got up and spoke passionately of the need for a magazine as a forum for new ideas, a place where Chicago writers and poets could be published and thereby advance the "liberation." The magazine was to be called *The Little Review* and she, Margaret Anderson,[1] was starting it.

A few months earlier she had attended a lecture by John Cowper Powys and felt inspired to start a literary review. She had asked everyone she knew for money, Then, using her passionate belief and startling beauty as weapons, she had assaulted the literary establishment and had collected enough cash for book ads to begin. The first issue came out in March of 1914 and was filled with the work of the Chicago School—Floyd Dell, Arthur Ficke, Margery Curry, Eunice Tietjens (assistant editor of *Poetry*), Sherwood Anderson and his wife Cornelia. Hecht was intrigued, but his involvement with the Renaissance was delayed.

Early that year the American novelist Winston Churchill's best-selling novel *The Inside of the Cup* was on the top-ten list. He was passing through Chicago on his way east, so Hecht along with reporters from the other dailies were sent to get an interview. In Churchill's hotel sitting room Hecht got his first view of Marie Armstrong, Chicago's only woman reporter. She was both attractive and intelligent, qualities Hecht thought incompatible in a woman.

A short time later, during a shakeup at her paper Marie was fired, then hired by the *Journal*. Hecht, taking his cue from Duffy, resented the intrusion of a woman into the city room, the two of them holing up in Duffy's sports department cubbyhole (where Hecht continued writing many of Duffy's stories for him), glowering at Marie whenever she got too near. To relieve the tension, editor Hutchins installed her in an unused office.

With Marie out of sight, Hecht still wasn't happy. The more he found out about her, the more intrigued he became. He noticed that frequently she stayed in the office at lunchtime reading novels in French, which he learned she had studied at the University of Chicago. Then he noticed that Duffy was watching her too. Neither of them dared make a move, so Marie invited them both to lunch. Duffy spluttered but Hecht accepted.

Before meeting Marie, Hecht hadn't had any serious affairs, his experience with women limited to the brothel, where he found sex without companionship, and the drawing room, where he got companionship but no sex. He had dated Jewish girls he met through his family but didn't have much time for these relationships what with working all day and going to shows, bars, and brothels and roaming the city by night. Nor were these casual relationships fulfilling, sexually, emotionally, or intellectually. Marie was a revelation. So was Hecht for Marie. If not conventionally handsome, with his mustache, curly brown hair, and Slavic features, he was mysteriously attractive. "His eyes were a deep blue and somewhat sunken," Marie recalled. "He did not look especially Jewish in those days. In fact, he could have posed as a Rumanian violinist, an Italian organ grinder in a Shubert musical, or a German student. He was under six feet, large-boned, square, with a loose, rapid walk." Marie had been impressed by stories of his reportorial exploits when she worked on Hearst's *American*, then when they met she was intrigued by his vitriolic intelligence and his convoluted epigrams. Regarded as a brilliant conversationalist—"a verbal Coney Island"—he was the writer of unknown potential who was expected to shoot up and tower over the rest of the Chicago literati.

Hecht spent his days at the *Journal* with Marie, they went on assignments together, and saw each other in the evenings. "Don't expect me to marry you," Marie remembered him telling her. "I'm not the marrying kind. I intend to be an artist. A great writer. I may take a mistress but never a wife."

"Then you don't love me?" Marie asked.

"Love has nothing to do with it! I do love you. I adore you more than

I ever thought I could care for anyone but myself. But I won't marry you. That's final. My intentions are not honorable."

They were too embarrassed, or rather Marie was, to solicit a friend's apartment for their assignations. Hecht didn't know any of the Fifty-seventh Street group well enough, and the only person on the *Journal* he was close to was Duffy—but Duffy was still sulking over Hecht's preference for a woman's companionship. On the top floor of the paper, abandoned except for a darkroom which conveniently had a cot in it, Hecht and Marie "fell into evasions that assumed a finality as complete as the thing itself." Hecht was intransigent in his insistence on love without marriage, however, and Marie was just as calculatingly adamant, for her part.

"Her behaviour confused me. It varied from passionate clinging to fanatic resistance. This was a technique not uncommon in that time when virtue held out like the Alamo, until the last bit of lingerie had been breached." To make Hecht jealous and to provide the romantic compli-cations that Marie said he was always accusing her of, she started openly flirting with Duffy. Hecht responded with increased ardor, trying to flesh out his favorite maxim of Rabelais—"The only proof of female virginity lies in its destruction."

Because they were at loggerheads over the question of Marie's virginity, their work suffered. Hecht wasn't turning out the stories he once had, and Marie alternated between flirtation with Duffy and "headaches." Then their darkroom assignations were discovered and Hutchins fired Marie, prompting Hecht to break off the affair and be rid of his frustration. Marie's mother, one of the few not charmed by Hecht's glib tongue, did everything she could short of locking Marie in her bedroom to keep her from trying to see Hecht again.

Marie was fired in July of 1914, and in August Hecht took a job at the *Daily News*, replacing his friend Harry Hansen, who had been sent to Berlin to cover the First World War, which had begun on the first of the month. Hecht wanted the extra money the *News* owner Victor Lawson was offering, plus he wanted to escape Duffy's acid tongue. As important was his desire to work for Henry Justin Smith, appointed *News* editor in 1913, who was gathering about him a staff of novelists and poets who also functioned as reporters when they had to. Smith "loved our paper with an interest that ignored circulation," Hecht said, "and saw it as a daily novel written by a wild but willing bunch of Balzacs."

With Marie out of his life, Hecht had both the time and the desire to become involved in other things. Once he was into the routine at the

News—which didn't take long since he was a seasoned reporter—he began to frequent the Fifty-seventh Street colony, especially Margery Curry's gatherings. It was there that he met and befriended a young man his own age who was to weave in and out of his life over the next forty years—the poet Maxwell Bodenheim. Raised in Hermanville, Mississippi, Bodenheim had arrived in Chicago during the summer of 1914 after being dishonorably discharged from the army, a result of frequent escape attempts culminating in a frenzied try at suicide by swallowing lye. He was tall and fair, with piercing blue eyes and russet eyebrows, and was determined to become a great poet. He had taken steps to that end immediately upon arrival, publishing a short verse in *Poetry* in August and another in *The Little Review* in September. Amiable and courteous, even "sweet," Bodenheim was also slovenly, outlandish, and a vicious wit. He seemed to be everywhere at once during his Chicago years—at the literary parties at Margery Curry's, writing both for Margaret Anderson and Harriet Monroe, as well as publishing in Alfred Kreymborg's magazines *Others* and *Glebe*, and in *The New Republic, Touchstone, Seven Arts, Pagan,* and *Egoist*. He lived in a succession of cheap rooms, drank heavily, tried to seduce almost every attractive woman he laid eyes on, and continually wrote poetry. Burton Rascoe remarked that he was America's Rimbaud, and one of Bodenheim's lovers compared him to Hofmann's paintings of Christ. His energy, his way with words, and his wit attracted Hecht from their first meeting and, though their paths were to diverge sharply a few years later, from the winter of 1914 till late 1916 they were the best of friends, bent on making names for themselves any way they could as long as it was with words.[2]

No Compromise with Public Taste

—MOTTO OF *THE LITTLE REVIEW*

When Hecht first encountered Margaret Anderson he felt she was deeply committed to an art she would never master: in conversation she omitted prepositions and sometimes verbs in her hurry to get her ideas out, and gestured frantically to fill in the gaps. Since Hecht was apolitical, he was further deterred by her sudden politicization three months after *The Little Review*'s inception, when Margaret came under the influence of firebrand political radical Emma Goldman. Goldman channeled

Anderson's energies and thoughts into anarchism, which meant *The Little Review* became rife with it, losing her the book ad revenue she had worked so hard to acquire.

Six months later, Margaret's anarchist sympathies had dried up and she switched to Imagism. Hecht hadn't been convinced that *The Little Review* could make it in February of 1914, but by the end of 1915 there could be no doubt: because of *The Little Review*'s success, Margaret was the most important literary editor in town.

Convinced of her commitment to literature from the beginning— although never of her ability to create it—Hecht was now convinced of her power. Not only was she a force on the local literary scene, he felt she was honest and had integrity as well—integrity evidenced by her publishing the Chicago School, honesty for sometimes refusing to publish them. "Not for us," her rejection notes read, "but I'm sure there are scores of other magazines that will be eager to buy it." Since Hecht was now an active member of the Fifty-seventh Street group, he wanted to publish in *The Little Review* and become recognized as part of the Chicago School. Bodenheim and Sherwood Anderson had "acquired a promiscuous audience for their talents" in the pages of *The Little Review*, the voice of the Chicago Renaissance heard worldwide, their names having "become synonymous with the assault of what was called the New Generation."

The only way to publish in *The Little Review*, Hecht knew, was to have Margaret enthuse over his writing, however inarticulately. Not prepared to go to her office in the Fine Arts Building, he sought her out at Margery Curry's parties, the only place outside her office she was to be found, and proceeded to envelop her in a web of opinion, epigrams, gossip, and flattery ("You can't possibly be as valiant as you look," he told her) till she was proclaiming his genius from atop the ramparts of Art, then located on the eighth floor of the Fine Arts Building in downtown Chicago. Shortly afterwards, he began publishing in *The Little Review*, his first piece, "The Sermon in the Depths," running in the May issue. ("Beware the hopelessly sane . . . freedom is fun but it means little. The artist who grows its wings becomes a mosquito nibbling on a billiard ball.") The June/July issue contained a book review and an article, "Slobberdom, Sneerdom and Boredom," about the annual dinner of the Walt Whitman fellowship, where Clarence Darrow expended "saccharine drool at the expense of a great man," Hecht admitting "it is rather a complicated matter this sneering business."

Fantasizing Margaret as "an immaculate and adoring companion," Hecht began to court her, a courtship made more than a little difficult since Margaret and a young friend, Harriet Dean, were living in tents north of the city along the Lake Michigan shore. Margaret came to the Fine Arts Building every day—which Hecht began to frequent—but she took the train back every evening. Convinced he was in love, Hecht made the trek on foot with Bodenheim one Saturday afternoon, but Margaret wasn't there. "I always had so little need of the humanity in people," Margaret Anderson wrote of herself decades later. She didn't respond to Hecht's seduction attempts, which only drove him harder despite his friend Wallace Smith's dismissal of her as "the idiot Sappho." Finally there was nothing for Hecht to do but accept defeat, although he was never to forget the experience. As with most things, it became grist for his typewriter. Almost a decade later, in his roman à clef *Humpty Dumpty*, this scene appeared:

> When he had started to embrace her he had felt her flesh stiffen, and her cheek as his lips touched it had seemed frosted. . . .
> "There's something queer about her. . . ."
> . . . he stood knocking at the door. . . .
> He heard someone walking inside and the door was opened slowly. A square-faced woman with black, glittering eyes confronted him.
> "What do you want?" she asked peremptorily. . . .
> The details of the woman's masculine clothes completed the dream in his mind. . . .
> "From the beginning," he mused, "an aversion for men. Anybody but a professional psychologist like myself would have noticed it. Her cold hands when I embraced her. I should have understood. She tried to love me. The spirit was willing but the flesh was tainted."

Unrequited love was one thing, career another. Hecht continued to publish in *The Little Review* for the next seven years.

During the spring and summer, Hecht frequented Sherwood Anderson's rooming house on Cass Street, which housed other writers and several painters Anderson had dubbed "the Little Children of the Arts." Anderson read stories from *Windy McPherson's Son* and a then unfinished and untitled work (which became *Winesburg, Ohio*), to the Little Children and the Fifty-seventh Street group. By 1915, though, it could no longer properly be called the Fifty-seventh Street group since Bohemia was shifting from the far South to the Near North Side. Anderson had moved to Cass Street, where *Poetry* was located and where Szukalski had a studio. Margery Curry was living in Oak Park, Bodenheim in a cheap room on the North Side; Hecht was still with his parents. *The Little Review*, the Little Theatre, and *The Dial* were all located in the Fine Arts Building near the Loop, and all the newspaper offices were in the downtown area as well. With the shift from south to north, the literary community was brought closer together geographically, while emotionally it began to draw apart. Sherwood Anderson, considered by New York and London editors and critics to be a writer of genius though his first book had yet to see print, had gathered round him a circle of the faithful, drawn by the power of his stories. Margaret Anderson was caught up in her own circle of women-without-men, and Margery Curry was in the throes of depression, a result of the breakup of her year-long affair with Sherwood Anderson.

In the late spring Hecht got a call from Margery's best friend, who told him she was afraid Margery might kill herself. Hecht went out to Oak Park, found Margery sitting by a railroad track in the rain, and listened as she told her story—Sherwood had walked out two weeks before and hadn't come back, refused to speak with her when she phoned his office (he wrote ad copy), and sent her letters back unopened. Hecht assured her he would talk with him and try to discover what had happened. Over lunch, Anderson explained, "I decided . . . that I wanted to see what it was like to have an affair with a thoroughly homely woman—with a homely face and a homely body. I wanted to see how a man would feel—pretending to be in love with that sort of woman, sleeping with a woman who bored you to death. Well, the experiment is over." In a note to Hecht a few days later, Anderson rejected his suggestion that he and Margery reconcile. "The truth is, Ben, that from my point of view it's interference and I can't do it. How do we know that all these mannerisms that sometimes make us impatient are but defenses set up by a spirit that is often at the breaking point. She has been defeated in health. She half wanted to write and that didn't go. She has a madness for a certain kind of social power and she had to see her influence over Floyd, me, and you wane. Let's let it rest, Ben. Dammit, man, it isn't in the cards."

Hecht had had a brief flirtation with Margery when they first met, which he now resumed. It provided a certain solace but only underscored his loneliness. Margery was thirty-two to Hecht's twenty-one, wasn't very attractive, and was too experienced sexually for his narrow morality. There seemed only one solution.

Hecht hadn't seen Marie since she had been fired from the *Journal*, but the failed affairs with Margaret Anderson and Margery Curry turned his thoughts back to her. He knew he couldn't call on her at home because of her parents' disapproval, but the problem was resolved in June when he discovered Marie was working at the *Herald*. They resumed their former relationship, which Marie kept secret from her parents. "Mother thought him a bad-tempered young man with a silly habit of saying things merely to shock people," Marie recalled. "Father said, 'He's just a smart-Aleck kid, clever enough, and probably a good writer—but I just don't like him.' " Hecht accused them of being "Anglo-Saxon, normal and nice." Loathing Marie's dependence on them, he pressed her to confront her parents and admit she had begun seeing him again. When she refused he decided to force the issue and wrote an article he titled "The American Family."

Harry Hansen thought that "Ben tried to satirize the typical American family" in the piece when in fact Hecht was writing "out of a concrete hatred" about only one family. He had Margaret Anderson run it in the August issue of *The Little Review*.

> The ambitious and educated American mother is a forceful creature, a strong, powerful woman. As an individual she is dead. . . . Moaning with a tyrannical lust for possession she enfolds her daughter in her arms. . . . In the night the daughter wonders and doubts. She would like "to get away"—to go forth free of certain fiercely applied restrictions and meet a different kind of folk, a different kind of thought. . . . It is all vague. Always revolt is vague for the daughters of women. . . . Something happens to crystallize the revolt. It is a man outside the pale. . . . Often the struggle is fought through little things too numerous to mention and the struggle itself too casual to classify. Sometimes it wages without a word; at other times there are blows. . . . [The mother's] first weapon (she uses it like a poison) is her love. She calls it that. "You are my only happiness," she cries. "I have given you everything, a part of me, all you have needed. I have sacrificed everything for you. All my dreams have been for you. O, how can you permit anything to come between us?" . . . Day after day

the mother strikes with this weapon. Her red, furious eyes dripping tears, she moans it out. Her voice is like the yelp of a frantic animal. . . . Her voice is cold and hard and hollow like an echo in a tomb. . . . The mother, moaning, shuddering, her eyes gleaming, folds her daughter in her arms. "I dare you to take her from me," she cries out to the man. . . . "Nothing can ever take me from you," the daughter weeps. Death. Tears, a form of decomposition, now roll from her cheeks. The struggle is over. The unit has been preserved and now one may look at the unit and see what it is. The rotted figures of the dead have dragged their shredded flesh back to the graves. . . . O, this daughter! She is the one who had the vision of beauty. She is the one whose soul sang for a day with the capacity for all the world's loveliness. Honesty, purity, fineness burned in her with their divine radiance. The lights are turned out. Death reigns supreme.

"It seriously hurt my father, who had begun to admire Ben's brain," Marie remembered. "This gesture of public insult outraged him, and justly. He said to me, 'It's a damn cheap trait in that young man rushing into print to wave a personal grievance in the face of a public. He has it in him to do something equally unsporting to you, if you are fool enough to marry him!'"

Hecht though was enormously pleased with the effect, "every sentence like a firecracker under the Armstrongs' seat," but Marie was miserable since her parents extracted a promise from her that she never see Hecht again. Torn between loyalty to her family and Hecht, she did nothing for the moment but wait for an ad to appear in the *Tribune*'s personal column, which was how she and Hecht had arranged to contact one another if anything ever went wrong. The ad didn't appear, but a cycle of poems in *The Little Review* did. In "Autumn Song" Hecht wrote, "It is cold. / I have lost my warmth. / I have lost thee. . . . / It is only she who hath died. / It is only she whom I loved with all my soul." "Death Song" spoke of "the white face of a dead love . . . a white face like a dim sorrow." Then the ad appeared: "Marie, do not judge me until we can talk. See me if you can and will. I am sorry. B." When a few days later Marie was able to slip away, Hecht explained that Margaret Anderson had persuaded him to publish the piece—not because she was jealous— but because he had been "unfaithful to the garrulous eunuch idea" she had of him. He promised to write a retraction and have Margaret publish it, but the retraction never appeared.

Because of Marie's parents' and even her friends' objections to Hecht it was difficult for them to spend much time together. Their furtive meetings had to be squeezed into office hours in out-of-the-way places lest they be discovered. They regularly met in unfrequented rooms at the Art Institute and a nook in the book department at Marshall Field's.

It was Wallace Smith who, by example, broke Hecht's resistance to marriage. Smith was "tall and dark, foppish and athletic . . . cynical as a coroner and disdainful of all humans except Mexicans," and Hecht's best friend. Marie had first encountered him when she worked on the *American*. "The telephone booths in the local room were always littered with papers which were bedecked with drawings of nudes, fearfully and astoundingly made. I soon learned that these were the work of one Wallace Smith who could write like a house afire but wanted to be an artist; he was handsome and snooty." Marie hadn't liked him then nor did she like him when she met Hecht; then Wallace got married and Marie's viewpoint changed. Now Hecht began to soften.

"I went out to see Wallace," he told Marie. "I can't tell you how funny I felt when I saw him with his wife. Maybe I've been wrong all along. Wallace was so proud of Hariot. He was always putting his arms around her. He said a lot of boob things about being married, but I knew in my heart they weren't boobish. When I left they both came down to the door with me.

"The last thing I remember—and, Marie, I can't get it out of my mind—is seeing Wallace with Hariot standing a little in front of him, he holding her to him and both waving good-by to me. Nutty thing to remember, isn't it? Doesn't mean a damn thing . . . only somehow it made me feel gone all over . . . like I knew I'd been born without an arm or leg or something." Hecht suggested they get married.

They foresaw either an elopement or an unpleasant struggle with Marie's parents when, in October, Marie's father died suddenly. Her mother took over his business, sold their house, and moved into an apartment, expecting Marie to share it with her. "I knew that if Ben and I were ever to be married, we must do it at once, for if I should settle with mother in a city apartment I would have to stay and share expenses. So we bought two rings, obtained a license, and planned the ceremony for the next day." On November 28th, 1915, they were married by an Episcopalian priest and moved into a four-room apartment on the South Side, where they installed a Mason and Hamlin grand piano (Margaret

Anderson's preferred instrument), which they bought on the installment plan.

A half dozen reporters were once interviewing Arnold Bennett. The cantankerous British novelist sat at the head of a long table. Flanking the table, we took turns asking questions of the great author. Only Starrett was silent. He had brought with him a suitcase filled with Arnold Bennett firsts. He kept sliding book after book down the table, with his calling card sticking out of each. In the tenth book, Bennett wrote, "To Charles Vincent Emerson Starrett, who is fast becoming an old friend." He signed it "Arnold."

—BEN HECHT
Gaily, Gaily

I met Arnold Bennett at the Press Club—or perhaps the Cliff Dwellers—where a luncheon had been arranged in his honor. . . . I suppose every living member of the club was on hand to greet the famous author, and there was a score of important guests. Some of them had brought books to be signed, among them Karl Edwin Harriman and myself. I had brought only one, but Harriman had brought close to a dozen. With the others, we sent our books down the long table with our cards in them, and for a time the English novelist toiled grimly. At length he paused for a sharper look at one of the cards. His eye brightened, an authentic smile twisted his lips under his ragged moustache, and he wrote, "For Karl Edwin Harriman, who is getting to be an old friend."

—VINCENT STARRETT
Born in a Bookshop

It was in Henry Justin Smith's salon, disguised as the *News'* city room, that Hecht came under the tutelage of fellow reporter Vincent Starrett, soon to leave the *News* to begin his career as critic, novelist, and literary biographer. Although Hecht's reading had been voracious, it had also been desultory, while Starrett, ten years Hecht's senior, had put in that many more years of assiduous reading and knew literature as well as anyone in Chicago. His taste ran to the modernists in fiction, to the genuinely American writers who had advanced the art of American letters, and to writers of any nationality he considered good. Starrett began guiding Hecht's reading and introduced him to Stephen Crane (Hecht then introduced Sherwood Anderson and Wallace Smith to *Maggie, The Red Badge of Courage,* and *Whilomville Stories*), Arthur Machen, Lafcadio Hearn, Ambrose Bierce, Edgar Saltus, and Havelock Ellis, as well as to such forgotten writers as W. C. Morrow, Richard Middleton, Hubert Crackenthorpe, John Davidson, Haldane MacFall, Arthur Crosslett Smith, and Young Allison. Since Starrett was an inveterate book collector, Hecht tagged along after him to McClurg's, Kroch's, Walter Hill's, and Powner's bookstores in search of first editions. Although he found nothing of antiquarian value, Hecht acquired complete sets of Walter Pater, Goethe, Sir Richard Burton, and Crébillon, which began to fill shelves in the new apartment and spill over onto tables, chairs, and the floor.

To pull the shy Starrett's leg, one day in the office Hecht began advocating the power of a planchette board. Starrett put it down as a toy, but Hecht maintained it could answer any question Starrett asked it. Phrasing it that way, Hecht figured he could dupe Starrett into asking where he could find some particularly valuable first edition. Skeptical but intrigued, Starrett had Hecht ask where he could find a first of Poe's *Tamerlane,* since each of the three existing copies was worth in excess of ten thousand dollars (in 1925, Starrett wrote an article for the *Saturday Evening Post,* "Have You a *Tamerlane* in Your Attic?", which turned up a fourth). The planchette, or rather Hecht, began to draw a map. Starrett said it resembled Madison Street where Powner's bookshop was. The planchette spelled out a "yes" and went on to describe exactly where in the store the book was to be found. Two hours later Starrett was back at the *News'* office complaining he'd searched the entire store and had only turned up a collected edition of Poe that contained the poem. Hecht suggested consulting the planchette again. This time it asked Starrett if he had checked the bookcases outside the shop. Starrett was off again. Next day, he told Hecht, "It's all subconscious. I knew that volume of Poe's collected works was there but my conscious mind had forgotten. And that pesky little board picked the memory out of my subconscious and made me accept it as information. Serves me right."

As a result of Starrett's influence, Hecht began contributing critical articles to the *Friday Literary Review,* and in mid-1916 when the *News* started running a two-page weekly book review section, he penned critiques for its editor, Henry Blackman Sell, about many of the authors Starrett had introduced him to, as well as on writers he was naturally drawn to—Gide, Proust, Nietzsche, and Dostoyevsky (for a time he proclaimed *The Idiot* the greatest novel ever written). Margaret Anderson had once remarked that Hecht reminded her of a Decadent poet, so he had sought out their work and now sang their praises in print. He hailed Dreiser as the greatest American novelist and deplored that a writer of Sherwood Anderson's ability couldn't get his books published. When, on September 1st, 1916, *Windy McPherson's Son* was issued, Hecht, was the first to acclaim its importance, in the September 8th *Friday Literary Review*.

Although Hecht had known Sherwood Anderson for almost two years, it wasn't until 1916 that they became close friends. Anderson would often accompany Hecht when he covered stories. They ate and drank together, walked and talked and argued together. "Sometimes he and I went forth to do our cursing," Anderson wrote ten years later. "Outwardly he was a more adept curser than myself but inwardly I felt I could outdo him and often we walked together, he cursing aloud our common fate and declaring dramatically that life was for us an empty cup, a vessel turned upside down, a golden goblet with cracks in the bowl, the largest crack being the fact that we both unfortunately had our livings to make, and I striving to cap his every curse with a more violent one. We went together into a street and stood under the moon . . . before us were many huge warehouses. 'I hope they burn,' I said feebly, but he only laughed at the weakness of my fancy. 'I hope the builders die slowly of a painful inflammation of the bowels,' he said while I envied."

Hecht was caught up in his marriage and the intensification of his efforts to make a career of writing while Anderson was enjoying the first fruits of his own efforts—his first three books were published in 1916, 1917, and 1918. He was frequently on the move during those years while Hecht stayed put in Chicago, so their respective "cracks in the bowl" drove them apart shortly after they'd become friends. Although Anderson was seventeen years his senior, Hecht, far more glib than Anderson, nevertheless gave him his due—thirty years later when he no longer felt threatened by Anderson's success. It was Sherwood Anderson, Hecht wrote, who turned "that Smoke House town into the new Athens."

Hecht and Kenneth Sawyer Goodman had continued collaborating, but by 1916 Hecht was devising the plots, Goodman helping with the staging and technical aspects of the plays. Their best, most complex play, the three-act *Hero of Santa Maria*,[3] was written that year, with most of the credit owing to Hecht. Produced by the Washington Square Players in

February of 1917, it marked the end of their joint playwriting. Hecht had outgrown Goodman, who died the following year. (In commemoration, Goodman's father built the Goodman Theatre next to the Art Institute in downtown Chicago.)

As an outlet for his own plays as well as works by local writers, Hecht and Bodenheim—along with Elizabeth Bingham and Lou Wall Moore, both of whom had been involved with the Little Theatre—created the Players' Workshop, an alternative little theatre housed in one of the Fifty-seventh Street Midway buildings. Hecht and Bodenheim cowrote several one-act pieces, but for his first offering Hecht did a one-acter by himself called *Dregs*. It was his earliest effort to show any individuality, to use ideas and language for their shock value, to be realistic yet cynical and mystical at the same time.

As the curtain rises, a derelict stumbles on stage and roars, "Jesus Christ, I'm a cross-eyed son-of-a-bitch if I ain't!" The opening night audience was stunned. The bum looks at his reflection in a saloon window on a cold winter night and thinks he's seeing Christ. He talks to him and tries to convince him to come along to a brothel where the girls will give them a warm bed for the night. Finally he realizes he's talking to himself.

Most of the audience at the first performance walked out after the first line, as did the second night's audience. When the third performance was reviewed by Percy Hammond, who deplored the "unbeliev-able squalor of the words," *Dregs* was replaced by another play. On the afternoon of the fourth day, Hecht dropped in on the rehearsal. "Nobody said anything to me so I sat down in one of the back seats and listened. The actors stumbled about in their lines, and now and then I thought someone was going to come up to me and explain why my play had been withdrawn. But no one did. Their courage had ebbed away. They were going on with something easy and surefire. After a while I felt chilled. I went out."

Refusing to accept defeat, Hecht submitted *Dregs* to a play tourney sponsored by the Washington Square Players, but it was rejected because of the opening line. Hecht then reverted to a sophomoric exercise in composition when he and Bodenheim collaborated on *The Master Poisoner*, the only play they wrote for the Player's Workshop still extant. Twelve pages long, it was replete with one-liners about art, beauty, and death, most of which were Bodenheim's. Under the superficiality of the writing and the flashes of the bizarre ("Your last poison of moth-blood produced an effect so exquisitely monstrous that even death was appalled. Ah, the bones of an old woman, dissolving within her, left her body a loose grimace") lay a deeper meaning for Bodenheim. He and Hecht had known an older woman named Fedya Ramsay, of whom Bodenheim was enamored. Fedya loved Sherwood Anderson, though, and couldn't be dissuaded by the best of Bodenheim's poetry. Anderson tired of her quickly, as he did with most women, so Fedya packed up and moved out of his Cass Street attic. When the Little Theatre invited her to go on tour with them, she accepted, but in Santa Barbara she fell from a horse and was killed. One of the Little Theatre group wrote Anderson of her death. The story he told his Cass Street followers that night was of Fedya. Hecht recalled that "Sherwood's voice was calm. He spoke of Fedya's death as if he had gotten rid of a rival for his affections. He now had the field to himself."

Bodenheim grieved over her death and never forgave Anderson, using him as the model for the play's master poisoner, who has created his masterpiece, a poison he believes will arrest Death. He administers the poison to his wife, Fana, who becomes inhumanly beautiful but doesn't die as expected. Death takes the master poisoner instead. (At a dinner the Hechts gave for the publication of Anderson's *Mid-American Chants*, Bodenheim purposely alienated Anderson forever: when Anderson asked him, a poet, what he thought of his book of verse, Bodenheim replied, "Oh, the corn, how it aches.")

Hecht and Bodenheim produced their plays through the fall of 1916, but the Workshop didn't last the season since there was little financial support forthcoming and there were not enough playwrights in Chicago to provide a repertoire, although people other than Hecht and Bodenheim did contribute, among them Elisha Cook, Sr.

Just as Hecht had once told Marie he could never be a husband, after their marriage he told her he could never be a father. Undaunted, Marie announced in late spring that she was pregnant. Hecht was still working as a reporter as well as free-lancing for the *Book Page*, but his forty-five-dollar-per-week salary was all they had to live on, Marie having quit her job on the *Herald*.

Slowly they went into debt. Although Hecht spent weekends writing plays and reviews, he earned little for them. During the summer of 1916 he and Marie managed to get away for a few weeks to Union Pier, Michigan, where they joined Sherwood Anderson and his clique, but by the fall Marie wasn't able to go out much. Hecht made an effort to spend more evenings at home, where they frequently had Marie's mother and Hecht's parents in. Then in November, Edwina Hecht was born, nicknamed Teddy after Theodore Roosevelt. When Marie got out of the hospital, Hecht delivered her to a new eight-room apartment by the lake, which put them deeper in debt.

4

"MONEY...
PROSE OF LIFE"

I have always had a picture of myself as a story teller. I have seen myself like those sunny and cackling fellows who once upon a time stood on the street corners of Bagdad and unfolded tales to the harassed citizens who paused to listen—and fling grateful kopecks at their feet.

—Ben Hecht
Introduction to
The Collected Stories,
1945

If I'd been an Arab I would have sat on a little rug with some kind of basket or pot in front of me—sat in a market and told stories and people would have thrown money into it. I know how to tell a story.

—Jed Harris
(ca. 1937)

The end of 1917 saw the Chicago Renaissance on the wane, a mere regional literary movement not strong enough to keep Chicago writers from drifting off to the publishing houses, theatres, and bigger checks to be found in the East. Maxwell Bodenheim left for New York in 1917, and Margaret Anderson and Jane Heap moved *The Little Review* there the same year. By 1918 Sherwood Anderson was in New York doing publicity for the movies and Ring Lardner had left his sports reporting job in Chicago for a similar position in New York; in 1919 Edgar Lee Masters would give up his Chicago law practice to relocate there.

The entry of the United States into the Great War helped undermine the Chicago School as well. Victor Lawson, owner of the *News*, refused a commission and went to war as a doughboy; Stanislaus Szukalski was drafted, refused to have his long hair cut, and was classified a conscientious objector; another news reporter, Charles MacArthur, fought in the trenches with the Rainbow Division. The war commandeered almost everyone's attention, but Hecht, true to himself, continued his life and work as if it didn't exist. There was a possibility he would be drafted, but with a wife and child it was a remote one.

What Hecht was concerned with was money. Since his marriage he had been getting deeper and deeper in debt. He had his newspaper salary but little other income since neither the Players' Workshop nor *The Little Review* paid anything. He had received a few dollars from his collaboration with Kenneth Sawyer Goodman and from his short story "Life," which had appeared in *The Best Short Stories of 1915*, but it was hardly enough. When the butcher came to their house demanding payment, Marie went crying to Hecht, "I owe the butcher thirty dollars but that isn't all I owe either. I owe the grocer and the milkman and the iceman, and you've been saying you'd give me more money. You never have, and I can't run this house and entertain all your friends on forty dollars a week!"

Hecht promised to do something about it immediately. Figuring the sale of one short story to a slick magazine would wipe out his debts, he submitted "The Unlovely Sin" to H. L. Mencken's *Smart Set*, one of the leading fiction magazines in the country, a magazine respected by writers because of Mencken's belief in literature as a way of life. Two weeks later Hecht received an encouraging letter from Mencken (signed "Yours in Christ") accepting the story.[1]

To Hecht's dismay the enclosed check was for thirty dollars. The only recourse was to write twenty stories to pay his debts, so over the next year and a half he cranked out an average of two stories a week, work he considered "second-rate stuff," since Mencken dictated the plots while he merely filled in the words. In 1918 Mencken wrote him, "Try a story about a Polish immigrant who works in the Chicago stockyards as a ten-dollar-a-week pig sticker, and who practices fiddle playing all night. So does the Mr. Swift who owns the stockyards and lives in a millionaire's mansion. Mr. Swift, the millionaire, is consumed with ambition to be a great fiddle player. And for an ending, have millionaire Swift sitting in his box in Orchestra Hall listening with seething envy to a great new fiddle player—the same ten-dollar-a-week pig sticker Polack who worked for him." Hecht dutifully wrote "Humoresque in Ham," switching Mr. Swift to Mr. Sloan.

Mencken suggested a story about a Mormon who decides he only wants one wife, so Hecht ground out "The Man with One Wife"; Mencken suggested a story about a woman pianist whose husband refuses to allow her to continue playing, so Hecht wrote "Caricature." Hecht's stories read "as if a sort of snorting amateur Mencken had written them," so he was assured an outlet through the *Smart Set* as long as he needed one. In his last book, *Letters from Bohemia*, Hecht wrote, "There is no successor for H. L. Mencken. Put together the ten most whooping critics of our current American scene and you won't have the beginnings of a Mencken. The sage of Baltimore is gone from our midst, and his boots remain empty."

During 1916 and 1917, as a result of his marriage to Marie, Hecht was out of favor with Margaret Anderson, who had warned him that "Marie was a snake that would coil about him and crush the genius out of him." Hecht, for his part, was equally unhappy with Margaret because of her liaison with one Jane Heap. An actress with the Little Theatre, Jane Heap had made her first appearance in Margaret's office in February of 1916, winning her immediate allegiance by informing a possible backer for the magazine that she gave her "a pain in the ass." With her wit and ability to extemporize brilliantly, she complemented Margaret's beauty, poise, and elegance, giving Chicago for a time its own Gertrude and Alice. The problem for Hecht was that "the fair-faced lad disguised as Jane Heap" (Sherwood Anderson's phrase) didn't like him and, worse, could out-talk him. Hecht shied away from her, unable to accept being verbally bested. Although he only published three poems in *The Little Review* during 1916 and 1917, he got the opportunity to edit an issue—while Margaret and Jane were in transit to California—and at the same time to pique Margaret by upsetting several of her important contributors. A sheaf of poems went back to Vachel Lindsay with a one-word rejection: "Rotten." A Galsworthy short story was returned with the notation "Cheap stuff." Although Hecht admired Theodore Dreiser, when he found a play of his with a note to Margaret explaining that he'd had it for a number of years but hadn't done anything with it, Hecht sent it back to him commenting that after reading it he understood why.

By 1918, though, Margaret had begun to warm to Hecht again, a partial result of two letters she received from Ezra Pound, her European editor. In 1917 Pound wrote, "Hecht is an asset. Hard reading and a bit heavy, but he has the root of the matter in him. He is trying to come to grips also. When he recalls the fact that Maupassant does not exaggerate, he can write *contes*—i.e. can (future) will be able to." And again the following year: "Hecht might write good de Maupassant if he didn't try to crack jokes and ring bells; and if he would only realize he DON'T need to exaggerate to be interesting." (In 1918, when a Chicago poet wrote Pound to ask him why he didn't return to America, Pound responded, "Why should I come back to that God-forsaken desert; there is only one intelligent man in the whole United States to talk to—Ben Hecht.")

Margaret was also aware that Hecht was getting his fiction published in *Smart Set*, thus breaking out of Chicago's regionalism and becoming known nationwide, so she wrote and asked him for stories—no money as usual but at least he could write whatever he wanted. Bored with Mencken's prefabricated plots, Hecht accepted eagerly. In 1918, he published an imaginary conversation with Pound—"Pounding Ezra"— and five short stories, which he considered the best pieces he ever wrote for *The Little Review*.[2]

In 1918 Hecht also collected twenty dollars for "Snow Monotones," his only contribution to Harriet Monroe's *Poetry*—"A great white leopard prowling / silently over the house tops. . . ."

Hecht would plagiarize Sandburg's poem "Fog" again in his own "Fog Patterns"—"The fog tiptoes into the streets. / It walks like a great cat"—and later in his novel *The Kingdom of Evil*—"The fog drifted into the city like a great blind moth."[3]

Hecht and Sandburg had first met in 1914 when Sandburg was a reporter for a radical sheet called *The Daybook*. When it folded three years later, Sandburg went to work for the *News*, where he and Hecht were in daily contact, without, however, becoming friends. Temperamentally, they were too dissimilar, the introverted Sandburg interested only in poetry, socialism, and the biography of Abraham Lincoln he had begun to write. To puncture Sandburg's dour seriousness—according to Harry Golden—Hecht hired an out-of-work actor, had him dress himself like Lincoln, then wait for Sandburg on a streetcorner the poet passed on his way home from the *News*. When Sandburg appeared, Lincoln walked toward him, tipped his hat and remarked, "Evening, Mr. Sandburg." In all probability, this was another of Hecht's storyteller's tales, made up later to enhance the reality, as was his account of Sandburg's coverage of an AF of L convention in Minneapolis:

"Carl's an expert on labor affairs. Why don't you send him up to cover it?"

"Good idea," said Beitler.

The next day Henry Justin Smith inquired of Beitler during their pre-Home Edition conference, "How much space are you giving the Sandburg story?"

"No space," said Beitler. "No story."

A second and third day passed without communication from our staff man in Minneapolis. Smith's scowl grew, but his loyalty to the stonily silent correspondent never waivered. On the fourth day a hair-raising story came over the wires from Minneapolis. It was not from Sandburg. It was from the A.P. It announced that an embittered labor delegate had drawn a gun during the forenoon session of the labor congress and opened fire on an orator, severely wounding him. This was a story of size and import—but Smith's heart was heavy as he took charge of the paper's remake for it. Not a word had come through from Sandburg.

"Any instructions for our staff correspondent?" Beitler asked.

"Tell him to come home," Smith said.

An hour later a wire from Minneapolis was handed to Smith. He stared at it with flushing face. It read: "Dear Boss. Can't leave now. Everything too important and exciting."

It was signed Sandburg.

"Ben Hecht says I was sent to a labor convention," Sandburg rejoined, "and over three days sent no story back; I have clippings of those three days with my byline big as a fence post."

Another source of income during the war years[4] was the Dill Pickle Club, run by Jack Jones, who "sounded like Tristan Tzara and Gregory Corso talking at once," said Kenneth Rexroth. Jones put on lectures, poetry readings (Bodenheim was a regular), and one-act plays (*Dregs* appeared on a triple bill with *Cocaine* and *Suppressed Desires*).[5] "I give them the high-brow stuff," Jones said, "until the crowd begins to thin and then I turn on the sex faucet." Hecht served as the "faucet" during 1917 and 1918, he and Bodenheim holding forth on various aspects of the sexual experience. In 1917, shortly before Bodenheim left for New York, they brought off their coup de grace—they arranged a debate, had Jones advertise it, and then on the night it was to take place revealed the subject: Resolved—That People Who Attend Literary Debates Are Imbeciles. The audience expected the usual fireworks that resulted from a Hecht/Bodenheim appearance, but were surprised when Hecht eyed them long and hard, then announced, "The affirmative rests." Bodenheim stepped to the podium, gazed at the audience, then conceded, "You win." It was the easiest money they had ever made, and they let it be known what they thought of the audience of slumming socialites and thrill-seekers. And the idea wasn't even original. Italian poet Emanuel Carnevali had told Hecht how he and Gertrude Stein had pulled it off in Paris.

Hecht also made a few dollars from Maurice Browne who, in an effort to keep his failing Little Theatre from going under completely, commissioned Hecht to write a play. Hecht, wanting to try something different from the European fare Browne had been providing, asked Michael Carmichael Carr, a frequent dinner guest, if he was interested in putting together a show for Browne. Carr was a painter who had designed puppets in Italy with Gordon Craig, Isadora Duncan's lover, so he built puppets for the two short plays Hecht wrote. Although the puppet shows were successful, they couldn't save Browne's Little Theatre, which gave up the ghost in December of 1917; the wealthy Chicagoans who had supported it, no longer interested in arty European drama, let their subscriptions lapse. Hecht had made some money, though, and added a little weight to his growing reputation.

During the war years, the Hechts' circle of friends expanded to include literary critics, magazine editors, artists, novelists, playwrights, poets, actors, and musicians, their apartment a "rendezvous for clever people who did nothing but talk," Marie remembered. Other than the omnipresent Bodenheim, there was Bartlett Cormack, who would later adapt a play of Hecht's for the movies; Anita Loos and her husband John Emerson, passing through town; Charlie Chaplin, working in Chicago for a few months; famous baritone Charles Clark, who sang to Hecht's violin accompaniment; John Farrar, editor of *The Bookman;* and Lawrence Langner, playwright and founder of the Theatre Guild.

Entertaining as the Hechts did, their debts couldn't help but mount, but "Ben absolutely refused to be annoyed with bills," Marie recalled. By the fall of 1918 they owed several thousand dollars and Hecht had no idea how he could make money fast enough to restore their credit so their life-style could continue apace. A solution appeared a week after the Armistice was signed: Victor Lawson offered the twenty-five-year-old Hecht the position of Berlin correspondent to cover the German reconstruction. Hecht accepted on condition he get an advance of several thousand dollars against his salary. Lawson agreed and Hecht used the "expense" money to pay his debts. Hecht also requested that Marie be allowed to accompany him, which Lawson wasn't averse to, so by early December, their furniture stored, apartment rented, and Teddy left in the care of their mothers, they were on their way to New York.

Stopping at the old Vanderbilt Hotel, Hecht arranged for passports and visas. He got his papers immediately, but at first the British consul refused Marie a visa on the grounds that the European situation was still too dangerous, that she would only be adding to the burden on the war-torn continent. They took advantage of the delay to visit Bodenheim, who presented Hecht with a copy of his first published volume of poetry, *Minna and Myself,* in which he had included their play *The Master Poisoner.* Bodenheim had dedicated the volume "By Both of Us to Fedya Ramsay," since most of the poems had been written to Fedya, not to his new wife Minna.

A week later the Hechts arrived in London, where they stayed at the Savoy while Hecht worked with Edgar Price Bell at the *News'* London office and paid social calls on Erza Pound and Arthur Machen. Anxious to get to Germany, though, the Hechts traveled up to Hull and located a captain willing to transport them to Amsterdam, where Hecht secured them diplomatic passports. Arriving in Berlin the following day, they discovered communist revolutionaries fighting in the streets with the forces of the newly formed republic, marauding bands firing at anything that moved. One night, on the way to the Alexanderplatz, their chauffeur-driven car was stopped by Spartacists (communists), and they might have been killed if Hecht hadn't snapped, "We're with the American Commission," a postwar investigating group then in the country. The driver was beaten up, but they were allowed to pass.

In April, when Hecht got wind that there was heavy fighting going on in Munich (Bavaria seceded from the German state to form an independent socialist republic), he jumped on the first train and arrived in Munich in time to scoop the entire international press corps with his story of how Junkers, Prussian military men headed by Gustav Noske (in charge of the army under the new regime), had toppled the new Spartacist government. Hecht inveigled the government to assign a plane to fly him to Freiburg, where he interviewed the newly deposed king of Bavaria. Back in Berlin, Hecht decided to buy the plane and fly around Europe to cover other stories, but the *News* wouldn't put up the twenty-thousand-dollar asking price.

By June the postwar government had been stabilized, Hecht filing stories on socioeconomic conditions, and growing steadily more restless. He bought a violin and had a piano installed in their suite at the Adlon Hotel so he and Marie could play duets. They also took up with the Dadaists for a time and attended several of their meetings, but Marie was unimpressed, finding them sad, while Hecht thought Dadaism the most important revolution he had witnessed in Germany. One night, at a Dadaist concert—where twelve poets read simultaneously, a woman at a typewriter raced another at a sewing machine, and a symphony was performed by half a dozen girls holding placards with musical notes painted on them—Hecht met George Grosz. Deeply moved by his drawings, Hecht had two hundred of them photographed. Back in Chicago in 1921, Hecht would have them exhibited in the window of Covici's bookstore on Washington Street and introduce America to Grosz.

Although they were traveling in limousines and drinking Château d'Yquem '93 (which Hecht had read about in George Moore's *Hail and Farewell*), Marie began pressing to go home because of the baby. Hecht wrote a fifteen-thousand-word article on the reconstruction and sent it off to the *News*, which put the lid on Germany for him.

"To get a bunch of growsing . . . from a man who is making a world reputation for his stuff almost knocks one over," Harry Hansen wrote him in June. "But if you've been feeling so rotten in Berlin you have certainly pulled some bully stuff in spite of it. You are the life of the party. After ten thousand lugubrious words from all ends of the earth, one cable from you will make everybody sit up and smile and feel that there's something after all in getting out a newspaper. . . . Smith shakes his head at your wanting to come back."

When Hecht contacted Henry Justin Smith to tell him he wanted to return, Smith said to visit the rest of Europe and not to forget Russia and China too. Hecht mulled it over for a few days then decided a "future full of bull-fights, pagodas and other alien barrooms" was not for him. Two days later he and Marie left Berlin. Unable to book passage to New York for two weeks, they holidayed at Scheveningen on the North Sea, then left on a troop ship from Rotterdam on July 26th. In New York they were detained by Customs officials who thought their German posters were communist propaganda. Released the following day, they went on to Toledo, where Marie's mother had moved, and picked up three-year-old Teddy. They were back in Chicago the next day.

In three books of reminiscences and one roman a clef in which Hecht wrote extensively of his German sojourn, he failed to mention that Marie had accompanied him.

5

THE GREATEST STORIES EVER RETOLD

Young women were going about in short skirts, exposing their legs and stirring the frightened libido of their elders. Youth was drinking moonshine, dancing in phallic embraces to the melancholy, aphrodisiacal strains of the "St. Louis Blues," conversing in racy epithets. Happiness was saluted as the cat's whiskers, the bee's knees, the snake's hips.

The nerve-hungry post-war generation was treating itself to the artifice of barbarism. Tomtoms beat in the cafés. Nigger shows, Russian dancers, Gauguinistic sceneries, jazz bands with gilded drums and gilded violins delighted the night throngs of the cities. . . .

The radio was supplanting the phonograph and nature found herself further coerced in the growing mania of society to bombard itself with caterwaulings and stupidities. Prohibition was routing drunkenness out of the saloons and spreading it through the homes of the nation. . . .

The serviceable and simplifying mold of Victorianism was beginning its second and bourgeois disintegration . . . and the symbols of it were Valentino, Fairbanks, Synthetic Gin . . . F. Scott Fitzgerald, Voliva . . . Nicholas Murray Butler . . . "He May Be Your Man but He Comes to See Me Sometimes," the Talmadges, "The Bat," the Winter Garden, "Lightnin'," the Ku Klux Klan, "Chauve Souris," Will Hays, Gilda Gray, the South Seas . . .

—BEN HECHT
Humpty Dumpty

Increasing debts and a taste for good living acquired in Germany determined Hecht to make a million dollars. He'd watched his father chase the illusive million and he'd been talking about it to his friends for years, but it was during the twenties that he began to pursue money in a big way. In the teens his activity had been ceaseless but he had just managed to make a living. Back from Germany, he not only had a wife and child to support, but a house that Marie had rented for them and a social life to keep up commensurate with his position as a well-known local writer and a former foreign correspondent.

"What can I do now?" he asked his friends. "I can't return and chase fire engines after covering political revolutions, international politics and interviewing kings and premiers." Henry Sell suggested he write for the "Book Page," which paid more than a reporter's salary but still wouldn't begin to meet his expenses. Not knowing what else to do, he took it.

In the spring of 1918, when he was free-lancing articles for the "Book Page," Hecht and Burton Rascoe, editor of the *Tribune's* book section, had got into a feud over James Joyce's *Ulysses*, then being serialized in *The Little Review*. Hardly anyone who read the *News* or the *Tribune* had ever heard of the book, but Hecht and Rascoe thrust and parried for weeks. A few days after they left off—aware of the interest they had stirred—Hecht began looking for a new target. Rascoe had proclaimed James Branch Cabell a brilliant writer. Hecht lambasted Cabell in the "Book Page," taking a few shots at Rascoe as well.

"Ben Hecht, annoyed that anybody should praise anyone but himself, wrote a brief diatribe against Cabell . . . which enticed me into some sarcasms about Hecht [in the *Chicago Tribune*]," Rascoe recalled in *Before I Forget*. "I had never met Hecht. Tennessee Mitchel, then the wife of Sherwood Anderson, invited Carl Sandburg, Llewellyn Jones,

Anderson, Hecht and myself to dinner. . . . Tennessee had purposely brought Hecht and me together without telling either that the other was to be there. Hecht and I were polite enough during the dinner; but we had no sooner gone into the drawing room than a heated argument arose between Hecht and myself over some matter of preferences in literature. We hurled epithets, quotations, names of European writers and titles of their books at one another's heads, our voices rising crescendo, for more than an hour, giving no one else a chance to say a word."

Finally, unable to endure any more, Rascoe spluttered, "You talk, you think you know something about life, about literature. But what do you know of life? You tell me. You answer me. What do you know of life? You look at him. This Ben Hecht knows nothing of life. Why, the man has never had but one mistress and she was a charwoman." Hecht broke out laughing at the bookishness of Rascoe's remarks, as did Anderson and the other guests. When Rascoe saw the ridiculousness of it, he joined in. "Hecht and I became friends after that night," said Rascoe, "and thereafter it was only with difficulty that we could appear to be enemies in print."

In 1919, Hecht saw no way to make money from being "enemies in print" with Rascoe, since Hecht was now employed by the "Book Page" and would not increase his salary by literary feuding. He did have a proposal to make Rascoe, however: hold literary debates and charge a fee for their services. Rascoe was more interested in the literature than the money, but agreed to go along if Hecht made the arrangements. A few weeks later, Hecht persuaded the Book and Play Club to pay them one hundred dollars to debate at the Loeb mansion. After the performance, Mrs. Loeb introduced Hecht to her son Dickie. "He's one of your most ardent followers, I think he has everything you have ever written, including all your *Little Review* articles." Marie remembered that the boy "shivered with the intensity of his hero worship, his eyes fired by Ben's audacious eloquence." Later Dickie Loeb would tell his best friend Nathan about meeting Hecht. Four years later their names were inextricably linked: they had become the notorious killers Leopold and Loeb. "Study the traits of these two young supermen who had lost the faculty of appropriate emotional reaction to experience," wrote Stuart Sherman in 1926, "who looked at the human pageant, including their own trial, as detached intellectual spectators, and who killed a fourteen-year-old boy 'for fun'; and you will find there every prominent feature of the type of mind described by Mr. Hecht in *Erik Dorn* and *Humpty Dumpty* [two novels Hecht would write in the early twenties]." Twenty-eight years after meeting Dickie Loeb, Hecht would be called in by Alfred Hitchcock to tighten the script of *Rope*, based on the Leopold-Loeb "thrill" murder.

When Hecht was notified that their house was to be razed, he told Marie to find them another one. She did—a large, expensive pile, which she cajoled her mother into advancing the down payment for, convincing her she and Ben planned to buy it. Hecht couldn't afford the payments on his salary alone, so Marie went back to work, as editor for a new entertainment guide. Between them they brought in one hundred dollars a week, still not enough to cover their increasing expenditures. Neither of them knew how to manage money, and they plunged further into debt, especially with a large, empty house to furnish. Hecht accused Marie of extravagance, buying a house the size of a summer hotel and hiring a servant. The way Marie saw it, Hecht was going overboard furnishing the place with specially designed lighting fixtures and three Lilliham carpets which alone cost $1,600. Hecht's rejoinder—"My God, can't you see I'm going to be rich."

In the new house they began entertaining regularly on Thursdays. These evenings at home drew the most interesting crowd in Chicago—drama critic Ashton Stevens, caricaturist Gene Markey, Jascha Heifetz, the Marx brothers, Lloyd Lewis, Harry Hansen, Wallace and Hariot Smith, and H. L. Mencken, in town for the Republican Convention. Because Marie was reviewing plays, she met theatre people constantly and invited whomever she liked to the house. Hecht, the omnipresent master of ceremonies, told stories and anecdotes, reveling in gossip and wit. He would sometimes write comic skits for the actors present, sing risqué songs he'd composed, and, with Jascha Heifetz present, saw his violin. Though Hecht knew how to play well enough as an amateur, grasping music, as he did most things, on a cerebral level, he wasn't a born musician. Marie called his playing a "tour de force of ambition."

Burton Rascoe summed up the ambience at the Hechts' gatherings and the conflicting outlooks that would ultimately drive Hecht and Marie apart: "Listening to Marie and Ben play duets, she at the piano and he at the violin, drinking Marie's homemade beer and watching Ben chuckle as he made some cynical observation or spun some fantastic yarn, coruscating with far-fetched similes and glittering with bizarre epithets and adjectives, while Marie would say, 'He doesn't believe any of that stuff, he's only talking for effect.'"

A way out of their financial difficulties presented itself during the summer of 1920 when Hecht, in the words of Henry Justin Smith, got himself married to "an overdressed, blatant creature called Publicity." (Some years later, when Smith became public-relations counselor for the University of Chicago, he insisted: "Don't call me a press agent.") Hecht quit the *News* and took a job with Grady Rutledge, a Southerner who had formed a public-relations firm to handle accounts in the Midwest for J. P. Morgan's China Famine Fund, Hoover's Near East Relief, and the Northern Baptist drive. With contacts in a fourteen-state area to do the canvassing, Rutledge needed Hecht to turn out brilliant copy to bring the whole thing off. They rented a suite of offices in the Willard Building, installed a switchboard, hired secretaries, and went to work. Hecht did the copywriting and local organizing since he knew Chicago better than Rutledge; in a whirlwind of activity he turned out street fairs, beauty contests, bazaars, lotteries, and parades.

Hecht and Rutledge became so successful so fast that they needed help, so Hecht hired Richard Henry Little, the *Tribune* reporter who had also been in Germany covering the reconstruction, and George Wharton, a newsman Hecht had known since his *Journal* days. In eight months they had raised $25 million for their employers and made handsome salaries themselves. For the first time in years Hecht was living within his means. "I don't know how much food our activities brought to those empty bellies, I only know that helping the world's needy was part of the American picnic spirit in 1920," Hecht wrote. To Bodenheim, Hecht's "interest in the famine gripping China at that moment was equal to the agony of an alligator over a brood of yellow chicks trapped in a bayou."

When their "Big 3" campaign ended, Grady Rutledge started looking around for comparable moneymakers to take their place. Not finding any, he devised some of his own. One was the Order of Camels, an anti-Prohibition club that would sell camel lapel pins, but he abandoned the idea when he got a hand-delivered message from Al Capone: "I like Prohibition just fine so lay off if you know what's good for you." His next project was an anti-KKK, anti-intolerance league, but he found little support for it in the Midwest. Desperate, Rutledge turned more and more to gin and pilfering the incoming money, what little of it there was, so George Wharton and Richard Henry Little quit. Hecht, however, stuck it out—he was still making money, and only putting in a few hours of work a week since there was little copywriting to be done.

A few months later, Rutledge took stock of his situation. His source of income had dried up and he had taken money illegally from the coffers, so he stuck his head in an oven and turned on the gas.

In 1918, several months before Hecht and Marie left for Germany, he had met a *City Press* reporter, a serious-minded, pretty young woman named Rose Caylor. (Rose and her parents had arrived in Chicago from Vilna in 1907, driven out of Russia along with thousands of other Jews.) Her parents were named Libman, but Rose was acting in little theatre groups and trying to write, so she had taken the stage and pen name of Caylor. Hecht had taken to her immediately, liked talking with her, and was pleased with her admiration. According to *News* reporter Larry Lawrence, Rose "aspired to be a Hecht the second."

Rose was working for the *Chicago Daily News* by the time Hecht returned from Germany. Although she had been offered a job at a much higher salary on the *Tribune,* she preferred being close to Hecht. It wasn't long before they became lovers. When Marie discovered there was a new girl reporter at the *News,* she asked Hecht about her and he promptly delivered a harangue about irksome females who gaze soulfully, spout Chekhov and revolution, and emote for little theatres. "She sits around with her head ducked shyly down over her typewriter, when as a matter of fact she's so damned intense she makes my back ache. And what's even worse, she acts in the Dill Pickle Theatre! You know we've always drawn the line at people who act in little theatres."

"But you used to write for little theatres once," Marie reminded him.

"That was when I was young and foolish. You've got to admit that I've steered clear of that arty gang since we got back from Germany. No, Marie, this Rose Caylor is the drama-sipping, tea-lover type. Synthetic emotions. Likes to clutch a man as a religion and demand the inner meaning of life."

Although Hecht and Rose were lovers, Hecht had no intention of causing a break with Marie. He saw no reason why he shouldn't have both a wife and a mistress, regardless of his statement in an essay on Dreiser written the year of his marriage: "I would like to argue with him the certain superiorities of monogamy for the artist." He wanted the two of them, but he wasn't prepared to face Marie with his decision until he had to. As far as Marie knew, Rose was just a lonely young girl among all the men at the *News,* so she invited her to several of the Hechts' Thursday-evening gatherings. When Marie and Rose began to get too friendly, Hecht put a stop to Rose's attendance, afraid of arousing Marie's suspicions.

Hecht found himself in the same position with Rose he'd been in with Marie before their marriage. Then, he'd had no place to take her because he was living with his parents, and now he had no place for his assignations with Rose. As he so often did in his writing, he reused an old plot element: he and Rose met at the Art Institute.

Marie had suspected Hecht of philandering in the past—there had been a German secretary in Berlin, and before the war she had heard rumors of a woman who accompanied Hecht on an out-of-town assignment—but she wasn't suspicious of Rose because of Hecht's denunciations. Marie thought Rose had "ugly, stocky legs and large feet" and Hecht had called her "pop-eyed." However, "Her eyes struck him as marvelously large and bright" was how he was describing them in the novel he had begun. "Unusual eyes . . . she gave him a sense of dark waters hidden from the moon . . . a morose little girl insanely sensitive and with a dream inside her."

As a result of Hecht's unwillingness to commit himself to her, when Rose was offered the opportunity to join the road company of Thomas Dixon's *Robert E. Lee*, she took it, playing engagements all over the Midwest and the South. Whenever the company stopped over in a town anywhere near Chicago, Rose would come to Hecht, or he would go out of town "on business" to be with her. (On one of those stop-overs, Rose became pregnant; following the advice of a woman doctor in New York, she tried hot baths, quinine, and magnesia to induce a miscarriage; only after her efforts met with success did she inform Hecht.) When the tour was over, Rose took lodgings in New York City, where she did some publicity writing for Metro Pictures while auditioning for Broadway shows. Eventually she landed a part with Al Woods, one of the top producers in the country, and went back on the road.

In the teens Hecht had written twelve short chapters of a novel about a "young dramatist" named Moisse, three of which were published in *The Little Review* ("Life," "Depths," and "Gratitude"). The manuscript he began in the fall of 1920, however, was his first sophisticated attempt at novel writing, and Imagism was the style he chose to imitate. As a poetry movement it was passé, but Hecht's use in prose of clipped phrases and incomplete sentences cut through the rococo phraseology of a great deal of the fiction of the day to a cleaner simpler style. The story he wrote had a main character based physically on Henry Justin Smith, but in every other wise on himself: the protagonist, Erik Dorn, is a newspaper reporter, married for seven years (Hecht had been married five) to an adoring wife, who meets and falls in love with a young girl named Rachel. He leaves his wife and runs off to New York with the girl (which Hecht would do in 1924). Dorn read Huysmans, de Gourmont, Flaubert, Gautier, Symons, and Pater, as did Hecht. When Hecht was in Berlin after the war he heard of a massacre that took place in the Moabit prison; in the novel Erik Dorn climbs a tree to witness hundreds of people machine-gunned. (Thirty-five years later, in his autobiography, fiction had become fact: "I climbed a tree a block away and sat in its branches with a field glass listening to machine guns still going in the prison yard. It was dark, but I could see an awful movement of dying, of chained human masses falling before gunfire.") Most of the characters in the novel were drawn directly from life—Crowley, an editor in the book, was a reporter Hecht knew on the *Journal*; Emil Telsa, an artist, was Emil Amin, who would work with Hecht on the *Chicago Literary Times*. Dorn knew a poet he called "Old Carl" (Sandburg) who was "a great poet—the greatest in America," and a novelist named Warren Lockwood (Sherwood Anderson), about whom he comments, "The fellow's content to write. I'm not. He's found his way of saying what's in him, getting rid of his energies and love. I haven't."

"Dorn's too damned clever," Lockwood drawls. "Things come too easily to him. He's got an eye but—I can't put my finger on it. You see, a fella's got to have something inside him. The things Erik says cleverly and prophetically don't mean anything much, because they don't mean anything to him."

A slightly expanded version of "The Yellow Goat," which had run in *The Little Review* in 1918, and two other *Little Review* pieces, "Shanghaied" and "Dog Eat Dog," were used to pad the plot. Hecht even inserted the fifteen-thousand-word monograph he'd written on the German reconstruction, but deleted it later. Even discounting this material, much of the novel was muddied by too little action and too much cynical psychologizing: Dorn is seemingly emotionless and faultless, a Michigan Avenue Nietzsche come down off the mountain.

I think of people frequently but always as a species . . . my wonder is concerned chiefly with the manner in which they adjust to the vision of their futility. Do they shriek aloud with horror in lonely bedrooms? . . . How are they able to forget their imbecility? What in God's name did he have to do with the masses raising their skinny arms from a smoking field and crying aloud, "Bread!"

Erik Dorn took six months to write and when it was finished Hecht sent it to Mencken, asking him if he could place it with a publisher. When G. P. Putnam's Sons accepted it for their fall list, Hecht repaid Mencken by letting him use *Erik Dorn* for a *Smart Set* subscription ad—four dollars a year and one of eight books free, "Eight of the most worthwhile books published recently"; *Erik Dorn* kept company with works by Sherwood Anderson, John Dos Passos, Edna Ferber, and George Jean Nathan.

In September, when *Erik Dorn* was published, it created a minor furor. Mencken brought out a review immediately in *Smart Set* criticizing it for being unintelligible in spots while in others reaching "an amazing clarity and balance." Harry Hansen called it "the romance of a disillusioned man," but some critics maintained it rested on cheap sensationalism. Mrs. Dawson, a well-known New York reviewer, said Hecht would do better if he confined his writing to lavatory walls.

"Mr. Hecht paints the logical conclusion of tendencies which he has remorselessly observed in his own mind," Stuart Sherman wrote in "Ben Hecht and the Superman," a chapter from his *Critical Woodcuts*, published in 1926.

> Mr. Hecht projects upon the screen of his imagination his own type of mind swollen to gigantic proportions by the disease incipient in it; he paints the elephantiasis of evil. Beneath the grandiose phrases and images of an occasionally impressive symbolism, one can trace readily enough the excitable, imaginative journalist, in whom excessive journalism and undigested modern literature have produced an atrophy of the normal emotional faculties, aspiring toward a super-humanity through the repudiation of all normal human sentiments and the untrammeled expansion of curiosity and libidinous desire. Mr. Hecht himself appears to have little sense of the necessity of the laws and conventions which more or less govern human society. The ordinary mortal, tolerably comfortable, moderately law-abiding, appears to his inflamed imagination as a pitiable, contemptible, horribly agonizing wretch.

Although pleased with the notoriety, Hecht was disconcerted by Sherwood Anderson's lack of enthusiasm. Anderson's book *The Triumph of the Egg* had been issued at the same time as *Erik Dorn* and Hecht had sent him a note questioning whether his book was "art," suggesting that since they had reservations about each other's work they should attack one another in print. Anderson would have none of it, explaining why in a letter to Hecht.

Dear Ben—

You are a strange guy. Why do you have to decide whether a thing I write is art or not. You aren't a critic. You don't have to justify your art sense to me.

You're a funny guy in another sense too. What do you think a friendship is. It's really a rather different thing than, say for example a love affair with some woman. I've no desire to be a hero to you. One can get that kind of thing rather easily.

The other day I came very near taking a shot at you something like "Well, Ben" I wanted to say, "I've always thought Henry Mencken was so nuts on the Puritans and talked about them so much because he's afraid that at bottom he's one himself and I'll begin to think that about you and the boobs if you don't quit being so sure everyone in the world but yourself and a few of your special friends are boobs."

Say Ben why not hook up for a moment anyway with a few other people. Just for a kind of vacation consider, just for a moment that you aren't as highly specialized a thing as you think. You and I for example are friends. Try the experiment of saying to yourself that there isn't any smart thoughts I may have that Anderson may not have them too, there isn't any love I have so deep that Anderson may not have had one just as deep.

This is a cinch. If you are a bigger or smarter or wiser man than I am or can ever be we can't be friends anyway and that goes both ways.

You may put this down as a fact. My friendship for you isn't based on my looking either up or down to you. I'm not impressed with the notion that you are a specialized thing. The things that get me about you is that you can write and that you are a damned site finer man and have more real stuff in you than 999 out of 1000 men I've met. I don't at all think you a finished artist any more than I do myself . . . Jesus Christ man you're only facing what every man who wants to do something has to face. The bluff you throw about being so full of energy and being so smart and fast don't bluff me. I've got your number on that because you're so very like myself.

The point is this—I'm ready to be friends but I'm not going to think you a heller. And I don't want to try to throw any bluff of being one to you. Anyway why do you have to bluff and bluff and impress me. Why are you so unsure of yourself. You can write man. You don't have to convince me of anything.

It is fact that every time I am with you I feel you liking me O K but at the same time I feel antagonism. Lets disarm. There aren't such a hell of a lot of people a man can talk to. If I am like another side of you perhaps you are like another side of me too.

—Sherwood

A year and a half later, in an article titled "A Pair of Windows," Hecht wrote an apocryphal account of these events in which he had Anderson make the suggestion that they become enemies. Hecht's response to Anderson: "I don't have to make artificial pacts to insure a supply of enemies. The trouble with you is you're trying to strangle a Pollyanna complex, and besides, all the books are boosting you and you're sore about it."

"Well," Hecht had Anderson reply, "you're scared of me." End of piece.

Anderson left for New York shortly afterwards and from there went to live in New Orleans and on the farm he bought in Virginia from the proceeds of his novel *Dark Laughter*. They saw each other only once more, twenty years later, at "21" when Anderson stopped off in New York on his way to South America. Two days later he died at sea.

Although *Erik Dorn* was a great stride forward for Hecht, Rose couldn't properly appreciate it. "I didn't like the book, of course (for personal reasons), and it was guiltily dedicated to Marie. It hurt me too much to read it—this fantasy of a changing 'Rachel,' of love dying, of life lessened and almost defeated by having dared to dream of love. *Dorn* was an attempt to exorcise me while enslaving me in his letters with certainties of our future lives together." As soon as Marie read *Erik Dorn*, she began questioning Hecht about the Rachel character. Who was she? Was she real? "Can't you differentiate between a man's actual existence and his imaginative one?" he demanded. The problem was that Marie knew from experience, from "The American Family" onward, how Hecht's fictions were almost always grounded in fact. An incident that occurred that fall convinced her Rose was his mistress. An old friend,

Sacha Kaun, telephoned to say he was on his way over. He had just returned from abroad and mentioned that he wasn't alone.

"Sorry to tell you this but he's bringing some woman with him," Hecht told Marie with the "cynical little grin" Marie remembered as always "heralding something unpleasant."

When Kaun showed up with his wife, Val, Hecht demanded, "Hey! What's the idea of telling me you had a mysterious woman with you?"

"I didn't say that," Kaun replied. "I said I had met someone abroad that I was very fond of and was bringing her, and you at once got excited and began to hem and haw and hint at things, so I thought it was a good joke on you and a lesson for you not to think the worst before you know it."

When Marie saw Hecht's delight turn to disappointment she felt her suspicions about Rose were correct. They were confirmed a week later when Kaun mentioned that he had had lunch with Hecht a few days before, when Marie thought Hecht was out of town on business. That evening and for many to follow, Marie quarreled and cried, then begged and pleaded with Hecht to break off his liaison with Rose. She threatened suicide; then one evening, when Hecht found her collapsed on the bed with the gas on, he decided he'd better play along. He comforted her and assured her that he loved her and would break it off with Rose since his marriage was more important to him. She calmed down and their life together went back to normal; he just had to be that much more careful.

The advance for *Erik Dorn* paid off their debts, but Hecht needed a job since he no longer had a regular income. Not long after he completed *Erik Dorn*, his former editor Henry Justin Smith asked him to come back to the *News*, offering him as an enticement the unprecedented job of writing a daily column about anything that struck his fancy. Hecht accepted, called the column "1001 Afternoons in Chicago," and turned out a daily piece for the next year and three-quarters without missing a deadline. More of the cityscapes, sketches, and word portraits he had been scribbling for years, "1001 Afternoons" ran on the back page of the *News* and shortly became the most popular column in town.

The opportunity to collect another advance presented itself when, in the fall of 1921, George Putnam asked Hecht to contribute a chapter to a book of essays he was planning on censorship. Putnam had already lined up a few Eastern heavyweights who wanted to do battle with book censorship, among them Dorothy Parker, Alexander Woollcott, and Heywood Broun, so Hecht, hungry for the company, spun a text out of nothing called "Literature and the Bastinado." As boring a piece of writing as he had ever cranked out, it rang hollow with empty denunciations.

The irony of Hecht's simulated anger over censorship came shortly after he had composed his space-filling essay: Putnam's told him he would have to delete several scenes from the novel he had begun if they were to publish it, because they didn't want a run-in with the censor![1] Hecht flew into a rage and wired Putnam's he'd brook no changes. They said changes or else. Hecht sped to New York where Horace Liveright, the owner and publisher of Boni & Liveright, agreed to take the book the way it was. Boni & Liveright edited out the same passage Putnam's objected to but didn't consult Hecht before they published the book.

> *In January 1921, the greatest living writer*
> *was said to be Eugene O'Neill.*
> *In February, Joseph Hergesheimer.*
> *In March, D. H. Lawrence.*
> *In April, F. Scott Fitzgerald.*
> *In May, Robert Charles Benchley.*
> *In June, George Santayana.*
> *In July, James Joyce.*
> *In August, Marcel Proust.*
> *In September, Sinclair Lewis.*
> *October, Heywood Broun.*
> *November 1–15, T. S. Eliot.*
> *November 15–17, Ben Hecht.*
> *November 17–30, Harry Kemp.*
> *December, Will Rogers.*
>
> —Christopher Morley

Having published one novel, Hecht was determined to get out of journalism altogether and make a career of book and playwriting. Knowing Imagism wouldn't work a second time, he had begun looking around for another style and subject when he met Sinclair Lewis at Schlogl's restaurant, the local watering hole for the literati.

In the teens, Henry Sell had begun gathering reporters and visiting writers together for luncheon parties at Field's Grill, several years before the Algonquin Round Table began in New York. When Sell left for New York in 1920 to assume the editorship of *Harper's Bazaar*, Harry Hansen moved the luncheons to Schlogl's, where Hecht and newsman Keith Preston presided over the weekday gatherings of reporters, which included Burton Rascoe, John Gunther, Ashton Stevens, Carl Sandburg, Charles MacArthur, Keith Preston, Lloyd Lewis, and Henry Justin Smith. In the spring of 1921 Sinclair Lewis was in Chicago to do research for *Babbitt* and attended several of the luncheon sessions where he held forth on his new book. His protagonist was to be called George Babbitt, an unimaginative, self-aggrandizing member of what Mencken dubbed the "booboisie." Shortly thereafter, Hecht began a novel called *Gargoyles* with a Midwestern boor named George Basine as its main character. Carl Sandburg showed up again, this time under the name Lief Lindstrum:

> Lindstrum was becoming known. His poetry printed in fugitive labor gazettes was attracting a slight attention. He was being identified as a poet of the masses. The masses, however, unable to understand, let alone appreciate the mystic imagery and elusive passion of *vers libre* phrasings remained oblivious to him.

Using the voice of one of his characters, Hecht spoke directly to Sandburg:

> What is your love of people but a blind infatuation with yourself? You hate them . . . but you're ashamed to admit that. The crowd . . . a monstrous idiot that devoured men, reason and beauty. Now it moved with a purr through the streets. People are foul. And you know it. They're not like you or me. They can't think even as much as a rat thinks. They're as rattle-brained as chickens, as greedy as vultures. And they lie all the time. You know all this better than I do. But you keep feeling things and you imagine they're things people feel.

Hecht also inserted two of the big news stories he had covered in the teens—the private banks scandal and the Morals Commission investigation[2]—as plot elements. These served to pad a plot that already was nothing much more than padding for an idea he didn't originate—yet it was Hecht who remarked that H. L. Mencken invented Sinclair Lewis. Lewis's *Babbitt* was a novel, however good or bad, whereas Hecht seemed to think a combination of witty turns of phrase, lengthy philosophical digressions disguised as a character's thoughts, little plot, and almost no dialogue made a novel. Mark Van Doren, reviewing *Gargoyles*, wrote that Hecht "does not convince me that he ever heard or saw, or felt, or believed his people. At most they are bundles of behaviour."

Hecht was a facile wordsmith but as a plotter he was constantly overruled by his intelligence. His quick turns of phrase, the information he had at his fingertips from wide reading, and his acentric ideas made him a fascinating conversationalist and fictioneer from an early age. "I'm the victim of too plastic a vocabulary. Its ability to defend any action of mine has deprived me of a conscience," he wrote in his 1924 novel, *Humpty Dumpty*. It seemed more to deprive him of the ability to plot a novel: he couldn't surmount the strictures of his intelligence to develop a natural style. Not that he couldn't spin plots when he had to work within a restricted form, namely the theatre and later the movies; but unconstrained he was singularly unable to hold a plot together. He had neither the self-assurance nor the ability to strike out in a new direction and felt compelled to assume someone else's ideas or style.

Liveright accepted *Gargoyles* for publication in 1922, shortly before Hecht met a fifty-year-old ventriloquist-turned-actor, Leo Ditrichstein, who was looking for a theatrical property. Hecht thought he could come up with something, since as usual he needed money (his advance from *Gargoyles* was already spent). Sequestering himself in his study for eight days, he turned out "Under False Pretenses," which had the same plot as *Erik Dorn* and *Gargoyles*: a man falls in love with a woman, marries her, then meets another woman and falls in love with her. . . . It was specially tailored to fit Ditrichstein, though, the protagonist an actor and the milieu the theatre.

Ditrichstein approved the play, so they struck a deal—Hecht would get an advance against royalties and a percentage of the box office. During rehearsals, however, Ditrichstein began to complain about other characters' witty remarks and good speeches, insisting Hecht cut them. Hecht fought this bowdlerization, but in the end had to submit because Ditrichstein threatened to drop the play otherwise. To circumvent Ditrichstein's objections, although weakening the play in the process, Hecht rewrote the speeches so that Ditrichstein got all the witty lines.

Even so, when "Under False Pretenses" opened in Toledo on September 28th, it rated a rave in the *Blade*—"It would seem the American stage has at last found its master satirist." Retitled *The Egotist*, the play then moved on to Chicago and San Francisco before

Ditrichstein took it into New York, where it opened Christmas Day and ran six weeks. George Jean Nathan wrote that it was "a witty, wise and delightfully worldly comedy," the first American play to "approximate Sacha Guitry's style."

One evening Ditrichstein's wife Josephine mentioned to Hecht that she was obsessed with mystery novels and never read anything else, promising she'd read Hecht's next book on condition it was a mystery. Marie had brought mysteries home from time to time, which Hecht had castigated her for since he considered mystery novels a low form of literature; but now Josephine Ditrichstein had given him an idea. Why not quickly hack out a mystery as his next novel?

Using Sardou's play *La Tosca* for the foundation, he wrote *The Florentine Dagger*, creating a jejune murder story around Sardou's play, actually incorporating it into the plot. To write it took him not eighteen hours, as Horace Liveright reported, but two months, and like *The Egotist* it was about the stage, with a middle-aged man in a major part. It would be a simple matter, Hecht thought, to turn it into a play for Ditrichstein, but since there was another principal—who would have been impossible to write out—Ditrichstein refused to act in it, even though Hecht had dedicated it to Josephine. (Liveright had rejected Hecht's original dedication: "To Warren Gamaliel Harding, with the affectionate hope that its reading will afford him the keen diversion that the reading of his speeches has afforded the author.") Liveright issued the novel in 1923, and it sold reasonably well, being reprinted three times in as many years.

Since Ditrichstein saw himself as a lover and man of action, Hecht decided to make one more stab at writing a play for him, adapting *The Autobiography of Benvenuto Cellini* for the stage. The first act took him only two weeks to write and Ditrichstein approved it, but with the second act Ditrichstein began to cavil once again about the witty lines given to other characters. Piqued by Ditrichstein's refusal to do *The Florentine Dagger*, Hecht told him he couldn't change *Cellini* since he was following the actual events of the subject's life. When Ditrichstein refused to accept the second act, Hecht abandoned the play.

In the early teens, Hecht had come under the influence of the Decadents. It had taken that long for the Yellow Nineties to turn Mauve and reach America, and Hecht had faithfully ploughed through Ernest Dowson, Arthur Symons, Yeats, Théophile Gautier, Verlaine,

Mallarmé, and Joris-Karl Huysmans. He had been so taken with *A Rebours* that when Mencken suggested he use a name other than Ben Hecht to publish under "because the Brahmins would never accept it," he had toyed with the idea of calling himself Joris Karl.

The preoccupation with "the dying fall, the gentle somewhat pallid languor, and the exquisite boredom"[3] that epitomized the fin de siècle writers appealed strongly to a young man of Hecht's character, eager to be taken as a serious, accomplished older man. Decadence was the perfect literary complement to the cynical world-weariness of the older reporters Hecht was aping. "Huysmans' decadence is the most virile and furious manifestation of beauty in any language. He is the rajah of writing," Hecht wrote in the "Book Page," and *A Rebours* was the ultimate Decadent work, which forced its author, in Barbey d'Aurevilly's phrase, to choose between "the muzzle of a gun and the foot of the cross." Huysmans chose religion. Hecht thought he had made a mistake and in 1918 had set out to rectify it by writing his own Decadent novel, *Grimaces*, a Trilby/Dr. Frankenstein story of a mad artist called Maldor (the name of his and Bodenheim's master poisoner, an obvious borrowing from Lautréamont's own bizarre hero Maldoror). He had sent the manuscript to Mencken, but when Mencken returned it, commenting that it was "a bit Poeish and strained," Hecht excerpted a short section of the long story for Margaret Anderson, who ran it in the September 1919 issue of *The Little Review*. Another section went to Henry Sell, who published it in *Harper's Bazaar*; then Maldor—renamed Mallare—showed up in "The Adventure of the Broken Mirror" in one of Hecht's *News* columns.

In 1922, when bookstore owner Pascal Covici decided to take advantage of the abounding local talent and become a publisher, he approached Hecht for a manuscript. To inaugurate his new regional publishing house, Covici wanted a volume with a lavish format, artwork, and enough sex to sell it, so Hecht dug out *Grimaces*, knowing it would have to be revised and expanded, but not drastically. He removed the original ending, in which he had Mallare murdered by his servant, and added a girl whom Mallare buys from gypsies. Mallare has no desire to have sex with her—he wants her to adore him as a god—but she provided the excuse for pages of epigrams on women and sex.

> As for those animals whose egoism has never escaped their testicles, their imagination discharges itself through their penis.

Ah, what loathsome and lecherous mouths women are: offering their urine ducts as a mystic Paradise . . . as an orifice to be approached with Gregorian chants.

Man is a collection of adjectives loaned to a phallus. . . .

The book's climax was an unintentional parody of Decadent literature: the girl strips off Mallare's hunchbacked servant's clothes and seduces him in front of Mallare. Driven mad by this vision, Mallare is left at the novel's end babbling to himself. Echoing Barbey d'Aurevilly's comment on Huysmans, the last line of the book read, "This is the cross." As a visual complement, Wallace Smith did a line drawing of Mallare hanging from an invisible cross, one eye rolled up, a grimace contorting his face.

Retitled *Fantazius Mallare* (which later Marie would lampoon as *A Malarial Fantasy* and Bodenheim as *Realismus Maloney*), Covici thought it walked the literary tightrope without missing a step, falling neither into pornography nor mundanity. Marie thought it brilliant. Hecht was not entirely pleased since he had meant to write a scandalous work and no one was shocked. To correct this he wrote a seven-page preface, "Dedicated to my enemies."

> *To the psychopathic ones*
> *who find relief for constipation*
> *in forbidding their neighbors the water closet.*
>
> *To the smug ones who walk*
> *with their noses ecstatically*
> *buried in their own rectums*
> *(I have nothing against them, I swear) . . .*
>
> *To the righteous ones*
> *who finger each other*
> *in the choir loft . . .*
>
> *To the proud ones who urinate*
> *against the wind . . .*
>
> *To these and to many other*
> *abominations this inhospitable*
> *book, celebrating the dark mirth*
> *of Fantazius Mallare, is dedicated.*

To make the dedication more outrageous, Hecht had Wallace Smith design a pen-and-ink border for each page picturing an erect penis entering a barbed-wire vagina. Marie finally told Hecht what he wanted to hear—he'd gone too far. Even Covici had reservations about the preface and the drawings, and Wallace Smith capsulized everyone's feelings: "Don't monkey with Uncle Sam."

Gargoyles and Fantazius Mallare were issued in September, then in December Covici brought out Hecht's collected 1001 Afternoons in Chicago, illustrated by Herman Rosse. Gargoyles was panned by most critics except for Mencken; 1001 Afternoons in Chicago was well-received, but not by Mencken; and Fantazius Mallare wasn't reviewed at all except by Mencken. Hecht, feeling blocked at every turn in his efforts to spark a reaction from Fantazius Mallare, had Covici send copies to reviewers, but to no avail; he then had fifty copies, opened to particularly inflammatory passages, displayed in the large front window of Covici's bookshop, but nothing seemed to work. Eventually Covici was warned by the postal authorities to discontinue sending the book through the mail because they had had complaints about its alleged obscenity. When Covici told Hecht, he responded, "Do you expect me to let that bunch of filth-eating morons dictate to me?" He insisted that Covici continue selling the book through the mail, which Covici wasn't averse to since the selling price was twelve dollars and fifty cents at a time when the average novel sold for two dollars.

Hecht had confided to Burton Rascoe several years earlier that he wanted John Sumner and his Society for the Suppression of Vice to try and censor a book of his. Sumner, although not an official government censor, was supported by many wealthy and powerful New Yorkers, thereby exercising enormous power over New York publishing houses, which meant over most of the book publishing in the United States. If Sumner tried to suppress a book of his, then Hecht would sue him for defaming his character and jeopardizing his income. The figure Hecht had in mind for damages was, expectedly, one million dollars. If he won he figured to put Sumner out of business by bankrupting him and thus end unofficial censorship in the United States. It wasn't Sumner that objected to Fantazius Mallare, however, but the postal authorities. Since Hecht had decided to disregard the warning, he, Wallace Smith, and Covici were slapped with a suit for sending "lewd, lascivious and obscene" literature through the U.S. mails. Three hundred bound copies and seven hundred still in sheets were seized.

Covici and Wallace Smith wanted to plead guilty, get a small fine, and be done with it, but Hecht refused. He intended to plead innocent, till their lawyer Charles Erbstein told him he stood a good chance of going to jail if the case were lost. Erbstein suggested they plead nolo contendere, which they finally agreed to do. Mencken volunteered to come at his own expense to testify in defense of the book's literary merit, as did Horace Liveright, but Hecht told them not to bother unless the nolo contendere plea wasn't accepted and it became a matter of a jury trial.

Because of the bad publicity the *News* was receiving, Victor Lawson fired Hecht, ending his "1001 Afternoons" column; Henry Justin Smith started a Hecht Defense Fund, and Hecht had cards printed that read, "There are no obscene words. There are only obscene readers."

At a hearing in the late spring, Erbstein entered a plea of nolo contendere but the presiding judge refused to accept it, contending Hecht and Wallace Smith were guilty or not guilty and must plead accordingly. Erbstein had the case delayed for nine months while he sought a more sympathetic judge. Finally, at a hearing held on February 4th, 1924, Erbstein again entered a nolo contendere plea, which the new judge accepted, fining them one thousand dollars each, to be paid in three months' time.

Even the loss of the court case didn't turn Hecht against his alter ego of eight years. "Mallare is my favorite character," he maintained through the twenties. Mallare would show up once more, played by Noel Coward, in *The Scoundrel*, a 1935 film Hecht would write and direct.

* * *

I have known him to be mistaken for a pickpocket, a Bolshevik, a Vaudeville acrobat, an errand boy, a theological student and a French aristocrat.

—BEN HECHT
"Allegro Pizzicato Window
Serenade to Maxwell Bodenheim"
Chicago Literary Times,
April 15, 1923

At Margery Curry's, Maxwell Bodenheim had met Alfred Kreymborg, a young poet from New York who had come to talk with Harriet Monroe about *Poetry* and to meet the Chicago School.[4] When Bodenheim first went to New York he lived with the Kreymborgs and in 1918 and 1919 helped edit *Others*, a poetry magazine devoted to publishing writers other than those represented in *Poetry*. Bodenheim also published in many of the little magazines of the day, among them *Reed's Mirror*, the *Modern Review*, and *The Quill*.

In his second collection of poems, *Advice*, brought out by Knopf in 1920, Bodenheim included a poem "To a Friend" (in a later edition changed to "To a Famous Friend"), marking his first portrait of Hecht in print.

> *Your head is steel cut into drooping lines*
> *That make a mask satirically meek*
> *Your face is like a tired devil weak*
> *From many vapid, unsought wines*
>
> *The sullen skepticism of your eyes*
> *Forever trying to transcend itself*
> *Is often entered by a wistful elf*
> *Who sits naively unperturbed and wise. . . .*

In the summer of 1920, sick and out of money, Bodenheim had written Hecht asking for a loan of two hundred dollars. Hecht, acquainted with Bodenheim's ruses for obtaining money ("He was the impecunious poet who was always around for a free lunch," is how Harry Hansen remembered him), sent him a letter reading, "I am very glad to be of service to you, enclosed please find check." There was no enclosed check. Not amused, Bodenheim wrote Marie asking her for fifty dollars, telling her he hoped "the Mountebank" hadn't reached her "with some of his subtle poison." When he heard nothing from either of them, he began referring to Hecht as "an enemy of mine."

Hecht took it all as a joke, but, a year later, when he heard that Bodenheim was seriously ill, he wrote a long piece in the *News* extolling him as one of America's major poets in danger of dying in obscurity. He also wrote to Horace Liveright suggesting he bring out a volume of his verse. Clarence Britten, a Liveright editor, had been pressing Liveright unsuccessfully for six months to take a volume of Bodenheim's poetry, but Hecht's letter changed Liveright's mind and he issued *Introducing Irony* in 1922 and would bring out *Against This Age* in 1923.

Late in 1922, Bodenheim was in Chicago to work on *Blackguard*, a roman à clef about his early life, his suicidal hitch in the army, and his escape to the hobohemias of Chicago. When Hecht learned he was in town, he sent him a note: "After seven years you and I are still the best hated men in American Literature. Why not pool our persecution mania?

My hate is becoming monotonous. I confess that yours lacks variety. I will be here Monday at 4 with a bottle of gin. I shall expect you. I salute the possibility of your fatheadedness."

Their friendship reestablished over the bottle of gin, Bodenheim told Hecht about *Blackguard*, so Hecht offered him a room in his house where he could work. Bodenheim settled in and had the novel finished before the year was out. Since Hecht was advising Covici about what to publish—he'd already taken him Henry Justin Smith's sketches of newspaper life, *Deadlines*,[5] and a volume of Stanislaus Szukalski's artwork—he submitted Bodenheim's manuscript. Covici issued it in March of 1923, Hecht in a review calling it "as definitive an experience as inhaling a quart of chlorine gas."

Before the book was published, Bodenheim returned to New York and with a small advance from Horace Liveright he and Minna visited London. On their return, Bodenheim found a letter from Hecht asking him if he would like to be associate editor of a new Chicago magazine that Covici was going to finance. He could write anything he pleased as long as it was witty, exciting, or insulting. Because Hecht was involved in the *Mallare* trial, and was hard at work on a new novel, *Humpty Dumpty*, he needed help with the magazine, and so had called on the most vicious wit he knew, the man who was "improvising the most brilliant lines to be heard in American conversation." Filled with spiteful glee at the thought of writing for a magazine that actually required him to attack his enemies, Bodenheim got his name on the masthead as the only editor other than Hecht, beginning with issue number 3.

First appearing on March 1st, 1923, the *Chicago Literary Times* proclaimed itself "a gazette devoted to the Sacred Ballyhoo," but Marie Hecht better caught its spirit when she described it as "the bastard child of a free union between *Vanity Fair* and the *Police Gazette*." During its brief lifespan, everybody and everything went under the knife. Hecht reduced *The New Republic* to "clichés on stilts," *Cosmopolitan* to "lost manhood ads," and Burton Rascoe (for whom Hecht had been reviewing books in the *New York Tribune*) to "a yesterday's orchid in Broadway's buttonhole," and attacked Floyd Dell for not fighting John Sumner when his novel *Janet March* was taken off the market. Bodenheim wrote that "H. L. Mencken suffers from the hallucination that he is H. L. Mencken. There is no cure for a disease of that magnitude." Hecht wrote, "In 1913 Americans thought that Art was men who wore long hair and talked like sissies; naked women in a garret; a Chinese kimono thrown over a chair in a vestibule; something they had in Europe; any statue in a public park. In 1923 Americans think Art is something that doesn't look like a photograph; marrying a negro in the South Seas; anything a Russian does; turning colored lights on the orchestra in the movie palaces; a rape scene in a motion picture."

Bodenheim said *The Waste Land* spoke "like an intellectual engaging in a drunken commotion, and erudition prattling with the husky candor of a vagrant in the back room of a saloon." Hecht wrote that "radio is established as a full sister of the movies in the business of emptying American heads," compiled a list of the world's worst books (which included *Pilgrim's Progress, Paradise Lost, Peter Pan, Das Kapital, Women in Love,* and *The Americanization of Edward Bok*), and regularly wrote anticlerical pieces such as "Another Professor Gives God a Haircut and a Shave" and "Hegel: The Man Who Bored God to Death." Bodenheim published selections from his "Merciless and Unabridged Autobiography," wondered if "a young woman who embraces a man while being assaulted by primitive drum beats and bacchanalian horn tootings, and pretends she is interested only in the technique of dancing, naked in bed with a man, would insist that she is only testing out the mattress," and kept up the attack on Mencken—"Your anaesthetic of malice has put your soul to sleep and set it to snoring in essay form." (Although Hecht and Bodenheim wrote seventy percent of the copy, there were other contributors—a Ring Lardner play, *The Upholsterers,* was reprinted, Ezra Pound contributed "The Duties of an Artist," Vincent Starrett and Lloyd Lewis reviewed books, Sam Putnam did translations from the French, and Wallace Smith served as art editor until he quit because he wasn't getting paid.)

Rather than comment directly on the *Mallare* trial, Hecht and Bodenheim composed a nine-part burlesque of censorship called *Cutie, A Warm Mamma.*[6] The main character was one Herman Pupick, "a wet smack from the take off" who "refused to nurse at his mother's breast" because "he considered it immoral and obscene." He was a government censor, "highly respected by old maids suffering from dementia menopause" and "like all censors had a foul mind and bad breath." He was married to an "autumn leaf named Emmaline" who suffered from virginity and who "couldn't pass a bathroom without blushing." "Herman used to pray every night before sliding into the hay alongside this kippered herring that God should keep him pure. Mrs. Pupick felt that the way God answered her husband's prayer every night was a miracle."

Then Herman met Cutie, who "offered an eyefull which would make a brass monkey run a temperature of 209 degrees." Herman thought she was trying to seduce him so he disappeared in a fright but couldn't get her out of his mind. He "wrestled with the devil for three weeks and lost two straight falls." Censoring in a nightclub one evening, Herman encountered Cutie again. She pulled him onto the dance floor where he felt her "shimmy begin to shake." Herman began behaving like "a clam with the hiccoughs" which got him tossed out. He found himself in Cutie's apartment the next morning dressed in silk lavender pajamas, looking like "a cross between a chop suey peddler and the inside of an Odd Fellow's coffin." Herman stayed at Cutie's, where "the days passed rapidly and the nights had no flies on them either." Finally he convinced Cutie to join him in his reforming. "We will burn down all the bookstores and blow up all the publishing houses and public libraries and arrest everybody. Everybody!"

"He closed up all the dance halls by writing letters to the papers and caused the arrest of 29 authors in Schlogl's restaurant, suppressed the *Chicago Literary Times*, wiped out all the bootleggers, and had all the abdominal belt displays taken out of all the drug store windows."

From the first morning when Herman "failed to report for his farina, Mrs. Pupick was worried. She feared he might have been run over by a kiddie car so telephoned a neighbor's husband, a dog catcher for a Greek restaurant, and asked him if he had seen our hero." Nine days later, Herman showed up with Cutie. "Before anybody could sandbag her Mrs. Pupick had run a hat pin into Cutie's left chest." Turning to Herman, she accused him of adultery; he admitted committing it twenty-nine times and was "tired of it." She stabbed him to death, staggered to a mirror, looked at herself and dropped dead. Herman's many admirers "presented him with a drainpipe for a coffin."

Hecht wrote free-verse ads about local businesses, printed them, then solicited the stores for money to keep the ads running: "It was amazing how pleased a guy would be if you printed a verse about his crummy store." In addition, Hecht had every theatre in town advertising by threatening to review their plays if they didn't. A year after the *Times* began it was selling over ten thousand copies each issue, Hecht pocketing three hundred dollars a week.

I'll take the mountains, you can keep the frying pan.

—BEN HECHT

The old soup bone was in the pot again.

—MARIE HECHT

Published in the fall of 1922, Hecht's second novel *Gargoyles* had had as its main characters one man and two women, just as *Erik Dorn* had, but none of the three were recognizable as Hecht, Marie, or Rose. This led Marie to believe her marriage was safe, that Hecht was keeping his promise not to see other women. When Hecht rented a studio in the same building in which Covici had his bookstore—as a place to write and as an office for the *Chicago Literary Times*—Marie chose the furnishings, content to think he was working there night and day through the spring and summer writing *The Egotist* and doing a brilliant job on his novel for Covici, *Fantazius Mallare* (he read her each "completed" section of the manuscript), when he was actually seeing Rose almost every day.

In fact, he had already written *Fantazius Mallare* several years before and needed but a few weeks to make the necessary changes he and Covici had agreed on. During this period he also wrote *The Florentine Dagger*, which took two months from beginning to end; the bulk of it was turned out in several long dictation sessions with a secretary at the *News*.

Marie knew he had written two novels, a play, and a daily column for the *News*, which deluded her into believing that it wasn't humanly possible for him to be seeing another woman. When this six months of frenzied activity came to an end, Hecht started another play, got sued by the government, plunged headlong into writing and publishing the *Chicago Literary Times*, and told Marie he had been seeing Rose all along. He meant to divide his time between the two of them, he said, spending four nights a week with Marie and the other three with Rose. Marie was aghast. She went to Peter Hecht's wife and told her what Ben intended. When her sister-in-law didn't commiserate, Marie asked Lloyd Lewis and Ashton Stevens what to do, and they both counseled her to do nothing, just accept the situation. The only sympathy she got was from Hariot Smith, who had recently divorced Wallace.

Marie had angered Hecht by running to other people with their troubles, but she hadn't budged him an inch, so she turned to other methods. She sought out Rose, despite Hecht's orders to the contrary, and made a scene, threatening to sue Hecht for divorce and name her as corespondent. She phoned Rose's mother and made the same threat, but she wasn't ready to carry it out yet. She threatened to take a lover herself, to which Hecht countered, "I know that no woman who had given herself to me could ever give herself to another man." Marie admitted that at that moment she was "lost in a genuine admiration of his ego."

Always at his best when involved with two women, Hecht published articles by Rose in the *Times*, then when Marie became furious he suggested she write something other than the theatre reviews she had been doing. Marie told Hecht she wouldn't write a direct rejoinder because that was what he wanted; instead she composed a series of short profiles of various types of women. One, called "Rosette," was a thinly veiled rejoinder nevertheless: "Rosette is notorious. When she promenades, men smile secretly into their memories and women sense her as an eternal enemy. But a fatigue has gathered beneath the mask of her face and she embraces an indifference. Her frock, of white lace, is a pretense of chastity, to flatter the egoism of the male."

Rose countered in "An Essay Concerning the More Maniacal Sex." In what was ostensibly a review of a book that Rose admitted was "laughably unimportant," she wrote,

> Woman, the theatre-goer [Marie was writing a theatre column for the *Times*], patron of concerts, acquisitive buyer, who caresses herself with silks until her dotage, who is obsessed with vanity and advancement, who often eats like a lumberjack [Bodenheim wrote that Marie "weighed over one hundred and eighty and her height was only medium; the result was inclined to be horizontal and impeding"] and sleeps like a nightwatchman, attempts an amazing fraud in her argument with man. She pretends that she is a creature tragically different. She does not live to gratify her senses. She lives to shed light . . . to create the moral traditions that govern us . . . to direct men and inspire them . . . to offer all. . . . Even her alimentary canal is altruistic. For her all is sacrifice and tragedy . . . it is the egomaniacal shriek of a pampered and deluded female, the sort of thing many a husband doubtless encounters in the sequestered torture-chamber of his home.

Hecht himself wrote a piece called "Amorous Fables," which he ran on the front page of the *Times*. It was divided into thirteen short sections; the second one read: "There were two kinds of women for him—his wife and Other Women. In his mind all women were naked but his wife. Thus she became the only woman he respected, because of all the women he saw she was the only one whom he did not desire."

Hecht told Marie that Rose thought her writing "infantile" and Rose that Marie thought hers "putrid." When Rose announced she was writing a novel about the three of them, Marie showed Hecht a sheaf of poems, entitled *Morte*, that she had written secretly. One of the verses, "To Him," ended with the line, "and my soul shall sing songs of passion to him, as he lies on my heart with her beside him." Hecht took *Morte* to Covici, who published the book in a limited, illustrated edition of 450 copies. Marie was convinced that not even literature was going to get her husband back. So she searched out the apartment Hecht and Rose had rented, filled with the furnishings from his office in Covici's building, and informed the landlady that the "couple" who lived there weren't married. They were evicted the same day. When he got home that evening, "Ben was white with rage," Marie recalled. "He cursed as only Ben can curse. He told me to get out, that he couldn't stand the sight of me. He beat me with his fists. I have never seen any human in such a rage. I stormed back at him until he threw me on the floor." In the roman à clef he had begun about himself, Marie, and Rose, Hecht—calling himself Kent Savaron—became the cuckold, Marie the unfaithful wife.

Rose edited the new novel for him, giving him a perspective he had never enjoyed before, since Marie had provided "an applause that didn't wait for him to perform." He had found the one woman for him, but Marie wouldn't consent to a divorce, telling him that as long as she lived Rose would have to be a kept woman. In February of 1924 Hecht left Marie and moved into an apartment on Astor Street with Rose. He had confided in his parents, who supported him in his decision to live with Rose, but Marie's mother was predictably incensed. She came from Cleveland and insisted that Marie put her and Ben's house up for sale, since she couldn't afford it on her salary alone. When it was sold, Marie moved into an apartment with Hariot Smith.

Hecht continued to edit the *Chicago Literary Times* but delegated much of the work to Rose so he could finish *Humpty Dumpty*, which had the same story line as *Erik Dorn* and *The Egoist*, but recounted the story of his life starting when he was a boy in Racine, through his arrival in Chicago, meeting Marie and her family, the publication of "The American Family" (called "The Humperdums Give a Party"), his marriage, success as a writer, publicity work with Grady Rutledge, the suppression of a novel, meeting Rose, and the breakup of his marriage.

Humpty Dumpty was finished by spring 1924 and sent off to Liveright, who issued it the following October. In it Hecht wrote about Chicago as he had for fourteen years, but now "he was no longer its intimate. The scenes in which he had once found a literary, mystic happiness saddened him now as if their outlines contained tender and inevitable gestures of farewell." The press was now "a monster with an endless howl in its lungs," H. L. Mencken "a soapbox orator," Sherwood Anderson "the wistful idealization of the masculine menopause," and bohemians were "snarly, incompetent egoists" with "alley holes, frowzy studios and repugnant sexual intrigues that he had sickened of." Ironically, he was now being lauded as one of the leaders of the Chicago School and considered one of the most gifted young novelists in America. Harry Hansen, who had taken over the editorship of the "Book Page," published a volume of essays on the Chicago writers, *Midwest Portraits*, in which Hecht was dealt with at length in a chapter titled "Pagliacci of the Fire Escape." Hecht also had a chapter devoted to him in *The Men Who Make Our Novels*.

One of the last to accept the demise of the Chicago Literary Renaissance, Hecht was now prepared to abandon Chicago in favor of New York. He needed money to make the move, though, as well as to pay his thousand-dollar fine. Haldeman-Julius's Little Blue Book series brought out two collections of *Little Review* stories—*Tales of Chicago Streets* and *Broken Necks and Other Stories*—and Mencken took a new story for *The American Mercury*, but Hecht netted very little money from either source, so he approached Covici with an idea for another high-priced sex novel. Covici was game, so over the summer Hecht penned *The Kingdom of Evil*, a sequel to *Fantazius Mallare*. Another moneymaking scheme was to publish a New York literary scandal sheet along the lines of the *Chicago Literary Times*. Boni & Liveright had published *Gargoyles* and in April had accepted *Humpty Dumpty* for publication, so Hecht reasoned he had a good chance of talking Horace Liveright into backing a *New York Literary Times*, since Liveright was a soft touch and a known gambler. Besides, it could double as the B-&-L house organ as the *Chicago Times* did for Covici.

In 1917, Horace Liveright had met Albert and Charles Boni, former bookstore owners who planned to publish cheap editions of Continental literature that the staid New England publishing houses, which then controlled the publishing industry in the United States, wouldn't handle.

Liveright was looking around for another project himself, since his scheme to manufacture toilet paper—Pick-Quick Papers—had recently failed. Together Liveright and the Bonis formed the Modern Library. By early 1918, though, they were fighting among themselves, Liveright wanting to publish new American writers as well as the Modern Library, while the Bonis preferred to steer clear of the new and stick with proven European successes, which could be counted on to bring in a steady income. By July, the three of them decided they couldn't continue together. They flipped a coin, Liveright won, bought out the Bonis, and immediately began issuing new titles under the Boni & Liveright imprint, primarily leftist political analyses. John Reed's *Ten Days That Shook the World*, published in 1918, was Liveright's first best-seller; Waldo Frank's *Our America* came out the same year, as did Eugene O'Neill's first book, *The Moon of the Caribbees*.

By 1920, though, Liveright was aware of the changing climate in affluent postwar America. A new generation, in revolt against nineteenth century values, was drinking, dancing, and making use of automobiles in ways engineers hadn't planned: the Jazz Age had begun. Liveright dropped most of the social-revolutionist titles from B & L's list and began issuing fast-paced novels of contemporary life, as well as European literary sex novels by James Huneker and George Moore, and also, that year, Freud's first American volume (which Freud had prepared at Liveright's request).

The twenties saw Liveright making a solid income from the Modern Library and his topical sex novels—his most successful was *Flaming Youth* by Warner Fabian, pseudonym of Samuel Hopkins Adams—which provided the capital to publish other more serious books, even though he would knowingly take a loss on many of them. From 1920 through 1924 B & L published *Winesburg, Ohio*; O'Neill's *Beyond the Horizon, The Emperor Jones, The Hairy Ape, Anna Christie,* and *All God's Chillun Got Wings*; *The Enormous Room* by e. e. cummings; *Terribly Intimate Portraits* by Noël Coward; *A Book About Myself* and a reissue of *The Genius* by Theodore Dreiser; *The Waste Land* by T. S. Eliot; and *Black Oxen* by Gertrude Atherton, the number 1 best-seller of 1923 and Liveright's only book ever to make the top position on the best-seller list.

By the mid-'twenties, Boni & Liveright had become the most prestigious small publisher in America. Knopf was issuing new European fiction, Ben Huebsch was shortly to merge with Harold Ginzberg and form the Viking Press, and Richard Simon had left Liveright in 1923 to form Simon & Schuster, but of all these houses B & L was publishing the most impressive list of American books, as well as taking more risks on new writers than all other American publishers put together.

On a trip to Chicago early in May, Liveright met with Hecht and Bodenheim in his suite at the Drake Hotel, Bodenheim wangling a thousand-dollar advance on a novel. Liveright, his publishing house a success, was looking around for new ventures to invest in, so he was ripe for Hecht's suggestion that he publish a magazine. A *New York Literary Times* was ill-fated, however, since Liveright wasn't interested. In the next issue of the *Chicago Literary Times* Hecht wrote, "Horace Liveright was in town last week and [was] almost talked into starting a great Chicago magazine," not wanting to admit to his readers that he was trying to bail himself out of Chicago on the merits of the *Chicago Literary Times*.[7] It would have been easy enough for Liveright to publish a magazine, since he already had a publishing house and a stable of writers who could write or be excerpted for it, but the venture was almost too obvious, it didn't involve any new form of excitement or risk for Liveright, so he turned Hecht's proposal down.

Liveright had a proposal for Hecht, though. He had decided to take a flier on an entirely new sort of enterprise—the theatre. Some time earlier he had commissioned Edwin Justus Mayer to write a play based on the life of Benvenuto Cellini, Liveright willing to gamble that Cellini's salacious sex life would be Broadway box office. In Italy, Mayer had researched Cellini's life and had returned to New York with a thoroughly documented serious play that Liveright found dull. Knowing that Hecht had written *The Egotist* for Leo Ditrichstein and had begun a play on Cellini for him as well, he proposed that Hecht rewrite the Mayer piece into a risqué modern play suited for the Broadway stage. It wasn't what Hecht wanted, but it would provide the cash to escape Chicago, so he accepted.

Flags at halfmast. Ben Hecht is leaving Chicago.

—Ashton Stevens

Hecht spent June and July writing *The Kingdom of Evil* for Covici, after which he began adapting *The Firebrand*, Mayer's play about Cellini. The income from the *Chicago Literary Times* was used to pay his bills while the advances for *The Kingdom of Evil* and *The Firebrand*, plus royalties from third and fourth printings of *Gargoyles* and *The Florentine Dagger*, were kept to finance the move to New York, planned for early August.

The "1001 Afternoons" column for the *Chicago Literary Times'* last issue was not a reprint from the *News*, as most of them had been, but Hecht's farewell to Chicago and his youth. He called it "My Last Park Bench" and described a walk he took in Grant Park looking "up at buildings which no longer interested" him; he sat on a bench to "recapture the flavor" of what was once a "romantic routine," deciding "it would be much more intelligent to put an end to this game of pretending the city panorama fascinates me as it once did." He meets a younger version of himself, but rather than "match epigrams" with him simply gets up and leaves the youth behind. "Let him sit till doom's day on this bench; he will never see me again. I have more important things to do. . . ."

6

NEW YORK: "THIN-LIPPED SCHOOLTEACHER OF A CITY"

I had arrived in New York in time to join a wild and premature fin de siècle *party.*

—BEN HECHT
A Child of the Century
(1954)

Hecht would claim thirty years later that during his first year in New York—his transition from Chicago and literature to Hollywood and the movies—he didn't write a word, when in fact he plunged headlong into the Roaring Twenties and not only cranked out plays and stories for cash but even resorted to writing publicity for a Florida real-estate developer.

Aware that he didn't possess the knack of constructing best-selling novels, he reasoned the theatre might provide the elusive million, although he was willing to give most anything a try. In Chicago he had set out to become a novelist and now, six books to his credit, he was being acclaimed as one of the finest, most important young fiction writers in the country. His books had sold moderately well but none had become best-sellers, nor could they have, considering Hecht's contempt for the average reader and his own inability to devise workable plots. Mass-market paperbacks were still years in the future, and this made the old saw of today even more true for writers then: You could make a fortune but you couldn't make a living. Money was now uppermost in his mind.

During his first year in New York, Hecht lunched occasionally at the Algonquin where, according to Gene Fowler, he "astounded the members of the Hotel Algonquin's *bon mot* club not only by his powers as a conversationalist, but also by the pancake hat and tennis shoes he sometimes wore." Former *Chicago Tribune* reporter Charles MacArthur sat in with the Round Tablers from time to time, as did Burton Rascoe, who, like Hecht, was not entranced: "The whole literary scene in New York seemed to me to be dominated by men and women who were shallow, pompous, uninformed, either frivolous or full of the wrong kind of solemnity. . . ." Johnny Weaver—a friend of Hecht's from Chicago who was reviewing plays for the *Brooklyn Eagle*—and his wife, actress Peggy Wood, were regulars, as was theatre critic Herman Mankiewicz.

The Round Table would have seemed the perfect milieu for Hecht's wit and conversational talents, but he was really still a displaced Chicagoan who had yet to adapt. "To us in Chicago," Hecht wrote, "there was an alien look and sound to New York—a smugness and silly strut. New York was a thin-lipped schoolteacher of a city, giving out marks. Its drone of criticism crossed the Alleghenys and buzzed in our bookstores and saloons. Visiting New Yorkers wore derbys, carried canes, smelled of cologne, spoke with a lisp and were loud with boasts of famous ladies they had toppled. I learned later that these flossy Gothamites were not necessarily homosexuals but normal New York literary types."

Still feeling this suspicion and contempt when he got to New York, Hecht was reluctant to seek out the Round Tablers with any regularity. In Chicago, he had once told Marie, "I'm going to show up those log-rollers of the Algonquin. If I ever fall for that racket, I hope to God you shoot me quick." (Once Hecht asked the Algonquin's manager, Frank Case, to lend him twenty dollars so he could take someone to dinner at "21.") Another problem for Hecht was adapting to a literary society in which he wasn't king or even crown prince.

The Round Table was incredible in that it brought together so many talented writers and bon vivants in perhaps the last decade in which conversation was practiced as an amusement, but the wit was often shallow, forced, and forgettable. "Among the Woollcottians," Hecht wrote,

> the bedazzling of the uninvited was made easy by the fact that nearly all of Alec's captains conducted gossip columns in the press and magazines. F. P. A., Broun, Ross, Frank Sullivan, Miss Parker, Corey Ford, and Woollcott himself wrote about each other swooningly. Though most of the talent of the day (in fact, nearly all of it) was missing from their salons, this Algonquin school of wags offered itself as the artistic vortex of the town. Among the missing at its tables were Thomas Wolfe, Sandburg, O'Neill, Sherwood Anderson, Willa Cather, Mencken, Nathan, Hemingway, George Luks, George Bellows, Edith Wharton, Edna Millay, George Grosz, Elinor Wylie, Vertès, Sinclair Lewis, Wyndham Lewis, Hergesheimer, Irwin Cobb, etc. The writer was wise who was absent. For a young novelist or playwright with his roots not yet down, to sit in such a clique of know-it-alls was to get the art frightened out of him. A pickpocket keeping company with a pack of boastful cops might feel similarly hesitant toward the practice of his profession. Any writer who makes critics his cronies is almost certain to quit writing. MacArthur had more critic

pals than any other writer in town. He didn't quit, but he went in for long hesitations.

During that first year in New York, Hecht and Rose also frequented magazine illustrator Neysa McMein's studio parties (at one of which Charles MacArthur first met Helen Hayes), Bob Chandler's house parties (Chandler was a millionaire who dabbled in the arts and threw lavish parties which he frequently didn't attend), as well as impromptu parties at the Boni & Liveright offices. Horace Liveright's gatherings were the most exciting groupings of different types of people to be found in New York during the twenties, Liveright's earlier propensity for political radicals having given way to one for Ziegfeld Follies girls, actors, newspapermen, movie stars, politicians, and, of course, authors. The mayor of New York, Jimmy Walker, was often in attendance, as were the movies' Jesse Lasky and Walter Wanger, millionaires Otto Kahn and Herbert Bayard Swope (himself formerly a reporter), actors and actresses John Barrymore, Paul Robeson, Anna May Wong, Kay Francis, and writers Sinclair Lewis, Theodore Dreiser, Edna St. Vincent Millay, and Elinor Wylie. "To recapture B & L's atmosphere, one would not, like Proust, dip a madeleine into a cup of tea, but a canapé into bathtub gin," Liveright editor Edith Stern quipped.

Hecht and Rose had rented a top-floor apartment at 233 West Fourteenth Street, in a building with a "fine aromatic hallway." Hecht quickly polished off his adaptation of *The Firebrand* and turned it over to Liveright, who had formed a production company with Broadway producer Laurence Schwab and Frank Mandel, author of *No, No, Nanette*. *The Firebrand* opened on October 15th, starring Joseph Schildkraut—a friend of Hecht's from Chicago who considered him one of his discoverers—and Edward G. Robinson, later to star in a film Hecht would direct.

With *The Firebrand* a hit—it would run 261 performances—Schwab, Mandel, and Liveright rehired Hecht to adapt *The Stork*, a comedy by Hungarian playwright Ladislas Fodor. Liveright, however—though about to enter his most successful year in publishing—was in financial trouble. Playing the stock market with tips given him by banker Otto Kahn, he had lost a lot of money, in addition to which he was deeply in debt to his estranged wife's father, which the following year would force him to sell the Modern Library to Bennett Cerf (whose father had bought him a vice-presidency at B & L). Even though Boni & Liveright was making money and *The Firebrand* was a success, Liveright didn't have the ready capital to finance another play, so he let Schwab and Mandel produce *The Stork* on their own.

It opened on January 26th, 1925, at the Cort Theatre, but despite Schwab and Mandel's faith in Hecht's adaptation, and the attendant publicity and promotional tricks (ushers passed out celluloid storks with cards around their necks reading, "Remember what the stork brought you"), the play was a flop. It lasted eight performances and was panned by John Anderson in the *Evening Post*, who branded Hecht "the playboy of the Middle Western world," and by Heywood Broun in the *World* as "a rowdy play yet a very dull one." (A few years later, Hecht would confide to Alexander Woollcott: "Broun, when I was young and moody, done me dirt and my small but honest heart refuses to relinquish its distaste for him.")

Not long after *The Firebrand* opened, Hecht and Herman Mankiewicz[1] became friends, attracted by each other's wit and lack of pretension. (They had first met in Chicago, at Schlogl's, when Mankiewicz was in town to address the Book and Play Club on the New York theatre.) Both eager to make as much money as possible for the least amount of effort, they decided to start a magazine. All that was needed was a backer. Mankiewicz suggested Otto Kahn, who speculated not only on Wall Street but in the arts as well ("Calling on Otto Kahn is a procedure that is getting to be by way of a habit for the neediest literates of the town," *The New York Times* had reported in December of 1924.) As Hecht would remark a few years later about Howard Hughes, Kahn was "the sucker with the money." Kahn's nineteen-year-old son Roger wanted to compose for Broadway, so Hecht agreed to help him write a show in return for which Kahn senior put up the cash for a magazine. Thus the Bozo Publishing Company was born in the back of Roger's Fifty-seventh Street nightclub, Le Perroquet.

Hecht and Mankiewicz dubbed the publication *The Low Down: A Magazine for Hypocrites* and proceeded to paste together an issue composed primarily of material that hadn't been used in the *Chicago Literary Times*. Hecht included the first segment of a *Cutie*-like story he and Bodenheim had written in Chicago, "The Love Affairs of Lesbia Lefkowitz, The Studio Siren," which he illustrated with drawings by George Grosz and Herman Rosse. The inevitable "1001 Afternoons" column, printed both in the *Chicago Literary Times* and the *News* under the title "Squatty," was rerun as "The Camel's Back." Blurbs Bodenheim and Hecht had written for the *Literary Times* were used on the inside cover—*The Low Down* is a magazine that Bites in the Clinches, Catches Flies in Church, and Whistles at the Molls on Main Street. It is published for Bozos, Gimps, Herring Destroyers, Goofs, Gazabos, Pot-wallopers, Frails with Swell Legs, Molls, Bimbos, Cake Eaters, White Wings, Sheiks, Shebas, Knee Nudgers—It is also Published for Wet Smacks Who Claim They Ain't Any of These Things."

Hecht and Mankiewicz took George Grosz drawings, added captions, and turned them into cartoons (one drawing pictured a middle-aged man in long underwear preparing to brush his teeth, while his wife, sitting on the bed, is taking her shoes off; the wife says, "Oscar, do you remember the first time you kissed me?"; he replies, "Hell, I can't remember the last time"). They cowrote three poems—"The Curse of Sin or Only a Pair of Hips," "Rhyme of the Very Best Way to Lead Pure Girls Astray," and "Toothpick Humoresque, Broadway Puts on Its BVDs," which they signed Alfred Pupick, his last name being that of the censor in *Cutie*—and a two-page spread composed of bogus gossip items called "On Main Street with High Holler," the name of a *Chicago Literary Times* column.

Hecht was the only named writer in the magazine—Mankiewicz being identified simply by his initials—so the opinions in the gossip column seemed exclusively his own. It started off with a jab at Heywood Broun: "Heywood Broun sprained his ankle last Thursday by falling off his stilts in front of Mazurine's Ice Cream Parlor." "Boom times are ahead," were predicted for Horace Liveright in what was to be B & L's best year. Alexander Woollcott, Robert Benchley, George S. Kaufman, and H. L. Mencken were kidded gently, while David Selznick, soon to join MGM, was reported saying he was "going to set up as a photographer as soon as he could find a proper location." The only biting item concerned Carl Van Vechten, known for his successful novels of life among sophisticated New Yorkers: "A lot of people are wondering what Carl Van Vechten is going to do with the new fangled manure spreader that arrived from the J. I. Case Tractor Works last Friday. Carl drove the contraption through town yesterday but folks don't think it will work when he gets it in the field."

In the second and final issue, Hecht's name was gone from the masthead, leaving the entire issue devoid of named writers, editors, or publishers. Incredibly, material from the first issue was reprinted, as well as "Definition of Art 1910–1924" from the *Chicago Literary Times* (Hecht undoubtedly hoped to capture some of the fanfare provoked by Ernest

Boyd's "Aesthete: Model 1924," just published in *The American Mercury*). Three-quarters of the issue was filled with Alfred Pupick poems, including reprints from the first number, which read like lyrics for Jewish vaudeville numbers—"Songs from a Yiddish Cowboy," "A Wolf in Sheep's Clothing or Why Yenta Had Her Shoes Re-Soled," "Who Will Protect the Woiking Goil or The Tragedy from a Socialist Picnic," etc.

The Low Down was a financial failure and not suprisingly, considering how it had been slapped together. It had reprinted material from the *Chicago Literary Times* but it had had none of the *Times'* style. The *Literary Times* was a tabloid, was printed on gaudily colored paper, and had eye-catching headlines. *The Low Down* was printed in a small format, had a dull red cover, had no visual continuity (there were no articles and no divisions between material), used huge print, and had none of the book, theatre, and film reviews that the *Chicago Literary Times* had had. It included no editorials or special features, was half-filled with Alfred Pupick poems, and had no flavor of person or place, whereas the *Literary Times* was specifically a Chicago magazine and the product of identifiable personalities. Hecht had got his New York magazine, but he hadn't bothered to make it a success.

When Hecht returned from Germany in 1919, he and another reporter, Joseph Patrick McEvoy,[2] had teamed up with illustrator Herman Rosse to write *The Yellow Mask*, a variety show they hoped to get produced on Broadway to make themselves a bundle. (Harry Hansen remembered that "there was a time when Ben was asking all of us if we had any plots that he could turn into theatre pieces with McEvoy for *The Yellow Mask*.") The original source for the show was Hecht's sketch "The Yellow Goat," which had run in *The Little Review*, had been inserted into *Erik Dorn*, and had been rewritten as "The Eternal Fugitive" for the *Smart Set*. Although Hecht, McEvoy, and Rosse didn't have any luck selling the show as a whole, they sold seven scenes to the Shuberts, who integrated them into Raymond Hitchcock's *Hitchy-Koo* and into *The Passing Show*, netting the authors a total of two hundred dollars, which they collected only after suing the Shuberts.

In 1924, with the proceeds from his play *The Potters*, McEvoy had bought a cottage outside Woodstock, New York, but was in Chicago in June of 1925 to work on another play, *It's the Old Army Game*. When Hecht was in town for a few days that summer,[3] McEvoy offered him the use of the cottage. Needing to escape the *fureur de vivre* of Manhattan in order to write, late in June Hecht and Rose moved upstate, where he began turning out short stories he described to Margaret Anderson as "tripe for the lower class magazines." *The Little Review* had paid nothing for contributions (F. Scott Fitzgerald had once told Margaret Anderson that he couldn't afford to write for her) and Mencken paid thirty to fifty dollars for a story, while the top magazines of the day, such as the *Saturday Evening Post*, paid three to four thousand dollars. Falling between these extremes were a number of popular magazines that were similar to the *Smart Set* in appearance—printed on cheap paper, with magnificent cover illustrations by Ralph Barton, John Held, Jr., and Neysa McMein—but which, along with fiction, ran articles on perennially popular subjects such as marriage, analysis, and divorce, and attracted better writers (Heywood Broun, Ring Lardner, Fannie Hurst, etc.) simply because they paid up to one thousand dollars for a short story or article.

By summer's end Hecht had sold nine stories to three of these middle-brow magazines—*Redbook*, *McClure's*, and *The Shrine*—for a total of $3,150. In July and August, though, a steady stream of visitors to Woodstock depleted his cash. Bob Chandler showed up frequently with an entourage from the city; Rose's sister Minna, a medical student specializing in psychiatry, visited; the Marx brothers arrived with wives and children in tow; and Herman Mankiewicz, on vacation from *The New York Times* and *The New Yorker*, appeared with no money—his wife Sarah having confiscated all his cash so he couldn't buy booze—but with a suitcase full of Scotch. In addition, Charles MacArthur had arrived broke, intending to spend the summer.

MacArthur had lived a libidinous, hard-drinking, carefree life after leaving home in his teens, driven out by his preacher father, and was "one of those men who never do what women call 'the right thing to do' in any circumstance," Rose Hecht wrote. He had survived some of the bloodiest campaigns of World War I with the Rainbow Division, then, upon his return to Chicago, had joined the staff of the *Herald Examiner* before switching to the *Tribune*. (MacArthur had begun his career in journalism on a suburban weekly, *Oak Leaves*, owned by his brother Telfer.) Hecht and MacArthur had known each other in Chicago in the teens, but Hecht had worked on an afternoon paper and MacArthur for a morning one, which made him and his brother reporters "a breed apart." "My memories of newspapermen are 95% confined to those who worked on the afternoon dailies," Hecht recalled. "Of the morning paper men I have a somewhat hysterical impression . . . to this day I am always somewhat startled on perceiving a morning newspaperman amid orderly, respectable surroundings."

MacArthur had preceded Hecht to New York by a year and a half and had become, as Burton Rascoe described him, "the darling of the Algonquin set." The first day Hecht was in New York he had met Gene Markey on the street (Markey had included Hecht in his book of caricatures, *Literary Lights*, published by Covici in 1923), and was warned, "If some important hostess with a diamond stomacher invites you to a party and promises that you'll meet the most captivating, thrilling, faunlike charmer of our time, don't get your hopes up. It's always that sonofabitch MacArthur."

Before his arrival in Woodstock, MacArthur had coauthored a play, *Lulu Belle*, with one of Broadway's most successful playwrights, Ned Sheldon, whose sister had married one of MacArthur's brothers. David Belasco planned to open *Lulu Belle* in the fall, but had postponed it until the following February, so nobody would lend MacArthur any more money on the strength of the opening. Since he had recently met and fallen in love with Helen Hayes—spending the summer with her mother at Percy Hammond's Syosset, Long Island, home—MacArthur even had to borrow the five-dollar train fare to visit her on weekends.

I had been ragging her about her appearance—the lip rouge, the green eyelids, the white powdered cheeks, the cape that trailed the ground, the skirt that came just to her knees, and above all, the puppet, that leering, degenerate-looking Count Bruga, which she was hugging to her bosom. . . .

—HENRY MILLER
The Rosy Crucifixion

During the week in Woodstock, Hecht and MacArthur played host to the ever-changing guests and collaborated on their first play together, *The Moonshooter*. (Sam Harris, former partner of George M. Cohan, and legendary Broadway entrepreneur Al Woods would both consider producing it that fall, but ultimately were not willing to take a chance on a comedy whose hero gets killed in the third act.[4]) But because of the debts he had piling up, Hecht put *The Moonshooter* aside temporarily to hack out a book for quick cash. Once again he was hard-pressed to come up with a plot when John Sumner and his Society for the Suppression of Vice decided Maxwell Bodenheim's new novel, *Replenishing Jessica*—which Boni & Liveright had just issued—was obscene.

Bodenheim and Horace Liveright were brought before the New York State grand jury, which concurred with Sumner, forcing B & L to withdraw the novel from bookstores. Although Bodenheim had pleaded innocent and the case wouldn't come to trial for three years, Hecht had found his subject: he spent the rest of the summer writing a thinly disguised comic portrait of Bodenheim called *Count Bruga*.[5] As with Hecht's earlier novels, there was little plot to bind the book's disparate elements. In an attempt to string episodes together, Hecht inserted a murder, which gave him the opportunity to write about criminals he had known and trials he had covered in Chicago. Bits and pieces of *Tosca* were cemented in. The story of real-life murderer Henry Spencer, whose trial Hecht had covered in the teens, was worked in, as were epigrams he and Bodenheim had written for the *Chicago Literary Times*—

> Sandburg is a moonstruck bricklayer who has fallen off his ladder and hurt his head.

> Pound is a yesterday's orchid in the Bloomsbury buttonhole.

> Carl Van Vechten is a sensitive barber out of work.

When an admirer of Bruga's poetry remarks, "There's a lot of talk this year about Michael Arlen," Bruga responds, "There is always a lot of talk whenever a butler takes to fiction." "I've always wondered," the admirer continues, "if a man of your type admired Henry James?" "I'm not interested in constipation or its struggles," Bruga retorts.

Hecht also inserted "The Shadow"—a short story he had sold to *Liberty* shortly before—as a yarn one of his characters relates. The mystery continued, with Bruga only brought in peripherally. To get him back in the picture, Hecht abruptly switched from the murder to a séance. Bodenheim was a striking man with blond hair and blue eyes, notorious for trying to seduce every attractive woman he met, so Hecht had Bruga attempt to rape a woman at the séance in full view of the other participants. When she begins to scream, Bruga, with his "lips in her ear," tells her to keep quiet since she's only attracting attention. Removed bodily from the séance, Bruga epigrammatizes the experience: "Sex is a

Public Comfort Station in which one may decorously pay hommage to certain impressive but unimportant needs."

At the end of the book, the mystery solved, Bruga is left at a dinner party cavorting as oafishly and outrageously as was Bodenheim's wont. Unwilling to leave him flayed in caricature, Hecht wrote two paragraphs near the novel's end that revealed the dichotomy of Bodenheim's character and Hecht's awareness of the violent oppositions that existed within him.

> Those who knocked at the door of his genius were greeted by a violent, unsavory and preposterous clown. A derisive ruffian assaulted them for their pains. Women pausing to murmur kindly and perhaps wistful words to Orpheus found themselves pursued by Jack the Ripper. Men responding in his presence to the urge of kinship found themselves crowned with a herring barrel.
>
> Yet there was a poet whose name was Hippolyt Bruga. There was a tender and curious man, gentle as a child who lifted his head in ecstasy to the color of a star; whose thoughts were as subtle and delicate as the utterances of nature. There was this man whose spirit sang at the touch of life, whose hands laid beautiful gifts upon altars. One caught a glimpse of him through the maze of poems he wrote—a lonely one, a vague silvered figure moving wraith-like behind the many-colored pillars of fairyland.

(What galled Bodenheim all his life was not that Hecht had caricatured him—in reality the book only enhanced the image of the wild bohemian that Bodenheim cultivated—but that Hecht had profited financially while he didn't make a dime.)

Leland Hayward's literary agency, the American Play Company, placed *Count Bruga* with Boni & Liveright for its spring list. Hecht wrote to Horace Liveright that the book was to be "the unreal and ironical history of a preposterous creature" that could best be illustrated by "showing Orpheus in a silk hat and a pair of soiled spats pursuing the regents of the YWCA."

Hecht and Rose also received an advance for *The Scoundrel*, a play based on Liveright, written in the spring and which producer Hassard Short planned to open in the fall. With the money from B & L and Short, the Hechts moved back to New York and rented a large old house on the Lower East Side across from the Henry Street Settlement. Hecht, Rose, and MacArthur had searched the city for a house to share but, finding nothing in Manhattan's upper reaches, had looked farther and farther downtown till MacArthur abandoned the quest at Fourteenth Street.

In December, Hecht sold a story to *McClure's* with a main character named MacArthur, and a few dollars trickled in from the publication of *The Wonder Hat and Other One-Act Plays* and a reprint of *Cutie* (shortly after its original publication in the *Chicago Literary Times*, Hecht had had *Cutie* privately printed in a limited edition). Then, late in the month, J. P. McEvoy came to Hecht with a proposal. Thomas Meighan, one of the top box-office stars of silent films, had asked McEvoy to polish the scenario of a film to be shot in Florida. Tom Geraghty, a scriptwriter for First National Pictures, had done a scenario, but Meighan, not satisfied, had inveigled Ring Lardner, one of his Long Island neighbors, into doing a rewrite. Still not satisfied, Meighan asked McEvoy to try his hand at it, but, never having written a movie, McEvoy wanted Hecht to accompany him to Florida and help with the scripting. When McEvoy offered to pay his and Rose's passage, Hecht jumped at the chance since there was a land boom going on in Florida, with men becoming millionaires overnight. By the end of the month they were on their way to Miami aboard the SS *Alexandria*.

In Florida, Hecht and McEvoy motored to Belleair, where the film was to be shot, and restructured the story and rewrote the dialogue to Meighan's satisfaction. Back in Miami, scouting ways to make a fast buck from "that diverting economic can-can known as the Florida boom," Hecht talked with a nightclub singer who lived across the hall from him and Rose at the Fleetwood Hotel. Quizzing him about the men who were making all the money, Hecht discovered that Charles Ort had come to Miami several months before with a few hundred dollars and had parlayed it into thirty million. Hecht figured he was the man to see. Two days later, the singer took Hecht to the Flagler Building and introduced him to Ort, "a short, reddish-faced man with an Ohio twang," whom Hecht smooth-talked into hiring him and McEvoy to do publicity for his Key Largo estates.

Impressed by the appearance of two heralded literary gents from up north—Hecht and McEvoy had been interviewed by reporters when the *Alexandria* docked—Ort readily agreed to pay them five thousand dollars a week. They fitted up an office in their hotel, hired one of the newsmen who had interviewed them, and began producing an eight-page promotional paper called the *Key Largo Breeze*, which so pleased Ort he read each issue aloud to his sales staff. "It is impossible even now," wrote Alva

Johnson[6] in the forties, "to read Hecht's prose without feeling the urge to rush south and invest a couple of hundred thousand dollars in the swamp that once was the town's Millionaire's Row."

Although the money was good, McEvoy tired fast of Miami and wanted to get back to Broadway. At a party on February 27th, 1926, he ran into Florenz Ziegfeld, who expressed an interest in the play he had begun, *Palm Beach Girl*. This resolved McEvoy to return to New York as soon as possible to finish it. When Hecht came up with a scheme for a bogus treasure hunt to lure Eastern socialites down to Miami on Kaiser Wilhelm's yacht, McEvoy returned to New York to make the arrangements and to resume his theatrical career.

People who knew Hecht in Miami began to remark on the weight he was putting on. Having no faith in Florida real estate—he hadn't invested a penny—and less in Florida banks, since he figured they would all go bust once the inevitable crash came, Hecht had been padding his body with layers of bills. When he had accumulated twenty thousand dollars, he contacted Marie and asked her for a divorce. If she was "nice and reasonable" she could have whatever she wanted, but if not he would disappear and not give her a cent. Within a matter of days, Marie had a lawyer push a divorce through on grounds of desertion. "I wired her asking if she would give me a divorce in return for ten thousand dollars in cash," was Hecht's version of events. "The divorce papers came a week later, containing a codicil requiring me to pay alimony for the rest of my life."

Marie wrote, "I made what I thought was a very modest demand of fifty dollars a week for the child and a quarter of his income, whatever it might be, for myself." *The New York Times* reported that Marie received $3,000 immediately plus $3,500 a year alimony and an undisclosed percentage of Hecht's literary works.

By the beginning of April the recession in Florida had begun, Ort losing money faster than he had made it. Hecht, with no work to do, decided it was time to clear out and counseled Ort to do the same. "I can't," Ort told him. "Someday this will all come back and what a fool I'd look like with a measly $800,000." Hecht and Rose left, and eight months later met an impoverished Ort on the street in New York.

With the remainder of the Florida money, Hecht refurbished the Henry Street house, which Rose had taken a fancy to. Rose had written in her novel that she had given up Bolshevism when she was fourteen; nevertheless she was still "on the side of the workingman," finding the immigrant Jewish ghetto where they were living sympathetic. "I lived in a

Trotzkyite dream of Freedom and Revolution," she said of herself more than forty years later. Hecht had imagined the house a social center, as his Chicago houses had been, and was disappointed when his and Rose's friends, whose lives centered around the West Forties, where magazine and publishing offices as well as the theatre district were located, declined invitations so far downtown.

In May, *Count Bruga* was published and promptly banned in Boston; *Gargoyles*, *The Florentine Dagger*, and *Humpty Dumpty* were reprinted for the eighth, fourth, and seventh time, respectively, and a short story of Hecht's, "Lindro the Great," was included in *The Best Love Stories of 1925*. To make ends meet, Hecht continued to turn out short stories for popular magazines and began preparing a collection of his stories for Covici. What with the inconvenience of living on Henry Street and this flurry of literary activity—Rose was adapting a Molnár play, *Riviera*, for producer Charles Frohman[7]—the Hechts abandoned their white elephant and in October moved to a top-floor apartment on Beekman Place, a lovely quiet area of Manhattan's Upper East Side, which in those years was not the high-rent district it was to become, but a mixture of well-kept brownstones and walk-up apartment houses.

In November, responding to Herman Mankiewicz's telegram offering him work in Hollywood, Hecht left for Los Angeles to write a movie for Paramount. That same month, Bodenheim's novel *Ninth Avenue* was published by Boni & Liveright. It contained a section on Hecht only slightly disguised as Ben Helgin.

> Ben was a robustly tall man in his early thirties, with a huge, half-bald head, and dark brown hair inclined to be frizzly. His long, pointed nose, severely arched eyebrows, and widely thin lips gave him the look of a complacent, pettily cruel Devil—a street urchin who had donned the mask of Mephistopheles but could not quite conceal the leer of a boy intent upon practical jokes and small tormentings. He was a master in the arts of dramatic exaggeration and belittling, never quite telling the truth and never quite lying, and his immeasurable vanity made him always determined to dominate any conversation. He had an Oriental volubility and people would often sit beside him for an hour or more and vainly try to insert a beginning remark or express an uninterrupted opinion . . . living in a dream world entirely of his own making, he loved to flirt with

visions, conquests, world-shaking concepts, and child-like boasts. On one morning he would appear among his friends, describing some plan or idea with a cyclonic enthusiasm, and on the very next afternoon no trace of it would remain in his mind. Again, he would loll in an armchair and announce that a famous actress of forty had implored him to reside with her and to become the leading man in her next play, but he would neglect to mention that the lady in question was renowned for her generous impulses and included truckdrivers and cigar-clerks in her overtures. These impositions caused most people to regard him as an eel-like *poseur*, when they were removed from the persuasive sorceries of his words, and they failed to see that his gigantic egoism had sincerely hoaxed itself into the role of a flitting and quickly ennuied conqueror.

For years he had followed the luring dream of amassing a large fortune through the creation of dexterously dishonest stories, plays, and press-agent campaigns, and while he had accumulated thousands of dollars in these ways, the dream of wealth persistently refused to be captured. He lacked the grimly plodding, blind instinct necessary for such a goal, and his financial harvests were always quickly gathered and dissipated. This babbling immersion in the garnering of money, however, gave him the paradoxical air of an esthetic Babbitt.

7

"BACKPORCH OF A DREAM"[1] TO *THE FRONT PAGE*

The son of a bitch stole my watch!

—LAST LINE OF
The Front Page

If Hecht hadn't decided to write for the movies, he would have been no more than a footnote to the literature of the teens and twenties. He'd had to scramble hard when he and Rose got to New York and had no money to show for it, good reviews not compensation enough for modest advances and minuscule royalties. Starting that summer of '25 in Woodstock, Hecht's reputation and glibness assured him and Rose frequent invitations to parties on Long Island, where Neysa McMein and Sam Harris had summer places and Otto Kahn a castle. Ring Lardner, whom Hecht had known in Chicago, had a house there, as did Thomas Meighan, George M. Cohan, playwright and Broadway entrepreneur Edgar Selwyn (soon off to Hollywood to become a director), Groucho Marx, Ed Wynn, Herbert Bayard Swope, Raymond Hitchcock, and Eddie Cantor. If Hecht had been unsure before, his year of hobnobbing with the rich and the famous decided him that making big money was more important than struggling to become a first-rate novelist. When Herman Mankiewicz's telegram arrived offering him three hundred dollars a week from the Paramount "Fresh Air Fund for New York Newspapermen," Hecht was more than willing to go Hollywood.[2] Once there, financial reward was almost immediate, Mankiewicz promoting Hecht a ten-thousand-dollar bonus for *Underworld*, which Mankiewicz promptly borrowed to pay off gambling debts.

Hecht's next assignment was to develop a full script for *Underworld*—from his eighteen-page "moody Sandburgian" treatment—for the film's director, Arthur Rosson and its producer, Howard Hawks. The three of them worked on a shooting script, then Rosson and Hawks cast the picture and had sets and costumes designed. Since some of the scenes were to be shot in a prison in San Francisco, Rosson drove up there, got drunk, disappeared for several days, and consequently was fired by the studio.

Josef von Sternberg, a former assistant of Rosson's, had salvaged *Children of Divorce* by reediting it and shooting additional scenes, so was given the direction of *Underworld* as a reward. He called in Jules Furthman's brother Charles, and Robert N. Lee—who, a few years later, would win an Academy Award nomination for his script of *Little Caesar*—to transform Hecht's hardboiled murder plot into his personal vehicle. "It was not von Sternberg," Hecht commented, "who put the script together but another director, Arthur Rosson." Neither Hecht, Rosson, nor Hawks received screenplay credit—Hecht's credit was for original story.

Jesse Lasky, cofounder of Paramount with Adolph Zukor, recalled that "*Underworld* was so sordid and savage in content, so different from accepted film fare, that the sales heads were afraid that no amount of effort could drum up business for it." They advised shelving it. After months of deliberation, B. P. Schulberg, the studio's production head, decided to take the risk and opened it at the Broadway Paramount at the end of August 1927.

It was an instant hit. Midnight screenings had to be added to accommodate the crowds; after a few days, it was moved to the larger Rivoli, where it made George Bancroft a star overnight and Hecht the latest white-haired boy of Hollywood. On May 16th, 1929, at the Hollywood Roosevelt Hotel, *Underworld* would win Hecht one of the sixteen Oscars presented at the first annual Academy Awards ceremony. As Hecht recalled, "*Underworld* was the first gangster film to bedazzle the movie fans; there were no lies in it—except for a half-dozen sentimental touches introduced by its director Joe von Sternberg. I still shudder remembering one of them. My head villain, after robbing a bank, emerged with a suitcase full of money and paused in the crowded street to notice a blind beggar and give him a coin—before making his getaway."

Sternberg, in his autobiography, *Fun in a Chinese Laundry*, wrote that Hecht

> did not consider me an able director, dismissing me, when he heard that I had been assigned to his notes, with, "There are thousands like that guy playing chess on Avenue A. . . ." The discerning Academy of Motion Picture Arts and Sciences bestowed one of their gilt statuettes on Mr. Ben Hecht for the best film of the year, and he must have been so overcome by that that he forgot to mention that he had requested that his name be expunged. He failed to show embarrassment of any sort, though he had previously stated in the presence of the press that when he saw the film he felt about to vomit, his exact words being, as quoted in print: "I must rush home at once, I think it's *mal de mer*."

After *Underworld* Hecht collaborated with Michael Arlen—whose *The Green Hat* had reached number five on the best-seller list the previous year, and who apparently hadn't taken umbrage at the quip about him in *Count Bruga*—on the script of *American Beauty*, which garnered them no screen credit since the studio had it rewritten. "In it," Hecht said, "we advanced the theory that a bright young woman could emerge from three sex affairs and still be fit to marry our hero. But we had gone too far. The script startled the sultans in the front office. 'We can't afford to alienate our movie audience by telling them the truth about themselves,' said Schulberg."

When Phillip Warren [Howard Hughes] came to Hollywood and announced his entry on a large scale as a producer of motion pictures, the czars and sachems of that fabulous town smacked their lips as if confronted by a large succulent herring, winked knowingly at their subsidiary potentates and fell to day dreaming. The arrival in Hollywood of so famous a bankroll was regarded as legitimate manna . . . he turned out to be a tall, lean aimless looking bonanza with a certain callow and effacive charm, a high-pitched, indecisive voice and full of a peculiar wall-flower modesty.

—Ben Hecht
"The Boy Pirate"

David and Myron Selznick and Lewis Milestone were frequent companions of Hecht's in Hollywood, David still a story editor at MGM, but about to be promoted to assistant producer. The Russian-born Milestone had first arrived in Hollywood in 1920 and had worked for Henry King, Thomas Ince, and Mack Sennett before he began directing. He had made two films previous to *The New Klondike* (the Florida picture Hecht and McEvoy had rewritten), after which he had returned to Hollywood to become enbroiled in a dispute with Warner Bros., who sued him for $200,000 for breach of contract. Milestone filed for bankruptcy, which got him out of paying the $200,000 but at the same time got him blacklisted by every studio in town. Depressed, he was seriously contemplating a return to Europe. At this point, Myron Selznick—out of work and obsessed with taking revenge on the movie business for ruining his father, Louis Selznick, one of the pioneers of the industry—decided to become an agent, allying himself with writers, directors, and stars against the studios at a time when agents had little power and were looked down on by the studios as interfering middlemen. Almost singlehandedly, Myron was to lift the agent to a position of power rivaling that of a studio boss and it was Howard Hughes who gave him his start.

In 1926, two years after he inherited his father's business, the twenty-year-old Hughes decided he wanted to make movies. He moved to Los Angeles, hired a friend of his father's, silent star and sometime director Ralph Graves, who produced a picture Hughes considered so bad he decided not to release it. His family then began to pressure him to turn his attention to more serious pursuits, which only determined him to succeed as a film producer. He hired Marshall "Mickey" Neilan, one of the top directors of the early twenties, who was having a hard time getting jobs as a result of his drinking, his contemptuous attitude toward the movies, and the advent of sound. Together they made *Everybody's Acting*, an immediate box-office hit. As Hecht later described it in "The Boy Pirate": "The vast success of [Hughes'] first picture came as a shock to the industry. [Hughes'] successful debut was discomfiting enough considering the already overcrowded ranks of Czars and Sachems. It was like the hatching of another Balkan state."

Shortly after the release of *Everybody's Acting*, a subsidiary of the Hughes Tool Company, the Caddo Rock Drill Bit Company, won a $500,000 suit against a competitor. Hughes used the money to form the Caddo Company of Hollywood, California, to manufacture motion pictures. Since Hughes was looked upon both as a novice moviemaker and an outsider by the studio bosses, Myron Selznick saw a chance to effect his revenge, or the beginnings of it, anyway, for he would make of it a lifelong project: turn Hughes into a success and hit the studios where it hurt most, their profits.

Myron contacted Neil McCarthy, a Los Angeles lawyer working for Hughes, to propose a number of deals, several of which Hughes accepted. Milestone was signed to a three-picture contract at a higher salary than Warner's had paid him. Thomas Meighan, whom Myron had known since Meighan was only a bit player for his father's studio, was signed to a two-picture contract. Hecht agreed to write two pictures and provide writers for four others, figuring he might as well get paid for what he had already done for nothing, having suggested to Mankiewicz— scouting for writers for Paramount—that he hire Oliver H. P. Garrett, and Wilson Mizner, whom he had met in Florida.

Hughes's first film under the Caddo banner was *Two Arabian Knights*;[3] to do the adaptation, Hecht had Hughes hire Wallace Smith, who had arrived in Hollywood shortly before Hecht to write *Venus of Venice* for Constance Talmadge. The Hughes deal had gelatinized so quickly that *Two Arabian Knights* was in production, with Milestone directing, by March of 1927, the same time that Sternberg began shooting *Underworld*.

Caddo was to produce nine films during its six-year lifespan, but for the moment Hecht had fulfilled his part of the deal. He had made a small fortune in Hollywood and returned to New York intending to write a serious novel, which *Count Bruga* hadn't been. He began a manuscript he called *A Child of the Century*, but other projects and New York social life intervened.

A play, *Such Is Life*, opened on August 31st, 1927, written by Marie Hecht and Peter Glenny. Originally titled *The Family Skeleton*, it was based, almost needless to say, on Hecht, Rose, and Marie. Before the year was out, Bennett Cerf's Modern Library reprinted *Erik Dorn*, Covici reprinted *1001 Afternoons in Chicago* and announced two of Hecht and Rose's plays in a single volume (*All He Ever Loved*—another name for *The Scoundrel*—and *Man-Eating Tiger*, written that summer), and Haldeman-Julius brought out five more Little Blue Book volumes of Hecht's short stories. Also, a study of Hecht's novels, "Ben Hecht and the Superman," was included in *Critical Woodcuts*, a volume of essays on contemporary authors.

In this theatrical neighborhood, full of dust and sunlight and stale perfumed drafts from the theatre alleys and stage door entrances, among the . . . theatre facades in front of which the audiences seemed always to be standing . . . in these streets that gave our senses all the life we knew, voluptuous girls marched, badly dressed, in costumes that exposed their legs and breasts like decorations . . . there we saw at times the incredible old actors, bespatted and moustacio'd, on their daily stroll . . . here our friends went by: the actor from the road show, the actress who had once been beautiful and famed, the little "sister act" . . . we recall the songs—the music of Broadway that is meant for feet and hearts . . . all day it spreads its din around us in the rehearsal halls nearby, it kept on patiently in the bedrooms and in the headquarters and the clubrooms of

*the vaudevillian trade, steadily it filled the streets and courtyards of our
little district with its gay, glib racket . . . just as the electric-lighted signs
above the buildings filled the night.*

—ROSE CAYLOR (HECHT)
The Journey

The American theatre was at its high-water mark in the mid- to late
twenties, before the sound film put it in permanent decline. (The 1927
season saw 263 shows open, but by 1933 the number of new productions
would drop to considerably less than 200; by the end of the thirties there
would be fewer than 100). In the spring of 1928 Herman Mankiewicz was
writing a play in Hollywood with George Jessel; McEvoy was working on a
musical for Ziegfeld, and MacArthur was in Maine writing *Salvation* with
Sidney Howard. Putting his novel aside for the moment, Hecht and
Roger Kahn finished *Hearts and Flowers*, the muscial they had been
collaborating on. Liveright announced it for the fall, but increasing
financial difficulties would force him to cancel it (Liveright's stage
production of *Dracula* was proving so costly he would also cancel a
musical version of *The Firebrand*).

The previous autumn, Hecht and Rose's play *Man-Eating Tiger*—
with a newspaper reporter as a major character—had opened in Allen-
town, Pennsylvania, and played a week. Hecht did rewrites before it
moved on to Philadelphia, but it still closed after three days. Al Lewis
announced he would bring it into New York after further revisions but
finally decided against opening it at all. Marie recalled that "Rose and Ben
had done a play together . . . it was being tried out on the road and
rumors reached me of trouble and more trouble. People who had seen it
came back and reported it was insane and impossible. Ben himself said
that if this play did not reach Broadway he would never write another." It
never did reach New York, but it motivated Hecht to take a stab at a play
with a reporter as a protagonist since plays about newspapermen were just
then coming into vogue. Like the hard-boiled detective, the newspaper
reporter was an indigenous American character—cynical, wisecracking,
without pretension—thus a natural subject for the tough romanticism
the theatre was then trading in. Surprisingly, the first successful newspaper drama, *Chicago*—which had opened in 1926—had been written by
a woman, Maureen Watkins, who, like Hecht, had worked on a play for
Leo Ditrichstein. Former Chicago society reporter Bartlett Cormack,
who had replaced Hecht on the *Journal* in 1914, had recently completed a

play, *The Racket*, with a reporter as a leading character, slated to open at the end of November. (Hecht had always tolerated Cormack but Charlie MacArthur had no liking for him: "Bart Cormack is a mental pee-wee and celebrity worshipper who is even a lousy newspaperman, and I don't know of anything more devastating than that.") To follow close on the heels of Cormack's play was *Gentlemen of the Press*, scripted by New York drama critic Ward Morehouse. Hecht figured if he was ever to write a play centering on the newspaper world he had better do it soon.

Since Rose didn't want to work with him on another play—"I preferred our marriage to collaborating"—Hecht began to look around for another writing partner. His first thought was J. P. McEvoy, who also had an apartment on Beekman Place and who dropped in on the Hechts most mornings. "It was I who called in Charlie MacArthur to collaborate on 'The Front Page,' " Rose recalled, "because I thought Ben and Charlie the better team."

Working mainly at the Hechts' and occasionally at the apartment MacArthur shared with Robert Benchley (where the closets were full of Brancusis, put there by MacArthur, who thought they cluttered up the place), Ben and Charlie condensed their combined twenty-five years of journalism into three acts about the adventures of a reporter and his editor, basing their characters on newsmen they had known in Chicago. The play's editor, Walter Burns, was Walter Howey, who had been MacArthur's editor at the *Chicago Tribune* and *New York Mirror* and was a legend in newspaper circles.[4] Hecht said of Howey that he knew him chiefly as "an invisible menace who sat in a Hearst tower, and with the aid of witches' brews, second sight, and other unethical trumperies, outwitted the town's honest news hounds." (The editor's patronymic came from another Chicago newsman, Walter Noble Burns, author of *The Saga of Billy the Kid*.)

Reporter Hildy Johnson, the play's other principal character, was based on a real reporter of the same name who, according to Jimmy Murphy, had been killed a few years earlier on Randolph Street when a truck jumped the curb. "If Hildy had been drinking as usual, he'd be alive today," alleged Murphy, who showed up in the play as a reporter from the *Journal*, where he actually worked when Hecht joined the paper in 1910. Vincent Starrett, however, claims that Johnson "died a few years after the play was produced—I saw him laughing in his box opening night—and it was said that his determined effort to approximate his reckless counterpart on the stage had hastened his untimely end."

Buddy McCue and Jack Schwartz, names unchanged and character traits intact, were written into the play, as was Roy Bensinger, the effeminate reporter in whose rolltop desk escaped prisoner Earl Williams is hidden. Bensinger's personality, however, was appropriated from another newsman, Spike Hennessey of the *American*, who, Hecht recalled, "lent a dignity to the premises as a result of an active germ phobia. Hennessey's mania for fresh air, germ protectors on telephone mouthpieces, individual towels and his aversion to whistling served to introduce a domestic note into the scene."

"It was one of the marvels of 'The Front Page,' " the play's producer Jed Harris recalled, "that although all the characters were actual people, nobody ever thought of suing us for invasion of privacy.[5] Indeed, they all turned up for the opening night in Chicago and simply wallowed in delight. When the curtain fell at the end of the first act, the roar that rose from the audience sounded like the bellowing of a herd of wild animals panicked by a fire in a zoo. Above this din one great monster of a voice could be heard yelling: 'MAKE IT MORE PERSONAL!' "

When Hecht and MacArthur got bogged down in the second act of *The Front Page*,[6] they showed what they had to Gene Fowler, who had been the youngest managing editor of a major American daily and who was still in Hearst's employ. Drawing on his own knowledge of the newspaper world and Walter Howey, Fowler gave them enough useful advice to put them back on track so that by spring *The Front Page* was finished. Gene Fowler's son Will remembered that "as a surprise during those deep Depression days, when the family was leaving Ben's one night, Charlie pressed an envelope into Mother's hand, telling her not to open it because there was something 'dirty' in it. When Pop got home, she gave it to him. He opened it to find two checks for one thousand dollars each from Ben and Charlie for his help on *The Front Page*. It was the most money Pop thought he had ever seen."

Hecht and MacArthur took *The Front Page* to Broadway's boy wizard, Jed Harris—who had produced Bart Cormack's *The Racket* and whom Hecht had met when he persuaded Cormack to sell his play to Howard Hughes for Caddo's second production.[7] When Harris read *The Front Page* he knew he had a hit on his hands, perhaps the best play ever written for the American stage. In his Introduction to the Covici edition of the play,[8] he wrote that "in an age when the theatre seems imprisoned in a vise of literal and superficial realism . . . in a day when the successful portrayal of a newspaper reporter is accomplished by attaching to the person of the actor a hip-flask and a copy of *The American Mercury*, it is soothing and reassuring to stumble on a stage reporter who begins an interview in this innocent fashion: 'Is it true, Madam, that you were the victim of a Peeping Tom?' " (This question was actually posed by the real Buddy McCue.)

The first thing Harris did was hire Broadway's top playwright, George S. Kaufman, to tighten the script and cut some superficial scenes involving gangsters from the third act. (Kaufman also provided the play its title.) After Kaufman read the script he told Harris he wanted to direct the play as well. Hecht and MacArthur were more than willing since it was the first time Kaufman wanted to take a directing credit, although he had directed other Broadway productions.

By late spring, Kaufman had cast it and put it into rehearsal. On May 14th, he previewed it in Atlantic City, but more tightening was needed, so Hecht and MacArthur rented a bankrupt girls' school in Nyack, New York, to do the rewrites. MacArthur had grown up in Nyack and had suggested it since it was a quiet little town only thirty miles from Broadway. Before they had finished their revisions, *Man-Eating Tiger* was put into rehearsal by Al Lewis, who once again thought he might open it. The rehearsals changed his mind, but not before Hecht began still another play, this time in collaboration with George Jessel.

Jessel and Mankiewicz had failed to finish *The Big Time*, the play they had begun writing on the Coast, so Mankiewicz suggested Hecht as a possible collaborator. When Jessel's picture contract was up he went to New York and sought Hecht out, recalling their first meeting in his volume of reminiscences, *So Help Me*:

> I had pictured Mr. Hecht as being a very aesthetic looking man, the type that wears a flowing black Windsor tie. The rehearsal of his show "Man-Eating Tiger" was in progress and Al Lewis motioned me to sit down. I was seated next to a man who was chewing on a cigar and wearing a loud red tie and a shirt that might have been used as a stage curtain for a troupe of very gay midgets. I sat through almost a whole act of the play and thought it very daffy. When the curtain fell Lewis turned to me and asked what I thought of it. I answered, "Well, my honest opinion is that when the keeper comes in, instead of coming for the character in the play, he ought to ask for you and Hecht and take you both back to the asylum." Whereupon Lewis hurriedly introduced me to the fellow with the red tie and said, "This is Ben Hecht."

After a few days of trying to work with Jessel, who not only couldn't write but couldn't organize a plot or think in dramatic terms, Hecht gave it up as a bad job. He told Gene Fowler that he had never met anybody "so eager to flaunt his stupidity, low-grade human values and jackass vanities to the world." Jessel took the play outline to budding playwrights Sam and Bella Spewack, who turned it into *The War Song*.

Having put aside his ambition to become a first-rate novelist to direct his energies toward the theatre and movies, Hecht was receiving more critical attention than ever from the literary establishment. *The American Novel Today* by Regis Michaud and *16 Authors to One* by David Karsner were issued, each with a chapter on Hecht's novels, and *Gargoyles* and *Humpty Dumpty* were reprinted once again.[9] This critical attention spurred Hecht into fits and starts of work on his new novel, *A Child of the Century*, but it wasn't coming easily. Besides, he didn't have the time to work on it, what with all his playwriting and socializing (one of his and MacArthur's habits being to spend Saturday mornings at Alexander Woollcott's breakfasts, where members of the defunct Round Table gathered).

Suddenly Hecht's growing reputation as a novelist was thrust into the background. After a successful tryout in Long Branch, New Jersey, *The Front Page* opened on the 14th of August, 1928, at the Times Square Theatre and, five days later, had been proclaimed a "hit" by *The New York Times*. Filling the front page of the Sunday drama section on August 26th was an essay by Brooks Atkinson:

> "The Front Page," which is one of the tautest and most unerring melodramas of the day, bruises the sensitive ear with a Rabelaisian vernacular unprecedented for its uphill and down-dale blasphemy . . . the story of "The Front Page" concerns a police reporter's sensational attempt to capitalize for his newspaper the escape of a condemned prisoner. After nearly a full act of unprogressive but highly entertaining verbal pyrotechnics, hilarious and blistering, the screaming jail siren announces the escape of Earl Williams, who, as the victim of political knavery, is about to be hanged as a murderer. With the frightful siren shrieking offstage, the searchlights flooding the pressroom and etching the hangman's noose in silhouette on the grimy walls, this scene—so rudely in contrast with the preliminaries of the play—makes a tremendous conclusion to the first act. During the rest of the melodrama Hildy Johnson divides his

time fairly equally between explaining to his fiancée just why he cannot meet her on the night train for New York, where they are to be married, and attempting to keep Earl Williams secretly locked up in a roll-top desk until his newspaper has printed the exclusive story. Throughout the rapid, breathless second act he appears to be successful. In the third act the police discover Earl Williams in the desk. But the play leaps along just as swiftly; and the curtain line finishes nothing except the current episode.

To leave the description of "The Front Page" like that would be to pass over the color, the pace, the incidents and the lusty humor that make it so vibrantly entertaining. Mr. Hecht and Mr. MacArthur, writing from personal experiences, have omitted none of the characteristics of their police headquarters press room. They have exaggerated, heightened the proportions of the profanity and the Billingsgate; but they have concentrated their material no more narrowly than good melodramas do. The bored reporter, the bully, the nauseated esthete who finds his shiftless comrades revolting and sprays his desk with disinfectant, the nervous and merciless managing editor—all go through their paces. The skepticism, the callousness, the contempt, the vague dissatisfaction with their lot, the boorishness, the brutal jesting and the omniscience are not invented. Hysterically funny as it may be to hear one of these newsmongers telephone the facts of the birth of a child in a patrol wagon, there is no gross perversion of the truth. Hilarious, gruesome and strident by turns, "The Front Page" compresses lively dramatic material into a robust play.

(The play was so "robust" that for weeks plainclothes police stenographers took down the dialogue because of complaints that it was pornographic and slandered the fourth estate. Notified ahead of time by a friend in the police department, Hecht and MacArthur "perfumed" the dialogue the evenings the stenographers appeared.)

The play's success was immediate and enormous, money and acclaim pouring in, reviews and interviews appearing in all the papers. Hecht and MacArthur were the Katzenjammer Kids of Broadway, as Jed Harris styled them. Two days after the play opened, MacArthur, a personality in his own right at last, married Helen Hayes.

In October and November, Harris sold the Central European and

Scandinavian rights for five thousand dollars and one thousand dollars, respectively, which was only the beginning. Covici published the play the week it opened on Broadway. Hecht and MacArthur dedicated it to "Madison and Clark Streets," and wrote in an epilogue, "We found we were not so much dramatists or intellectuals as two reporters in exile"—a feeling that would grow stronger as they got older. The book was so successful that Covici had a second printing run off in September.[10]

A month after the New York premiere, when *The Front Page* opened in Los Angeles, Herman Mankiewicz reviewed it for *The New York Times*:

> Not even the oldest Hollywood inhabitant whose memory goes back as far as seven or eight years can remember a theatrical opening which engendered as much enthusiasm as was manifest at the Belasco Theatre on Sunday when "The Front Page" was first revealed to West Coast theatre goers. The audience was entranced from the opening curtain and there was an outburst of applause and whistling after the second act such as is rarely seen in these semi-tropical parts.

Around this time Hecht was also paid for *The Green Ghost*, a movie treatment he had written about a British regiment decimated by mysterious deaths, which Leland Hayward had sold to MGM. Released as *The Unholy Night*, it was directed by Lionel Barrymore, who, along with his younger brother John and sister Ethel, had become friends of the Hechts. They had been brought together by Gene Fowler, a drinking companion of John's since 1918.

As soon as Lionel was finished shooting the picture, French director Jacques Feyder, then working in Hollywood, stepped in and made the same story in French (a common practice in the early days of sound before pictures could be dubbed into other languages), reinstating the original title, *Le Spectre Vert*.

After two years of frantic activity, Hecht entered 1929, the year of the stock market crash, with more equanimity than he had ever felt, having written a box-office smash both for the movies and the theatre—*Underworld* and *The Front Page*.[11] With some of the proceeds from *The Front Page*, the Hechts purchased a 198-year-old six-room house on a one-acre plot in Nyack, one hundred feet of the property fronting on the Hudson River. (Although Hecht was to buy a house in Oceanside, California, and a duplex apartment on West Sixty-seventh Street in New

York City, the Nyack place would be his real home for the rest of his life.) His best play behind him, his greatest achievements in Hollywood still to come, 1929 served as an interim. His writing output decreased sharply while he and Rose supervised construction of a new wing on their house and Hecht did some writing sheerly for the fun of it.

Hecht had first met Gene Fowler in 1918 when Fowler was arrested in Chicago for not having his draft card on him. In transit from Denver— where he had been reporting for the *Post*—to New York to cover the Jack Dempsey–Fred Fulton fight and to check on job possibilities in the East, Fowler had stepped off the train to stretch his legs and was arrested. When Hecht learned there was a fellow reporter in jail, he had him sprung. In New York six years later, Hecht became reacquainted with Fowler, then sports editor on the *Daily American*, which Walter Howey was managing and MacArthur was reporting for.

Although Fowler had ambitions to become a novelist, he never mingled with the literary crowd, forswearing the Algonquin for the newspaper and sports clique at Billy LaHiff's tavern on West Forty-eighth Street, where Toots Shor was the bouncer and the regulars included Bugs Baer, Ed Sullivan, Louis Sobol, Leonard Lyons, and Walter Winchell (who lived upstairs). Like Duffy, who taught Hecht Chicago's inner workings, Fowler was an intimate of New York's politicians, sports figures (he had grown up with Jack Dempsey), cops, and mobsters. Through Fowler, Hecht came to know the inside of the Great White Way as seen from Park Row.

Fowler's son Will recalled that "like Pop, Ben always had a great regard and sense of wonderment at vaudevillians, members of the burlesque, and others who really were artists but not regarded as such by those guardians of the Holy-of-Holies of the American theatre. Ben and Pop were often to be found backstage with their cronies at the Palace, etc., where there would be impromptu performances by the greatest dancers, pianists, and other specialists of the vaudeville theatre.

"They were not alone in this liking for the very special tribe of people known as variety artists. Not infrequently there could be seen near an old and battered piano at the Friars Club in New York, George M. Cohan, James J. Corbett, Jack Lait, Damon Runyon, and occasionally Ring Lardner. Ben and Pop would sit for hours with them while these great dancers and singers would try out new dances and songs for no price whatsoever except the applause of their fellows.

"Then Ben and Pop would go to Billy LaHiff's to see another class of their favorite persons, the men of the sports world. Jack Dempsey, his manager Jack (sobriquetted 'Doc' by Dempsey) Kerns, Mickey Walker, Sid Mercer, Walter Winchell, who then was a rangy young fellow with his skull full of notebooks and his nose full of news, and a great many men who since have become known as columnists. Indeed, it was in the cellar kitchen of LaHiff's that Pop wrote several chapters of his first book while Spooner the headwaiter served him food and drinks off the cuff. Bugs Baer had a room overhead and Joe Magurk the artist and Pop and Ben slept on the floor there. Occasionally Harrison Fisher, Leo Gordon, Horace Liveright, and others, including Tommy Meighan and Eddie Foy, Sr., would be Pop's and Ben's companions of an evening."

A witticism current on Broadway in the twenties was that a whore's breakfast consisted of a cup of coffee, a cigarette, and a copy of the *Morning Telegraph*. In December of 1928, when Walter Chrysler and Joseph Moore bought the famous old racing and theatrical paper with a view to turning it into a high-class sporting sheet, they hired Fowler to manage it and he rounded up a crowd of his old newspaper cronies to write for him—Westbrook Pegler, Lois Long (the *New Yorker's* "Lipstick"), Ring Lardner, Whitney Bolton, Walter Winchell, and Hecht.

Early in 1929 Hecht covered half a dozen boxing matches at Madison Square Garden for Fowler. In a piece titled "The Rights That Failed," Hecht wrote that a fighter whose face "looked like a dish of crushed strawberries . . . sent his opponent sprawling on his spine with a triphammer smash on the button . . . then when Braddock appeared unable to do more than shake the dewdrops out of Lomski's hair with his famed right wallop, the faithful registered depression." (Rose Hecht, who didn't share Ben's fascination with boxing, was dragged along to a bout and, upon hearing that a certain fighter was Catholic, suddenly became enthused, yelling, "Kill the Papist!")

Hecht also wrote several spot news stories for Walter Howey, but gave up reporting for the fun of it after writing a piece about a woman who claimed she was raped in a canoe. Hecht submitted that normal intercourse wasn't possible under the circumstances but "canoe-lingus" was. He had written the story to amuse Howey and Jack Lait, but the copy editor let the story go to press, the woman sued, and Hecht personally had to pay damages of seven thousand five hundred dollars.

In midyear Hecht published two articles, one looking back on his literary career, the other his first published reflections on writing for the movies.

"Farewell My Bluebell" appeared in the final issue of *The Little Review*, which was comprised of pieces by many of the original *Little Review* regulars.

> I saw my name in print for the first time in *The Little Review* in 1914 or 1915 . . . . during these sixteen years I have avoided mellowing, sure-footedness, deeper understanding, honest simplicity, real insight into men and women and all the other bogus coin for which a writer trades in his personality. These are the good things. As for the other side, my novels and collections of short stories which have been published give me a bellyache. I do not keep them in the house. . . . In the thirteen years that have passed since I became an Author I have never answered a letter from an admirer, never written a response to a critic, never been present at a literary dinner, never invited a book plugger, claque hound or important literary horse's hind end to my house; never delivered a speech, never answered a request for interviews, photographs or biographies such as this, never sucked around, played yogi, acted dignified, or rubbed noses with the god damn fools who run the literary billboards of the USA. In short I have been a model of egoism.

The other piece appeared in the June issue of *Theatre* magazine, reflecting an attitude Hecht would expand on vociferously over the next three and a half decades:

> I am an unmercenary literary man and have never invested my prose with a sales angle. Well, hardly ever. Out of the millions of words I have written I doubt whether I have averaged a half-cent a word. This lack of financial reward has given me quite a standing in my own eyes as a fellow full of literary integrity and a sort of fanatic insistence on art.
> My attitude toward the movies, therefore, strikes me, at least, as a very uncharacteristic one. I am chiefly interested in how much money I can wangle out of them. I charge from $15,000 to $25,000 for a scenario or, as they are fantastically called in Hollywood, an "original."
> A scenario or "original" takes from one to five afternoons to dictate.

The greed which fills my bosom when I am approached by a movie magnate is a psychologic rather than an economic one. The fact that the movie magnate is going to make an enormous pile of money out of my story and that I am therefore entitled to a creditable share of it, seldom, if ever, occurs to me. I am, to the contrary, convinced that my contribution is nil. The story I will provide will be a piece of hack-work, containing in it a reshuffling of familiar plot turns and characterizations. . . .

What does occur to me when I am asked how much I want for an "original" is that I am being asked to participate in a species of hoax. The hoax is one which the movie magnates have put over on themselves.

When a decade or more ago a group of uncultured and almost untutored gentlemen found themselves at the head of what was being called a "New Art Form"—namely, the movies—they turned, rather pathetically, to the literary personages of the country for corroboration. They began shelling out large sums of money to "big writers" for movies.

The introduction of "big writers" into the movie scenario department was and remains pure farce. But the movie magnates continue to ignore this factor because it flatters them to think that talent, effort, big brains, etc. go into the creation of the product they sell.

Thus the movie magnate approaching me for an "original" appeals fundamentally to me as being a sucker—a sucker who, strangely enough, is perfectly willing "to be taken." He prefers that I ask huge sum for a few afternoons' work and derives a peculiar thrill when I do.

When I go into conference with this movie gentleman, he prefers that I pose as a genius and that I give him the illusion a "Big Brain" is going to work for him in the creation of the quite inane and often idiotic scenario he is going to buy. How he is able to bamboozle himself that it takes more intelligence than he has himself, or even half as much as his stenographer has, to concoct one of the successful movies he sells, is a problem I leave to his own capacity for rationalization. I am content to play his game, and at the proper time remark that it will cost $20,000.

In May 1929, Hecht received his first Oscar, which he put to use as a doorstop in the tiny guesthouse perched at the north corner of his front lawn in Nyack. Earlier in the year he had sold a short story, "The Rival

Dummy," to James Cruze's newly formed independent producing company Sono Art World Wide Pictures, where it was directed by its star, Erich von Stroheim (although Cruze took the directorial credit), and released as *The Great Gabbo*. He also scripted *The River Inn* for Walter Wanger, head of Paramount's Astoria studios, and for Helen Morgan, who was to star. One evening at Big Jim Redmond's Parody Club (another of Fowler's hangouts), Hecht and Wanger caught the week's headliners, the Three Musketeers—Jimmy Durante, Lou Clayton, and Eddie Jackson. Wanger thought Durante perfect for the picture, signed him, and had Hecht rework the part of Helen Morgan's accompanist for him. The picture was renamed *Roadhouse Nights* and released the following February. Although Hecht was credited with having written an original screenplay, the source for the picture amazingly was Dashiell Hammett's novel *Red Harvest*, sold to Paramount in 1929; very little of Hammett's novel survived, however, except for certain resemblances between Hecht's protagonist, a reporter, and Hammett's Continental Op.

Hecht and MacArthur then teamed up to write their first movie together, *The Homicide Squad*, which Leland Hayward sold to Universal for twenty thousand dollars. Hecht and MacArthur's story went through the Universal script mill and had so many writers on it that they didn't get screen credit when it was released more than two years later.

That September, Helen and Charlie MacArthur moved to Los Angeles, where Charlie went to work for MGM, lured there by the huge salary offered him by Irving Thalberg, the studio's young head of production. Left without a collaborator, Hecht began plotting a story for Harpo Marx and his brothers. Since their first two films had been stage adaptations, Harpo wanted something written specifically for the screen, so Hecht did an outline for a picture he called *Monkey Business*. He was still working on it at the end of the year,[12] and on the novel he had begun two years earlier. He had retitled the novel *A Jew in Love*, and considered it the best novel he had yet written, by far his most serious work since *Erik Dorn*. He also returned to short-story writing and turned out two long tales in rapid succession, "The Champion from Far Away" and "Baby Milly and the Pharaoh," which Leland Hayward sold to the *Saturday Evening Post* for $2,500 each. In January he finished *Monkey Business* and Leland Hayward sold it to Paramount on the thirtieth. (The film would be made the following year, but Hecht wouldn't receive credit, since the story was further developed by S. J. Perelman, who wrote the dialogue.)

In Nyack, on the 30th of January, 1930, Hecht was visited by David

Selznick, who was in the East on business for Paramount, where he had been working since he left MGM in 1928. Selznick was unhappy at Paramount, though, and was looking around for other job possibilities. Hecht thought he'd make a great Broadway producer and tried to convince him to take a stab at it, but Selznick wasn't interested. Book publishing did hold a certain fascination for him, so Hecht arranged a meeting with Pascal Covici; nothing came of it, however, since Selznick was really committed heart and soul to the movies. Selznick recounted his visit with Hecht in a letter to his fiancée, Irene Mayer, daughter of Louis B. Mayer.

> Today I spent with Ben Hecht at Nyack. I found him ninety
> per cent of my conception of him these several years since
> we have met. And thus he is the only one of all my Eastern
> figures that has not been shattered. We had a delightful
> afternoon walking through the snows over bleak roads along
> the Hudson. He has bought a house a century and a half old
> and added to it an incongruous, amazing assortment of
> things, including swimming pools indoors and out; a gym-
> nasium, odd little reading rooms. . . . The house sounds
> romantic, but is not, but rather like a junk shop for
> incompleted dreams. Hecht is less jovial but more pictur-
> esque when without his present affluence.

8

SCARFACE

Ben Hecht is the best screenwriter I have ever seen.

—Jean-Luc Godard

Ben in my opinion was the greatest of all scenario writers.

—David O. Selznick

Hecht was surprised to find Charlie grinning at him one day when he answered his front door in Nyack, since the last he knew MacArthur was in Los Angeles working for Irving Thalberg. MacArthur had in fact written dialogue for two of director Sam Wood's pictures, *The Girl Said No* and *Way for a Sailor*, dialogue for a musical, *The King of Jazz*, and had been in the middle of *Billy the Kid* for King Vidor. Helen was pregnant, though, and had returned to New York several months earlier, so MacArthur had come back East to be with her for the birth of their child. (Traveling on a United Fruit Line ship bound for New York via the Panama Canal, he had got drunk in Havana, missed the ship, and had to wire Anita Loos for money.)

In Nyack, Hecht and MacArthur decided to write another play, announcing to the newspapers they would be scripting one for producer Chester Erskine. As soon as Jed Harris got wind of this, he phoned his press agent, Dick Maney. "He had read in the *Times* that Hecht was to write a play for Chester Erskine," Maney recalled in his memoirs, *Fanfare*.

> Erskine had achieved genius rating for staging *The Last Mile*. Hecht must be in desperate circumstances to thus play the apostate, said Harris. It was less than two years since Harris had enriched him and MacArthur with his production of *The Front Page*. It was less than four months since he cheered Rose Caylor (Mrs. Hecht) for her adaptation of *Uncle Vanya*. What ingratitude!
>
> I tracked Hecht down in an East Side hotel. He was playing gin with MacArthur. I pressed $5,000 in cash into his hand. "A token from the Darkling," I said. "For what?" asked Hecht. "Advance royalty on your next play." "What next play?" they choroused. "And where's *my* five grand?" chirped MacArthur. "Looks like discrimination!"

Having accepted a fat advance on a phantom play, Hecht's conscience started to gnaw him. To appease Harris, he and MacArthur wrote a fifteen-page synopsis of the life and times of Big Jim Colosimo, a Chicago hoodlum recently ventilated in his own saloon. This outline could be spun into a three-act melodrama if Harris found the sample to his liking. Harris wanted no part of a Cook County hood. He resorted to a pocket veto.

During the Colosimo debate, Charles Bruce Milholland came to Harris with "The Napoleon of Broadway." Milholland had been Morris Gest's press agent. . . . Exposure to Gest all but demented Milholland.

The central character in "The Napoleon of Broadway" was a lunatic producer, a paraphrase of Gest. Harris was fascinated with this maniac, but found the other characters tiresome. He persuaded Milholland to let Hecht and MacArthur coin a new plot and write new dialogue. [According to Rose Hecht, Ben and Charlie didn't even bother to read the Milholland play.] Ten days later, Hecht and MacArthur were cloistered in a Charleston hotel. Three weeks later they laid two acts of *Twentieth Century* on Harris' desk. . . . Oscar Jaffe, the moody producer about whom the plot swirled, was a composite of Belasco, Morris Gest, and the Gitano [Harris], with all of whom the authors were familiar.

The work had gone so smoothly in South Carolina that Hecht and MacArthur thought it would only take another week to ten days to write the third act, which they intended to do in Nyack. In New York, however, they met Sam Goldwyn in an elevator in the Pierre Hotel, where Hecht, unable or unwilling to stop himself from bamboozling a Hollywood mogul, launched into a movie plot for MacArthur's amusement, making it up as he went along. Goldwyn said he'd buy the story for $10,000 and the script for an additional $125,000, so Hecht and MacArthur decided to finish the play in Hollywood. But, before leaving for California, Hecht wanted to find someone to write the Goldwyn movie for them. By chance, on the train to Nyack, where he was headed to pack for the trip West, Hecht ran into an aspiring young writer named John Lee Mahin.

"Charlie and I are going out to Hollywood," Hecht told him. "How would you like to come along? You can work for us as our secretary. We'll give you two hundred dollars a week and when we leave we'll see that you have a job. We're going to have a story factory, you'll do a movie while we finish our play."

Mahin threw over his advertising job and went. In Los Angeles, they made their way to a seventy-five-acre avocado ranch Hecht and MacArthur had rented from New York. "They paid twelve hundred dollars a month for it, which at that time was godawful rent," Mahin remembered. Located on a hill overlooking MGM's back lot in Culver City and called the Youngworth Ranch, it had once belonged to a high degree Mason. Mahin, overwhelmed to be working for Ben Hecht, never forgot the night they arrived.

"It was the darnedest thing—suddenly the house filled with everybody, David Selznick and Irene, Phillips Holmes, Lewis Milestone, and a lot of Hollywood stars. I was out in the kitchen when I heard David Selznick calling Myron, saying, 'Come on over here and we'll fight MacArthur.' I went up to Ben and said, 'Jesus, it's gonna be rough here.' 'Never mind,' he said, 'Nutsy can take care of himself.' Nutsy—that's what he called MacArthur. So Myron showed up and they started to argue. You could see that they were picking a fight. Charlie said, 'Come on in my room and we'll have this out.' Well, they both went in the room and David and Myron started going after Charlie. And Charlie was doing pretty good. Irene tried to get in to stop it but they slammed the door. Ben and I were watching, he standing next to a chiffonier, smoking a cigar. I said, 'Jesus Christ, Ben, let's stop this.' And he said, 'Don't worry about Nutsy.' I tried to stop David and when I tried to stop Charlie he said, 'Get away from me, you fairy!' and he hit Dave again. They're all on the bed and Irene is banging on the door, saying, 'They're killing my husband!' Finally, Irene did get in and put a stop to it by beating Charlie over the head with the spike end of one of her slippers."

Helen Hayes called it "one of the worst brawls that Hollywood had known," but Hecht was simply amused. Rose wrote that MacArthur, in a fight, was "doing what he wanted; he was in his element . . . in his eyes there was a keen concentration and alertness rather than the reminiscent gaieties of the war, or boredom, and his laugh when he met his opponent's rushes, and measured him with his opening punches, was so realistic, so hard and unaffected that all his laughter and hardness before this might have been some effeminate masquerade."

Knowing how much MacArthur relished brawling, Hecht would spur him on. Once, years later, sitting in Sardi's after a play of theirs had opened, Hecht spotted a certain theatre critic, a known homosexual, who had panned their show. Hecht suggested MacArthur go over to his table and sock him. MacArthur, older and out of shape, quipped, "It's not worth it, I'll just send him a poison choir boy."

The day after the fight at the Youngworth Ranch, Hecht and MacArthur began work on the third act of "The Napoleon of Broadway," retitled *Twentieth Century*, but John Gilbert showed up drunk. As Mahin recalled, "Gilbert adored Ben and Charlie, but they said to me, 'Here's your first job. Take him off our hands.' So they sent me out with Gilbert, which lasted five days. I was really Merton of the Movies. We stayed at Gilbert's house and there were a lot of lovely girls around but I didn't realize until later that they were Lee Francis' girls. [Francis was Hollywood's most renowned madam of the period.] I didn't realize it until they left and the phone rang and Gilbert said, 'Yeah, I'll send you a check.'"

Hecht and MacArthur made little progress on *Twentieth Century*, since Sam Goldwyn, once he heard they were in town, began hounding them for a script. Also, Howard Hughes—who had finally finished his $4 million airplane epic, *Hell's Angels*—wanted Hecht to write Caddo's next picture since it was right up his alley: gangland Chicago. The original source for Hughes's movie was a pulp novel published in 1929 called *Scarface* by Armitage Trail (pseudonym of one Maurice Coons), which told the story of two brothers, one who becomes a cop, the other a hoodlum, and the inevitable conflict that followed. In 1930, Hughes bought the rights to the novel and had a script prepared, as John Lee Mahin recalled, "by a lot of hack movie writers," primarily W. R. Burnett, whose first novel, *Little Caesar*, had also been published in 1929.[1]

Hecht agreed to script *Scarface*, but he told Hughes he would do it only on condition that he receive a thousand-dollar bill every evening at six o'clock in payment for the day's work. "In this way," wrote Hecht, "I stood only to waste a day's labor if Mr. Hughes turned out to be insolvent." In reality, Hecht's demand was only a furthering of the legend he was building for himself, the idea of the thousand-dollar bill suggested by Myron Selznick, who remembered when silent screen star Alla Nazimova had demanded one thousand dollars from his father at the end of each day's shooting when she appeared in *War Brides*.

Hecht also wanted Howard Hawks to direct the picture, but Hughes at first refused to hire him. Hawks had had a run-in with Hughes over a scene in his picture *The Dawn Patrol* that showed a fighter pilot vomiting blood after being shot during a dogfight. Hughes had a similar scene in *Hell's Angels* and had wanted Hawks to edit his out. Hawks refused, and consequently Hughes didn't want him to direct *Scarface*. When Hecht cavalierly declined to write the gangster story otherwise, Hughes gave in, since Hecht was being touted as the best screenwriter in Hollywood. He had just won an Academy Award for *Underworld*, and Hughes, at odds with the Hollywood establishment, wanted him that much more because of the award they had presented him. Also, Hughes, aware of the mediocrity of the script he had, rightly thought a writer with Hecht's background as a Chicago crime reporter would be able to deliver a superior script. "Howard Hughes wanted to top all the gangster pictures," said Hecht, "so I had my secretary go out and see all the gangster pictures playing. She counted up the dead people in each picture. In one film nine were bumped off so I went to Howard and said, 'We're going to kill twenty-five people.' "

During a weekend at Hawks's Palm Springs house, Hecht and MacArthur confided to Hawks that they had sold Goldwyn a story in New York but couldn't remember what it was, so the three of them came up with what John Lee Mahin has laughingly described as "some cocka-mamie thing about a couple of thugs in the Sahara desert." Back at the Youngworth Ranch, Hecht and MacArthur delivered the plot to Mahin with instructions to write a story around their outline. Hecht went to work on the gangster story for Hughes while MacArthur, persuaded by Thalberg to put his wife in pictures, rewrote *The Sin of Madelon Claudet* for Helen, since he considered the script Thalberg had "so bad it would sink Garbo." *Twentieth Century* receded further and further into the background.

"Ben's work on *Scarface* was brilliant," Hawks recalled. "Of course, he knew a lot about Chicago so he didn't do any research." Mahin, who was to write some additional dialogue on the set, corroborated: "Real guts were put into the thing. The basic story was Ben's. Without his material there was nothing because I saw some of the stuff Hughes had." "It took Ben eleven days to write the story and the script," Hawks says. "I know it was eleven days because Ben had been offered twenty thousand dollars by Hughes and he had told him he wanted a thousand dollars a day so when he finished he knew he'd only get eleven thousand dollars and was sore as hell. I told him, 'We'll drive back to New York and add some more scenes so you can get your money.' " After twenty days the script was delivered to Hughes.

"Where the hell's the brother?" Hughes demanded.

"There isn't any brother," Hawks replied.

"Well, it's a good story anyway," Hughes conceded.

*　*　*

"*Scarface* was really the story of Al Capone," Hawks admitted. It has often been commented that Hecht wrote the story of *Scarface* from the headlines of Chicago dailies, Hecht himself confessing that many of his ideas for movies came from Chicago mobsters he and MacArthur had rubbed shoulders with. Alexander Woollcott wrote that "MacArthur and Deanie O'Banion, the last of the first class killers, used to ride up and down the boulevards at dawn in Deanie's automobile, Deanie shooting at the arc lights to keep himself in practice and Bugs MacArthur singing 'Nobody knows my name, poor boy, nobody knows my name.'" Hecht too rode around with the flower-loving killer.

In real life, Al Capone and Johnny Torrio had "Big Jim" Colosimo killed in their bid to take over Chicago. (Colosimo was the mobster, Hecht said, who summed up his success in the white-slavery racket by saying, "You gotta wholesale them cunts.") In *Scarface*, Tony Camonte and Johnny Lovo kill "Big Louie" Costillo to gain control of the South Side. They then rub out another mobster, O'Hara (read O'Banion); subsequently, O'Hara's gang tries to mow down Tony in a downtown hotel with a machine-gun fusillade.

"In 1926 the O'Banions, still unrepentant despite the loss of their leader, introduced another novelty in gang warfare," Frederick Lewis Allen wrote in *Only Yesterday*.

> In broad daylight, while the streets of Cicero were alive with traffic, they raked Al Capone's headquarters with machine-gun fire from eight touring cars. The cars proceeded down the crowded street outside the Hawthorne Hotel in solemn line, the first one firing blank cartridges to disperse the innocent citizenry and to draw Capone forces to the doors and windows, while from the succeeding cars, which followed a block behind, flowed a steady rattle of bullets, spraying the hotel and the adjoining buildings up and down. One gunman even got out of his car, knelt carefully upon the sidewalk at the door of the Hawthorne, and played one hundred bullets into the lobby—back and forth, as one might play the hose upon one's garden. The casualties were miraculously light, and Scarface Al himself remained in safety, flat on the floor of the hotel restaurant.

In *Scarface*, the one difference is that Tony's friend Rinaldo shoots the kneeling gunner and grabs the machine gun. Tony has never seen a portable machine gun before, precipitating one of the film's best scenes:

CAMONTE: Hey, Johnny, look what I got.

LOVO: You dirty murdering mug, you bumped off O'Hara.

CAMONTE: Who me? That's foolish. You told me to stay out of the North Side, so I stay out. I been home all day. Right, "Little Boy"?

RINALDO: Sure.

LOVO: Oh, so that's it. I told you to lay off.

CAMONTE: I don't hear so good sometimes.

LOVO: You won't be hearing anything if you go on like this. Look what happened to me. They hit me.

CAMONTE: Look it, Johnny, you can carry it around like a baby. (*Tony holds up the machine gun*)

LOVO: Aw, shut up. We gotta get organized. This is only the start of it. They'll be back after us.

CAMONTE: What d'ya mean. We won't give 'em time. This town's up for grabs.

LOVO: Yeah. Keep runnin' around and you're gonna get your head blown off.

CAMONTE: Yeah, and who's gonna do that?

LOVO: O'Hara's mob, Gaffney's runnin' it now.

CAMONTE: We're goin' up to the North Side, like I always told ya.

LOVO: You can't do that.

CAMONTE: What d'ya mean, can't. Who's stoppin' me?

LOVO: I am. I'm givin' you orders for the last time.

CAMONTE: There's only one thing that gets orders and gives orders and this it it. (*Holds up machine gun*) That's how I got the South Side for you and that's how I'm gonna get the North Side for you. Some little typewriter, huh? I'm gonna write my name all over this town in big letters.

LOVO: Hey, stop him somebody.

CAMONTE: Get outta my way, Johnny. I'm gonna spit. (*Tony fires the machine gun into a rack of pool cues.*[2])

Because Hecht was in a unique position to write realistically about Al Capone, which he did with very little alteration of fact, he received a visit in Hollywood from two of Capone's henchmen wanting to know just exactly what Hecht was writing. (Hecht later remarked, "Their dialogue should have been in the script.") He appeased them by explaining that the film was a generalized account of mob leaders he had known in Chicago during his days as a reporter. They were impressed by the figures he named but were still disturbed that the picture's title was *Scarface* (Capone's nickname because of the long scar that ran along his jaw and across his neck where someone had bungled the job of cutting his throat). Hecht replied that the title was certain to draw good publicity for the film since Al Capone was one of the most interesting and prominent figures of the day. The thugs pondered this, then asked who this "fella" Howard Hughes was. "He's got nothing to do with anything," Hecht replied, "he's the sucker with the money." (When the film was finished, Capone liked it so much he got his own print.)

The germ for *Scarface* exists in *Underworld*, which is a loose telling of the rise of Capone during the early and mid-twenties. The trio in *Underworld*—the mob leader, his girl, and his number-one henchman—have metamorphosed into *Scarface*'s incestuous threesome: Tony, his sister Cesca, and Tony's best friend and right-hand man, Rinaldo. Bull Weed, the boss in *Underworld*, is trapped in a room with his girl just as Tony and Cesca are caught at the end of *Scarface*. Another earmark linking the two films is the steel doors that don't work when they're needed to shield Bull Weed and Camonte from the cops. As well, there are the signs that blink in the night: THE CITY IS YOURS (in *Underworld*) and THE WORLD IS YOURS (in *Scarface*).

Feathers McCoy in *Underworld*, the film's only female interest, is split into two women in *Scarface*: Poppy, Lovo's wisecracking moll, and Cesca, the modern good girl. In *Underworld*, Feathers started out as Poppy but ended up as Cesca. As Poppy, all she could be was a dumb blonde because she couldn't crack wise except through the occasional title. In *Scarface*, Poppy speaks with well-honed sarcasm. The first time she and Tony meet, Tony tells Lovo that they have their pictures in the paper. Poppy asks, "What did they run it in, a razor ad?"

Time passes and Tony gets more powerful. They meet accidentally on the stairs to Lovo's office.

TONY: Hi, Poppy.

POPPY: Hello.

TONY: Hey, what's all the time bitin' you? You afraid of me?

POPPY: Well, that outfit is enough to give anyone the yips.

TONY: I got myself a new house. You come up sometime.

POPPY: With my grandmother.

Then Lovo is on the way out; Tony and Poppy have dinner in a fancy restaurant.

TONY: You know every time I see you you look better. That's a cute hat.

POPPY: Please! My stockings.

TONY: Whatsa matter?

POPPY: Well, don't do that, Tony. They're brand new.

TONY: Hands off, huh

POPPY: No. Feet.

Through these brief encounters Hecht was able to relay the changes that were taking place in their relationship in the fewest possible words, no long speeches, nothing uncinematic, which was why Hawks enjoyed working with him. "He was so good because you could talk to him. The average writer hasn't the slightest idea how to tell a story on the screen. And Ben had an eye for it, if you told him something he could go write it down. And write it so it sounded good to someone else. He spoiled you for other people to work with. And I think Ben enjoyed working with a director who knew a little about the story because then he didn't have to do it for some producer and he didn't like to work with producers very much."

A theme central to the movie was the love triangle—Tony loved his best friend Rinaldo, Rinaldo loved Tony, Cesca loved both of them, and they in turn loved her. Amazingly, the censors demanded the relationship between Tony and Cesca be played down, not because it was incestuous, but because it was "too beautiful to be attributed to a gangster." One day Tony catches Cesca being kissed in the front hall of their mother's house. "I caught you," he bellows.

CESCA: What do you mean catch me. I wasn't doing nothing.

TONY: You was kissin' him.

CESCA: Sure. What of it.

TONY: I don't like it.

CESCA: You're missin' lots of fun, Tony.

TONY: Lissen, I don't want anybody kissin' my kid sister.

CESCA: You're hurting my arm.

TONY: I don't want anybody puttin' their hands on you.

CESCA: What do you think you're doing.

TONY: Well, I'm your brother.

CESCA: You don't act it. You act more like . . . I don't know . . . some kind of . . . sometimes I think. . . .

TONY: I don't care what you think. You do what I say.

Another time Tony catches Cesca in a nightclub and drags her home: "Runnin' around with fellas, huh? Lettin' 'em hold you like that. Lettin' 'em look at you. Dressin' up like that for fellas to see, huh?" Then in Tony's steel-shuttered room, only minutes before they'll both be killed, Cesca emerges from the shadows intending to shoot Tony since he has killed Rinaldo—he thought Rinaldo had seduced Cesca, when actually they were secretly married. Police sirens distract her from her purpose. She exclaims, "Tony, quick. Tony, they're coming. The police."

TONY: Cesca.

CESCA: They're after you. They're going to get you, Tony.

TONY: Why didn't you shoot me, Cesca, why didn't you shoot me?

CESCA: I don't know . . . I love you. I think because you're me and I'm you. It's always been that way.

Hawks said they couldn't shoot the scene in full light because it would have been too intimate to show their faces, so they did it in silhouette against a window for back-lighting. "We just couldn't take a chance."

Hecht's ending was to have Tony walk into the street, through a hail of bullets, up to Guarino—the cop who has been pursuing him—point his gun at his face and fire. His revolver is empty though. Guarino shoots him and Tony falls dead still clicking his empty gun. (Hecht facetiously suggested that Tony collapse onto a pile of horse dung.) Hawks reworked Hecht's overly melodramatic climax so that when Tony exits the building, he is hit by a fusillade and immediately falls dead in the street, the camera panning up from his body to the electric sign in the night sky: THE WORLD IS YOURS. Hawks had Lee Garmes shoot this ending but was unable to get it past the Hays Office. Hawks said he had been allowed to get away with murder the way it was—fifteen of them—but the Hays Office wouldn't pass the final sequence because it was too violent. The film was finished by then and Paul Muni (who played Tony Camonte) was working on another picture, so Hawks had to devise a new ending without him, finally settling on a sequence picturing a man's legs and feet shuffling to the gallows, then a final shot of the dangling feet after he has been hanged.

"Gangsterism must not be mentioned in the cinema . . . *Scarface* will never be released," the Hays Office told Hughes. Unless changes were made. Changes more profound than the relatively simple matter of changing the ending. First of all the Hays Office demanded that the subtitle *Shame of a Nation* be appended, and that a scene be inserted, neither written by Hecht nor shot by Hawks, to lessen the effect of the brutality and near mass murder. A group of citizens complains about the violence resulting from mob rule of their city in a ridiculous sequence totally out of synch with the rest of the picture. A newspaper publisher responds, "Don't blame the police. They can't stop machine guns from being run back and forth across state lines. . . . Make laws and see that they're obeyed, if we have to have martial law to do it. The Governor of New Mexico declared martial law to stop a bull fight. The Governor of Oklahoma to regulate oil production. . . . The army will help, so will the American Legion. They offered their services more than two years ago and nobody called on them."

Allegedly, a number of Hollywood moguls, in an attempt to sabotage Hughes, had pressured the Hays Office to try and stop *Scarface*'s release. But after Hughes complied with the Hays Office's demands, he had to be given a seal of approval to show the film.

That wasn't the end of his troubles, though. Next, he had to submit *Scarface* to each individual state's censor board for approval. In New York, where he wanted to premiere the film in January of 1932, he was turned down. Since the head of the New York Censor Board, Colonel James Wingate, was known to be an ally of Will Hays—together they would toughen up the existing production code—Hughes appealed to the press: "I am convinced that the determined opposition to *Scarface* is actuated by political motives. . . . It has become a serious threat to the freedom of honest expression in America when self-styled guardians of the public welfare, as personified by our film censor boards, lend their influence to the abortive efforts of selfish and vicious interests to suppress a motion picture because it depicts the truth about conditons in the United States which have been front page news since the advent of Prohibition."

Although *Scarface* was being shown in New York in the altered Hays Office version (those New Yorkers who wanted to see the uncut picture had only to cross the state line into New Jersey, where it had met with no opposition from the censor board), Hughes sued the New York Censor Board, as well as all the other state boards that had refused to approve the film. After a lengthy legal battle Hughes won the New York case—and a majority of his suits against other state boards—and the film was shown without cuts, and with the original ending restored. Although *Scarface* was made before *Little Caesar* and *Public Enemy*—the two films for many years heralded as the first real gangster films—it wasn't released until 1932 because of Hughes's legal difficulties. Then, after its initial run, Hughes withdrew it from circulation and up to the time of his death it was not shown legally in the United States.

Finished with *Scarface*, Hecht checked on John Lee Mahin to see how the Goldwyn film, *The Unholy Garden*, was progressing. "You couldn't write for Ben Hecht," Mahin admitted. "I tried. I made a little stab here and there but I didn't know anything about picture form. Ben said, 'Just write the story,' but I didn't know what he wanted." Hecht and MacArthur had already been paid $10,000 for the story, but when Hecht learned that the additional $125,000 Goldwyn had promised them for the script was to come out of the film's profits, he hired two secretaries and dictated it in two days, although he claimed to have written it overnight "in a pet." Leland Hayward delivered the finished script to Goldwyn with a blue bow tied around it, and when Arthur Hornblow, Jr., Goldwyn's right-hand man, read it, he congratulated Hecht for his brilliant work. The script was produced as written and, Hecht noted, "was one of the worst flops ever turned out by a studio."

Back in Nyack, Hecht spent the summer and early fall of 1930 finishing *A Jew in Love* (which he had considered calling "Monkey Heart"), socializing with the Fowlers, and pursuing his new hobby, photography. In the fall, Rose's adaptation of *Uncle Vanya*, staged by Jed Harris, opened on Broadway,[3] and Harris sold the film rights to *The Front Page* to Howard Hughes for $125,000 (Hecht wondered "if we could have gotten $150,000"); Lewis Milestone was hired to direct and Bart Cormack to adapt it for the screen.

His novel completed, Hecht returned to Los Angeles to help MacArthur doctor *The Sin of Madelon Claudet*, which had been previewed and panned by the Hollywood trade papers. After reading the reviews, MacArthur broke down and wept, "Helen has been a star for twenty-five years and I've ruined her in an hour and a half." He and Hecht did what they could, new scenes were added, and the film was finally released in October 1931. It became a box-office hit and won Helen an Oscar for Best Actress, but, ironically, MacArthur didn't receive screen credit.[4]

9

USED BY WORDS

Men are animals used by words.

—JAMES BRANCH CABELL
Beyond Life

A *Jew in Love* was published by Pascal Covici in January of 1931 and either horrified or delighted its readers. Banned in Boston, it nevertheless was reprinted five times in six weeks. Expert at "hooking" his readers—whether the general public with a novel or a studio mogul with a script—Hecht opened the book with a frank discussion of Jewishness:

> The Jews now and then hatch a face which for Jewish-ness surpasses the caricatures of the entire anti-Semitic press. These Jew faces in which race leers and burns like some biologic disease are rather shocking to a mongrelized world. People dislike being reminded of their origins. They shudder a bit mystically at the sight of anyone who looks too much like a fish, a chimpanzee or a Jew. . . . Jo Boshere was not quite so bad as this. The racial decadence which had popped so Hebraic a nosegay out of his mother's womb was of finer stuff than that glandular degeneration which produces the Jew with the sausage face; the bulbous, diabetic half-monsters who look as if they had been fished out of the water a month too late.

A *Jew in Love* grew out of an unfinished and unpublished novel called *Deliaga* that Hecht had been working on for years, in which Jo Boshere was not the protagonist. "But the colorful Jo refused to remain a minor character," Donald Friede remembered, "and it soon became obvious to Hecht that the whole book was slowly becoming dominated by him. So he pulled him out of the book entirely and wrote a long story about him, under the title of 'A Jew in Love.' This was to be the lead story in a collection of Hecht's short stories that Covici-Friede planned to publish. But when Covici read the manuscript he got terribly excited about the title story and suggested to Hecht that he expand it into a novel." Hecht was game.

In 1925 Hecht had written a play about Horace Liveright, *The Scoundrel*, then two years later he began *Deliaga*, using Liveright as the model for Jo Boshere. Hecht didn't find Liveright rich or complex enough to sustain a long novel, however, so he began grafting Jed Harris's personality onto that of Liveright, till in the end the composite character was more Harris than Horace Liveright. The melding of their personalities was easily accomplished since the two men were strikingly similar in many respects. They were both Jews who had become successes in the arts but not as artists. As young men they had had vast ambition and energy but no specific end to turn it to until they happened on their ultimate professions: producing and selling the work of artists, Liveright through publishing and Harris through play producing. Boshere, the protagonist of *A Jew in Love*, a publisher who had made a fortune in the stock market (Liveright had lost one), was a portrait of Harris only slightly exaggerated.

> Boshere . . . had a face stamped with the hieroglyphic curl of the Hebrew alphabet. For his face, however, he had invented such un-Jewish expressions, surrounded it with such delicate mannerisms (although he never quite outgrew the semi-onanistic activities of his hands) that his personality had lost its Semitic flavor. He had a way of standing, one hand spread genteely [*sic*] over his epigastrium, his skimpy shoulders hunched forward, his slightly enlarged eyelids drooped in an artificial and brooding smile, his red-lipped mouth widening in an actorish grimace of meditation; a way of posturing, purring and smiling in the teeth, as it were, of his Jewishness, that gave him the look of a Prince Charming in the midst of a pogrom.

Boshere was married but had a mistress named Alice Sterns. (Liveright had an editorial assistant named Edith Stern; Arthur Stearns was a character in *Erik Dorn*, and several years later Hecht would call himself Alexander Sterns in a play.) Throughout the novel, Boshere alternates between Alice and a more recent acquisition, Tillie Marmon. The usual turgid description, character analysis, and rambling philosophy were somewhat redeemed by Hecht's phrasing. Tillie Marmon is a "lackadaisical Broadway nymph" for whom "sex is little more than routine and a little less than a novelty." Her seduction: "Like a child finally flattered into running an errand, Tillie accompanied him into the bedroom." Boshere wants to know about her previous lovers, "the geography of her past," and discovers she loves another man who "walks like a shadow through her organs." Boshere approaches her "as if he were an empty nest pursuing a dove," and talks to her "as if his words were walking on eggs."

Harris had tried to cheat Hecht and MacArthur out of their full share of the profits from *The Front Page*, so Hecht homed in on Harris's shady financial manipulations.

> Boshere had a trick, even in business relationships, of personalizing a transaction to such an extent that the introduction of money-talk sounded like an unfriendly attack on him. Throughout most of his financial dealings he gave the impression of living in a world of spirit, of having whisked his fellow transactor to some higher plane, where faith and beauty of soul were a substitute for contracts.
>
> Occasionally, among the authors with whom he did business he ran foul of a tartar, a mercenary clod who refused to soar alongside him out of the business department. Boshere, confronted with such coarseness, passed from disillusion to contempt and from contempt into a fever of bargaining which would have shamed a push cart vendor. He drew up contracts full of traps and jokers, delayed payments, juggled sales figures and—the deal closed, the check changed hands—laughed pityingly at his author. He had, said Boshere, saved a great deal of money by that gentleman's disgusting venality. For had that gentleman trusted him, he, Boshere, would have done as he usually did, allowed him to walk off with his eye teeth.

Although he alienated Harris by this characterization, Hecht always claimed his reason for writing the book—other than the royalty checks— was the same as it had been with *Count Bruga*: he liked and respected his subject but enjoyed writing a book about him—altering fact to make the portrait more amusing—for his friends' and his own amusement, since the reading public at large he considered "simpletons." In his Preface to *Broken Necks* he had written, "I am certain I know the names and addresses of nearly three-fourths of the intelligent men and women who read my books. I would say they number in all about fifty. This I consider an excellent public."

But Hecht did paint a miniature in *A Jew in Love* not redeemed by amusement. It was of George Jessel, called Gabe Solomon:

. . . a semitic pagan; vulgar, lecherous, sentimental. . . .
He was a man with a compact body, graceful as a pugilist,
with coarse features, a spatulate Jewish nose, large red lips,
cold eyes, black and glittering with ennui. His black naturally kinky hair was greased and plastered into little waves
that gave it the semblance of a too carefully manicured
toupé [sic]. Lean, overgroomed, reeking with expensive per-
fumes, slobbering when he laughed and showing a set of
heavy white teeth, Solomon was of the tribe of Jews who
dominate the night life of Broadway, who stamp their
legendary sophistication as a trademark on American entertainment. . . .

Gabe Solomon was more than a lay figure in this
Parnassian gutter. He was one of its most accomplished
annotators. He was full of encyclopedic information concerning the depravities, sexual habits and two-timings of its
denizens. His talk of women would have abashed a gyne-
cologist. . . . Solomon's social small talk was like a breath
from a vaginal sewer. He boasted of having slept with three
hundred women, all of them beauties, all prominent at one
time or another in the Arts, if you included nymphomania
and diamond filching, and all of them bitches. But his
information extended beyond these personal contacts. He
told tales of perversion involving famous names in a reckless
manner . . . he prattled of orgies as if they were part of
some daily routine; blasted reputations, hung filthy and
withering epithets on unsuspected celebrities and filled his
talk with a contempt for women and a disbelief in their
honor, truthfulness and chastity that would have delighted
a Saint Paul. . . . He embraced all women who came near
him, jiggling their breasts in lieu of a handshake, standing
behind them, one hand pressed into their stomachs, and
whispering obscene remarks into their ears in a tender,
mocking voice.

"When Ben wrote the story of *A Jew in Love*," Harry Hansen opined,
"I think he made a very serious attempt to write in the upper echelon, like
Henry James, but Ben was too close to events. He was much too close to
life as it is lived to be reflective on all that. Ben was the life of the party,
everybody wanted to talk with Ben, wanted him around. There was a
running comment that Ben had no dull moments. He was greatly
endowed and, of course, we rather looked to him to become a major
author."

Covici was convinced *A Jew in Love* was a great book. "He assured us in the office it was by far the best thing Hecht had ever written," Donald Friede recalled in his memoirs, *The Mechanical Angel.*

> We would see just how great it was when we read the completed manuscript. It would not be fair to it, he said in answer to our requests that we be permitted to see some part of it, to read the book until it was finished. He even refused to tell us what it was all about. The result was that when the manuscript finally reached us we were panting with excitement. We all cleared our desks of any work that happened to be facing us, and soon four of us were reading the book, passing pages of manuscript down the line as each finished reading them. And suddenly, at about page one hundred, we all stopped as if on a signal. We looked at one another and we could see that we were in agreement. We did not like the book. And we were certain that the more we read of it the less we would like it. And yet it was our lead book for the spring and a certain big seller. . . . There were still four months before we would have to go out and sell it. We would spend that period of time in a Coué-like trance, telling ourselves and each other what a great book it was, how infinitely superior to anything Hecht had ever written, what a certain best seller it was bound to be, how lucky we were to be publishing it. We did a pretty good job of persuading ourselves. Our advance sale was the biggest we ever had on any novel, and we ended up by selling close to fifty thousand copies of the book, a phenomenal sale in those days.

Six months after *A Jew in Love* was issued, a transparent roman à clef titled *Duke Herring* was published by Maxwell Bodenheim, who had chosen to see himself caricatured once again by Hecht. Angry, he had decided to exploit Hecht as he felt Hecht had exploited him with *Count Bruga.* Where for the most part *Count Bruga* had been gentle satire, *Duke Herring* was embittered invective. Like Hecht's book, there was little plot, and what there was—Hecht's life from 1922 through 1924, the *Chicago Literary Times* period when Bodenheim had lived with the Hechts—served only as a backdrop against which Bodenheim could comment on, parody, and attack Hecht's personality and life-style.

His face . . . the long, pointed nose, wide lips, hem-stitch mustache, and arched eyebrows, converged to the epitome of slyness. The head was too huge in its proportion to the remainder of the figure—a head already one-third bald and sheering into a rag of dark brown hair. Dominating the narrow shoulders and bottom-heavy body, it reminded the beholder of a street-urchin and Faust incongruously welded by a faint touch of rabbinical meditation. The vestige of a Jew, denying its own existence, smoldering a bit under the juvenility and malice of a devilish Boccaccio hero. . . .

Mr. Arturo Herring looked like a Gentile when he remained silent, but the moment he opened his mouth he became a Semite shrouded but incarnate. . . .

Although the Duke's ambition was to be sardonic and malicious at the expense of other men, he had cataracts in both eyes whenever he looked at himself. In his effort to disrobe other men, he was forced to imagine himself immune to their own sores, frustrations, and hysterias. Otherwise, he would have discovered that he was also exposing and dissecting parts of himself, and the discovery would have robbed him of the petty transports and superiorities of his labors. Again, the frantic attempt to make laughing-stocks out of other men and vindicate his grudges against them made it impossible for him to laugh at himself. With all humility artificially driven out of his nature, he visualized himself as the patronizing untouched bystander to other people's mishaps, blunders, frenzies, and sprawlings. The missiles and trippings, which he himself suffered, were never recognized. The custard pie changed to rose pulp on his cheek. . . .

He wanted to be an affluent, luxurious, commercial panderer tossing off flashy bilge with his tongue in his cheek, and also an unruly, brilliant, slashing intellect in more serious talk and creations . . . he wanted to be supreme in both camps, commercial and artistic, without pledging allegiance to either one . . . the deadlock between Babbitt and the artist. . . .

His favorite boast was that he intended to accumulate a million dollars in the following year, and though this goal had eluded him so far, he did amass thousands of dollars annually through the sale of meretricious short stories, shallowly clever plays with short runs, and epileptic novels, whose malicious brilliance always held one eye cocked toward the adding machine in the publisher's office.

"It was lousy and not nearly as successful as mine," was how Hecht chose to remember *Duke Herring* in the early sixties. "I daresay it wasn't read by more than eighteen people. But Bodie was satisfied; somehow he'd thought he'd won a victory. He always thought he'd won. If you kicked him downstairs, he'd stand at the bottom and look at you triumphantly as though he'd beaten you."

Bodenheim had reached the pinnacle of his career in the late twenties and was slipping slowly down the other side. He'd published two best-selling novels in 1928, *Georgie May* and the book pulled from the shelves in 1925 by John Sumner, *Replenishing Jessica*: it wasn't until 1928 that the court case was finally held and the book adjudged nonpornographic. The attendant publicity put both novels on the best-seller list, prompting young girls to seek out the libidinous Greenwich Village poet. Three short-lived affairs resulting in two suicides and one near miss brought Bodenheim even more publicity and sales.

Flush with money for the first and only time in his life, Bodenheim spent lavishly. In 1930 he visited Paris, where, dressed in a Bruga-esque tailcoat, he hobnobbed with Ezra Pound, Ford Madox Ford, and Kiki of Montparnasse. In 1931, *Duke Herring* and *Naked on Roller Skates* were published, then in 1932 he went to Hollywood to try to sell his novels to the movies. Hecht, unamused by *Duke Herring*, gave him no help, and Bodenheim met only with failure on his own. Several more novels and volumes of poetry followed. In 1935 he worked for the Federal Writers' Project assembling information on polar expeditions, but was dismissed when it was discovered he'd lied when he'd sworn that he had never been a member of the Communist Party. The FBI promised him his job back if he would turn informer on other party members. Bodenheim vehemently refused the offer, referring to the government agents, in a letter to Hecht, as "white-washed rodents in the service of Tweedledum Roosevelt." Renouncing the novel, he returned to the "purity of writing poetry," but began drinking more and writing less. He saw an edition of his collected poems published, but would be able to complete only one more book during the remainder of his life. His writing had gone out of fashion, which he would never recover from.

In 1931, Dorothy Parker, reviewing Dashiell Hammett's *The Glass Key*, put down Hecht's novels as "smiling and swaggering savageries"; a pamphlet entitled *The Pseudo-Realists: A Critical and Comparative Analysis of Ben Hecht and William Faulkner* was issued. Hecht's story "The Ax" was included in *The Best Mystery Stories of the Year*, and *The Champion from Far Away*, a Covici-Friede collection of Hecht's short stories, was published. (Earlier in the year, Covici had announced a collection of Hecht's *Chicago Literary Times* pieces, *Journalese*, to be illustrated by Peter Arno, but that volume never appeared.[1])

Also, that fall, Hecht signed a six-story contract with *Liberty*. "In the Midst of Death" and "The Mystery of the Man with an Accordion" were immediately accepted for two thousand dollars each, then a few months later two more pieces were taken—"The Boy Pirate," the Howard Hughes story that was also a lampoon of Sam Goldwyn (called "Leo Spangleman" here), and "The Mystery of the Fabulous Laundryman," a tale of Czar Nicholas of Russia, allegedly executed but who (in Hecht's version) escaped to the United States, where he lived for eighteen years in Harlem under a Jewish alias, based on the real-life story of Isidore Fink. When *Liberty* informed Hecht that his fifth story, "Actor's Blood," would have to be cut by two thousand words, Hecht had Leland Hayward submit it to the *Saturday Evening Post*, where on January 6th, 1932, it was accepted intact.

Fulton Oursler, *Liberty* managing editor, wrote Hecht on the eighteenth complaining that "Actor's Blood" had been sold to the *Post* without some compromise being reached with *Liberty*. Oursler also told Hecht that his earlier submission, "The Mystery of the Man with the Accordion," was being rejected since it wasn't an original. Six months earlier, a tale with the same plot, "The Man with the Concertina," had been submitted by the American Play Company, written by one Charles Samuels. (Not long after the Florida real-estate crash, Samuels—the young reporter who had worked for Hecht on the *Key Largo Breeze*—had moved to New York to try his hand at writing fiction. He reestablished contact with Hecht, who sent him to Leland Hayward's agency, which placed several short stories for Samuels, and a novel, *The Frantic Young Man*. After "The Man with the Concertina" had been rejected by *Liberty*, Hecht, with Samuels's permission, had rewritten it and submitted it under his own name.) A few weeks after receiving Oursler's letter, Hecht turned over a final story to him, which was accepted, fulfilling Hecht's contract for a minimum of four acceptances, ending his association with *Liberty*.

To fulfill his part of the deal with Howard Hughes, Hecht had created a writing factory. Not a new idea—Dumas *père* had done it, and Dumas was a favorite of Hecht's—but one that had yet to be realized in Hollywood outside a studio. Unlike Dumas, Hecht didn't take credit for other men's work; they simply worked for him rather than for a studio, although Hecht would supply story ideas and polish scripts. Of the Chicago friends Hecht had used as writers for the Caddo films, Bart Cormack was still working for him doing screenplays, dialogue, and adaptations for Paramount productions. In 1928, Hecht had also recruited Johnny Weaver, who worked for him for three years and turned out six films, quitting in 1930 to go back East, where he wrote a novel about Hollywood, *Joy Girl*; he later became drama reviewer for *Esquire* magazine. In 1928 and 1929, Gene Markey had labored in the Hecht factory, writing two films for Paramount, then got himself hired directly by the studio. Wallace Smith, who had worked on one Caddo film for Hecht, was another matter. An accomplished short-story writer and novelist (five books in print by 1930), he felt he was Hecht's equal and couldn't accept a role as a subordinate, especially since he'd had two of his stories turned into movies before Hecht's *Underworld* even went before the cameras (one, *Upstream*, was directed by John Ford). He continued writing for publication and made a career as a scenario writer on his own.

When Hecht began looking around for a new collaborator— MacArthur no longer reliable—he thought of Charlie Lederer, whom he had met on one of his first trips to Los Angeles. At that time, Hecht had written to Rose, "I have met a new friend. He has pointed teeth, is nineteen years old [he was actually several years older], completely bald and stands on his head a great deal. I hope to bring him back to civilization with me." In a letter to Gene Fowler, Hecht called Lederer "a sort of poisonous bud—very tender soul—a Peter Pan weaned on distilled cunt and with a moonbeam for a cock." With Lederer in tow, Hecht had returned to New York where Charlie captivated the New York literati just as the other Charlie (MacArthur) had a few years earlier. His wit and dislike of sham, hypocrisy, and work delighted Woollcott, Benchley, Alice Duer Miller, Howard Dietz, and MacArthur himself. Lederer was an incessant practical joker, too, which endeared him to Hecht. (Several years later, Lederer and Hecht returned an inebriated MacArthur to his house in Nyack, placed him unconscious but fully clothed in a tubful of water, then dumped in several pounds of gelatin. When MacArthur awoke, unable to move, he noticed the spoon and attached note: "Eat your way out.")

Hollywood was home to Lederer, where for most people it was a place they moved to in order to work for the movies. Virtually none of the film community had grown up in Los Angeles, but Lederer had been brought there when he was eleven by Marion Davies, his mother's sister and the mistress of William Randolph Hearst. Lederer thus knew the movie colony inside out as seen from the top and wasn't impressed—another plus in Hecht's eyes. Lederer, who considered working for a living a waste of time, had once been berated for his lack of ambition—during lunch in a fashionable restaurant—by his current lady friend, musical-comedy star Marilyn Miller. Lederer had listened attentively, but when she finished her scolding he had stood up and handed her his trousers, remarking, "Here, you wear these," then strode out of the restaurant.

When Hecht asked him if he wanted to try his hand at scriptwriting, Lederer agreed, thinking it might be fun. After Hecht had finished the *Scarface* script, Lederer helped John Lee Mahin with on-the-set rewrites, and Hawks recruited him to play the bit role of a reporter—MacArthur of the *Tribune*. Next, Hecht teamed him with Bart Cormack, who was adapting *The Front Page*. Then, in mid-1931, Hecht put him to work on *Cock of the Air*, the last Caddo film he had to provide a writer for.

Gene Fowler, who had just completed his first novel, was of a mind to tackle something new as well. On July 4th, at a party at Billy Rose and Fanny Brice's Fire Island home, Hecht suggested he write for the movies, telling Fowler he would see what he could do for him since he was leaving shortly for Los Angeles. Since Hecht had last been on the Coast, David Selznick had left MGM, as he had told Hecht he planned to do when he'd visited Nyack the year before. He had tried to set himself up as an independent producer but had been thwarted by his father-in-law, Louis B. Mayer. Then, when David Sarnoff's Radio Corporation of America took control of RKO and needed an experienced Hollywood film man to run the studio, Selznick was offered the job. Needing competent scenario writers, Selznick turned to Hecht for help. Hecht promptly got Fowler a job writing *State's Attorney* for John Barrymore. When Fowler finished the script, he and Hecht spent two weeks rewriting the scenario of Fannie Hurst's best-seller *Back Street* for Universal. Then Fowler, Hecht, and Rowland Brown—who had also worked on *State's Attorney*—polished the dialogue for *What Price Hollywood?*

Bart Cormack was switched from Paramount, where he had been doing mediocre genre pictures (*The Spoilers, Woman Trap* for William Wellman, adaptations of S. S. Van Dine novels, et cetera) and put to work for RKO, where he continued in the same vein, the only exception being *The Half-Naked Truth*, an early Gregory La Cava film. Hecht also suggested to Selznick that he hire Herman Mankiewicz to rewrite a picture Wallace Smith had scripted, *The Lost Squadron*, that was ready to be released but which Selznick thought could be improved. (Rewritten by Mankiewicz it became a financial success.)

Since *Scarface*, original factory worker John Lee Mahin had been having a hard time scaring up another assignment. Hecht had promised to find him work once *Scarface* was completed, so he turned to Mac-Arthur, who had just scripted *The New Adventures of Get-Rich-Quick Wallingford* for Jimmy Durante and MGM. Still close friends with Irving Thalberg, MacArthur wangled Mahin a job on a Jean Harlow picture, *Beast of the City*. The original story for the Harlow film had been written by W. R. Burnett, but Paul Bern, the picture's producer and Miss Harlow's financé, wasn't satisfied with it, so he called in Hecht and together they changed and elaborated the Burnett plot. (Hecht be-musedly named the picture's heavy Belmonte, playing on Camonte, Scarface's patronymic.) With the new outline, Bern turned the job of producing a shooting script over to Mahin, who, after working with Howard Hawks, had got "the hang of picture form" and was able to flesh out the Hecht/Bern outline and earn his second screen credit.

That fall Hecht also began making notes for *The Devil's Dilemma*, a morality play structured like *Christmas Eve*, but in verse. As for plot, Hecht intended a *Cutie*-like tale in three cantos, the first to be "an ode to female lust," the second the story of the heroine's affair with and marriage to a doctor; in the third she was to "go to Hollywood—have her meet Hollywood producer ['director' crossed out] who wants to put her in pictures." Covici's partner Donald Friede had one copy of a book bound, *The Devil's Dilemma* printed on its spine, the pages blank. Hecht jotted in twenty-five pages of notes before giving it up, completing only the introductory verses to "The Reader."

In February of the following year, 1932, the first issue of *Contact* magazine—which a few years later would publish selections from Natha-nael West's *The Day of the Locust*—ran a verse of Hecht's titled "Ballad of the Talkies." Hecht had penned "The Reporter's Litany" in the teens to complain about city editors, and both Hecht and Gene Fowler had written obscene poems denigrating Hollywood that had circulated through the studios, but Hecht wanted a public shot at the film capital, so when *Contact* asked for a contribution he composed his "Ballad."

> *Come flicker forth you squawking hams,*
> *You pasteboard hearts and candied woes*
> *You little gibbering diagrams*
> *Of silly plot and infant prose . . .*

Your gags and wows and slapstick shams,
And all your pansy Romeos
And all your billboard oriflammes
And all you Zuckors, Myers and Lowes . . .

Late weaned on penny arcade shams,
Oh idiot child tricked out with Bows
Whose adenoidal yapping crams
These Paramountish pattios—
The ash can waits your mechanams
Art never yet turned up its toes—
There shivering on his outcast gams
Our gallant Thespis thumbs his nose.

After MacArthur had finished the Durante picture, Thalberg assigned him the task of scripting *Rasputin and the Empress* for the three Barrymores. Hecht helped Charlie block out the action, then teamed up with director Harry d'Abbadie D'Arrast to write a picture for Al Jolson. (Herman Mankiewicz had worked, with and without credit, on many of D'Arrast's films, one of which—*Laughter*—got D'Arrast, ironically, a nomination for Best Original Story in 1931.) Warner Bros. had had Jolson under contract since 1927 when they had produced *The Jazz Singer*, the first widely distributed talking picture. They had paid Jolson an enormous sum to sign with them, so to recoup part of their investment they loaned him out to United Artists. Hecht and D'Arrast devised a story about a vagabond, living in Central Park, who wasn't unemployed because of the Depression but because he refused to go to work, finding life joyous and satisfying as a bum. (Hecht's inspiration derived from Floyd Dell's short story "Hallelujah, I'm a Bum!" published in 1926, and from his association with Charlie Lederer.) In an era when intellectuals and writers were becoming increasingly social conscious and even pro-communist—a position Hecht was never to take—*Hallelujah, I'm a Bum* stood out as a film that was both anti-establishment and apolitical.

With a bulging bankroll, Hecht returned to New York while D'Arrast began preparations for *Hallelujah*. After the first day's shooting D'Arrast told Joe Schenck, who was producing, that he couldn't work with Jolson and wanted him replaced. D'Arrast was replaced instead, by Lewis Milestone.

Hecht and D'Arrast were to collaborate once more, on a script of Rostand's *Cyrano* for Hungarian producer-director Alexander Korda, who intended to produce it in England, where he was then working. Korda had made a movie out of *The Private Life of Helen of Troy*, a pseudohistorical comic novel popular in the twenties. He was shooting *The Private Life of Henry VIII* at the moment, and would go on to make a career as a producer of historical films, although he was never to film *Cyrano*. By the time he was ready to mount the lavish production—almost ten years later—Hecht was writing propaganda for the Irgun, one of the revolutionary groups attempting to force the British out of Palestine in order to form a Jewish state. Afraid of strikes during filming or boycotts afterwards because he was using a Hecht script, Korda cancelled the project and sold the rights to the Rostand play to Stanley Kramer, who hired Carl Foreman to adapt it.

Lewis Milestone had been nominated by the Academy for Best Director and Adolphe Menjou for Best Actor (in *The Front Page*)—neither would win—and *Scarface* had opened at the New York Rivoli by the time Hecht returned east. *Scarface*, though winning critical acclaim, was regarded as almost too much to bear by many critics. *Film Daily* reported that it would "send the average movie patron home with a sick feeling in his stomach" because of its unprecedented violence. Many communities banned the picture, cutting into the grosses, but as *Variety* assessed it, "To keep people away from the theatres it plays will be about the same as keeping 'em out of the speakeasies."

In New York's most renowned speak, Jack and Charlie's (later known as "21"), Hecht and Gene Fowler decided to write a play, Hecht remarking, "We discussed a plot which I made up on the spur of the moment [actually lifted from Ferenc Molnár's *Liliom*]. Strikes me, on the whole, Fowler would make a much better collaborator than MacArthur."

Hecht had become resentful of Charlie's growing friendship with, and seeming preference for, Irving Thalberg.[2] He was also sore about Thalberg's interference earlier when he had trained west to help Charlie salvage *The Sin of Madelon Claudet* for Helen. During their rewrites, Thalberg, who had been out of town, returned and assured MacArthur the picture could be saved but only if he got rid of Hecht. Accepting Thalberg's advice, MacArthur told Hecht he wanted to return to New York to finish *Twentieth Century*. They decided to slip out of town secretly, but when MacArthur met Hecht at the Pasadena train station he pretended to be drunk. Dr. Sam Hirshfeld, who accompanied Charlie, convinced Hecht that MacArthur was ill and should stay in Los Angeles. Hecht wasn't to learn of Thalberg's machinations till he was back in New York. MacArthur, however, had his own reasons for wanting Hecht out of town. When Hecht had arrived at the Youngworth Ranch to work on *Madelon Claudet*, he wasn't alone. Because he was with another woman, Helen Hayes packed a bag and moved into the Santa Barbara Biltmore, refusing to return to the ranch as long as Hecht's companion remained.

Fowler moved to Nyack on June 9th and remained through the middle of July, by which time he and Hecht had completed a first draft of *The Great Magoo—A love-sick Charade in three Acts and something like eight Scenes, recounting the Didoes of two young and amorous Souls, who nigh perished when they weren't in the Hay together.* Nicky, the play's male principal, is a sideshow barker for a Coney Island girlie show and a songwriter on the side, who has written what he believes to be a great love song, "It's Only a Paper Moon." (In a footnote in the published play, Hecht credited Billy Rose as lyricist; Ian McLellan Hunter, however— who was present during the play's production—claims Hecht himself wrote the words to the song.) Julie, the female lead, is "the Isolde of the back stages, the Nicolette, the Héloïse. She is the Great Magoo. A bit loose in her morals, a bit selfish, ambitious, susceptible rather than intellectual, with a rather sad knowledge of men and their bedrooms, our *Julie,* though she play a lot of easy tunes with her heart, can make cymbal music, can moan with the Valkyries, can, in short, die for love." Nicky and Julie are in love, but since Nicky is forever gambling away his money, Julie leaves him. She wants to be a singer so, to further her career, she becomes the mistress of an orchestra leader. When a rich "angel" offers to back a Broadway show for her, she drops the band leader and marries her rich suitor. When he finds out about her past, he closes the show and she goes off to live with still another man. In the interim, Nicky has become part-owner of a traveling show and comes looking for Julie, whom he finds beaten up and abandoned in a cheap rooming house. He persuades her to marry him and they exit to join his troupe.

Billy Rose, a frequent visitor to Nyack, wanted to produce the play and Hecht wanted to direct, but before he and Fowler could rewrite and polish the script, Hecht was again caught up in the imbroglio that *Twentieth Century* had turned into. In December of 1931, Hecht and MacArthur had been sued by Jed Harris for breach of contract since they hadn't finished their rewrite of "The Napoleon of Broadway" (the previous year they had agreed to deliver the third act to Harris no later than August 15th). Harris, impressed with the first two acts, had lined up a tentative cast and had even approached legendary theatrical producer Morris Gest for the role of Oscar Jaffe. The two options Harris had taken on the Milholland play then ran out, along with his patience. Harris had even trailed Hecht cross-country to the Youngsworth Ranch to squeeze the third act out of him and Charlie but, according to Sam Marx, he was refused entrance and "lurked outside the hacienda night and day, hammering on the doors, screaming epithets and helping disrupt the work that was only rarely in progress." Washing his hands of the project, Harris sued Hecht and MacArthur for the recovery of the five thousand dollars he had advanced them.

When Harris gave up on the play, other producers tried to step in, but there was a serious legal stumbling block; the contract between Harris and Milholland stipulated that the rewrite be done by Hecht and MacArthur, thus barring anyone else from providing a third act. At this point, writer-director-producer George Abbott and his partner, Philip Dunning, extracted a short-term option from Milholland, but they couldn't get Hecht and MacArthur together to produce a third act before their option ran out. At this juncture, Billy Rose decided that a professional director was needed for *The Great Magoo*, since Hecht had yet to direct a Broadway play, and the director Rose wanted was George Abbott. Abbott agreed to take on the play providing Hecht came up with a last act for *Twentieth Century*. Putting *The Great Magoo* aside for the moment, Hecht secluded himself at Nyack for ten days in August and turned out the long-awaited act by himself, MacArthur still in Hollywood. Abbott and Dunning then drew up still another but final contract with Milholland, who was to receive one-third of all royalties, Hecht and MacArthur the other two-thirds, plus twenty percent of all profits. Abbott and Dunning also repaid Harris his five thousand dollars.

In October, at David Selznick's request, Hecht and Charlie Lederer adapted Marcel Pagnol's *Topaze* for John Barrymore; then on the twenty-sixth *The Great Magoo* went into rehearsal with unknown principals, although Billy Rose had tried to sign up Lee Tracy and Claudette Colbert. Rehearsals for *Twentieth Century* followed on its heels. *Topaze* completed, Hecht and Fowler knocked out *Catastrophe* for Paramount, at the same time selling them the screen rights to *The Great Magoo*. On December 2nd, 1932, *The Great Magoo* premiered at the Selwyn Theatre to a star-studded audience that included Noël Coward, Eddie Cantor, Groucho Marx, Fannie Hurst, Sophie Tucker, Fanny Brice, Leland Hayward, Martin Beck, Horace Liveright, and Beatrice Kaufman. The audience loved the show but the next day's reviews spelled disaster. Brooks Atkinson in the *Times* called the play "stale and malodorous" and the *American* said it was a "sleazy vaudeville." Robert Garland in the *World-Telegram* wrote that "when all has been said and done, you're reminded of a pair of precocious boys showing off before company, plotting and planning just how far they'll be allowed to go." Burns Mantle in the *Daily News* said the play's language should be cleaned up but that "the disappointment is likely to come after that, when the boys find that without its physiological and biological bases, its tough talk and its gutter talk, there will be little left of the play."

Most of the critics attacked it for its "gutter talk" or, as Garland phrased it, "its pungent, if not precisely Presbyterian lines." Although frank in its references to biological functions, the play was hardly obscene. A typical example of the gutter talk: three men are conversing, one a professional flagpole sitter—

> SAM: Finally going up, eh? Say, it's always been on my mind—what kind of plumbing do they provide?
>
> HANRATTY: That's a trade secret.
>
> BILL: Thank God my folks gave me an education. I could never go that long on a flagpole. I'm too hot blooded. Does the doctor give you anything?
>
> SAM: I suppose love finds a way.

Later, a chorus girl remarks, "That's burlesque—they always want you to sign on the dotted couch . . . it's unbelievable what men have done to me. I wish I could write." The play ends with Nicky and Julie leaving her squalid room, Julie exclaiming, "Oh, darling, it's like a fairy tale," since she has just been rescued by Nicky from a sordid fate. Tante, an old woman from Nicky's show, comes running after them holding up a douche bag, calling "Hey Cinderella. You forgot your pumpkin!"

The Great Magoo closed aften eleven days despite positive audience reaction, two revolving stages, five pianos, and a stuffed whale (part of the Coney Island Midway), grossing a total of $2,500.[3] On December 18th, the *Herald Tribune* printed a letter Hecht wrote Percy Hammond, who liked the show but didn't give it a rave.

> Sir: Where were you during the pogrom "The Great Magoo" unloosed? Sulking around the leaves of your dictionary, egad, and mumbling in your beard about literature!

I missed you at the tar-pots, and later when the posse turned the corner with the hounds in full cry I missed you. And so did my breathless and beleaguered pal, Mons. Gene Fowler, who was wading up a creek trying to confuse the pursuit.

When we finally dived into a corn-crib, outwitting the vigilantes, one of whom displayed a noose, we peered through the slats at the night full of torches and whispered to each other, "Where in God's name is Sheriff Hammond?"

I am writing this from the corn-crib to inquire after your health and to ask you to find out for us, if you will, what has become of Billy Rose, our producer, whom we last saw drop into a pit silo an inch ahead of Cotton Mather, brandishing a pitchfork. Herr Rose is a dapper fellow, with flashing Broadway eyes and a penthouse pallor, in case you should see him.

Also, if your absence from the posse the other night was not due to some oversight or previous engagement; I mean if you are a really sincere advocate of letters, could you smuggle us some chalk so we can finish our next opera? Inflamed by the suggestion of your baying colleagues, we are writing it on a barn door and out-of-the-way fences by the light of a leering moon.

Fowler wanted to lie in a coffin at Campbell's Funeral Parlor after inviting the critics to be pallbearers. Since the play had been partially backed by New York mobsters—who would also back Billy Rose's Casino de Paree—Rose had to dissuade them from bumping off the three critics who did hatchet jobs on the play.

While *The Great Magoo* was dying on the boards, Philip Dunning restructured the third act for *Twentieth Century*, tightening Hecht's plot to further accentuate his rapid-fire dialogue. On December 22nd, MacArthur appeared at the Broadhurst Theatre demanding to know "what the hell was going on." Hecht pointed to the stage, where the third act was being rehearsed and replied, "See what Hecht has done, unaided." Seven days later, *Twentieth Century* opened—starring Eugenie Leontovich, Moffat Johnson, and William Frawley—but to a different set of reviews than had greeted *The Great Magoo*. Burns Mantle called it "the most striking production of the year," Gilbert Gabriel said it was "a monumental Bronx salute to the Titans of Times Square," and Robert Garland dubbed it "a *Grand Hotel* on wheels." Hecht's anger with the critics quieted in the face of his second Broadway hit, but he never gave up thinking *The Great Magoo* would have been a hit too if not for the same critics.

David Selznick resigned from RKO in December of 1932 because of eastern interference in his production plans, even though he had built RKO into a successful studio. Irving Thalberg, production head of MGM, had suffered a heart attack that December and by February was in Europe recuperating. Louis B. Mayer, impressed with how Selznick had turned RKO around, began to warm to him, prompting the famous quip that "the son-in-law also rises." A good part of Mayer's *volte face* was a result of Thalberg's growing influence and increasing demands. To keep power at MGM firmly in his own hands, Mayer hired Selznick to head a production unit of his own, giving him his pick of stars, directors, and stories—plus a salary of four thousand dollars a week.

One of the first things Selznick did was to get Hecht to return to the Coast to help him out. Thalberg had had a film made from a story written by Salka Viertel and Margaret Levino about a seventeenth-century queen of Sweden; Selznick wanted it rewritten and reshot. Hecht's first assignment was to do a complete rewrite of *Queen Christina* for Greta Garbo. (Fowler collaborated with him, and Walter Wanger—to whom Hecht had dedicated *A Jew in Love*—was brought in to produce.) Next, Hecht was teamed with playwright-turned-director Edgar Selwyn to write a Lee Tracy comedy, *Turn Back the Clock*. On the heels of that, Hecht dashed off a story outline that Leland Hayward sold to Warner Bros., a murder story centering around the familiar Hechtian trio—a man, his wife, and mistress. Facetiously titled *Upperworld*, it was directed by Roy Del Ruth later in the year. With Selznick at MGM, Rose Hecht was hired to adapt Antoine de Saint-Exupéry's *Night Flight* for Helen Hayes, and Hecht switched both Bart Cormack and Johnny Weaver from Paramount to Selznick's MGM unit.

Then Hecht undertook to adapt Noël Coward's play *Design for Living* for Ernst Lubitsch, one of Hollywood's most successful directors. A good deal of the dialogue in the play was unusable because the Hays Office—the motion picture industry's self-imposed moral guardian—wouldn't pass it. Hecht decided to use only one line from the play ("For the good of our immortal souls") to josh Lubitsch, who had made *Lady Windermere's Fan* without including a single Oscar Wilde line. For *Design for Living*, Hecht excerpted dialogue from two other Coward plays, *The Vortex* and *Hay Fever*, and composed the rest himself. "In writing with Mister Lubitsch on *Design for Living*," Hecht recalled,

> I was confused by what seemed to be at first glance a sort of manic-depressive psychosis on its upswing. Mister Lubitsch, when he creates those delicate touches for which he is notorious, has a way of flinging himself around the room like an old-fashioned fancy roller skater. He pirouettes, leaps, claps his ankles together in mid air, screams at the top of his voice, and bursts into tears if contradicted. If Mister Lubitsch doesn't like something you suggest in the way of a line (or half a line) or a piece of business, he falls ill, takes to his bed. His elfin face fills with reproach and he lies tossing for sometimes as long as several hours, moaning, "Dull, dull, oh so dull." On such occasions he can be coaxed out of bed by questions about his early life as an actor. There were three particular reminiscences which he loved to tell, and once I got him started on any one of them, he was on the road to recovery (his, not mine). When Mister Lubitsch composes scenes he always acts them out as if they were written for a calliope. He takes all the parts regardless of the sex of the characters. Whenever I tried to act a scene out, he would sink into a chair, wrinkle his upper lip and remain sneering even after I had finished. If you sneer back at Mister Lubitsch for anything he does, he takes to his bed again and is ill for a day. He is very sensitive.

On his return to New York, the Lubitsch picture completed, Hecht became romantically involved with another woman. Rose Hecht was still in Los Angeles, where Hecht was scheduled to return shortly to script *Viva Villa!*—but, intent on making the most of his fling, he with his lady friend departed for South America. Neither of them spoke Spanish, so Hecht invited Ian McLellan Hunter, a Nyack neighbor's son who spoke the language fluently, to accompany them. They embarked in New York on July 16th and arrived in Rio a week later. From there they traveled on to Buenos Aires, flew over the Andes to Santiago, Chile, took a train to Valparaiso, then a fruit boat up the coast. Quito was their ultimate destination, but the boat was taking too long for Hecht, who had commitments in Hollywood. In late August he debarked at Lima and hopped a plane for Los Angeles, leaving the other two to proceed to Quito and on to the United States, Hunter to New York and the lady to Los Angeles.

Back in Hollywood Selznick assigned Hecht a quick rewrite of *Riptide*, which MacArthur had begun scripting when he and Helen, Irving Thalberg, and Norma Shearer had returned from Europe in July. The first project Thalberg slated upon their return was Michael Arlen's *The Green Hat*, which MacArthur considered a dated hack work. Thalberg refused to change his mind about producing it, so MacArthur, after beginning a script, walked out on the project. Selznick had Hecht and director Edmund Goulding rough out the rest of the story, then Goulding did the shooting script while Hecht went on to yet another adaptation—*Two Thieves*, a novel by Manuel Komroff, a former vice president at Boni & Liveright—before beginning *Viva Villa!* In the midst of the adaptation, Hecht received a phone call from George S. Kaufman's wife, Beatrice, who informed him that Horace Liveright had died.

Over the years Liveright had lost so much money in the stock market that he had been forced to sell more and more stock in B & L to his business manager Arthur Pell, who in 1929 took control and forced him out. Liveright spent nine months in Hollywood as a story consultant for Paramount, hired by Adolph Zukor, then, unwilling to work for someone else, he returned to New York where he announced a number of projects, among them his autobiography, none of which were realized. At the end of 1931 he married Elise Bartlett, Joseph ("Pepi") Schildkraut's first wife and a close friend of Marie Hecht's, but the marriage lasted only a few months. In September of 1933, Liveright died of pneumonia, broke and alone in a cheap hotel on West Fifty-first Street, just a short walk from the Boni & Liveright offices. Twenty years later, Hecht wrote his tribute to one of the greatest publishers in the history of American letters.

> Though he seemed to do nothing but pursue women and drink himself into nightly comas, Liveright was actually a hard worker and a brilliant one. He published scores of fine books and produced a number of successful plays. He loaned courage and money to many fumbling talents. He fought ably against censorship and was one of the chief forces that freed the literature of the Republic from the strangle hold of its old maids. He launched the Modern Library—the first introduction to the larger public of the world's fine writing. There was in New York no more popular and exciting figure than Liveright. Beauty, success, and admiration attended him like a faithful retinue, and hundreds of hangers-on were proud to boast of his friendship.

Early in 1933 David Selznick optioned a biography of Pancho Villa (by Edgcumb Pinchon), the option not to be exercised until Selznick received script approval from the government of Mexico, since he wanted the picture shot on location there. To adapt the book and do a rough-draft screenplay Selznick hired Hecht. Hecht had been hearing stories about Villa for years from MacArthur, who had been a soldier with the American Expeditionary Forces chasing Villa through Mexico, and from Wallace Smith, who had ridden with Villa as a Hearst correspondent. Hecht got Smith hired as a consultant.[4]

According to MGM story editor Sam Marx, L. B. Mayer had Joe Schenck, who knew some of the higher-ups in the Mexican government, "assure the country's powerful politico, Plutarco Elías Calles, that the film would be a faithful picturization. Schenck reported back that Calles, who had fought against Villa in the revolution, wanted the movie to show the bandit-hero as an almost mindless peon, arrogant in victory, groveling in the dust before his captors." Selznick had Hecht revise his first draft to try to please both the pro- and the anti-Villa officials, then in June of 1933 sent Ramon Novarro's brother, Carlos Samaniegos, who was familiar with the upper echelons of Mexican politics, to Mexico City with the revised draft. Both Calles and President Rodríguez approved it. "However, Samaniegos reminded them that an election was drawing near and would occur while the picture was in production. 'What if President Rodríguez is voted out of office?' he asked. Calles called army headquarters to send over Lieutenant Cárdenas. He signed, and Calles told Samaniegos, 'Now you have our next president's signature too!' "[5]

Selznick then paid Hecht fifteen thousand dollars to write a full screenplay, promising him a five-thousand-dollar bonus if he completed it to his satisfaction within two weeks. Selznick justified the high rate of compensation to Mayer in a memo: "I do not think we should take into consideration the fact that we are paying him a seemingly large amount of money for two weeks' work . . . as this would be merely penalizing him for doing what would take a lesser man at least six or eight weeks, with infinitely poorer results." In September of 1933 Hecht and Selznick revised the screenplay, adding so much new material Selznick briefly considered releasing the picture in two parts.

Leaving Los Angeles on October 10th, Hecht accompanied the film's director, Howard Hawks, and a caravan of cast and equipment down to Mexico where Hecht and Hawks worked on final revisions, interrupted only by Rose's unexpected arrival. Since he and the lady from his South American sojourn were registered as Mr. and Mrs. Hecht at their hotel,

Hecht in a panic rushed to Hawks to ask him what he should do. "He didn't know Rose was planning to come," Hawks remembered. "He was forewarned just in time. When he asked me what to do I said, 'Well, Christ, you figure it out yourself, you got yourself into it.' 'Give me some kind of help,' he said. And I said, 'You'd better be perfectly honest. Be a reporter and tell her the story of her husband who's down here with another woman and what's she going to do about it?' And he did and by God he got away with it. Rose said plenty to him, I don't think she liked it a bit, but God knows she must have known what he was. I think Ben amused me most when he got into a real bind, when he got in trouble with some girl and Rose found out about it. Then his mind would really begin to function. I would always ask Charlie MacArthur, 'Is he in any trouble? No? That's too bad.' He enjoyed being the brunt of trouble. It kept him very busy thinking how to get out of it. He was a Romeo but he was in love with Rose and liked her jealousy. He was a pretty devious guy with a lot of different sides to him. It's as though the other women were appealing to what his imaginative mind would work out and Rose appealed to what he was. Rose checked him on everything, she took care of him, otherwise he would've gone off to California without any clothes if she didn't pack them. With other women he wasn't trying to make anything that was lasting. Ben had to adore Rose, she was not a nagging person at all. He was a genius in his way and she treated him as one."

The young lady in question left for parts unknown, and when the script was complete Hecht and Rose returned to Hollywood while Hawks stayed on to direct the picture. When it was finished, Hawks and Louis B. Mayer had a falling out over Lee Tracy, who played the MacArthur role of the newsman who rode with Villa ("I'm a reporter—all brains, no dough"). "Tracy was perfect during the picture," Hawks maintained, "but when it was over he got drunk and got into trouble. He peed on the Chapultepec Cadets during the Independence Day parade in Mexico City and got put in the can. I was on the train by that time and didn't hear about it until I got to the border. When I got to the studio, Louis Mayer wanted me to say that there'd been a great deal of trouble during the shooting but I told him to go to hell."

Mayer insisted that Hawks not only tell the newspapers that Tracy had been impossible to work with but that he turn around and go back to Mexico to reshoot all of Tracy's scenes with another actor. Hawks refused and quit on the spot. Mayer fired Tracy, and Selznick wired the Mexican president that "MGM has removed him not only from the film but has dismissed him entirely from its employ." The studio also claimed that twenty thousand feet of film—the Tracy footage—had been lost in an air crash outside El Paso, necessitating extensive retakes. Hecht substantiated this story in a *New York Times* interview, remarking that he didn't think the loss as tragic as MGM was making out.

Selznick brought in director Jack Conway to complete the film with Tracy's replacement, Stu Erwin. A second unit was left in Mexico but most of the new footage was shot in the mountains outside Los Angeles and on the MGM lot in Hollywood where the Mexican town was reconstructed. By this time Hecht was back in Nyack, but the never-satisfied Selznick had him rewrite the second half of the picture to reduce the reporter's importance and mail the scenes to him as they were completed. Thus, the extensively restructured final cut of the picture presented a very different vision of Villa than had the Hecht/Hawks version. Howard Hawks felt that some of the best material he and Hecht devised had ended up on the cutting-room floor.

"It really could have been one hell of a picture. We had a great death scene. We made it but they didn't use it. Villa was shot in a butcher shop where he'd gone to get some pork chops for a new girl he had. The reporter Johnny found him there. Villa said to him, 'Johnny, I've been reading about what great men said when they died. What am I going to say, Johnny?' And Johnny says, 'I'll think of something.' Villa says, 'No, I want to hear it now, Johnny.' So Johnny went into a spiel about a great man shot and dying, faithful followers coming from far and near. The last thing he says is 'Forgive me, my Mexico! If I have harmed you it was because I loved you.' Then Villa said, 'That's okay, Johnny, but don't let my wife know I was buying pork chops for that girl.' And then he died. I tried to make a strange man, humorous but vicious, out of Villa as he was in real life, but Conway's version had Wallace Beery playing Santa Claus."[6]

Hecht and Hawks had enriched the mythos of the American cinema with *Scarface* but their efforts to do the same with *Viva Villa!* were thwarted. Nevertheless, Hecht was nominated for an Academy Award and offered a scripting job by Joseph Stalin, who loved *Viva Villa!* Stalin was prepared to send a battleship to fetch Hecht back to the USSR but Hecht refused when he learned that the film Stalin wanted to make would only be shown in the Soviet Union.

Hecht returned briefly to Los Angeles to adapt *The Prisoner of Zenda* for Selznick, Hecht and Fowler preparing a treatment that Rowland Lee and

John Farrow based their shooting script on. (This shooting script was completely ditched for a new one when Selznick finally made the film for Selznick International—not MGM—in 1937.) Hecht made a quick five thousand dollars from MGM for his labor then headed back to Nyack where he, MacArthur, and Hawks had arranged to meet to adapt *Twentieth Century* for the screen.

BEN HECHT BUILDS DOLL HOUSE IN NYACK

A friend of ours tells us that old literary master of sensation, Chicago's own Ben Hecht, has been building a doll house in his beautiful home in Nyack.

The hillside garden by his house slopes down to an unusually beautiful ice-bound Hudson. But he is oblivious to the out-of-doors and has been since his trip to Mexico.

For it is said, now don't quote us, that Mr. Hecht brought back with him from Old Mexico some small but sophisticated, almost too sophisticated, dolls fashioned by Aztec artisans.

Friends help him build, and you may be sure these long winter evenings are not without laughter and good fun in the Hecht home.

—*New York Evening Post*
February 15th, 1934

Before he left Mexico, Hecht had ordered six miniature wax tableaux to be made, asking Hawks if he would pick them up for him when he finished shooting *Viva Villa!* The statuettes arrived at Hawks's hotel packed in a suitcase minutes before his departure for Los Angeles. Since he hadn't had time to examine the contents, Hawks became apprehensive as he neared the border, and hired a Mexican to carry the suitcase across for him. From Hollywood, Hawks went on to Nyack (after the *Twentieth Century* porters lost then found the case in Chicago), where he delivered the package to Hecht.

"He opened it and there were six boxes of little wax statues that were the dirtiest things I'd ever seen in my life—a mother going down on her son, things like that. They were really horrible but they were fabulously done by this erotic, crazy family down there who were great artists. Well, I was going to kill him. I got cold perspiration thinking about what could have happened if I'd got caught with those things. But Ben was delighted with them." Hecht and Hawks spent the day visiting Hecht's artist friends in the area, including Ernest Poole, to show them the statues. Hecht then had niches constructed in his library to display the figures, soliciting artists to paint colorful backgrounds for them. "Ben was always up to some crazy thing like that," said Hawks. "You could never trust him at all, he was liable to do any damn thing but it was always funny."

Gene Fowler's son Will remembered an experience he had with the figures.

> When I was a boy we used to go up to Ben's quite often. I was about thirteen and I was to sleep in Ben's library one night. At one end there were some cornices that were concave and when I went to bed on the couch that night and turned out the light, I saw these little slits of light like you would see coming through a closed door except it was in small cabinets which weren't over ten inches high. Being an inquisitive boy I opened them and found these little models of people screwing and doing all sorts of things. At thirteen I had never seen anything like that. I came from a sort of prudish midwestern family and they made me sick to my stomach. So I said I wanted to sleep in another room. I wouldn't tell anybody why. In the other room, I started to look for something to blow my nose on and I reached into the night table and there were some twenty woodblock prints. The first one showed a farmer carrying a gal in his arms and her skirt was up. As I went on, everybody was screwing and little boys were masturbating. "Oh my God," I thought, "how the hell am I going to get away from all this stuff!"

In *Twentieth Century* on the stage the principal female character was a Russian actress, but for the film version Hawks told Hecht and Mac-Arthur they would have to change the "theory" of her lines and "make her into a Sadie Glutz."

> We worked from eight in the morning until eight at night, [Hawks recalled.] I'd stay in Nyack for a couple of days then go back to New York to get some clothes. But Ben worked best when I kept plugging at him. If he went off for a day I knew it would be a couple of days to get started again. Both he and Charlie worked very fast. They made such a great team that I thoroughly enjoyed working with the two of them. Ben seemed to thrive on Charlie's suggestions, that's why he worked with fellas like Lederer, why he had Johnny Mahin around, anybody who would feed him and keep him going. I don't think Ben enjoyed working all by himself.

I remember when we'd finished the script, they figured we were all done. I said, "Now we start on new, different ways of saying the same thing." We had more fun for three days just twisting things around. I asked them, "How do you say this—'Oh, you're just in love'?" Ben came up with "You've broken out in monkey bites." If there were three characters in a scene, we'd sit around and each of us would be one of the characters and we'd try to stump the other person. When a good idea came up, Ben would go off and write, leaving Charlie and I to play backgammon. They taught me how to play. We would work for two hours and play backgammon for an hour. I started winning from them so they got together and decided that when I was their partner they'd lose so that I would always be on the losing end of it. They were so gleeful about this, but I saw what they were doing. If I threw a six and a three and I wanted a six and a four, I'd move it six and four. They never noticed. I won about forty thousand dollars in IOUs from them and they never knew why the hell they were losing.

It was an easy transition from the "ornate and sibilant" speech of Broadway entrepreneur David Belasco, the original model for the character of Oscar Jaffe, to John Barrymore's equally theatrical delivery. Barrymore, however, hadn't been consulted. The burden of informing him fell on Hawks. Back in Hollywood, he was counseled that Barrymore would never play comedy, but, undaunted, Hawks phoned Barrymore anyway to tell him that he wanted him for the part.

"Why do you want me to play this thing?" Barrymore wanted to know.

"Well," Hawks drawled, "it's the story of the biggest ham on earth and you're the biggest ham I know."

"I'll do it, I'll do the picture," Barrymore answered without hesitation. (He would come to consider it his favorite film: "It's a role that comes once in a lifetime.")

"The reviews at the time were generally good," Hawks recalled, "but a number of them said they thought the film would only appeal to a specialized audience. They seemed to think it would be difficult to understand, but later on it became a classic."

Hecht and Hawks created another genre and started another trend— one that was not to endure the way the gangster film has—when they made *Twentieth Century*, since it was the first talking picture in which an established star played comedy. "Notably the first comedy," Andrew Sarris wrote, "in which sexually attractive, sophisticated stars indulged in their own slapstick instead of delegating it to their inferiors." John Barrymore was a male lead on the wane and Carole Lombard was appearing in her first starring role when they acted in this prototypic screwball comedy. The idea caught on and soon most big stars were playing zany parts. Frank Capra's award-winning *It Happened One Night* with Clark Gable and Claudette Colbert was made shortly after; Billy Wilder and Charles Brackett wrote hysterically funny screwball comedies throughout the thirties, such as *Ninotchka* and *Midnight*; Leo McCarey made his classic *The Awful Truth* with Cary Grant and Irene Dunne in 1937. The list is a long one, considering that the genre didn't last much longer than a decade, culminating in the brilliant comedies Preston Sturges wrote and directed in the early forties. Nevertheless, the screwball comedies of the thirties are without question the funniest, wittiest, most sophisticated comedies made in the English language, and *Twentieth Century* was the first.

"The best way to get a play finished," says MacArthur, "is to leave Hecht strictly alone while he is doing our writing."

—MICHAEL MOK
New York Post

Before Hawks left Nyack, Hecht was off and running on another project—a play for Billy Rose, who wanted to awe Broadway with something spectacular.

"What's the most spectacular type of theatre you can think of?" Hecht asked.

"A circus," Hawks supplied.

"And the most spectacular plot?"

"Romeo and Juliet," MacArthur uttered.

Hecht immediately began plotting a story about two rival circus families. When it came to dialogue, Hecht, Hawks, and MacArthur began improvising while Billy Rose, who as a young man had won first place in a world championship shorthand competition, took it down as fast as they invented it. Hawks left long before the play was finished—he had to get back to Hollywood to shoot *Twentieth Century*—but Hecht and MacArthur continued working on *Jumbo* through the early months of 1934 (writing part of it in Charleston, South Carolina) and had it almost finished by spring, when the MacArthurs left for Europe. By that time, Billy Rose was involved in opening the Billy Rose Music Hall and the Casino de Paree, the first theatre-restaurant in the United States, so he delayed his plans to stage *Jumbo*.

When, in 1935, he was finally ready to produce the play, Rose had the old Hippodrome gutted to accommodate the two circuses that figured in the Hecht/MacArthur story—which, typically, wasn't quite finished. Jock Whitney, who at the same time was forming Selznick International Pictures with the Selznick brothers and Irving Thalberg, put up the money for the show in partnership with Herbert Bayard Swope. George Abbott was hired to direct, Rodgers and Hart to provide the songs, Paul Whiteman to conduct, and Jimmy Durante to star. "It seems," Durante recalled, "that Hecht and MacArthur always showed up in time to save me from some dillemia; first with *Roadhouse Nights*; next when Mac-Arthur gave me *Get-Rich-Quick Wallingford*; and now they concocted *Jumbo* for me. It is Hecht and MacArthur who gave me lines in *Roadhouse Nights* that I am always fond of, like 'It's the gallows!' and 'I'm just a tool for a beautiful dame!'"

As soon as Hecht and MacArthur knocked out the last pages of the play, they presented them to Billy Rose. Interviewed by the *New York Post*, Hecht maintained he couldn't recall the plot, although MacArthur remembered that the story told "the adventures of the bibulous Irish owner of a bedraggled one-ring circus. It is his careless habit to share his jags with his elephant. On the boss's birthday the elephant gets the d.t.s and sees pink men." "Billy Rose, our esteemed maestro," Hecht added, "objected to this idea. Billy has a curious fetish. He is obsessed with the notion that a musical spectacle, to be successful, has to have a lot of pretty girls in it. So now the elephant sees an army of wriggling chorines."

Rose, rehearsing the show not only at the Hippodrome but at the Manhattan Opera House and the Venice Theatre in Brooklyn, had to postpone it five times because of the enormousness of the preparations. He ran ads in all the New York papers reading, "I'll be a dirty name if I open 'Jumbo' before it's ready" and had huge billboards in Times Square erected that read, SHH! "JUMBO" REHEARSING. Finally, on November 17th, it opened. Paul Whiteman came riding in on a white horse and Jimmy Durante dangled from the neck of Rosie the elephant. There were two acts and eleven scenes with tightrope walkers who worked over an open lion pit, clowns, trapeze artists, bareback riders (the Rodgers and Hart song "The Most Beautiful Girl in the World" was sung while Romeo and Juliet rode around the ring), ax throwers, and trained bears.

The reviews in general were favorable, Percy Hammond calling the show "a sane and exciting compound of opera, animal show, folk drama, carnival, circus, extravaganza, and spectacle." Many of the critics, however, put down Hecht and MacArthur's contribution as minimal and banal. What they didn't know was that following a preview, Billy Rose had cut most of Hecht and MacArthur's dialogue since it was difficult to hear in the vast Hippodrome. Hecht, furious over Rose's bowdlerization, never went back to the Hippodrome after the preview. He sent Dick Maney, the show's press agent, a telegram on opening night: "It never should have opened and it would have been a great hit, thanks to you." The show nonetheless was a popular success, running nine months in New York and an additional two at the Texas Centennial in Fort Worth.

10

THE ASTORIA FILMS

Better than Metro isn't good enough.

—BEN HECHT AND
CHARLES MACARTHUR

A Hollywood screenwriter under the studio system was an assembly-line worker: he wrote scripts based on novels, plays, or ideas previously developed by the studio; other writers rewrote his scripts and still others rewrote the rewrites. Then a director was assigned to make a film of the script with actors that had been assigned by the producers. Every step in the process was isolated from the next, which stirred up discontent among many writers, who resented the loss of control over their material. Their dissatisfaction was unheard or disregarded by the front office.

When F. Scott Fitzgerald predicted that in some distant future screenwriters would oversee the production of their scripts from filming through editing, Hollywood writers were incredulous. Yet in 1934 Hecht and MacArthur contracted to do just that. In May of that year, Leland Hayward sold *Erik Dorn* to Universal, *The Florentine Dagger* to Warner Bros., and Ben and Rose's play *The Man-Eating Tiger* to Fox, and Hecht did the impossible: he and MacArthur signed with George J. Schaefer (president of Paramount and a friend of Hecht's since the 1920s) to write, direct, produce, and edit four pictures at Paramount's Astoria studios in Queens, where Walter Wanger was in charge of production. Hollywood writers considered it a dream come true, one that they hoped would liberate them from their own impotent positions in the studios.

Needing a professional crew to make the pictures, Hecht asked David Selznick to lend him a cinematographer and an editor. Selznick sent him Lee Garmes—one of Hollywood's top lighting cameramen, who had worked with Hawks, Sternberg, and Mamoulian—and Slavko Vorkapitch, a montage expert Selznick thought was a film editor. Arthur Rosson, *Underworld*'s first director, was hired as the business and production manager, and Charlie Lederer was asked to come east and lend a hand as well, since he had had another of his periodic fights with David Selznick and was out of a job.

"When Ben started to make pictures, when he wanted to direct them," Howard Hawks recalled, "he got me on the phone and said to me, 'For God's sake, will you come back here for a week and help us. We don't know a god damn thing about it.' I came to New York and helped them get started. When they began to feel comfortable I got out of there and they finished it. I didn't direct the picture, I just told them what I would do."

The night before they began production, the Hechts and the MacArthurs, Charlie Lederer, Billy Rose and Fanny Brice visited Coney Island. One of the attractions in the freak show was a Negro pinhead dressed in a grass skirt. Hecht and MacArthur hired him, had him dressed in a business suit, and installed him in Adolph Zukor's old office at the Astoria studios. Then they held a press conference to introduce their new executive producer from Hollywood.

When avant-garde composer George Antheil was hired to score their second picture, the question of salary arose. "Let me introduce you to our president," Hecht told Antheil. "He and he alone decides matters of this kind." "Ben took me to the room next door," Antheil recalled in his memoirs, "which was marked PRESIDENT—HECHT-MACARTHUR PICTURES, INC., and told me to go in. I advanced to the desk, where a little pinhead gentleman in a high wing-collar was writing. He did not even look up. I looked at what he was writing. He was doodling. He looked up then jumped right over the desk at me! He always jumped right over the desk at all visitors, jabbering incoherently. Otherwise he was harmless."

"There were three doors into Ben's office," Lee Garmes recalled. "There were two desks, Ben had one and Charlie had one. Ben asked the assistant director to go out and get life-sized photographs of three different nude girls, nice poses of good-looking girls on sepia-tone print. They fitted them onto the three doors. People would come in to be interviewed and they'd see this nude girl in the doorway and they'd say, 'Gee, I beg your pardon.'"

For their first picture, Hecht and MacArthur adapted a short story of Hecht's published by the *Saturday Evening Post* the year before. *Crime Without Passion* told of a brilliant criminal lawyer who mistakenly believes he has murdered his former mistress during a quarrel; his attempts to cover up his crime metamorphose the cold-blooded defender into a terrified, sweaty-palmed petty crook. The picture's budget was $150,000, an impossibly small amount for a Hollywood film, but one that Hecht was determined not to exceed, convinced as he was that it was possible to make good movies for far less money than the studios deemed necessary.

One cost-cutting measure was to use stage actors and unknowns rather than stars. To play the attorney, Hecht and MacArthur hired Claude Rains, who had been top-billed but hardly appeared in one previous film, *The Invisible Man*. A young singer and dancer named Margo, then appearing at the Waldorf, was persuaded by a friend to audition for the part of Rains's mistress. As soon as Hecht set eyes on her, he exclaimed, "That's the girl I've been looking all over New York for," signing her up on the spot. Ben and Charlie changed the character Margo was to play to a show-girl and filmed her Waldorf act, saving production time as well as money. When she began reading her lines like a Broadway starlet, Hecht yelled at her, "Hey, sweetie, stop it! Don't act. There's thousands of lice who do that."

When they needed chorus girls for a nightclub scene, Hecht phoned Jack and Charlie's and had them pile their eighteen girls in cabs and send them over to Astoria. When an orchestra was called for, they borrowed one from a Harlem nightspot for the afternoon. Not having to pay a director cut costs enormously, too, since Hecht and MacArthur were directing, with the occasional assist from Lee Garmes. "On the set," *Photoplay* reported in October 1934,

> Hecht will sit cross-legged on top of a table, directing a difficult emotional scene as calmly as if he were watching a slow game of tennis. Just off the set MacArthur is spinning a yarn for a group of extras. He will interrupt himself suddenly to yell at Hecht, "Hey, Ben! Shouldn't Claude pause longer between those two sentences?"
>
> "No."
>
> "Okay." And he goes back to his story.
>
> In a moment Hecht climbs slowly off the table.
>
> "Take it over, Mac. I'm going across the street for a cup of coffee."
>
> "Let Lee handle it. I'll go with you." So the director-producers leave and Lee Garmes takes over the scene.

As well as doubling as director, Garmes saved them enormous outlays of capital. Because Hecht and MacArthur's Broadway art director was designing sets forty feet long, Garmes suggested they buy his sketches but discontinue his employment. Garmes then scaled the designs down to ten- and fifteen-foot interiors, but never had complete sets built. He had wheels put on set walls so they could be shifted quickly to create new sets. Garmes would light a set for a certain scene, then after he had photographed it, he would have the next interior rolled in front of his previously positioned lights, an enormous timesaver since it regularly took hours in Hollywood to light for a single shot. Sometimes he barely had sets built at all; the nightclub where Margo works was effectively suggested with only twenty dollars' worth of materials.

Shortly after the picture started shooting, Hecht discovered that his editor, Slavko Vorkapitch, was in reality a montage expert. "There is no Slavko Vorkapitch," Hecht joked, "he's just one of his own special effects." Hecht set him to work anyway, devising an opening montage in which three Furies descend to Earth to wreak their havoc. Vorkapitch had three actresses wrapped in long gauzy swatches, suspended them with wires, and turned a wind machine on them to give the impression they were traveling at great speed. Vorkapitch completed the sequence in ten days—as well as photographing the titles and taking some "atmospheric" background shots of New York—then returned to Hollywood.

Both to save money and to amuse themselves, Hecht and MacArthur played reporters who interview Rains outside the courtroom where he has successfully pleaded a case. They also appeared in the background of the nightclub, seated at a table. In another scene, Helen Hayes, Fanny Brice, and Gertrude Lawrence showed up in a hotel lobby. Still another economy measure, and a somewhat cruel amusement, was to hire Oscar Levant at fifteen dollars a week to write some of the film's background music. He was given the title of Assistant President of the Music Department and was required to play duets with Hecht. When he asked for more money, Hecht and MacArthur sent him a memo stating that his salary was to be doubled. Nevertheless he continued to receive only fifteen dollars a week. Finally he quit, telling Hecht and MacArthur, "I can't afford such a high salary, I'm starving to death on it."

Crime Without Passion was shot in June, edited by Garmes, and on August 31st, 1934, opened at the Rialto in New York. *Variety* reported that Hecht and MacArthur's "first made in the East production is a promising starter for them. They show themselves to be adept in all the major departments of picture making. It's also a boost for Eastern producing, showing that geography can have little to do with quality and results in film-making." Most of the New York reviewers were extremely enthusiastic, and the picture played to capacity crowds in Manhattan, convincing Hecht and MacArthur their movie was a hit—but this was not to be the case, since outside the larger cities there was no audience for the film at all. Director Don Siegel thought so highly of it, however, that he had Universal buy the rights to it in the fifties; he and John Cassavetes prepared a script for a remake that Universal was then unwilling to produce. In 1965, film historian Herman Weinberg wrote, "Thirty years ago when I first saw *Crime Without Passion*, I thought it ten or fifteen years ahead of its time. Seeing it recently again I feel we still haven't caught up with it."

Hecht and MacArthur's next picture, *Once in a Blue Moon*, which they adapted from a story by Rose Hecht, told of a small traveling circus that has lost all of its performers during the Russian Revolution. The shy little circus owner meets a family of fleeing aristocrats, hides them, and turns them into performers. They travel the length of Russia, cross the border secretly, and make their way to Paris. There, the naive circus owner learns that his companions are wealthy beyond his wildest imaginings. Realizing his love for the family's pretty young daughter can never be requited, he slips away from the ball they are giving for him, never to return.

Hecht and MacArthur had seen "Chaplinesque" comic Jimmy Savo perform at Billy Rose's Casino de Paree, hired him, and adapted the part of the circus owner for him. For the female lead they held auditions, announcing they were looking for a type not to be found in Hollywood: five feet tall, weighing one hundred pounds, with a "Dresden china quality." The part went to Hecht's nineteen-year-old daughter, Teddy, who had been living in New York with Marie for five years. Hecht rehired Whitney Bourne, who had played in *Crime Without Passion*, and got Nikita Balieff, creator of the internationally famous *Chauve Souris* revues, to play a Russian aristocrat. Needing extras to play Russian soldiers, Hecht and MacArthur advertised in New York's Russian-language newspapers. They received more than four thousand replies, from which they chose four hundred, among them a grandson of Leo Tolstoy and a former governor-general of Siberia. Screenwriter-to-be Ian McLellan Hunter, who worked for Hecht and MacArthur that summer, had the job of paying the extras. He remembered that gypsies were paid five dollars a day unless they were sleeping with a member of the company; then they got twenty dollars.

The story took place largely outdoors, in rural Russian settings, so for location shooting Hecht and MacArthur got permission to use the estate of J. P. Morgan's sister in the Tuxedo Park area of New York. In August the huge cast occupied eighteen local hotels and shooting commenced. Rain cancelled five days of exteriors, but, not to be put off their schedule, Hecht and MacArthur cut the scenes to be shot on those days and bused the cast to Astoria to do interiors.

One morning, preparing to shoot a scene in the studio, Hecht got a call from Adolph Zukor: he was sending over a Wall Street financier who controlled a large block of Paramount stock and who had decided to take personal control of the studio. Zukor's son and the financier arrived an hour later to find the studio dark. Hecht and MacArthur were sitting silently beside Jimmy Savo. Zukor's son introduced the financier.

"I hope you'll excuse us but we're working very hard and in all fairness shouldn't be disturbed," MacArthur told them. The man sat down and waited, hoping to see how a movie studio functioned, but nobody moved or said a word.

"We better knock off for lunch," Hecht said, breaking the silence.

"What do you suggest?" MacArthur asked.

"The Colony is all right with me," Hecht replied.

"A secretary can have a waiter sent over to take the order."

The financier, aghast at the idea of ordering lunch from one of New York's most expensive restaurants, suggested they at least place the order by phone. Hecht and MacArthur ignored him.

"We have dignitaries visiting so it seems to me we owe it to them to serve champagne," MacArthur said.

"It wouldn't look good," Hecht responded. "We'd be sitting around drinking champagne while the crew drank beer."

"Well, in all fairness, we must order champagne for the crew as well," MacArthur concluded.

"Might as well order lunch for everybody while we're at it," Hecht added.

An hour and a half later, lunch was delivered for forty people by a fleet of taxis.

After lunch, Hecht and MacArthur told the Wall Street man that they had to get back to work. "First thing, we better look at Jimmy's rushes. We've got one of the funniest scenes ever filmed. You'll die laughing."

They adjourned to the projection room, ordered whiskey, and screened a scene in which Jimmy Savo steps over a windowsill and enters a room. Hecht and MacArthur howled with laughter. They had the scene run again. "Funniest thing ever made," Hecht said. "It was your idea Charlie and will go down in history." Hecht ordered the scene rerun. He and MacArthur once more emitted side-splitting laughter before ordering the projectionist to run it again. The financier departed in a fury.

When *Time* magazine owner Henry Luce needed a newsreel made of him pitching his favorite charity, Hecht offered him Astoria, assuring the vain Luce he had one of Hollywood's best cameramen working for him there. Luce agreed and went over to Astoria, where Garmes shot the charity appeal. After Luce spoke the last words in his prepared speech, twelve nude girls ran out and surrounded him. Ian McLellan Hunter, who was a witness, recalled that "after an appalled moment Luce recovered quite well." Shocking Luce was nothing new for Hecht, however, since Luce had once worked as a sixteen-dollar-a-week legman for him when he was writing his "1001 Afternoons" column for the *Daily News*.

Hecht and MacArthur budgeted *Once in a Blue Moon* at $350,000— more than double the cost of *Crime Without Passion*—but the picture allegedly was foiled from the beginning by bad sound. With the exception of the principal characters, all the other speaking roles were played by Russians with heavy accents. When they were on location near Tuxedo Park, the soundman told Lee Garmes he couldn't understand a word of the dialogue; Garmes reported this to Hecht, who insisted he could understand every word. Garmes reminded Hecht that he had written the dialogue and wasn't in the best position to judge, but Hecht continued to demur, so Garmes approached MacArthur only to be told the movie was "Ben's baby" and he wouldn't interfere.

In November the picture was turned over to Paramount for distributions, but Paramount shelved it because of the unintelligibility of the actors. In December of 1936, it finally played second-bill in the few theatres that could be convinced to show it. "There's no sense kidding about *Once in a Blue Moon*," said *Variety*, "or mincing language, or being cute about it. It's a bad picture. Jimmy Savo is featured and is very unfunny in what was intended to be a new Chaplin performance. Late Nikita Balieff [who died shortly after the film's completion] is featured and it is impossible to understand a word he says. There's an interesting musical score marred by bad sound."[1] One Chicago theatre advertised it as the worst film ever made, and Hecht quipped that it opened and closed on a transatlantic liner. It played briefly in New York City in December of 1936 only because of a product shortage.

At the end of the year, Hecht announced that their next picture would be *The Scoundrel*, adapted from his and Rose's play of the same name. The story concerned a sophisticated, heartless publisher— modeled after Horace Liveright—who has never loved anyone in his life, although he has had a succession of mistresses. It was the same picture of Liveright Hecht had painted in the ironically titled *A Jew in Love*. In *The Scoundrel* the publisher, killed in a plane crash, is granted a heavenly reprieve to find one person who will cry for him, or otherwise suffer eternal damnation.

To play Liveright—named Anthony Mallare after the mad artist of *Fantazius Mallare*—Hecht hired Noël Coward, whose play *Point Valaine* had just closed. Coward was only offered five thousand dollars but, needing the money and not wanting to spend months in Hollywood, where he had been offered several roles, he accepted the part. Hecht and MacArthur had promised him Helen Hayes as a leading lady but then they decided she wasn't right for the role; a younger, more ethereal girl was needed to play the poetess who becomes Mallare's latest conquest. George Jean Nathan's friend, Julie Haydon, just returned from Hollywood, got the part.

Haydon and Coward took an instant dislike to one another. One morning while watching the previous day's rushes, Coward objected to the dress she was wearing in the scene in which he tells her he's through with her. "Of course, it's too late to do anything about it," Coward remarked. "Not at all," Hecht replied, "we'll put in a line saying he's leaving her because of the dress."

Lionel Stander played a cynical poet based on Maxwell Bodenheim. In one scene, Stander mimics a poem written by the young poetess, the same Bodenheim poem Hecht had satirized years earlier in his novel *Humpty Dumpty*—"I am a stranger wandering always. Only the dark trees know me and the dark sky and the winds that come to warm themselves in my heart."

Alexander Woollcott did a cameo as one of Mallare's authors, Vanderveer Veyden, a caricature of Boni & Liveright popular historian Hendrik Van Loon. Alice Duer Miller, the real poetess who during World War II would compose her famous verse on Dover's white cliffs, played another Mallare author, and Hecht and MacArthur did cameos as bums in a Bowery flophouse. (Hecht is seen briefly when a hotel clerk walks down an aisle past rows of beds pointing out the various occupants to Mallare. When the clerk gets to Hecht he says, "Here's a professor." MacArthur is sitting on the next cot, scratching his head.)

The film was shot during February and March, edited in April, and released in May 1935. The reviews were excellent, as they had been for *Crime Without Passion*, but this time the critics pointed out that the picture wasn't likely to be a commercial success. (It later became an art-house favorite, so impressing writers-to-be Adolph Green and Betty Comden that they would act out entire scenes.) "Noël Coward's stellar film debut is good Hotel Algonquin stuff but not for the automat trade," *Variety* assessed. "It'll appeal to the palates of the pseudo, near-and-full fledged sophisticates but it'll leave the average film fan bewildered. It's not box-office in the accepted sense."

Audiences found Noël Coward effeminate and, as *Variety* predicted, were "bewildered" by the story. Hecht and MacArthur had scored two critical successes but were failing at the box-office. Not only that, making the Astoria pictures was actually costing them income! They had a percentage of the profits, but since the films weren't doing much business, Hecht and MacArthur weren't earning more than fifty to sixty thousand dollars per picture.

In January of 1936 André Sennwald, movie critic for *The New York Times*, included *The Scoundrel* on his list of the ten best films of 1935, calling it "hilariously bizarre and so far outside the normal cinema pastures that it confused and annoyed all sorts of people and died an agonizing death." (It had cost $172,000 and grossed $500,000, a small profit in Hollywood bookkeeping.) *The Scoundrel* was nominated by the Academy for Best Original Story, and would win MacArthur his first and only Oscar, Hecht his second and last (although Hecht had been nominated the year before for his script of *Viva Villa!* and MacArthur the year before that for *Rasputin and the Empress*). Though their Astoria films were commercial failures, at least their fellow film artists awarded them the industry's highest token of approval the same year that Dudley Nichols picked up the Best Screenplay award for *The Informer*, beating out Jules Furthman's *Mutiny on the Bounty*. A screenwriter's renaissance was once again looking to be a figment of Scott Fitzgerald's imagination.

On March 20th, 1935, to bolster their bank accounts, Hecht and MacArthur signed a one-picture deal with Sam Goldwyn. They remained in New York, though, until after the May premiere of *The Scoundrel*, then headed west, elated with the reviews but dejected about returning to Hollywood to make money. The only bright aspect was that Howard Hawks was to direct the Goldwyn film.

The script was to be adapted from a journalistic account of political corruption in San Francisco in the 1890s, *The Barbary Coast: An Informal History of the San Francisco Underground*, but Hecht and MacArthur only used the book as background for a tale they had told before. "It was more trouble than any of the others we did together and not as good," Hawks said of the picture, a touchy subject for him since it was one of the few times Hecht and MacArthur put something over on him. Over lunch at "21," Leland Hayward told Hawks that he had sold one plot of Ben and Charlie's three times. "He was laughing and laughing about it," Hawks recalled, thinking something sounded uncomfortably familiar.

"Was the guy's name in the story Chamalis?" Hawks asked.

Hayward stopped laughing: "Did they sell it to you too?"

"Yeah, they just sold it to me."

Hawks believed it was "a lousy picture, a contrived thing done more or less to order. There were some pretty good scenes in it but the whole thing was pretty mawkish. As Ben said, 'Miriam Hopkins came to the Barbary Coast and wandered around like a confused Goldwyn girl.' I was no good on it or else it wasn't really any good. It was popular but I don't know why. It was a lot of romance, a lot of bird calls. Ben always leaned toward that kind of wild love story, like *To Quito and Back* and *The Great Magoo*. Those pictures are very difficult to do, but if left to his own volition, Ben would be inclined to do things like that. We really didn't enjoy *Barbary Coast*."

With one more film still to make at Astoria, Hecht and MacArthur returned to New York in midsummer. They got Lee Garmes, working with Alexander Korda in London, to come back to the States and shoot it for them, then began rehearsing *Hearts and Flowers*, the musical Hecht had written with Roger Kahn. An ill-fated project, it was cancelled after two months of preparation because of Hecht's infatuation with a young New York socialite, Mary "Mimsi" Taylor.

Hecht's love affair with Taylor would be his most serious outside his two marriages. Mimsi was a top fashion model whose father was the youngest man ever elected a governor of the New York Stock Exchange. Her aunt, Countess Dorothy di Frasso—formerly married to an Italian nobleman—lived in Los Angeles, where she was known for her "discoveries": she and Gary Cooper had been lovers before he became a star, and Hecht later claimed that di Frasso had discovered Rudolph Valentino working in a dime-a-dance parlor in New York and had taken him to Hollywood.

Hecht and MacArthur then reworked an unfinished play of theirs into a vehicle for Miss Taylor, renaming it *Soak the Rich* after Huey Long's political platform of the same name that enjoyed a certain vogue in the social-realist thirties. Their story concerned a rich young college girl (type-casting, some would say) who falls in love with a student radical played by John Howard, hired by Hecht and MacArthur partly because of the similarity of his name to that of Communist screenwriter and organizer John Howard Lawson.

The script was written and all preproduction work completed by the end of September when it went before the cameras. The smooth progress of the film was marred for Hecht when on October the 10th he learned that his parents had been struck by a car on Wilshire Boulevard. Peter Hecht remembered, "Both our parents had been hit by a car turning against the red light. Both were hospitalized. Mother died two days later, having had several ribs pierce her lungs. Rose Hecht, who was on the Coast at the time, did not want to leave Dad alone in the hospital and, against the doctor's wishes, abducted him and brought him to Nyack. Mother came along in the baggage car."[2]

Soak the Rich was edited by the end of the year and released in February 1936 to unenthusiastic reviews. The miracle in Astoria had turned out to be a counterrevolution for many, for rather than liberating writers, if anything it had retarded their control over their own scripts.

Alfred Hayes, in the March 1936 issue of *New Theatre*, summed up the disenchantment felt by many writers regarding the Astoria films.

> I remember how eagerly we awaited the first production of Ben Hecht and Charles MacArthur after their break with their Hollywood paymasters. . . . With the establishment of the Long Island studios . . . a rumor and a belief circulated that Mr. Hecht had at last stopped chasing the elusive dollar-sign and was about to make an aesthetic comeback. We believed . . . that the Hecht of *Erik Dorn* and *Humpty Dumpty* . . . the iconoclastic and metaphoric Mr. Hecht, the champion of Life (in capital letters) and the foe of the smug bourgeoisie . . . was about to rise out of the graveyard. True, he might be a slightly aged and withered Lazarus . . . but nevertheless the idol-smasher of old.
>
> At last, *Crime Without Passion* appeared . . . the clichéd and motheaten murder mystery with Nietzschean trimmings which "the boys" had turned out as their first offer to an expectant public. . . . The whole thing sounded as though a skillful and talented man was amusing himself writing unusual *Saturday Evening Post* stories, pitifully thin and pretentiously decorated. . . .
>
> *The Scoundrel* was *Crime Without Passion* without the crime, without passion, with a phony ending. . . . Surprisingly, Mr. Hecht seemed to have developed a strain of religious mysticism which must have caused acute pain to the copy desk of the *Chicago Daily News*. . . .
>
> Thus, the . . . Hecht-MacArthur productions were . . . distinguished by their irrelevance, their pretentious emptiness, and their failure to approach even the cinematic standards of the Hollywood product. . . .

And so, after all, it was no Lazarus who arose out of the Hollywood grave when Hecht-MacArthur left. The corpse simply moved to Long Island. We may remember years and years ago that Mr. Hecht refused to evade charges of literary obscenity in Chicago and valiantly defended the freedom of the artist from censorship, that Hecht himself once showed signs of being an artist. But that was in another country, and besides the wench is dead.

The Astoria films didn't advance the freedom of the scriptwriter in the Hollywood factory system but to many they admirably demonstrated that excellent movies, not restricted by Hollywood's predigested plots, could be made to appeal to more literate segments of the filmgoing populace. Nevertheless, the experiment was at an end, and Hecht and MacArthur were back to writing according to the rules.

11

WHY DO THEY MAKE ME WRITE LIKE THAT?

*If in one of those guessing games currently popular the country over . . .
the question was as to the identity of the two most publicized scenario
writers in Hollywood, it would probably be a backward moron indeed who
would not promptly either write down or speak up with the names of Hecht
and MacArthur.*

—George Jean Nathan

Disgruntled and frustrated by his forced return to Hollywood to do run-of-the-mill scripting chores he'd thought himself done with forever, Hecht wrote a funny, vicious poem attacking the kind of work writers were assigned by the studios. Bound in blue velvet wrappers and illustrated by Fanny Brice's son Billy, *Hecht's Prayer to His Bosses* was published by Stanley Rose. (Rose—who had opened a bookshop early in 1935 next door to Musso and Frank's restaurant, the gathering place of the film community literati—was a local character, half confidence man, half aesthete, who turned the back room of his shop into a meeting place for writers and small-time hoods. His sometime practice of selling pornography was used as a plot element in Raymond Chandler's *The Big Sleep*; Rose's regulars included Hecht, Fowler, Nathanael West, Horace McCoy, Dashiell Hammett, Scott Fitzgerald, and William Faulkner.)

The poem was directed at the studio system in general and specifically at L. B. Mayer (referred to by Gene Fowler as Louis B. Manure) and MGM. Mayer, the production head of the most powerful studio in Hollywood at the time, was the most hated of all the moguls. *Variety* has commented on his "monumental pettiness, his savage retaliation, the humiliation he heaped upon old associates." Hecht had never been the butt of these indignities, since he usually worked for David Selznick when he worked for MGM, but he had witnessed Mayer's bullying turned on others. A few years earlier, to belittle Mayer, Hecht and MacArthur had taken a young man with a British accent to the studio, introduced him to Mayer as "the well-known British novelist Kenneth Woollcott" (in reality he was a gas-station attendant), and got him a year's contract at one thousand dollars a week. When the year was up—during which time the young man hadn't written a word—MacArthur ghostwrote a letter to Mayer from him:

I wish to thank you for the privilege of working this year
under your wise and talented leadership. I can assure you I
have never had more pleasure as a writer. I think if you will
check your studio log you will find that I am the only writer
who didn't cost the studio a shilling this year beyond his
wage. This being the case, would you consider awarding me
a bonus for this unique record. I leave the sum up to you.

Mayer was furious, but not half so furious as when he read Hecht's
Prayer.

> *Good gentlemen who overpay*
> *Me fifty times for every fart,*
> *Who hand me statues when I bray*
> *And hail my whinneying as Art—*
> *I pick your pockets every day*
> *But how you bastards break my heart.*
>
> *Knee deep in butlers, smothered half*
> *In horse shit splendors, soft and fat*
> *And worshipping the Golden Calf*
> *I mutter through my new plush hat*
> *"Why did you steal my Pilgrim's Staff?*
> *Why do you make me write like that?"*
>
> *I kowtow to you day and night*
> *In conference I'm always glad*
> *To kiss your ass a rosey white*
> *And wipe it with my writing pad*
> *But when I get alone to write*
> *Oh, gentlemen, I go half mad!*
>
> *My chateaus turn sheiss house fawn,*
> *My gardens fair stink in my nose*
> *When sitting down I start to spawn*
> *Those jelly fish scenarios—*
> *Those drooling tales of Came the Dawn*
> *And Virtue sweet beshat her foes . . .*
>
> *No human beings dare intrude*
> *Upon my plots, no truth rebuke*
> *The moron, cretin, or the prude,*

Why Do They Make Me Write Like That?

I write of servant, clerk and duke
All slobbering with platitude
And half-assed ninnies etched in puke.

My heroine must be so nice
So full of dainty tweedledums—
Her gimlet ass a cake of ice—
So delicate she feasts on crumbs
And full of smirking sacrifice
Farts bonbons and shits sugar plums.

This Venus of cliché and slop
Must nary imbecile affront,
Must suffer and come out on top,
Must love and die and bear the brunt
While Will Hays like a traffic cop
Barks signals from inside her cunt.

And what about the dreary hick—
My hero with his marcelled hair—
So noble, cute and politic,
So winsome—Holy God is there
In all of lit'rature a prick
As flaccid and a mind as bare.

He must be fashioned without juice
No thinking must disturb or shock
This last pale drop of self abuse—
This human cypher run amok
Whose balls are full of Mother Goose
With Bo Peep tattooed on his cock.

These are the lovers I must link
Two eunuchs panting prettily
Whom censors have forbade to drink
To fuck, to shit, to take a pee—
Just to make goo goo eyes and stink
Of cinema nobility.

But not enough that I must limn
These hypo thyroid Launcelots
And fungus headed virgin quim—
These mentally arrested tots

But must exercise their wit and whim
In what are known as Sure Fire Plots.

Who envies me my swimming pool,
My esne, servitor and slave
My mameluke and royal fool
And Miss Luella Parson's rave—
That one has never played the ghoul
At every mildewed drama's grave.

Has never dallied with the bones
Of long dead tales or tried to woo
A zombie plot-turn from its stones—
Has never poured his soul into
Cadavers or retyped the moans
Of corpses for a camera crew.

Good Gentlemen I only trace
With cautious word the horrid chore,
The tribulation that I face
In playing literary whore—
That little nuance of disgrace
That one gets so much money for . . .

Yet hear my prayer—the timid plea
That trickles from my venal bed,
The echo of integrity
That still wails in my empty head.
Attend! And please don't fire me
For not being altogether dead.

O Molochs of the Movie Set
O Geniuses whose violence
Has tamed the Lion for a pet,
O Mighty Wizards who dispense
Amusement to the world—please let
Me write a movie that makes sense.

Before I die or go berserk
Oh let me write once Not To Fit
Some big box office movie jerk
Some million dollar piece of tit,
Oh let my battered talents work
On something besides baby shit.

Why Do They Make Me Write Like That?

Oh let me grow one leaf of grass,
One breath of truth, one cry of man's
Travail and quest, one peal of brass
To drive Art from its crapping cans—
One tale that doesn't kiss the ass
Of ninety million movie fans.

Not given to frequent socializing with the movie colony elite—the bosses, producers, and actors—especially now that he felt he had been driven back to the movies for money, Hecht spent his time with MacArthur, Fowler, and Lederer. He also began frequenting the Bundy Drive studio of artist John Decker, where many of his and Fowler's friends would gather, among them Jimmy Durante, Thomas Mitchell, former art critic Sadakitchi Hartman, Sidney Skolsky, W. C. Fields (dubbed Uncle Claude), and John Barrymore.

Starting in 1935 and continuing till his death in 1942, John Barrymore was looked after by the Decker group. As Gene Fowler wrote in his biography of Barrymore, *Good Night, Sweet Prince*, "These were the last seven years of a lifetime. The personal phases of that lifetime were a Gothic holiday of flowers, of verses, and of wine, with rains and thunders, too, when, towards the close of day, the landlord spoke above the storm to remind the unthinking guest that no one feasts for nothing or is sheltered free at the inn."

The studios were less and less willing to hire Barrymore because of his drinking, erratic behavior, and bad publicity. In 1935 he had become entangled with a Hunter College student, Elaine Jacobs, whom he maintained he was going to mold into an actress. (He must have had in mind Oscar Jaffe's similar remolding of Mildred Plotka into Lily Garland in *Twentieth Century* since he and the newly christened Elaine Barrie did a scene from that play on the radio in May of 1935.)

Barrymore was fifty-three and Elaine Jacobs Barrie nineteen when he decided to marry her. He was in Los Angeles, as were Hecht, MacArthur, and Fowler, who, at the Countess di Frasso's, pleaded and argued with Barrymore not to go through with the marriage. Fowler claimed they gave him fifty-three reasons why he shouldn't. When he wouldn't yield and they demanded to know why he was going ahead with it, Barrymore simply replied, "It fits." The marriage took place the following day.

Hecht, however, was in no position to advise Barrymore about young girls, since he was involved with one himself and about to commit an indiscretion of his own. He was in Hollywood to promote *Soak the Rich*, to do some polishing on Selznick's *Little Lord Fauntleroy*—which Johnny Weaver had been working on—and to spend some time alone with Mimsi. Will Fowler remembered the evening Hecht and MacArthur presented Mimsi and *Soak the Rich* to Hollywood society:

> One night Ben came to the house and wanted Pop to go to a big party. He and Charlie were in Hollywood to introduce a young actress who was in their film *Soak the Rich*, which they had just finished. Ben wanted Pop to go to this party at the Countess di Frasso's, who used to give the biggest parties in Hollywood. Ben was wearing that little bow tie that gave you the impression you were looking at a great nineteenth-century poet. Pop didn't want to go so Ben asked if I'd like to go with him and I said, "God, I'd love to!" I had a grey suit, nothing formal, so I stood out like a sore thumb but I'll never forget the party. I'd never been anyplace with such an enormous amount of actors, the biggest stars in the world. Ben and I, for dinner, were seated with Edmund Lowe and his wife. From the Countess di Frasso's we went up to Pickfair, Mary Pickford's and Buddy Rogers' home, where there was a preview of the picture. Charlie Chaplin, John Barrymore, Gary Cooper, Carole Lombard, just all the big stars of the day were there, and this elderly gentleman in a walrus mustache and white tie and tails. We got in a wonderful conversation with him and Ben told me he was H. G. Wells. I wasn't exactly a court jester to Ben but Ben liked to do strange things like showing up with a young guy or a hunchback.

Previous to his affair with Mimsi, women had only been bit players in the drama of Hecht's life, and came and went as such—frequently and with no billing. Mimsi was different, though, and Rose knew it, so she couldn't remain unaffected. Howard Hawks recalled that Rose, who had taken boxing lessons, went over to Mimsi's apartment building, waited till she came out, then "went up and knocked hell out of her." Rose then returned to New York and took a boat to Newfoundland to be alone and think things out. Hecht, typically employing a previously used plot turn, took Mimsi to Quito. Helen Lawrenson recalled, in her memoirs, that "Condé Nast's parties attracted hoity-toity socialites, debs, blue bloods, and wits with sarcastic repartee who talked about Mimsi Taylor, a young socialite model with an exotic Balinese face who had gone to Quito with Ben Hecht. . . . 'To Quito! But why Quito of all places? My dear, her family must be wild. Why couldn't he have taken her to the Riviera?' "

In Ecuador Hecht began *To Quito and Back*, a play about a forty-year-old writer named Alexander Sterns who leaves his wife to run off to Quito with a young society girl named Lola Hobbs. There they became caught up in a people's revolution against the upper classes, all the while staying at the villa of an American countess modeled on Mimsi's Aunt Dorothy. Sterns has told the girl that his wife promised him a divorce, but as the play progresses Lola discovers that he has been lying.

> STERNS: I came away with you because I had that mania, peculiar to middle age, to live again. I admit I fell in love with you . . . when you're young, love fills the world for you. When you get older, it merely fills your heart.
>
> LOLA: You try and leave me. . . .
>
> STERNS: You remind me wonderfully of my wife. . . . I'm not a man full of superior attitudes whom you've loved so flatteringly. I'm a goddamned child half-frightened to death of life and all its realistic practitioners who are able to crawl through the panic of existence like turtles. . . .
>
> LOLA: All you wanted was to live on two stages and be perfect on each. You're unhappy now because you can't bear being admired by just one woman.

Lola and Sterns grow further and further apart as he becomes more involved with the successful revolution, a friend of the new president, Zamiano, who likes him because of a film he once wrote, *Pancho Rides Again*. Sterns has Zamiano close all the movie theatres on "the theory that the education of the masses begins with the abolition of the movies." "They'll suffer for a while," he tells Zamiano, "but in a week or two their complexions will clear up and the brain cells will begin to stir— faintly. . . . The People have only one amazing characteristic that has never changed. It's their inability to think. They knit their brows, they grunt, they screw up their faces, they shoot a few of their fellows in the name of freedom now and then and presto! The light goes out."

> ZAMIANO: Yeah, I know that. They're pretty dumb. But even a dog doesn't go back to where he gets kicked all the time.

STERNS: But he stays a dog. He doesn't find himself walking around on his hind legs with his head full of very undoggish philosophies. . . . The Proletariat is strutting around on its hind legs and the strain is beginning to tell. They want to get back to their garbage cans.

A fascist counterrevolution is planned by the former ruling class, led by the countess's lover, who had been a barber. Sterns goes to fight with Zamiano, Lola to the American embassy. In the ensuing battle Sterns is killed, neatly avoiding the choice he otherwise would have had to make between his wife and Lola.

In real life, Hecht chose Rose. In the play Lola asks Sterns, "Do you want to go back to her?" "No," he replies, "I want never to have left her."

"I think I experienced as much agony as possible," Rose said of Hecht's affair with Mimsi. "To me the . . . discovery of an infidelity was shattering. He had disappeared into another continent. . . . Alone in Newfoundland I believed I had lost him. It was his birthday, and I sat alone on some strange promontory, a terrace?—before the sea—and like a mirage! like some young Noël Coward play, I saw his life, still alive before me and I felt the joy that it was not over. I suppose it was like a mother's joy—this discovery. I wrote him a letter—a letter with love in it, for his birthday. It ended the dangerous amour."

The revitalization of his marriage and the split from Mimsi energized Hecht, who threw himself into scriptwriting with a vengeance, producing rewrite after rewrite as well as the occasional original, all the while steadily turning out pages of what he would consider his favorite work of fiction, *A Book of Miracles*.

In Hollywood, Hecht and MacArthur scripted *Murder at "21,"* the picture they had contracted to write the year before for Sam Goldwyn. An unexceptional gangster yarn with the obligatory reporter hero, it was filmed by Robert Florey and released as *King of Gamblers*. Shortly afterwards, Sam Goldwyn took a look at the rushes of John Ford's *Hurricane*. Although he was satisfied with how Ford had handled the exterior action sequences, he wanted all the interiors reshot and new dialogue written. He had the footage screened for Hecht, then asked him what he thought.

"I think it stinks," Hecht told him. "So do I," Goldwyn concurred. "I want you to rewrite it and you've only got seventy-two hours to do it." Hecht shut himself up in his study and rewrote the dialogue in return for twenty-five thousand dollars. Goldwyn had the interiors already shot scrapped and Ford started over with Hecht's new material.

Hecht then bounced to David Selznick, who was ready to start shooting *A Star Is Born* but wasn't really happy with the script. *Star* derived from *What Price Hollywood?* (produced by Selznick at RKO), the story of a waitress who is made a star by an alcoholic director whose career wanes as hers ascends, driving him to suicide. Since *What Price Hollywood?* had been scripted by Rowland Brown and Gene Fowler, Selznick had hired Brown to rewrite the *Star* script prepared by William Wellman and Robert Carson. Brown told Selznick the script was fine and needed no changes, but Selznick always believed that any script could be improved if rethought by different writers: "The script is perfect, tomorrow we start rewriting." Thus, Selznick asked Hecht and Fowler to take a look at it. The Wellman/Carson story had switched the director from *What Price Hollywood?* to a silent-screen star who can't make the transition to the talkies, based on the life of actor John Bowers, who had committed suicide in November of 1936. Bowers had rented a sailboat, telling a friend he was going to "sail into the sunset" and never return, which is how the Wellman/Carson script ended.

MacArthur and Hecht had been friends with silent-screen idol John Gilbert, whose career was allegedly ruined by talking pictures because his tenor voice didn't jibe with the romantic, swashbuckling roles he was known for. (In fact, his life and career were sabotaged by L. B. Mayer, but that is another story.) One evening in the fall of 1935 when Hecht and MacArthur were socializing with Gilbert and a few friends at his Malibu beach house, Gilbert had jumped up and announced he was going to kill himself by swimming out to sea. He rushed out of the house before anyone could stop him but was back an hour later, drenched. Opening his mouth to talk, he vomited instead, then collapsed on the floor. "Always the silent star," MacArthur quipped. In 1934 Gilbert had made his last picture, adapted from Wallace Smith's novel *The Captain Hates the Sea*. A few months after his "suicide" attempt, "he went to a gay Hollywood party. While he was dancing with a movie queen," Hecht wrote, "his toupee fell off. Amid shouts of laughter he retrieved it from under the dancer's feet. He was found dead the next morning in bed—in his castle on the hill." Based on their knowledge of Gilbert, Hecht and Fowler polished the *Star* script, changing the ending so the protagonist walks into the Pacific when he commits suicide. Selznick then turned the script over to Dorothy Parker and her husband, Alan Campbell, for further rewrites.

* * *

HAZEL: I don't suppose newspapermen get married as a rule?

WALLY: Not after they're fourteen or fifteen. That's the dangerous age for the journalist. His ideals are not yet formed and he falls easy prey to every waitress. But once his finer side is born, he waits.

HAZEL: Waits for what?

WALLY: For the sound of the fire alarm, Miss Flagg— waiting to go rushing off to the fire.

HAZEL: What fire is that, Mister Cook?

WALLY: Love . . .

HAZEL: Are you looking for a big fire, skipper, or just a little one made out of strawberry boxes and lies?

WALLY: It doesn't matter. It's usually out before your hook and ladder gets there.

When David Selznick's principal backer, Jock Whitney, wanted him to produce a screwball comedy starring Carole Lombard, Selznick commissioned Hecht in April of 1937 to write an "original" for her and Fredric March (born Frederick Bickel in Racine, Wisconsin, where his sister and Hecht had been high-school classmates). After a few weeks, however, Hecht had only completed an outline about a group of rich tourists "devoid of all human problems, with neither ideals nor morals," one of whom falls in love with a nightclub singer in Havana. He convinces her to return to New York with him, then, when he goes bankrupt, starts grooming her to marry one of his friends. "He'll fix her up with a history of family connections and if it's the last thing he does, he'll put her over." Of the script itself, Hecht had only completed the opening scene, in which his group of socialites, on board an ocean liner, passes through the Panama Canal, which Hecht had done on his return to the United States from Quito.

Selznick rejected Hecht's outline, in part because the Hays Office would never pass the New York sequences—the nightclub singer co-habiting with the playboy—but mainly because there wasn't enough time for Hecht to complete the script before the shooting was to begin. Selznick's brother Myron was Carole Lombard's agent and since she had previous commitments, he had only agreed to let her do the picture if photography began in mid-June, six weeks off. On top of this, Selznick had contracted March (also through Myron) at fifteen thousand dollars a week. At the end of April, with nothing on paper other than Hecht's outline, March's contract lapsed, and Selznick had to pay an additional thirty-five thousand dollars to renew it.

Selznick proposed to Hecht that they take a trip to New York so they could work with director William Wellman on a script. Hecht, David and Irene Selznick, the Jock Whitneys, William Wellman, Robert Carson, and the latest addition to Hecht's writing factory, Charlie Samuels, entrained for New York on the *Santa Fe Chief*. The Whitneys and the Salznicks secluded themselves in their private car, taking their meals alone, David not emerging to work either with Hecht or with Wellman. When the Whitneys and the Selznicks left the train in Chicago to fly to the Kentucky Derby, Hecht and Wellman had the Whitneys' private store of vintage champagne broken out, Charlie Samuels instructed to round up all the attractive women he could find for a party in the Selznicks' private car. Piqued by David's snobbery, Hecht and Wellman made sure every bottle of the wine had been consumed by the time they arrived at Pennsylvania Station.

In New York, Selznick engaged a suite in the Waldorf Towers, renting rooms on a lower floor for his entourage. There, Hecht and Wellman tinkered with a new story that they couldn't get to work. Selznick then had to return to the Coast, so Hecht retired to Nyack to work on *A Book of Miracles*. In desperation, Selznick sent his story-conference secretary to New York to get Hecht back to work on the plot he and Wellman had devised. In the meantime, Val Lewton (Selznick's story editor and Alla Nazimova's nephew) came across a magazine short story, "Letter to the Editor," that Selznick thought had possibilities. He bought the rights for $2,500 and had it read over the phone to his secretary in New York, who transcribed it and passed it on to Hecht.

After settling on a fee of thirty thousand dollars—if the script were completed no later than the end of May—Hecht went to work immediately, amused by the tale of a small-town girl, allegedly dying of radium poisoning, who is exploited for her human-interest value by a large New York daily. Hecht had a deal in the works with Sam Goldwyn necessitating his return to Hollywood, so he wrote a first draft during the four-day train ride west on the *Twentieth Century* and the *Super Chief*. By the end of the month Hecht had finished the script—retitled *Nothing Sacred*. Then, also for Selznick, he did a quick polish job on *Tom Sawyer*, which Johnny Weaver had adapted. Selznick approved Hecht's *Nothing Sacred* script except for the ending, which he wanted changed so the Walter

Burns–like editor is not a heartless manipulator but the foil of the cynical reporter. Hecht reacted with exasperation. He had written in a part for John Barrymore, in failing health and desperate financial straits, but when Barrymore couldn't remember his lines Selznick refused him the role. For Hecht that was the last straw.

The climax of Hecht's version had the New York reporter, who had sought out the dying girl, fall in love with her; then, after she has been given the key to the city, been fêted by New York society, and wept over by thousands of the newspaper's readers, she and the reporter discover that she really isn't going to die. The editor, who has used her plight to sell papers, exposes her as a fraud to get his paper off the hook—and, of course, to sell more papers. Selznick, afraid of the bad press the picture would receive at the hands of the slandered fourth estate, rejected the ending. Hecht facetiously proposed the film end with the birth of quintuplets in the United States, the public immediately forgetting the dying girl. Then he quit, leaving Selznick without an ending. Forced to begin principal photography, Selznick hired Ring Lardner, Jr., and Budd Schulberg to devise an acceptable climax. They had the girl and the reporter sail secretly for Europe, the editor reporting the girl's death to the public. Selznick really didn't like their solution but, under time pressure, approved it and had Dorothy Parker polish the dialogue.

Hecht then turned his attention to Goldwyn, who wanted to sign him to a year's contract at six thousand dollars a week. (Hecht offered to have his script factory write all of Goldwyn's films, but Goldwyn ultimately turned him down since it would give Hecht too much power in the studio.) Goldwyn planned to produce a Ziegfeld-style extravaganza and needed a story line to thread the different acts together. Spoofing L. B. Mayer and Lillie Messinger, an assistant Mayer consulted about the popularity of movie plots, Hecht devised a story about a movie producer who, beset with problems caused by temperamental actors, hires an unsophisticated young girl he dubs Miss Humanity—the embodiment of mass taste—to view his variety-show acts and tell him whether she likes them or not.

Months later, the film in the can, Hecht turned up at the studio with several friends to screen the picture but Goldwyn refused them entry to the projection room. Hecht asked him if it was "a desperate attempt to save it from the public," but admitted that "the significance was lost on him."

"I left in a childish huff," Hecht said. "I packed my luggage, crossed off a couple of zeros on my next year's income and went to New York." In retaliation, when Goldwyn wanted to buy the rights to *Jumbo*, Hecht sold them instead to Goldwyn's arch-rival, Louis B. Mayer.

Their falling out, however, wouldn't prevent Goldwyn from later acquiring the rights to Hecht and MacArthur's adaptation of *Wuthering Heights*. After Hecht and MacArthur made *Soak the Rich* at Astoria in 1935, Walter Wanger had resigned as head of Paramount's East Coast studio and gone into independent production, releasing his films through Goldwyn–United Artists. The first project he wanted to film was the Emily Brontë novel.

While Wanger tried to locate the capital, Hecht and MacArthur sailed up to Alexander Woollcott's island in Vermont to knock out the script. Woollcott, a longtime admirer of the Brontës, plagued them with questions about the adaptation. Hecht told him, "You know that part of the story were Heathcliff leaves England and goes off to make his fortune? Well, we thought that had good picture possibilities. You know: Heathcliff among the Indians, his adventures crossing the plains. Maybe striking it rich in California. We're developing the story from that angle." Every day after they finished work, Hecht and Charlie would type out a few pages about Heathcliff fighting Indians and read them to Woollcott, who ranted, "You have raped Emily Brontë!" "She's been waiting breathless for years," Charlie rejoined. Woollcott wouldn't find out the truth until four years later when the film was released.

While Hecht and MacArthur were adapting the book, Wanger tried to sell Goldwyn on the idea of producing it, but he refused. When Wanger demanded to know why, Goldwyn told him, "Because I don't like stories with people dying at the end." With Leland Hayward, Hecht and MacArthur then decided to produce *Wuthering Heights* as a stage play, but when Sylvia Sidney, whom Wanger wanted to play Cathy, interested William Wyler in the film project, they dropped their plans to put it on Broadway. Wyler, on loan to Warners, showed the script to his leading lady, Bette Davis, who took it to Jack Warner and insisted he buy it for her. When Goldwyn got wind of the fact that Warners wanted the project he asked Wyler, one of his house directors, whether he thought Merle Oberon could play the lead. Wyler assured him she could, reminding Goldwyn that she was British. Goldwyn bought the script and produced the film he was to consider his personal favorite, tacking on an ending unbeknownst to Wyler in which Heathcliff and Cathy are reunited in heaven. The film won the New York Critics Award for best picture of the year but lost money at the box office and wouldn't recoup its costs until it was reissued in the fifties.

*   *   *

Early in September of 1937, Hecht returned to New York for the rehearsals of *To Quito and Back,* scheduled as the first production of the season by the Theatre Guild. (Hecht also began work on two new plays he foresaw on Broadway after *To Quito and Back—A Handful of Isoldes* and *The Maladjusted.*) Covici bought the play, then on October 6th, after a two-week tryout in Boston, it opened in New York starring Sylvia Sidney, whom Hecht had known since the twenties, when Horace Liveright had had an affair with her. Hecht told the press, "I have decided to come back and marry the stage, if it will have me. I'm through writing pictures for good." The reviews, however, changed his mind. Brooks Atkinson wrote that "the pampered passenger is likely to suspect that the round-trip is not to Quito and back but to the dictionary and back to the thesaurus," and the *Herald-Tribune* opined that "it talked itself to death in a suicidal sort of frenzy." George Jean Nathan was not so kind: "The result was a play that . . . was so boozy with rhetoric and so bibacious with Brown Derby animadversions . . . that even the most loyal theatre-goer suffered a painful ringing in the ears before the evening was half over and battled with an impulse to get out, run around to a film parlor, and seek some less pretentious, less verbose, less postureful, and more relieving entertainment in one of Hecht's melodramatic Hollywood movies."[1]

Hecht stopped work on his two other plays and by May of 1938 was back in Hollywood, where he now announced to the press, "I'd rather do a movie any day than a stage play—it's far more fun."

Rowland Brown, reputedly a member of the Purple Gang during the twenties, had been down on his luck for years, no longer directing and having a hard time wangling scripting assignments. When Warner Bros. gave him the chance to write *Angels with Dirty Faces* for director Michael Curtiz, he didn't want to bungle it, so he went to Hecht and MacArthur for help, which they willingly gave. (The following year Brown's script would receive an Academy nomination for Best Original Story.)

Around this time, Hecht's and MacArthur's script of *Gunga Din* went into production as well. William Faulkner had worked on an earlier script, and Lester Cohen had done a treatment for King Vidor, but when Howard Hawks was hired by RKO in 1936 he had thrown out the earlier material and had Hecht and MacArthur do their own adaptation of the Kipling poem. They had a finished script at year's end, but by that time

Hawks was in the middle of shooting *Bringing Up Baby*. When he went over budget Sam Briskin, head of RKO, fired him. Briskin then left RKO, replaced by Pandro S. Berman, who hired George Stevens to direct *Gunga Din*. "There was never a more ludicrous Hollywood assignment," Donald Ogden Stewart thought. "Imagine putting Hecht and MacArthur on a movie about British imperialism! They were always for the underdog. One of the preliminary scripts was turned back with the notation: 'You just don't seem to understand the white man's burden.' To which Ben and Charlie wrote back, 'The white man's burden seems to be making lots of money. Since we're both white, how about an advance of $20,000?' "

Walter Wanger had been convinced by the Hecht/MacArthur productions at Astoria that it was possible to make pictures of much higher quality than the assembly-line products the studios manufactured. After at first failing to sell *Wuthering Heights* to Goldwyn, he went on to produce Fritz Lang's *You Only Live Once* and Frank Borzage's *History Is Made at Night*, two impressive films by exceptional directors. His next project was what appeared to be a routine Western John Ford wanted to make from a pulp short story, "Stage to Lordsburg." A script had been prepared but Ford, unhappy with it, had Wanger invite Hecht for a weekend cruise to Catalina on his yacht. Constrained by a tight budget, Ford and Wanger wanted Hecht's help without paying fifty thousand dollars for it, so Ford left a copy of the script where Hecht was sure to spot it. When he did, Ford told him, "Well, go ahead and read it."

When Hecht had finished, Ford asked him for his opinion. "It's a good story fundamentally," Hecht ventured, "but it lacks color. Why don't you make the boy a kid just out of prison who's out to revenge his three brothers, and instead of the namby-pamby ingenue why don't you make her a prostitute."

"That's a good idea," Ford agreed.

"Hecht made some other very valuable suggestions on it, he practically laid the whole thing out for me," Ford admitted. "Years later I met him and I talked to him about *Stagecoach*.

" 'I saw the picture. It's damn good,' he says. 'It sounded familiar. Did I ever read it? Was it from a book, a short story?'

" 'It's from a short story,' I said.

" 'I must have read it, it sounds familiar.'

" 'It should. You wrote it,' I told him.

" 'Why, you son of a bitch, I never got paid for it,' he said.

" 'I know, but you were working on something else at the time getting paid.'

" 'I didn't get any screen credit,' he says.

"I says, 'Well, that was beyond me, I had nothing to do with that.'

"And he laughed. He thought it was a big joke."

Hecht had done a stint at MGM before the Astoria period and returned there in 1938 with his collaborators. Rose Hecht worked uncredited on *Dramatic School* for Mervyn LeRoy and helped adapt Robert Sherwood's play *Idiot's Delight*; Charlie Lederer wrote *Broadway Serenade* and *Within the Law*, while Charlie Samuels roughed out stories. Hecht himself scripted *Let Freedom Ring*, a typical Western in plot—a young man returns home from college to find a cattle baron terrorizing the local ranchers; he organizes a group of workmen and takes over a newspaper to fight the evil cattleman's strong-arm methods—which on another level was an anti-Nazi, anti-fascist parable, the Spanish Civil War having just been lost, the invasion of Poland imminent. *Variety* commented that the film was "in line with the current tide of patriotism . . . the first in the cycle of film offerings to stress the American type of democracy and freedom for the classes and the masses." Hecht, inspired by the events taking place in Europe, nevertheless took part of his inspiration from a play of the same name done on Broadway three years earlier, adapted from Grace Lumpkin's proletarian novel *To Make My Bread*, published in 1932. The novel told the story of two families, driven from their homes by big business, who became involved in labor strikes. Hecht played on the same themes of righteousness, patriotism, and equality for the masses, but neatly switched the villain from the capitalist at home to the fascist abroad.

In December of that year Hecht did a quick rewrite of *I Take This Woman* for MGM, which MacArthur had plotted six months earlier. Determined to make Hedy Lamarr a star, L. B. Mayer was producing the film personally, the only time he was ever to do so. Josef von Sternberg had been hired to direct, but when he read MacArthur's story, "New York Cinderella," he quit. Mayer replaced him with Frank Borzage, who had to leave when a previous commitment intervened, so "Woody" Van Dyke, known for his speed, was hired. (Shooting was going on so long that around Hollywood the picture was being called *I Retake This Woman*.) Mayer hired Hecht at the same time, since his speed was also legend; by the end of January he had completed a forty-nine-page synopsis, which Mayer used to complete the film.

That same December Hecht and Herman Mankiewicz teamed up to write *It's a Wonderful World,* also for MGM. Mankiewicz had left Paramount for MGM in 1933, shortly after David Selznick quit RKO to head his own MGM unit. By the end of the thirties, Mankiewicz had become an alcoholic and had brutalized so many producers with his wit that MGM was the only studio in town where he could work and then only because L. B. Mayer respected him. Hecht wrote of Mank that he "could puncture egos, draw blood from pretenses—and his victims, with souls abashed, sat still and laughed. The swiftness of his thought was by itself a sort of comedy. Never have I known a man with so quick an eye and ear—and tongue—for the strut of fools. Once Mayer had offered a five-thousand-dollar bonus to anyone who could come up with a slogan that would increase audience attendance at MGM films. Mankiewicz had suggested, 'Show the movies in the streets and drive them into the theatres.'" (Nunnally Johnson claims this quip as well.) Together Hecht and Mankiewicz wrote one of the decade's funnier screwball comedies, the story of the mad exploits of a private detective (James Stewart) and a poetess (Claudette Colbert). Hecht named one of the characters Willie Heyward and another Herman Plotka, the first a reference to Leland Hayward, the second a combination of Herman Mankiewicz and Mildred Plotka, Lily Garland's real name in *Twentieth Century.* Mankiewicz plotted the story with Hecht, then Hecht turned it into a screenplay, finishing it at the beginning of February.

At dawn on Sunday, February 20th, 1939, David Selznick—Genghis Selznick, as Hecht called him in a letter to Fowler—and director Victor Fleming shook Hecht awake to inform him he was on loan from MGM and must come with them immediately and go to work. On the drive to the studio Hecht agreed to a fee of fifteen thousand dollars, only then informing Selznick that he hadn't read the Margaret Mitchell novel, *Gone With the Wind,* which Selznick had been preparing for three years and which he had begun shooting five weeks before.

> David was outraged . . . but decided there was no time
> for me to read the long novel. The Selznick overhead on
> the idle *Wind* stages was around fifty thousand a day. David
> announced that he knew the book by heart and that he

would brief me on it. For the next hour I listened to David recite its story. I had seldom heard a more involved plot. My verdict was that nobody could make a remotely sensible movie out of it. Fleming, who was reputed to be part Indian, sat brooding at his own council fires. I asked him if he had been able to follow the story David had told. He said no. I suggested then that we make up a new story, to which David replied with violence that every literate human in the United States except me had read Miss Mitchell's book, and we would have to stick to it. I argued that surely in two years of preparation someone must have wangled a workable plot out of Miss Mitchell's Ouidalike flight into the Civil War. David suddenly remembered the first "treatment," discarded three years before. It had been written by Sidney Howard . . . after an hour of searching, a lone copy of Howard's work was run down in an old safe. David read it aloud. We listened to a precise and telling narrative of *Gone With the Wind*.

We toasted the dead craftsman and fell to work. Being privy to the book, Selznick and Fleming discussed each of Howard's scenes and informed me of the habits and general psychology of the characters. They also acted out the scenes, David specializing in the parts of Scarlett and her drunken father and Vic playing Rhett Butler and a curious fellow I could never understand called Ashley. He was always forgiving his beloved Scarlett for betraying him with another of his rivals. David insisted that he was a typical Southern gentleman and refused flatly to drop him out of the movie.

After each scene had been performed and discussed, I sat down at the typewriter and wrote it out. Selznick and Fleming, eager to continue with their acting, kept hurrying me. We worked in this fashion for seven days, putting in eighteen to twenty hours a day. Selznick refused to let us eat lunch, arguing that food would slow us up. He provided bananas and salted peanuts. On the fourth day a blood vessel in Fleming's right eye broke, giving him more an Indian look than ever. On the fifth day Selznick toppled into a torpor while chewing on a banana. The wear and tear on me was less, for I had been able to lie on the couch and half doze while the two darted about acting. Thus on the seventh day I had completed, unscathed, the first nine reels of the Civil War epic.

In fact, Hecht worked for two weeks on the script, part of the time with playwright John Van Druten. Hecht's account of Selznick suddenly "remembering" the Sidney Howard "treatment" that he had "discarded three years before" is apocryphal, since the Howard script was the only one Selznick had, although extensively revised by Oliver H. P. Garrett, with minor emendations by F. Scott Fitzgerald. Also, Hecht, Selznick, and Fleming couldn't "toast the dead craftsman" since Howard was alive! Six months after Hecht worked on the script Howard was killed in a tractor accident on his Massachusetts farm. Richard Harwell in his essay on the preproduction for *Gone With the Wind* reduces Hecht's contribution to next to nothing (except for writing the titles that introduce the major divisions of the movie). "Historians of *Gone With the Wind* have given too much credence to Hecht's account in his *Child of the Century* . . . Hecht's account is so full of demonstrable untruths and exaggerations (as is the rest of that autobiography) that it should be heavily discounted."

It is impossible to determine exactly how much Hecht scripted. In all likelihood it was not the nine reels he claimed but certainly more than Harwell believes. In the official credits filed with the Screen Writers' Guild, Sidney Howard was of course awarded the sole screen credit, but four other writers were appended under the heading "Other Substantial Contributors (writers whose contribution represented more than 10% of the value of completed screen play)." Jo Swerling was noted as contributing to the treatment, Oliver H. P. Garrett and Barbara Keon (Selznick's scenario assistant) to screenplay construction, and Hect to dialogue, so it would appear Hecht's influence was not insubstantial.

The film Hecht was working on when he was interrupted by Selznick was *Day at the Circus* for the Marx brothers (shortened to *At the Circus* when released). He only did an outline, which MGM had rewritten—to little avail, since it remains one of the Marx Brothers' lesser works. Next, Hecht wrote the original story and scenario of *Lady of the Tropics*, with a part in it for Pepi Schildkraut.

In the middle of the scripting, a writer Hecht knew from the back room of Stanley Rose's bookshop, a hack writer of Westerns for Republic, sent him the galleys of his fourth (and what would be his last) novel. Nathanael West had six proofs of *The Day of the Locust* bound and sent to Scott Fitzgerald, Aldous Huxley, Edmund Wilson, Erskine Caldwell, George Milburn, and Hecht to see what they thought of his Hollywood tale.

*   *   *

The Front Page had begun a cycle of newspaper pictures that continued to the end of the decade, with Lee Tracy—who had starred in the original stage version—as the pattern from which the reporter was cut. In the mid-thirties, though, girl reporters had been introduced to provide romantic interest. It was only natural then for Howard Hawks to think of switching the play's tough male reporter to a woman—which wouldn't even entail changing Hildy Johnson's name.

Hawks always maintained that Hecht and MacArthur's dialogue was the best that anybody had ever written for him, as well as being the most modern dialogue written for the screen at that time. To prove his point—at a party at his Hollywood home one evening—he decided to read a scene from *The Front Page*. He took the editor's part but needed someone to read the part of the reporter. He got a young actress to read Hildy's part and got an idea at the same time. The day after the party, Hawks phoned Gene Fowler to ask him if he would work on a story for him.

"What are you going to do?" Fowler wanted to know.

"Ben's story, *The Front Page*, in terms of a girl."

"I wouldn't be a party to such nonsense," Fowler replied. "Why don't you call up Ben and see what he thinks about it."

Hawks telephoned Hecht: "What would you think about changing Hildy Johnson and making him a girl?"

"I wish we'd had that idea," Hecht responded.

"Well, I want to buy it and remake it as a picture if that's all right with you."

Hecht agreed and with Charlie Lederer drove to Hawks's Palm Springs house to begin work on a screenplay. They figured it would increase the pace of the already incredibly fast-moving story if they made the two main characters a divorced couple with editor Cary Grant trying to lure his ex-wife, Rosalind Russell, back to him and the paper. They edited out the more risqué lines because they didn't fit the changed conception and also to avoid any censorship problems. (When Lewis Milestone shot the original version ten years earlier he had neither of these problems so had done the play almost verbatim.) After Hecht and Lederer had plotted the new story line, Hecht returned to Los Angeles while Lederer stayed in Palm Springs to write the shooting script. Hawks acquired the film rights from Howard Hughes, who retained them from the 1931 production, then got Columbia to produce.

Why Do They Make Me Write Like That?

In the fall of 1938, *A Book of Miracles* was finished after more than two years of work, the longest time Hecht had ever taken to write anything. He received a two-thousand-dollar advance from Covici-Friede in October, but shortly afterward Pat Covici's publishing house went out of business. Donald Friede had sold his stock in 1935 to move to Los Angeles, where he set up shop as an agent; then at the end of 1938 Covici's printer called in all Covici's notes, forcing him to close his doors. Covici went to work for Viking, which issued *A Book of Miracles* in June of the following year. Not only was it Hecht's favorite, it is arguably the best work of fiction he was ever to produce. Years later, he commented that he was "proudest of the *Miracle* book. The critics praised it greatly. But hardly anyone read it. Even in London where it was identified as one of the important books of our time, it remained unread."

The book is made up of seven long stories, each involving a miracle. "The Missing Idol" tells the story of a movie star playing Christ in a Biblical epic. The star is transported to Heaven for an audience with God. Because God has confused the movie set with events that took place involving His son some eternal seconds earlier, God imbues the actor with his heavenly light, reasoning He'll do things differently this time and use the movies to spread His glory. Unfortunately, the actor, when returned to the set, is glowing with God's light to such an extent that he is invisible on film. His contract is cancelled—the producers insured against "acts of God"—and his career ruined. "He had felt in his bones something of this sort would happen when God had begun asking those questions about the inside of the movie business. God had tumbled another idol, which in its debris, was in no mood to spread the Almighty's fame."

Another story, "The Heavenly Choir," was a scathing indictment of advertising based on the career of Albert Lasker, the founder of Lord and Thomas, the most successful and powerful ad agency in the world during the twenties and thirties. (Lasker is the man who, when asked how his campaign to sell a new product called Kleenex was coming along, replied, "Fine. Women are beginning to waste it.")

"The Adventures of Professor Emmett," the last tale in the collection, was the most revealing. The first section recounts the life of a professor of entomology, Gifford Emmett, who is mysteriously metamorphosed into an ant. Gifford the ant discovers that the world is in the process of being destroyed by a new breed of termite that eats stone.

Through a series of fantastic events, Gifford warns the world of the peril before he is inadvertently squashed when a book is snapped shut on him.

When Gifford first learns of the stone-devouring termite, he decides to let man perish. Then he changes his mind. His reasons are Hecht's, the clearest exposition of his feelings and ideas about life and its purpose he was ever to write.

> The humanity that he had condemned was speaking to him. . . . Consider, it went on softly, consider who we are, and the darkness out of which our mind was born. Consider how ancient the beast is beside the little furrow of thought that has come to mark its brow. Though in our ignorance we have spilled a great deal of blood, we have also wrestled a little wisdom out of the dark. In the midst of our lusts and bigotries we have found time to draw maps of the heavens, to examine the roots of plants, to peer through microscopes at our bacterial forefathers, and to pry open a fraction or two the doors of mystery.
>
> And listening to this cajoling voice in him, Gifford beheld slowly another vision of humanity. He looked at its science. Behind the political diseases of its centuries, hidden in the ugly shadows of its religions and conquests, he beheld the isolate mind of man—a never-dying light that gleamed through the ogreish history of the race. . . .
>
> Though we have come forward only a small way, it is a noble inch we have moved. . . .
>
> And Gifford thought of the scientists, of the eyes that had kept everlastingly peering out of the human shambles at the ways of the moon, the sun, the stars, winds, birds, beasts, and all the elements and exudations of Nature. . . .
>
> And Gifford recalled these immortal heroes of the mind whose names were written on the small scroll of wisdom. Where the many others had butchered and lusted and left behind the gaudy, vanishing tracks of conquest, these few had toiled and died and left only some tiny fact to mark the small road of learning. But how much brighter this little way shone than all the tracks of glory. . . .
>
> These are the mind of man, thought Gifford; these are the law-givers and the rulers of the world. These are the soul of the race. All the rest is a froth of hunger and ego, lust and lies and actors sick with the need of applause. The light of these remains to deny the most abominable darkness. I have judged wrongly. . . . The list of human

evils is long and the record of human honor small and scattered. But it is worthy of survival.

Late in 1939, Hecht decided to make another stab at independent, East Coast film production in order to retain creative control, remain in the East, and keep a percentage of the grosses. To accomplish this though he had to raise the money. "After several conferences with a bank president, I had been assured that the bank would put up half the finances needed were I able to lay hands on the other half. This is not such a bonanza as it sounds. It is exactly like being promised the Lackawanna Railroad, providing you can go out and buy the New York Central first." During the latter part of the year and the early months of 1940, he tried to scare up the other half of the cash, announcing to the press regularly that production was about to begin. To publicize the project, he met with Mayor LaGuardia, himself trying to interest Hollywood studios in making films in New York City. Hecht also asked New York's flamboyant former mayor Jimmy Walker to appear in the picture.

He got plenty of publicity but no backers for a film titled, ironically, *Angels Over Broadway*. In January, he worked out a distribution deal with Columbia Pictures, then in February announced that photography would begin March 10th at the old Biograph studios in the Bronx—but once again he failed to raise the necessary cash. As a last resort, he turned to Columbia for financing. Columbia's president, Harry Cohn, had made his studio stand for pictures of quality, and a Ben Hecht film would add prestige. Also, since it wouldn't cost much, he was more than willing to accept Hecht's proposal, but he made one condition: Hecht had to shoot the movie on the lot in Hollywood. Hecht agreed, since it was that or not make the picture at all, though it meant giving up an East Coast production and tied him back into studio financing. Hecht, in compensation, made one condition of his own: total control. "Cohn looked at me with very sad eyes, sighed heavily and stood aside," Hecht said.

The germ of *Angels Over Broadway* came from an encounter Hecht had had in Chicago in 1923. Lunching at Schlogl's, he, Sherwood Anderson, and several reporters couldn't quite finance a bottle of wine. When a man at an adjoining table offered to treat them, they accepted readily. The man joined them, and for the next two hours recounted the story of his life, how he'd come from Russia and made a success as a box manufacturer. When he'd finished he bought them another bottle and left. The following day Hecht phoned Anderson to tell him that their host had been found floating in the Chicago River. What he'd told them about being a box manufacturer had been true, but a success he was not. He'd lost his business and had withdrawn the last of his savings the day before, paid his debts, lunched at Schlogl's (because he'd always admired writers), then killed himself. Hecht wrote the story up as "Don Quixote and His Last Windmill" for his "1001 Afternoons" column, and Anderson related it in his *Memoirs*, considering it "one of the classic stories of American life." For his film, Hecht metamorphosed the box manufacturer into an embezzler, his crime newly discovered, who decides to have a last night on the town before committing suicide.

In June, shooting began, with Lee Garmes doing the cinematography. George Antheil wrote the music, and Douglas Fairbanks, Jr., starred, coproduced, and assisted with the casting. Hecht played his violin between scenes and, working closely with Garmes, who was codirecting with him, finished the picture eight days ahead of schedule.

When Harry Cohn saw the final cut, he decided to reedit it himself, a frequent practice of his that infuriated writers and directors. Cohn insisted that he had a "fool-proof device for deciding whether a picture is good or bad—if my ass squirms, it's bad; if my ass doesn't squirm, it's good." (Herman Mankiewicz had lost a job at Columbia by remarking, "Imagine, the whole world wired to Harry Cohn's ass.") Apparently, Cohn's ass squirmed when he ran *Angels Over Broadway,* or he found the film too offbeat for Rita Hayworth, whom he was intent on making a star. When Hecht, back in New York, learned what Cohn was doing from a filmcutter at Columbia, he reminded Cohn that his contract gave him final cut and that if Cohn didn't keep his hands off the picture he'd sue. Harry wasn't fazed, so Hecht decided to take the matter up with the studio's business manager, Jack Cohn, of whom George Jessel quipped, "His bark is no worse than his brother." In his memoirs, Dick Maney recalled the meeting.

Facing Jack Cohn, head of the cartel, Nate Spingold, Columbia pooh-bah, and one of their legal beagles, Ben refused to sit down. Indicating me with a wave of his hand, he said: "This is Richard Maney. He is a press agent, widely and favorably known in the amusement world. I have told him that your West Coast mercenaries have mutilated *Angels Over Broadway.* Unless it is restored immediately to the form I approved last Tuesday, Mr. Maney will wire every movie editor and critic in the land of your infamy tonight.

He'll brand you as vandals. He'll detail your treachery. He'll blast your pretensions and spotlight your ignorance."

"Come, come, Ben. Be reasonable," chorused Spingold and Cohn. "You wouldn't do that. Let's talk it over. We'll . . ."

Signaling me to precede him, Ben stalked to the door, then turned to deliver his valedictory: "You have two hours to think it over and confer with your hatchet-men in California. Mr. Maney and I are going to '21' for refreshments. You can reach me there. If I do not hear from you by four o'clock I'm turning Maney loose."

At "21," Hecht composed his press release:

A movie minus one arm, one ear and with its feet bashed is about to come limping into your ken shortly. The picture is called *Angels Over Broadway* and was written, directed and produced by me. A number of fine actors including Doug Fairbanks, Jr., and Thomas Mitchell are in it. After I had completed my work the picture was taken into the operating room by Harry Cohn, president of Columbia. Mr. Cohn, giddy with his artistic labors in the Blondie Series, fell upon my work with the most mysterious illiterate fervor I have ever encountered in Hollywood. He recut my movie in such a way as has left me and it and all my actors and associates shuddering. The cyclonic stupidity which Mr. Cohn turned on my work leaves me with no redress other than this. I humbly submit that I worked hard to make this picture worthy of your more serious attention and I apologize in advance for the garbled Harry Cohn version of my work with which your eyes are to be assailed shortly. If you are interested in further details of my seemingly desperate stand against Columbia's unholy sabotaging tactics I am to be reached at Nyack, New York. Ben Hecht.

"Ben and I had been in '21' about forty minutes when one of the Kriendlers approached. There was a telephone call for Ben. He came back from the booth, his face wreathed in a triumphant leer. 'They've thrown in the sponge,' he said." The film was released in October 1940 the way Hecht had made it.

The critical reaction to *Angels Over Broadway* was phenomenal,

Morton Thomas in the *Hollywood Citizen* enthusing that "*Angels Over Broadway* is a hit, a very definite creamy hit. And the experiment of putting a good writer in a three-way spot is going to mean till-music at the box office. Ben Hecht is launched on a new phase of a very brilliant career." *The New York Times* called it "the most satisfying of Hecht's work that we have seen." As with *The Scoundrel*, though, Hecht won the critics but not the movie-going public. (It was to get Hecht an Academy nomination for Best Original Screenplay, although Preston Sturges's *The Great McGinty* proved the winner in that category for 1940.) *Angels Over Broadway* would play for the next fifteen years in big-city art houses—it appeared regularly at the Thalia in New York City—but by 1955 it was still twenty thousand dollars short of recouping its production costs.

While preparing *Angels Over Broadway*, Hecht and Charlie Lederer took twelve days to rewrite Herman Mankiewicz's *Comrade X* script (from a story by Walter Reisch, coauthor of the very similar *Ninotchka*); then on the heels of that, Hecht rewrote the script of Vincent Sheean's autobiography *Personal History* for Walter Wanger and Alfred Hitchcock. Sheean's career as a foreign correspondent, redolent of the turn-of-the-century exploits of Richard Harding Davis, had intrigued Wanger with its film possibilities. But when Hecht updated the story, concentrating the action on Nazi intrigues in Europe, Wanger wanted him to redo the entire picture from that angle. Hecht had to refuse, since he was already committed to helping Howard Hawks with the *Billy the Kid* script he was preparing. Wanger dropped *Personal History* and had the film rewritten to fit Hecht's idea of a foreign correspondent haphazardly falling privy to a Nazi assassination plot. During the shooting of the film, retitled *Foreign Correspondent*, Hecht got a call from Wanger and Hitchcock: they were desperate for an ending. Hecht stayed up most of the night and delivered the final pages to Wanger the following morning for a fee of two thousand dollars.

Hecht did a preliminary treatment for Hawks, then began the shooting script based on a story Hawks had heard in New Mexico: Pat Garrett kills another man, purposely blasting his face so he is unrecognizable, permitting Billy the Kid to escape, assumed killed in the shootout with Garrett. "Then Ben went off on something else," Hawks recalled, "and I got Jules Furthman to come in and work on the script."[2] The "something else" Hecht had become involved in was politics. For the first time in years, Hecht's foremost concern wasn't making money through storytelling.

12

THE FORTIES: PROPAGANDA WARS

That Ben Hecht and Gene Fowler and other hardboiled fellers that never before believed passionately in any human causes are now out thundering vehemently has its meaning.

—CARL SANDBURG

Once a revolutionist, always a hack.

—BEN HECHT

"Politics," Hecht said, "is the magic wand that changes people into beetles," an attitude derived from his years as a reporter privy to the inner workings of city hall in the capital of the Middle West, a city notorious for its political corruption. He had infused *The Front Page* with tolerant cynicism toward politics, but by the time of *To Quito and Back* his contempt had turned merciless, even though he killed off his hero fighting alongside a band of revolutionaries. Hecht and his protagonist were as cynical as ever but, a result of the rise of Hitler and Mussolini, they had become involved with an antifascist, anti-imperialist cause, which was in no way typical of them.

The First World War hadn't stirred Hecht's patriotism, and the left-wing activism of his peers during the thirties hadn't engaged him either. During the Depression, when proletarian themes were explored and exploited in the novels of John Dos Passos, John Steinbeck, Dalton Trumbo, Sinclair Lewis, B. Traven, Mike Gold, and Edward Dahlberg, Hecht's books and stories included no social-realist themes, no stories with worker heroes, labor disputes, or political radicals. *Hallelujah, I'm a Bum!* was an exception in that it dealt with the Depression, but at the same time it was an antiproletarian film since it supported the individual, the loner, in opposition to literature's latest hero, the Masses. In *To Quito and Back* Hecht treated proletarians only to savage them.

> In my day when I was a reporter in Chicago, radicalism had something to do with going on a picnic on the first of May . . . no, radicalism has changed from a picnic into a religion. The poor have fallen out of their old heaven, howling and jabbering there is no such place. And the new piety has located the face of God in the mob. . . . There comes a time in all revolutions when the masses get a little punch drunk. A mysterious yearning rises in them, a yearning to surrender to some iron-faced leader who'll rid

them of the necessity of thinking and dreaming. And being heroes. The slide from communism to fascism is on the whole a happy one for the proletariat. It's like exchanging a weird headache for the more familiar pains of servitude.

In the thirties the Hollywood literary community was split into hostile camps by politics, with the formation of two unions to protect writers as other guilds protected the technicians—the cameramen, soundmen, etc. John Howard Lawson, the Broadway playwright and Hollywood screenwriter Hecht had satirized in *Soak the Rich,* was the prime mover behind the organization of the Screen Writers' Guild, which throughout the thirties and early forties agitated for a minimum wage for writers and for a more just system of determining screen credit—since, up till that time, screen credit was decided by the head of the studio or by the film's producer and frequently was neither fair nor accurate. In response to the Guild, the studios formed another union, the Screen Playwrights, in an attempt to retain control over their writers, which caused a long, bitter struggle that made enemies of friends. Hecht's response to the imbroglio was terse: "All those fatheads do is keep voting."

Most writers allied themselves with the Screen Writers' Guild—which in 1938 was certified as the sole bargaining agent for motion picture writers—but Hecht knew writers on both sides. Irving Thalberg, L. B. Mayer, and Jack Warner had founded the Screen Playwrights, whose numbers included John Lee Mahin (who, consequently, became a partial model for Budd Schulberg's Sammy Glick), Laurence Stallings, Rupert Hughes (Howard Hughes's uncle), George Oppenheimer, and Herman Mankiewicz. ("I think Herman did it less out of political commitment than out of plain orneriness," Sam Marx said later; Budd Schulberg: "I think he may have also believed that it was simply not an appropriate activity for writers to organize like workers in other industries. Mank took out an ad in the trade papers saying, 'Writers of the world unite. You have nothing to lose but your brains.'") The Guild's membership included Nathanael West, Dorothy Parker, Lillian Hellman, Ring Lardner, Jr., and Dashiell Hammett. "Stop yelling for your rights because somebody's likely to give them to you, and we'll all be working for $75 a week," Herman Mankiewicz bantered, and Gene Fowler wrote in the *Hollywood Reporter* that writers playing at union organizing would "bring down the papier mâché walls of this rookery like the collapse of an opera hat . . . the threat of strikes and public battle will inspire a Congressional interference that will throw everyone to the ravens."

But Hecht refused to become involved with either faction, especially with the Guild since many of its members were communists. Hecht's feelings about his friends' newfound sympathy for the masses were shared by S. J. Perelman, who wrote, "The noble piety of the Hollywood folks, as they immersed themselves in the plight of the migratory workers and the like, was pretty comical. One couldn't fault them for their social conscience, but when you saw the English country houses they dwelt in, the hundred-thousand-dollar estancias, and the Cadillacs they drove to the protest meetings, it was to laugh."

The right wing was equally ridiculous to Hecht—the profascist groups springing up in Hollywood in response to the pro communist ones, e.g., Victor McLaglen's Light Horse—"It is all ready to ride down the crimson hosts," wrote Alva Johnston, "the moment they start marching on Hollywood"—and the Hollywood Hussars, which Gary Cooper rode for (a partial inspiration for Hecht's use of Dorothy di Frasso in *To Quito and Back* as the character whose lover becomes the leader of the counterrevolutionary forces). Hecht, however, refused to submit to political factionalism, which was not an easy position to hold in the ideologically embattled thirties. The highest-paid, most prolific, and most highly regarded scenarist in Hollywood, Hecht successfully risked noninvolvement, although this isolationism embittered many of his fellow writers. To Hecht, most of the writers and intellectuals of the period, both in Hollywood and New York, were "full of purrs for the new Russia of Lenin and Stalin. My lack of love for the Bolsheviki and all their noble slogans made me seem very callous. My non-communism has nothing to do with the prospect of the Russians conquering Europe, Asia and the world, or with their Marxist notions of how to run factories. It was founded on the single personal fact that in a Communist state I would be either jailed or shot for speaking my mind. I could understand almost anybody espousing Communism except a writing man or a man of active intelligence."

Being duped by the American Communist Party and Herbert Biberman—who was to become one of the Hollywood Ten—contributed to Hecht's distaste for the "comrades." In 1938, Biberman was the party organizer for the Committee of 56, which met once in December at Edward G. Robinson's house to hear Clark M. Eichelberger, director of the League of Nations Association and of the American Union for Concerted Peace Efforts. At the meeting a letter was drafted to President Roosevelt and Congress entreating them to place a boycott on trade with Nazi Germany. John Ford, Charlie Chaplin, Henry Fonda, and Hecht were among the fifty-six signers, most of whom were unaware of the pervasive influence of the Communist Party in the committee's organizing group, the Hollywood Anti-Nazi League. Eight months later, Hitler and Stalin signed a nonaggression pact and Biberman, still collecting signatures to add to the list already sent to Roosevelt, completely reversed his position on Nazi Germany—a move dictated by the party—accusing the committee of warmongering. (As a result of the nonaggression pact, the party charged "England and France with responsibility for the war," "supported Hitler's proposals for . . . settlement of the 'Jewish problem,'" and "sought to defeat all measures intended to aid the powers which were opposing Hitler."[1])

One of Hecht's responses to the split over guilds was to go into independent production in Astoria for a year and a half, but when that experiment failed economically he was forced back to Hollywood. There, he wrote one politically oriented movie, *Let Freedom Ring*, which was nonpartisan in relation to the American political scene and was political only in the sense that it was pro–American democracy and anti–German fascism. Hecht became more explicitly anti-Nazi a year later in *A Book of Miracles*. Politics was on Hecht's mind for the first time in his life as a decade of depression bled into a decade of war.

* * *

"My my, what big teeth you have, Adolf!"

Adolf tore his shawl off his head, let out an awful Nazi snarl and answered:

"The better to eat you with, you good-for-nothing! You and all the Americans who are nothing but Jews with broncos and bows and arrows."

Saying this, Adolf leaped forward with his fangs glistening, and you could see bits of Belgium, Holland, Norway, Denmark, Greece, Czechoslovakia and France hanging from his teeth.

—Ben Hecht
"Johnny, Get Your Gun"
PM

In the spring of 1940, Erich von Stroheim had asked Hecht to work on *Abri: 50 Personnes*, an anti-Nazi screenplay he had outlined in Paris the previous year. The story took place in the basement of an exclusive whorehouse during a Luftwaffe raid on the French capital. Hecht, Stroheim, Irish literary critic Ernest Boyd, and Thomas Quinn Curtis met several times at "21" to discuss adapting Stroheim's story for the stage, changing the setting from Paris to London. Stroheim brought Paul Kohner from Hollywood to produce the play, but Hecht dropped out of the project after a few meetings since he wanted to write about the war in Europe himself, not be a rewrite man for Stroheim. He got his wish and was put back in harness as a newspaperman in 1941 when he became a columnist for the left-wing New York tabloid *PM* (where, as some wag quipped, "Man bites underdog" was the rule). The paper was edited by Ralph Ingersoll, who had been a *New Yorker* editor during the twenties.

Hecht felt the isolationist position the United States was taking was wrong, that the Nazis had to be stopped at all costs, the sooner the better. To this end he used his column, writing emotionally loaded stories and blistering attacks in order to stir people out of their noninterventionist lethargy. Pétain was pictured as a seagull dying on a beach with "shadows from an alien hill drifting over him"; the Hearst press was attacked for "slyly demanding that we stop worrying about such nonsense as helping England," Charles Lindbergh because he kept "hosannaing for the Nazi air force and its invincibility." An open letter to Winston Churchill, noting wryly that at the time the Battle of Britain was being fought twelve thousand complaints of cruelty to animals were lodged and investigated in New York City alone, was signed, "Hoping that these tidings will help the morale of your brave people in these desperate times, I beg to remain one of the proud race of turtle, chick, flea and horse-tail lovers—your American ally, Ben Hecht." In "Wreath for a Little Girl," Hecht pulled out all the stops and told of a little girl and her dog who lived in Plymouth, England. "Betty listened to a screech coming closer. Her arm tightened around her musty old dog. Then Betty and the dog and the street in which they had played other games all disappeared. Two days later the diggers found the remains of a child and her dog. The child was blood-caked. Its legs were missing. Its face was torn. Its eyes were gone. It looked like something fetal and unborn. The diggers found a dog's head in the crook of the stiffened little arm." But Hecht's most forceful piece of moral blackmail as well as his most cutting criticism of American foreign policy occurred in "Prayer to Someone," in which he attempted to shame America into the war.

> We are the loud-mouths of fear. We cower behind an ocean and watch the lights go out, watch the dream of freedom die, watch the hard-won towers of liberty crumble. And our guns are not yet there. . . .
>
> O Lord of battle, we have a statue in our harbor. Hide us from her. . . .

And loud among us is only one voice—the voice of the coward. It is his tongue that clacks the highest in the twilight. The tongue of the coward is the stairway to calamity. We are on those steps. . . .

Our brothers die for an old dream, and our guns are not there. Hunger is in their bellies and our ships are not there. They look to us for the arm that smote Goliath, and we are a mist far away. Their bodies make a wall against our enemy, and we remain pale and timorous behind an ocean. . . .

In September 1941, Hecht rewrote the script of *Ten Gentlemen from West Point* for Darryl Zanuck at 20th Century–Fox, and he and MacArthur collaborated on a one-act play, *Fun to Be Free*, for Fight for Freedom, Inc., a group headed by Herbert Agar agitating for the entry of the United States into the war. The play worked on a purely emotional level, playing on people's patriotism by making the then current situation in Europe analogous to America's decision in the 1770s to fight a war of independence against the British. On September 26th, Rose arrived in Los Angeles to write *Fingers at the Window*, which Charlie Lederer was slated to direct, and at the beginning of October Hecht returned to New York, where Billy Rose staged *Fun to Be Free* at Madison Square Garden. It then went on tour and was published with an introduction by Wendell Willkie denouncing Nazism.[2]

When the Japanese attacked Pearl Harbor on December 7th, Hecht wrote "Uncle Sam Stands Up," bringing the first phase of his propaganda writing to a successful close. It ran in *PM* the following day.

> *The great big gabble-headed*
> *Red, white and blue galoot*
> *Has drawn his Forty-four*
> *And started in to shoot. . . .*
>
> *He sat around and gabbled*
> *And fiddled with his gun*
> *And sort of half regretful*
> *Watched half the world undone.*
>
> *He huffed and puffed and argued,*
> *He yodeled and he sighed,*
> *And watched his fine blood brothers*
> *Get taken for a ride.*

The Forties: Propaganda Wars

But dry your eyes, good Poland,
And lift your head, Paree,
And grin with hope, old England—
He's drawn his snickersnee. . . .

With the U.S. finally in the war, Hecht began gathering Hollywood talent to produce a number of short films on air raids, plane spotting, and possible attack of the U.S. mainland. "One of those Washington three-letter agencies that flourished in such abundance then was in urgent need of these films," George Oppenheimer recalled.[3] "Ben assembled quite a group—Clifford Odets, Lillian Hellman, Maxwell Anderson, George S. Kaufman, Moss Hart, Gene Fowler, and myself among others, with Burgess Meredith as director. We had a meeting at which Ben gave out assignments and asked that the finished scripts be back to him within a week. George Kaufman and I collaborated on our two and in the time specified every script was in Ben's hands. A month or so later the three-lettered agency was disbanded and our scripts disappeared somewhere in the limbo of Washington bureaucracy."

When Stanislaus Szukalski returned to the United States in 1941, a refugee from his native Poland, Hecht used his old friend's experiences with the Nazis to make a further case against Hitler in the pages of *PM* in a piece titled "Hitler's Lost Cause." "For twenty years my friend Szukalski experienced disasters which would have killed off a dozen businessmen," Hecht wrote. "Sickness, hunger and poverty yipped everlastingly at his heels. Defeat stood constantly in his doorway." (In the twenties, Marie Hecht described Szukalski's return to Europe differently: "Stanley married an heiress worth several million dollars; they went to Paris, where he is going on with his work under the most ideal conditions." In 1953, Alson Smith, in *Chicago's Left Bank*, presented another variation: "The Polish wild man walked off with all the marbles, winning a Chicago heiress out from under the very noses of her horrified parents and whisking her off to Hollywood and a life of leisure on the Golden Shore.") Hecht's article described how Szukalski had become a well-known sculptor in Warsaw, his studio open to the public as a museum. Then came the Nazi invasion. The studio was bombed and everything Szukalski had ever drawn, sculpted, or painted was destroyed. In New York, Hecht asked him what he planned to do. "Work," Szukalski answered. "I start over. Poland will need beauty and art when it is free again."[4]

Another old friend Hecht hadn't seen in years showed up in *PM* as "A Poet Out of Yesterday"—Maxwell Bodenheim. Bodenheim hadn't had a book published for almost ten years, his wife Minna had divorced him in 1938, and he had become a Greenwich Village drunk who traded poems for a shot of whiskey. Toothless and ragged, he was agurgle with belief in communism as the solution for all ills, his talk revealing "the radical contortionist trying to poultice a Hitler-bruised rump with a Muscovite valentine." Despite Hecht's dislike for Bodenheim's politics, he painted a sympathetic portrait, calling him "a mathematician of words . . . with a vocabulary as mystic and nimble as the second law of thermodynamics." What was important about Bodenheim was "that so harassed and battered an ego had been able to fall so deeply in love with life. Bodenheim, the butt of hunger and calamity, had taken to singing of the woes and hopes of others." Nevertheless, Bodenheim was only further embittered by Hecht once again capitalizing on him. In retaliation he composed "Sonnet to B.H.," published in *The American Mercury* in July.

> He swung the small, blunt knife of ridicule,
> To hide the effervescence of a soul
> Immersed in gaudy tatters and the rule
> Of those who dropped a condescending dole.
> In parlors he could jeer at poverties
> And label them the natural breath of dumb,
> Neurotic men forever on their knees—
> Laughing before he picked the next stray crumb.
> Eventually he snared the trick of wealth—
> Thin novels, brittle swaggering of plays,
> Cartoons of enemies, with malice, stealth:
> The fashionable wise-cracks, slanting gaze.
> Yet in this ease he found himself still poor.
> Begging for friendship, shivering, insecure.

Hecht also wrote columns about friends Charlie Lederer, Moss Hart, Henry Varnum Poor, Peter Arno, and Harpo Marx. He had convinced Gene Fowler to write a column three times a week for *PM*, and when Fowler arrived in New York from Hollywood Hecht did a piece about him as well.

"Where you from?" said Gus. . . .

"Culver City, California, a stone's throw from Hollywood," said the Fowler. "Been working the MGM lode there. . . ."

"Yes," said Gus, "run by Louis B. Mayer, ain't it?"

"Well, I don't know who runs it," said the Fowler. "Some folks say it's run by a ghost in a long white beard with a noose around his neck. On the other hand, I've heard tell it's operated by an unhappy fellow who at sundown turns into a timber wolf. Maybe they're both legends—but I don't know. . . ."

"Must be fun digging up all that gold and diamonds," said Gus.

"No, son, it's no fun at all. . . . For instance, how would you like to spend your nights robbing graves? . . . Every worker in the MGM lode has got to have seven corpses in his tent just to show he is not a snob. Well, after you've been sitting around with these grinning cadavers week after week, and the Indians burning up your wagons every night . . . Where was I?" The Fowler voice broke off. "Oh, yes, I was telling you about the bleached skulls that line the corridors of old MGM. Just skulls lying there in the moonlight. And some of them talk. Surprises you at first, but you get used to it. Everybody's mighty kind to them— letting 'em pretend that they're running the outfit and supervising production. Here, I've brought one of them back with me." The Fowler smiled tenderly. "I'm going to make him into a tobacco jar."

Charlie Samuels, who researched many of Hecht's stories for him, recalled, "I had some of the most comical and goofy experiences of my life when I worked as a news-digging legman for Hecht's column. He kept up the column when he went to Hollywood, telling me to read all the papers and send any likely-looking items to him. I got all the papers and spent six hours a day clipping them and sending him the items by special delivery air mail. . . . While he was still in California he sent me a mysterious telegram: FIND OLD BOWERY VENUS AND INTERVIEW HER AT ONCE. I went to the missions on the Bowery, the police stations, talked to bums, the owners of flophouses, old reporters. None of them had ever heard of any Bowery Venus. In despair I called him up . . . 'There is no Bowery Venus,' I said.

" 'You're certainly getting dopey,' he said. 'Didn't you realize I meant you should find the oldest prostitute in New York, and get her life story?'

"I found the lady and, take my word for it, the assignment was tough work. She was sixty-three." [In his column Hecht described her as "a pile of fat that kept walking."]

"Things like that were happening all of the time. Ben would decide he wanted a story about someone who had attempted suicide and failed, a tattoo artist who wanted America to declare war so he'd have more sailors to work on, an interview with a wealthy recluse who lived on the Bowery to save money. Fortunately, in New York you can find anything."

In February of 1941 Hecht had also used the *PM* column to defend Herman Mankiewicz and Orson Welles against William Randolph Hearst's top brass when they tried to suppress *Citizen Kane*, alleging it was an unflattering portrait of their employer. The Hearst organization didn't put pressure directly on RKO president George J. Schaefer, but threatened to publish biographies of L. B. Mayer and other movie moguls in the Hearst press if *Citizen Kane* were released. Mayer went to the RKO board of directors, the bankers who controlled the company, and to other studio heads and convinced them the bad Hearst publicity would lose their studios money by alienating a portion of the moviegoing public. RKO instructed Schaefer to shelve the picture.

In "Louis B. Mayer Defends His Bell Jar," Hecht attacked his favorite enemy and revealed the real reasons behind the suppression of *Citizen Kane*, wondering why the studios were "afraid of a little literature in the Hearst press. Hollywood's great men taking to a bomb shelter at the sight of Mr. Hearst pointing a cap pistol at them is a baffling spectacle." Hecht did deny that the story of *Kane* was based on Hearst—"It has no more to do with WR than with Prester John"—when it very clearly was based on what Mankiewicz had gathered over the years about him. Not long after Hecht's column ran, *Citizen Kane* was released.

Hecht and Orson Welles had first met in the mid-thirties when they both stayed occasionally at the Algonquin, though Hecht had first heard of Welles in the twenties from drama critic Ashton Stevens, a friend of Welles's family. Then, early in 1939, Hecht tried to get Welles an acting job at MGM, assuring L. B. Mayer that Welles could be had for fifty thousand dollars. When one of Mayer's subalterns persuaded him it would be ridiculous to pay so much for an actor who had never appeared in pictures, Mayer phoned Hecht and told him he could only offer thirty thousand dollars. Another Metro executive then told Mayer he knew an actor who'd play the part for ten thousand dollars. Mayer phoned Hecht back and told him not to offer Welles more than ten thousand dollars; while they were still on the line, Mayer received word that Welles was calling from New York. At that point, Mayer yelled at Hecht, "I'm hiring a fellow right here in Hollywood to do that role for us. Tell that friend of yours that he's fired."

A few months later, Hollywood was flooded by press coverage of the unique three-picture contract Welles had signed with RKO: he had been given complete control as writer, director, and player in whatever films he chose to make. With the exception of Hecht—writer-producer-codirector of four of his own pictures—no one had been given such complete control over a film by a Hollywood studio since the silent era. This predisposed the movie community against Welles, since he wasn't one of them as Hecht had been—he was from Broadway, the theatre, the effete East. Hecht entertained no such prejudice, however, nor did Welles hold it against Hecht when Hecht's friend Charlier Lederer informed Hearst of the Mankiewicz script about him that Welles was preparing to shoot. In May of 1940, Lederer married Welles's first wife, and during July and August Hecht and Welles saw each other often since Welles was a frequent visitor to Hecht's set at Columbia during the shooting of *Angels Over Broadway*. Welles was there to call on the film's female lead and his new girlfriend, Rita Hayworth.

For his second RKO production Welles adapted Booth Tarkington's *The Magnificent Ambersons*. During the shooting, he conceived of a four-part film he wanted to make next—the first part was to be "My Friend Bonito," written by Robert Flaherty—so he despatched director Norman Foster to Mexico to begin preparations. When RKO turned thumbs down on the project because of the foreign locations and large budget, Welles decided to do a thriller. (Before settling on *Citizen Kane* as his first RKO picture, Welles had considered filming *The Smiler with the Knife* by Nicholas Blake, the pseudonym C. Day Lewis used for his mystery thrillers.) Both he and Hecht were mystery enthusiasts—a few years later Hecht would wallpaper the bathroom of his Oceanside, California, house with dust jackets from mysteries—so together they chose an Eric Ambler novel, *Journey into Fear*, for Welles's third film. On July 23rd, 1941, while Welles was still shooting *The Magnificent Ambersons*, Hecht signed with RKO to adapt the novel, receiving a first payment of ten thousand dollars. By the end of August a script was ready, but Welles was still in the midst of production. At the end of the year he called Norman Foster back from Mexico to begin shooting Hecht's script, since revised by Richard Collins and Ellis St. Joseph, while he edited *The Magnificent Ambersons*. "Don't read the book," Welles advised Foster. "We've changed it."

Hecht had written the script knowing he wouldn't receive screen credit, well aware of Welles's penchant for grabbing credit for everything he touched. When Welles tried to buy Herman Mankiewicz's screen credit for *Citizen Kane*, Hecht counseled Mankiewicz to "take the money and screw Welles" by claiming credit anyway. (Hecht even offered to write an article for the *Saturday Evening Post*, revealing how Welles was trying to steal Mankiewicz's credit.) Welles didn't take a writing credit for *Journey into Fear*, nor did he list himself as director, assigning credit to Norman Foster, who did much of the on-the-set direction following Welles's explicit instructions. Welles assigned script credit solely to actor Joseph Cotten, a member of his New York theatre company, the Mercury Players, who had acted in *Citizen Kane* and starred in *Journey into Fear*. Since it was common knowledge in Hollywood that Welles actually directed *Journey into Fear*, though at a remove, his assignment of the sole scenario credit to Joseph Cotten assured that Welles would be considered scriptwriter as well as director. For many years Welles's belief was borne out. *The New York Times* on March 19th, 1943, ran an article that noted, "Mr. Welles, in collaboration with Joseph Cotten, has written the adaptation." Joseph McBride, in his study of Welles's films, wrote, "*Journey into Fear*, a war thriller set in the Near East, directed by Foster from a script by Welles and Joseph Cotten. . . ." In his Museum of Modern Art monograph on Welles, Peter Bogdanovich said *Journey into Fear* "was scripted by Joseph Cotten (supposedly with Welles' assistance)." As Charles Higham summed up in his biography, *Orson Welles: The Rise and Fall of an American Genius*, "This hatred of giving credit to anyone else was typical of Welles: his ego could not or would not tolerate the idea of anyone's sharing . . . the applause."[5]

Hecht's prophecy of a coming genocide[6] in "The Death of Eleazer," one of the stories in *A Book of Miracles*, along with his *PM* columns about Nazi persecution of Jews, brought him to the attention of a committee of European Jews agitating for the establishment of an autonomous Jewish state in Palestine. Representing the committee, Peter Bergson contacted Hecht in September of 1941 at the Algonquin, where he was finishing a play, *Lily of the Valley*, to ask him to join their campaign for a free Palestine. Hecht told him he "disliked causes and public speaking," that he "couldn't bring himself to make orations nor listen to them," and that he had no interest in a "Jewish homeland." Bergson—also a member of the Committee for an Army of Stateless and Palestinian Jews—then informed Hecht that there were some 200,000 young Jews in Egypt, Syria, and Palestine ready to fight the Germans in Africa. To mobilize this force permission was needed from General Wavell, the British commander of the Allied African campaign, but thus far the British had rejected the plan because they didn't want a large Jewish fighting force in Palestine after the war. Since this project coincided with his own war efforts, Hecht joined the Committee, determining to go to Hollywood and raise money while Bergson went to Washington to present the plan to the War Department.

Before Hecht left for the Coast, though, he put *Lily of the Valley* into rehearsal, directing it himself. The play was another cynical/mystical work in the same vein as *The Scoundrel*; its main characters were eight dead Bowery bums who related their life stories in a morgue. Among Hecht's sources for this were five anecdotes he had bought from a former Chicago mortuary worker. He also inserted "Dregs," the story of the bum who thinks he sees Christ in a saloon window, which he had written in the teens. To put some action in the recitations by the eight "stiffs," a subplot concerning a Salvation Army missionary who gets murdered was worked in. By the end of the play, the missionary is convinced there is no god, that people just "howl like murderers and end up moaning on the cross." When the missionary admits his atheism to one of the derelicts, the accordion he uses during his services begins playing "Lily of the Valley" all by itself.

The critical reaction was murderous. The play closed six days and eight performances later. George Jean Nathan in *The American Mercury* summed up the general feeling about Hecht from Broadway's point of view:

> Ben Hecht was once, as almost everyone knows, a valuable playwright. As author in his early years of the highly amusing comedy, "The Egotist," and as co-author somewhat later of that best of all newspaper farces, "The Front Page," and that gay travesty of a well-known theatrical magnifico, "Twentieth Century," he made a position for himself in the theatre. Hollywood thereupon lured him with its copious mazuma to the post of movie scenario writer.
>
> Time passed and Hecht, now rich, deemed it meet to regain his lost self-pride in a return to his old love. He came

back and wrote "To Quito and Back," which had nothing of his former talent in it and failed both critically and popularly. He betook himself sadly to Hollywood once again, but presently the old urge was once more upon him. Again, he came back and wrote "Lily of the Valley," which indicated even less of his former talent and which failed in both directions even more signally. He is . . . now sobbing wet tears over his defeat and indignantly blaming everyone but himself for it.

Angry, Hecht struck back at his critics for killing the play. On January 28th, 1942, in *PM* he published "Sonnet to the Critics," which began

> *Good critics who reject my fairest song*
> *And spatter my fine shirt with printer's ink*
> *I'd bellow bitterly you do me wrong*
> *Were I not suffocated by your stink. . . .*

On the first of February, the day after *Lily of the Valley* closed, he wrote "Lament for the Living" for *The New York Times*, in which he did "bellow bitterly" against critics, whom he characterized as "a group of esthetically exhausted old men with literary nerve centers worn out from too much slapdash service . . . a fungus ego'ed coterie of fretful and wearied scribblers at whom our modern drama must aim itself . . . persnickety and callous and wearily groping gentlemen of the aisles full of some prep school mumbo jumbo about playwrighting and literature." (Later in the year, a proletarian novel by Maxwell Bodenheim was published that was a last jab at Hecht and his play full of dead characters—*Lights in the Valley*.)

Hecht's displeasure with theatre critics was hardly surprising, since the literary establishment had turned on him several years before. In 1937, in *Books and Battles of the Twenties*, Irene and Allen Cleaton had written,

> Hecht was the leader of the Chicago literary school which for a few years was the most exciting group of writing men in the country. He seemed able to do anything. Several of his news stories . . . and his sketches called A *Thousand and One Afternoons in Chicago* are by way of being journalistic classics. His novel *Erik Dorn* was a brilliant *tour*

de force in irony, wit, and disillusionment. He turned to the stage with great popular success, and when Hollywood lured him he proved he could put more box office appeal into a scenario than anybody else on the lots.

Hecht has now given himself up altogether to the pursuit of popularity and riches, and it is doubtful if he will ever again produce much of literary dignity. He seems destined to be a literary lost hope like Robert W. Chambers and Rupert Hughes, though he is never as insipid or as obvious as Chambers and Hughes got to be at the height of their money-making powers. . . . His literary work degenerated from the brilliance of his early books to the point where it became almost unreadable. In this and other cases, however, the movies only provided the sliding board; the primary defect was in the artist.

Back in Hollywood by February, Hecht spoke at a fund-raising meeting for the Jewish Committee, organized by Rose Hecht and held in the commissary at 20th Century–Fox. Hecht had already approached several studio heads seeking support but had been refused; Harry Warner even threatened to call the police. Many of the studio bosses thought Hecht unpatriotic and refused to help the Committee because of the secret meetings Joseph Kennedy had held with them in 1940 at President Roosevelt's bidding, to ask them not to publicize the Nazi persecution of Jews lest the war in Europe be labeled a Jewish war.

The rally at 20th Century–Fox wasn't very successful, but it did activate a few members of the movie colony. Charlie Chaplin, normally a recluse, showed up though he had never before attended any "Jewish affair" for fear it would give credence to gossip that he was Jewish. Ernst Lubitsch as well as actor/director Gregory Ratoff and Sam Spiegel pledged support, but many members of the audience left before the meeting was over, and of the $130,000 pledged, only $9,000 was actually collected. This setback convinced Hecht that his best weapon was his pen, not his oratory.

To raise money for his own bank account, Hecht signed a four-picture contract with 20th Century–Fox. Leland Hayward remarked, "You've never worked there before, I figure we ought to be able to take them for three or four hundred thousand before they get wise to us." His first assignment was to write two of the six tales comprising Sam Spiegel's production of *Tales of Manhattan*,[7] followed by an "original"—*China Girl*—about Flying Tiger squadrons in China and Burma. Hecht plotted the story, then turned it into a screenplay, but original story credit went to one Melville Crossman. Darryl Zanuck, who had the option of selling four stories a year to Twentieth, took the story credit under the Crossman pseudonym and Hecht acted as *China Girl's* producer, earning them both more money. To fulfill his obligation Hecht hired Henry Hathaway (who had just directed *Ten Gentlemen from West Point* and was known as an action-film director), helped with the casting, and was on hand during the shooting, a rare practice since his involvement usually ended when the script was turned in. (During July and August, Hecht would complete his contractual obligation to Twentieth by adapting Rafael Sabatini's pirate novel *The Black Swan* and scripting *Voyage to Nowhere*, which was not produced at the time.)

When shooting on *China Girl* was over for the day, Hecht—who had never learned to drive—would have Hathaway motor him to the West Los Angeles apartment of a young actress he had become entangled with. So Rose wouldn't know he was spending money on other women, Hecht had Leland Hayward's agency keep two sets of accounts of his earnings, one with the actual amounts received for scripts, and a second set with lesser amounts recorded, both bearing the instruction: "Be sure that you do not under any circumstances give information to Mrs. Hecht without first consulting me—Leland Hayward." Hecht soon tired of the lady, and when asked by her for a sum of money (the inference being that she'd tell Rose about their affair if he didn't come through), he had his lawyer write her that all financial matters were handled by Mrs. Hecht, to whom she should address herself. Hecht never heard from her again.

Insatiable wordsmith that he was, Hecht outdid himself in the fourteen-month period from late September of 1942 to December of the following year. Secluded in his bedroom/study at Nyack he did nothing but write stories, books, and plays, but not a single film.

Six of the long stories he wrote were published in *Collier's* magazine through 1943. "Miracle of the 15 Murderers" told of a secret society of doctors that meets to confess the murders they have committed, either by surgical error or mistaken diagnoses;[8] "Concerning a Woman of Sin" was a spoof of Hollywood and L. B. Mayer which Hecht would turn into a movie ten years later. The other four stories were all concerned with politics and the war in Europe. "The Doughboy's Dream," in which a soldier dreams he and Hedy Lamarr capture Adolf Hitler, was purely a propaganda effort and consequently the only story of the six that was shallow, obvious, and, surprisingly, clumsily written. (Hecht's own dissatisfaction with the story was evidenced two years later when he selected the other five pieces for inclusion in his *Collected Stories*.) "God Is Good to a Jew" told of an old man who, having twice escaped death at the hands of the Nazis, dies happy in the United States, where "goodness does not vanish where the Jew stands." "Café Sinister" was a tale of revenge in which a European nobleman kills the informer who turned his sister over to the Nazis because she was half Jewish.

"The Pink Hussar" was an amusing tale about the community of Hungarian artists relocated in New York as a result of the Nazi occupation of their country, playwright Ferenc Molnár serving as model for the story's protagonist. Ladislas Fodor, who worked on *Tales of Manhattan*, has had a play roasted by the critics and is "still in bed moaning." A Bodenheim quote is slyly attributed to Schopenhauer, the Countess Rividavia from *To Quito and Back* turns up, the title of Hecht's unfinished play *A Handful of Isoldes* becomes the title of a Hungarian play, and Broadway critics come in for some gentle criticism, in comparison to Hecht's vituperations of the previous year: "The critics run an elevator service between wizardhood and oblivion—with no stop-overs." Hecht remarked in the story, "It is of these sprightly Hungarians I write—a task a little hazardous, for sitting among them I have heard a thousand and one tales, plots, jests and ironies—and do I put one of these on paper I will be sued for plagiarism instanter. For plagiarism suits are as firm a part of Magyar culture as double-decker pastries. In fact, the joke runs that in the golden days of Hungarian letters the first thing a Budapest playwright said to his valet on awakening with a Pilsener hangover was, 'Well, Rudolph, whom do I sue today?'" Hecht had had firsthand experience of this aspect of "Magyar culture" when Hungarian playwright Ladislas Bus-Fekete, while staying at Nyack to work on *Lydia* with Hecht and Julien Duvivier, sued Hecht for failing to properly credit him for the original story of *Ladies and Gentlemen*, a play Hecht and MacArthur had adapted from his *12 in a Box*.

"Miracle in the Rain," the longest story Hecht wrote during his reclusion in Nyack, was published by the *Saturday Evening Post* and issued as a novella by Knopf. When Pascal Covici at Viking rejected the manuscript, Hecht wrote to Fowler of Covici's "gurgling ways," complaining that he "waves a sword made out of tin foil," and that he was "basically no more than a cut above a jellyfish." "Miracle in the Rain" told of a homely young girl who dies of grief when the soldier she loves is killed in action. Just before her final collapse, she meets the spirit of the dead soldier on the steps of Saint Patrick's Cathedral, where he gives her an old Roman coin he carried for luck. She is found dead on the steps by a friend who, prying open her clenched fist, finds the coin and "was unable to speak because something like fright pounded in her heart . . . her face grew radiant. She smiled widely at the coin and at the gentle face of her dead friend. Then she fell to her knees and began praying." The story was not typical of Hecht in that it depended on a miracle unrelieved by cynicism, but for Hecht it was just another propaganda effort.

For a *Redbook* novellette-of-the-month, Hecht churned out "Imposter in Heaven," a story that fell into the "popular swill" category, Hecht even proferring an introductory apology: "This story bears so little relation to the world being reshaped by bombers and submarines that its telling is almost like the spinning of a fairy tale. Like many writers, I would rather be using what talents I have to shout whoever reads to battle, and to celebrate the valour of our youth at Armageddon. Yet I turn my back and whistle at ghosts in an empty house, and set my mind to matters as far away as a grasshopper's dream."

During the writing of the story, John Barrymore died of alcoholism and Hecht appended a new opening.

> They're dying off, all my exuberant and artistic friends who were the landmarks of a mirage known as Happy Days. They came bounding into the Century like a herd of unicorns . . . they were part of the last high old time when news was made by madcaps rather than madmen, and they were sustained through hunger, calumny and hangovers by the conviction that they were improving the world. Now whenever one of them falls, brought down not so much by the barrage of years as by disillusion and a drop too much of alcohol, I mourn doubly. I mourn the passing of another of the moonstruck gentry, and of the era that specialized in hatching their dwindling tribe. Every time one of these battered old iconoclasts waves good-bye, that era grows dimmer and all its carnival fades a little more.

In his last years Barrymore had taken more and more to drink. He lived at John Decker's house part of the time but Hecht, MacArthur, Fowler, and Thomas Mitchell were frequently called to the rescue when he escaped and got into trouble. The year before Barrymore died, Hecht gave a birthday party in his honor, inviting the Hollywood elite without telling them who the guest of honor was for fear they would refuse the invitation. Barrymore arrived sober and spun stories all evening to an entranced audience. His friends had been terrified he would commit some outrage as was his wont in his declining years—once he had leapt over the counter of a diner and tried to ravish a waitress, demanding "to see Epping Forest once more"; another time he urinated publicly at the opening of a nightclub—but the evening of his party he behaved impeccably, finally nodding to Decker that it was time he be taken home.

Of all Hecht's politically motivated writing during World War II, his most powerful, and most historically important, was "Remember Us," written to call America's attention to the mass slaughter of Jews by the Nazis, which at the time was not widely known. Hecht, Peter Bergson, and the Jewish Committee produced a memorial pageant, *We Will Never Die*—part three of which was "Remember Us"—with a threefold aim: "The creation of an army of Palestinian and stateless Jews; the immediate initiation of any possible transfer of Jews from Hitler-dominated countries to Palestine or any temporary refuge; the immediate appointment of an intergovernmental commission to determine a policy of action to end the slaughter of the European Jews." The program was mounted on March 9th and 10th, 1943, at Madison Square Garden, with Paul Muni and Edward G. Robinson reading two of the principal parts. "Remember Us" dramatized the genocide then taking place.

> In the town of Szczecin in Poland on the morning of September 23rd, which was the Day set aside for our Atonement, we were all in our synagogue praying God to forgive us. . . . Above our prayers we heard the sound of the motor lorries. They stopped in front of our synagogue. The Germans tumbled out of them, torches in hand. The Germans set fire to us. When we ran out of the flames, they turned machine guns on us. They seized our women and undressed them and made them run naked through the market place before their whips. All of us were killed before our Atonement was done. Remember us.
>
> Remember us in Wloclawek. Here also the Germans came when we were at worship. The Germans tore the prayer shawls from our heads. Under whips and bayonets, they made us use our prayer shawls as mops to clean out

German latrines. We were all dead when the sun set. Remember Us!

Remember us who were in the Ukraine. Here the Germans grew angry with us because we were costing them too much time and ammunition to kill. They devised a less expensive method. They took our women into the roads and tied them together with the children. Then they drove their heavy motor lorries into us. Thousands of us died in this way, with the German military cars running back and forth over our broken bodies. . . .

In Odessa, the Germans led five thousand of us out into the country roads. We were mostly old men, old women and children—some too old and some too young to walk. Above our heads the Germans flew their bombers and dropped their bombs on us. The German officers yelled that we should be proud for we were serving Germany by helping their fliers improve their marksmanship. But their marksmanship was good. Of the five thousand, none of us remained alive. . . .

When the German delegates sit at the peace table with their monocles restored to their pale eyes, no sons or survivors or representatives of these myriad dead will be inside the hall to speak for them. And by that time, it will be seen that the Jews are Jews only when they stand up for the hour of extermination. Once dead, it will be seen that they are left without a government to speak for their avenging and that there is no banner to fly in their tomorrow.

Only this that I write—and all the narratives like it that will be written—will be their voice that may drift in through the opened window of the judgement hall.

The American Mercury reprinted "Remember Us," the first piece in any major American publication to reveal the Nazi genocide.

In June of 1943, Hecht wrote the Fowlers that the Nyack house would be empty from the middle of July to the middle of August and would be at their disposal. The Hechts would be in New York, where on July 30th Ben and Rose's only child, Jenny, was born. Three days later Hecht wrote a poem to Jenny as the dedication for one of the two books he had written "while lurking like a sea bass, motionless for more than a year." *A Guide for the Bedevilled*[9] was a potpourri of Jewish history, recollections of Chicago, New York, and Hollywood, portraits of friends, anecdotes, philosophical rambles, and chunks of undigested rhetoric used to analyze anti-Semitism.

> I write of fools, pipsqueaks, social imposters, spiritual harelips, tormented homosexuals, lonely sadists, intellectual bankrupts; of unctuous gossip-mongers for whom speech is a form of masturbation; of bile peddlers, and invalids whose teeth ache, whose bladders drip and whose hearts are a sackful of worms; of religious zanies who woo God by spitting in His eye, and anti-religious zanies who fill the dark of their heads with ugly screams; of cunning rabble-rousers lusting for a nickel's worth of power, and of the dough-headed rabble ever ready with its false coin and its sickly cheers; I write of all that mincing and bepimpled, clapper-tongued and swivel-brained tribe of lame ducks who make up the ranks of the anti-Semites.

The book would be published in March of 1944 to mixed reviews. Gene Fowler began a laudatory critique, "I have just spent two evenings with a prophetic artist. He has written a book called *A Guide for the Bedevilled*. This I think is at once a spear in the side of Ignorance, and, as well, a prime torch for the lost ones who grope in the grottoes of Hope. It holds our time in a suspensory glimpse." Elmer Rice, in a *Saturday Review* piece, "The Pitchfork with Prongs at Both Ends," was more reserved in his enthusiasm: "Mr. Hecht has written an earnest book, worthy of the most serious consideration. It is shot through with flashes of wit, penetrating observations, passionate indignation, entertaining self-revelations. My quarrel with it is that it is discursive, over-abundant in irrelevancies and oblique paradoxes and, chiefly, that it ignores the practical realities of race hatred in the world."

In July of 1946, Hecht would negotiate with Herbert J. Yates to write and direct a film for Republic based on the life of Ignaz Semmelweis, the Hungarian doctor who discovered a connection between the spread of disease and the fact that doctors didn't wash their hands before performing operations. Semmelweiss's ideas were scorned in his time, so in desperation he cut open a finger at a medical convention and plunged it into a corpse to prove once and for all that there could be fatal organisms transmitted from doctors' hands to patients. He died in 1865 without having convinced anyone.

Hecht had included an outline of Semmelweis's life in *A Guide for the Bedevilled.*

> I offer it to my mogul movie-making friends as a work for the screen. It has nothing to do with Jews so they need not wince in advance. It has to do, however, with a mood which a Jew can understand a little more quickly than other people. . . . I wrote it in order to dramatize the backwardness and stupidity of the world. Semmelweis is only an accident I use . . . there is a villain I want to expose who is vastly greater than any anti-Semite . . . this is the character of the world itself. Utter, blank, wooden-headed indifference to all truth, is the world's deepest quality. There lies its rotten spot. The Bible says that it was the Devil who entered Eden as a snake and tempted man with knowledge. This section of the Bible must have been written by the Devil himself. What the snake brought Adam and Eve was ignorance. He handed them an apple full of worms. And their descendants are still chewing on it.

In *A Guide* Hecht had even fantasized a script conference in which studio moguls gutted his story: "The thing that needs licking in this Semmelweis story is a sort of lie that's in it. You've got the public and the Authorities playing the villain. . . . I think we can make the whole thing more understandable by underlining the fact that Semmelweis is actually his own worst enemy. It's his character that defeats him. You say yourself that he was insolent, snarling, hot-headed—in fact, a thorough heel. And that's why he doesn't put his discovery over—because there's a rotten spot in him."

"That," answers Hecht, "is hogwash. Semmelweis doesn't put his discovery over because there's a rotten spot in the world. Because Audiences are idiots and Authorities are all swindlers." The argument goes on but in the end the studio turns the script down because Hecht wouldn't allow it to be changed. Republic turned it down, just as Hecht had forecast.

The point of the Semmelweis story for Hecht was that the mentality that persecuted Semmelweis was the same one that persecuted Jews and allowed them to be massacred. An irony unrealized by Hecht, who took his information from *La Vie et l'oeuvre de Philippe-Ignace Semmelweiss,* was that its author, the celebrated French writer Louis-Ferdinand

Céline—one of the twentieth century's most virulent anti-Semites—was in prison in Denmark for collaborating with the Nazis at the very time Hecht proposed the story to Yates.

* * *

> Devlin entered, as Jimmy Durante says, "unannounced!"
>
> "Is there any significance in your occupying an office next to the gents' toilet?" he inquired in his solemn drawl.
>
> "A literary accident," I said.
>
> "I thought it might be a quest for inspiration," Devlin looked owlishly around. "You were always an artist who liked to keep close to his subject matter."

The other book Hecht wrote during 1943 was *I Hate Actors!*, his first novel since *A Jew in Love* in 1931. A spoof of Hollywood with some of the same characters who appeared in his short story "Concerning a Woman of Sin," it was dedicated "To My Friend Leland Hayward Who In No Way Resembles Any Of The Characters In This Story." Hayward nevertheless appeared as Orlando Higgins, a Hollywood agent, as he had in the short story. The narrator is Hecht himself and the main character is Gene Fowler, called Devlin after a former editor of his. L. B. Mayer, as J. B. Cobb, was again the butt for Hecht's demeaning comments on movie moguls. John Barrymore appeared as Laurence Bison, and a host of characters from other Hecht works showed up—Bertha Fancher changed from Amy Fancher in *Soak the Rich*, Bensinger from *The Front Page*, and Hecht's near-omnipresent character, Egelhofer. (Egelhofer was the name of the psychiatrist in *The Front Page*, *His Girl Friday*, and *Nothing Sacred*, as well as the name of the mother in "A Woman of Sin." Among the variations on Egelhofer were: another psychiatrist, Englemeyer, in "The Boy Pirate"; the two characters Engle and Hopper in *Angels Over Broadway*; and a character in *Hazel Flagg*, a musical Hecht was still to write.)

Although Hecht wrote Fowler that in *I Hate Actors!* he had revealed all he knew about "how, why and under what hellish circumstances movies are made," the book nevertheless was a light-hearted task after the more serious business of writing about the war in Europe. Like *Count Bruga*, *I Hate Actors!* had a murder gratuitously inserted to enliven the plot. Still, it was not Hecht's usual potpourri of philosophical and psychological maunderings but a genuinely amusing novel written more like a film—i.e., with action and ideas carried forward through dialogue. An inspired description of the inner workings of Hollywood—writers, agents, stars, studios, moguls, sex, ego—it was more accurate and telling than most books written about the movies. It contained neither the tragedy of *The Last Tycoon* nor the macabre brilliance of *The Day of the Locust*, but Fitzgerald and West hadn't attempted to present the entire panorama of Hollywood, whereas Hecht deftly painted a complete picture of the moviemaking machine, with essays in miniature integrated into the dialogue, furthering rather than disjointing the plot.

A Hollywood day is the quickest of all time phenomena. Before you can get around to doing fifteen minutes of honest work—it's gone. A second breakfast in the studio commissary in company with a group of literary beach-combers (earning two thousand a week and dreaming sadly of a better life), a little game of gin rummy with a pigeon who fancies himself a Cagliostro of the cards, a chat in the corridor with a scrivener who is having producer trouble (one is never tired of listening to tales of producer-idiocies), a small bet placed on a horse; a shave, shine and confab with an admirer who thinks you are the only able man in the studio and wishes you would do something beautiful to raise the standard of the movies—and it's time for lunch.

Lunch kills the afternoon. Lunch at the Writers' Table, seating twenty-four, taps the more serious side of your talents, involving as it does, debates on international policy, military strategy, memoirs of Hollywood frustration, astonishing sidelights on sex, plus a dice game. It being impossible to work after you have had a third cocktail, lost your morning horse bets and a fifty dollar bill on the dice, and exhausted yourself, to boot, proving why the Russians are better (or worse) than the English, you go back to your office and put a telephone call in for New York, and look over a line of ties, handkerchiefs and mufflers a Mr. Schultz is allowed to peddle inside the studio gates.

Knowing all this, I seldom "went to work" at all but clung to my hotel chamber in pajamas and slippers. My so-called employers, not seeing me at the studio—that combination pool room and drugstore corner for mental zoot-suiters—imagined me honestly a-toil somewhere—a fine, healthy illusion.

By December of 1943 Hecht was yearning for activity after his fourteen months of isolation. He wrote Fowler that he was coming to Hollywood to raise the capital to produce *Miracle in the Rain*. The massive flirtations with bankers he wrote Fowler about came to nothing, however, making it impossible for him to make a film of his novella, so he sold the book to Warner Bros., where it was filmed eleven years later with a changed ending in which the heroine doesn't die! In March and April *I Hate Actors!* was serialized in *Collier's*, and at the end of March William Powell read Hecht's eulogy for Myron Selznick, who had died on the twenty-third: "He was a little boy who never grew up! . . . We loved him for his courage. We admired him for the quickest mind of anyone since the pioneer days of his great father, whose name he and his brother perpetuated with energy and honor. He was both brilliant and wise. . . ."

Not wanting to write "shoe-shine scenarios," Hecht resisted the lure of easy money from the studios and devoted his energies to writing propaganda plays, a short film for the State Department, and part of a Broadway show. A one-acter called *The Common Man* was presented one night only at the Henry Hudson Hotel in New York on a triple bill with Arthur Miller's *They That May Win* and *Untitled* by Norman Corwin, all produced by Stage for Action "to educate people on the home front." *The Common Man*'s setting was a side show like that in *The Great Magoo*, but its attractions were somewhat different. A poster showed an elephant labeled GOP covered with patches, another pictured Hoover and Dewey as monkeys swinging from a trapeze. The play's thrust was the "necessity" of electing Roosevelt to a third term: A cooch dancer outside the GOP tent picks up a young soldier and, after money changes hands, leads him offstage; the common man, not so easily seduced, resists her advances in favor of the clean life with Roosevelt. A one-act fund-raiser with a cast of three hundred, *A Tribute to Gallantry*, written for the New York Committee of the National War Fund, was performed at the Waldorf, featuring Helen Twelvetrees and Dean Jagger. *Miracle on the Pullman*, a radio drama presented over the Blue Network on November 19th, 1944, with Franchot Tone and Myrna Loy, was done for the Sixth War Loan Drive. Another of Hecht's patriotic plays, it concerned the spirit of a dead GI who inspires passengers on a train to buy war bonds. For an "entertainment" called *The Seven Lively Arts*, a colossal variety show with ballet music by Igor Stravinsky, popular songs by Cole Porter, and sketches by George S. Kaufman and Moss Hart, Hecht wrote the comic speeches for a comedian named Doc Rockwell, who made jokes about young people trying to break into show business and gave a speech on female anatomy. The show opened at the Ziegfeld on December 7th to rave reviews and ran 183 performances.

That same month Hecht put together a script for the State Department about the United Nations, first titled *The World of Tomorrow* but released as *Watchtower of Tomorrow*. "Its purpose," Hecht explained, "was to make the citizenry who gaped at it in the movie theatres fall in love with the wonders of the United Nations. What those wonders were no one in the State Department seemed to know. I finally put some scraps of information together, larded them with rhetoric and war episodes and sent the script on to Hollywood for production." MGM produced the film, with Alfred Hitchcock directing. Then, in April of 1945,[10] Hecht was commissioned to write a radio play for the opening session of the United Nations in San Francisco, to be broadcast over the Mutual Network. To read the principal parts, Hecht hired Edward G. Robinson and Harold Stassen.

But of all Hecht's political playwriting, the one piece he felt most deeply about was not to be produced. *Call the Next Case* was to open in a local theatre and run as long as the United Nations' delegates were in session. The purpose of the play was "to explode the Jewish issue in the face of the entire United Nations." For Hecht, the "Jewish issue" meant not only the mass murder of Jews by Nazis but President Roosevelt's "betrayal" of them. In the winter of 1943, Kurt Weill had read a short news story to Hecht from a Swiss newspaper announcing that the Rumanian government would be able to evacuate seventy thousand Jews before the imminent German occupation if it were to receive fifty dollars per person transport money. Hecht confirmed that the story was true, then placed a full-page ad in *The New York Times*:

For Sale to Humanity
70,000 Jews
Guaranteed Human Beings at $50 a Piece

He also contacted the State Department to verify the report (it did), but the American Jewish Congress announced to the press that the story was unconfirmed and the Jewish Agency in London denied its truth, so nothing was done and the seventy thousand Jews were massacred by the Germans. Hecht put the blame on the official Zionist organizations that had refused to be associated with any of his Jewish pageants and had, in fact, scotched the proposal for putting a Jewish army in the field in Africa.

"All these matters failed to turn me against Franklin Roosevelt," Hecht wrote. "I remained an ardent drum beater. He was not on the side of the Jews, but he was on the side of the angels. A Jew can imagine that this is the same thing. Besides, what proof did I have other than the logic of events. Believe in logic and your sweetheart is unfaithful every time she lies to you. It's better to wait till you can look in, unexpectedly, through the bedroom window and see something besides logic."

Hecht saw something else in September of 1944 when the Moscow Declaration was issued promising the Germans would be punished for their war crimes. The document listed atrocities committed against sixty-two different groups of people, with no mention of Jews. It was signed by Franklin Roosevelt. "This was a pretty omission," Hecht commented, "the greatest race murder in history, omitted from the official Allied statement on German atrocities. Reading it I knew that British policy preferred that all the Jews die incognito in the German furnaces rather than a single Jewish refugee enter Palestine. I knew that my American President was of similar mind in the matter. He was on the side of the angels, but he looked now a little too red with Jewish blood for my further hosannahs."

Late in 1944, Hecht placed another full-page ad in newspapers—"My Uncle Abraham Stands Up." Uncle Abraham—a Jew killed by the Nazis—attended the Moscow Conference. He "came away considerably depressed" but, not giving up hope, went to Washington, to Roosevelt's study, where he was still waiting, but "had small hopes of hearing anything about Jews dead or alive worth writing down."

The piece so upset Roosevelt that he had Bernard Baruch ask Hecht to discontinue his criticism, since the president was going to the Near East soon and would settle the "Jewish problem" to Hecht's satisfaction. Hecht held off as requested, but turned against Roosevelt when, a month later, he returned from his trip abroad without having talked with a single Jewish leader, consulting instead with Ibn Saud of Saudi Arabia, a rabid Jew-hater who had announced to the press a few weeks before Roosevelt's arrival that "the only way to solve the Jewish situation in the Near East is to take all the Jews out of Palestine and send them into Central Africa, where they won't be able to bother anybody. If they refuse to go, the only other alternative is to exterminate them where they are." In March of 1945, in a report to Congress, Roosevelt said he had "learned more about the Moslem problem, the Jewish problem, by talking with Ibn Saud for five minutes than in the exchange of two or three dozen letters." If this wasn't enough, Hecht learned that during the time the seventy thousand

Rumanian Jews could have been saved, Roosevelt had directed the State Department to reassure Ibn Saud and other Arab leaders not to fear an influx of Rumanian Jews into Palestine.

Call the Next Case was to be a long one-act play in which Roosevelt is summoned before the Bar of History to state what he had done to save the European Jews from extermination. The jury would be twelve murdered Jews. On April 12th, however, Hecht heard over the radio that Roosevelt had just died. He tore up *Call the Next Case* and went to San Francisco with his elder daughter, Teddy, to produce the UN radio play.

In 1945 David Selznick was consulting a psychiatrist—he was breaking up with his wife, a result of his involvement with a young actress, Jennifer Jones—which prompted him to buy the film rights to *The House of Doctor Edwardes*, a mystery novel about an amnesiac who assumes the identity of a murdered psychiatrist. The movie version was to be called *Spellbound*. Selznick slated Alfred Hitchcock to direct, hired Salvador Dali to design a dream sequence, and Hecht to write the script (Hecht added a minor character named Mr. Garmes, who insists he murdered his father). Hecht never read the novel, working instead from an adaptation of Angus MacPhail.

Immediately afterward, Hecht and Hitchcock collaborated on a script about Nazi scientists in South America trying to develop an atomic bomb. In the fall of 1944 David Selznick had asked Hitchcock to read a short story from his files, "The Song of the Dragon" by John Taintor Foote. Since the plot involved a woman's change of identity (an earmark of Hitchcock's work) as well as her sexual enslavement for the purpose of secretly gathering information about the Nazis, Hitchcock gave Selznick the green light to hire Hecht. At Hecht's Nyack house, the three of them wrote the script of *Notorious*. As Hitchcock recalled,

> I wanted to make a film about a man who forces a woman to go to bed with another man because it's his professional duty. The whole film was really designed as a love story. The politics of the thing didn't much interest me, but I realized we had to have a reason for the Germans to be in Brazil. We thought of jewel mining, precious minerals, that sort of thing, and then one day I said to Hecht, "What about uranium?" and he shrugged and said he didn't think it mattered, that one MacGuffin was as good as another if we

(Above, top to bottom): Ben Hecht, his mother, Sarah, and his younger brother Peter. (COURTESY OF PETER HECHT)

(Above right): Hecht's father, Joseph. (COURTESY OF PETER HECHT)

(At right): Ben and Peter Hecht, Chicago, circa 1900. (COURTESY OF PETER HECHT)

LEO

DITRICHSTEIN

in a New
Comedy
by

**BEN
HECHT**

Author

of

**ERIK

DORN**

AND

GARGOYLES

"THE EGOTIST"

"Mr. Ditrichstein is **a** uniquely great dramatic artist."
—*James Gibbons Huneker in the New York Sun*

Playbill for The Egotist, *Hecht's first three-act play, which played New York City in late 1922 and early 1923.*

Caricature of Hecht by Ralph Barton, which accompanied Hecht's essay "Literature and the Bastinado" in Nonsenseorship: Sundry Observations Concerning Prohibitions, Inhibitions and Illegalities *(G. P. Putnam's Sons, 1922).*

Caricature of Hecht by fellow Chicago Daily News *reporter Gene Markey, included in his collection of caricatures of then contemporary authors,* Literary Lights *(Knopf, 1923).*

(At right): the standard publicity photograph of Hecht during the twenties and thirties. (CREDIT: MAURICE GOLDBERG)

(Below): director Art Rosson and Hecht during the preproduction for Underworld, *1926.* (CREDIT: MUSEUM OF MODERN ART FILM STILLS ARCHIVE)

Charles MacArthur and Hecht in Adolph Zukor's former office at Paramount's Astoria, Queens, studios, where Hecht and MacArthur wrote, produced, and directed four pictures. (CREDIT: MUSEUM OF MODERN ART FILM STILLS ARCHIVE)

Charles MacArthur and Hecht in disguise on the set of their second Astoria studios picture, Once in a Blue Moon, *1935.* (CREDIT: MUSEUM OF MODERN ART FILM STILLS ARCHIVE)

Edwina Armstrong, Hecht's daughter by his first marriage, and actress Whitney Bourne on the set of Once in a Blue Moon; *Edwina (Teddy) had a featured role in the picture.* (CREDIT: AMERICAN MUSEUM OF THE MOVING IMAGE)

(Above, left to right): Hecht, Charles MacArthur, John Barrymore, and Noël Coward during the shooting of The Scoundrel, 1935, in which Coward starred.

(Below, left to right): Hecht, Walter Connolly, and Charles MacArthur in the credit sequence of Soak the Rich, 1936; the artwork was painted by George Grosz. (CREDIT: AMERICAN MUSEUM OF THE MOVING IMAGE)

Some of the more striking pieces of artwork that accompanied Hecht's writing: (above) the title page of 1001 Afternoons in Chicago, *Hecht's 1922 collection of* Chicago Daily News *columns; (left) the art deco dust jacket for* Count Bruga, *Hecht's 1926 roman à clef based on poet Maxwell Bodenheim; and (right) Hecht's book plate designed by fellow Chicago newspaperman Wallace Smith in 1924.*

were really putting together a love story. By the end of
March . . . I'd decided on the uranium angle—uranium
hidden in wine bottles seemed like a good idea. . . . It
seemed to me that ever since Rutherford split an atom of it
[uranium] and released a lot of energy, that someone,
someday, would make a bomb out of it. And with all the talk
in 1945 of some devastating secret weapon we were supposed to be developing, my angle sounded topical. Selznick
thought the whole thing was somewhat harebrained. I
insisted that even Hecht had agreed with me.

Hecht and Hitchcock put together what little they knew about the
possible existence of superbombs with a lot of science fiction and made
an educated guess. Their story hinged on the fissionable material being
small enough to fit into a wine bottle, so they decided to consult
Dr. Robert Millikan, the Nobel Prize winner who had discovered cosmic
rays, about how to make an atom bomb. Not wanting to risk being
refused an interview on the phone, they drove to Dr. Millikan's house
and knocked on the door.

"I guarantee he will go white at the question," Hitchcock said. "The
worst he can do is throw us out on our ears," Hecht thought.
Dr. Millikan, more than a little taken aback by their question, told them,
"If I make the slightest response to your question we'll all be arrested."
They did get the needed bit of inforamtion, though—the "substance"
would indeed fit into a wine bottle. They returned to RKO and finished
Notorious, for which Hecht would receive his last Academy Award
nomination.

Several months after Hecht and Hitchcock talked with Dr. Millikan,
the United States dropped atomic bombs on Hiroshima and Nagasaki,
Hecht now remarking, "Who could ever forgive the dirty scientific work
done under the grandstand at Stagg Field that in 1940 produced the
Doomsday Bomb?"

In the latter part of the year, Hecht polished the script and added
new scenes to a Rita Hayworth picture, *Gilda*. He then adapted his short
story "Specter of the Rose" for the screen and convinced Herbert Yates,
president of Republic Pictures, to let him direct and produce. Yates had
made his money from film processing laboratories, which in 1935 enabled
him to form Republic, a small studio in the San Fernando Valley.
Grade-B Westerns were the standard product, but Yates occasionally
produced a class picture. (He had recently hired an A-picture director,

Frank Borzage, to direct *I've Always Loved You,* commissioning Artur Rubinstein to record the music, which alone cost Republic eighty thousand dollars.) Hecht, though, had proposed a budget of only $200,000 for his picture; Yates said it was the first time anyone had suggested a film to him for under a million.

"All I want is a pinch of the profits and no interference," Hecht told Yates (he got 50 percent of the profits).

"All right," agreed Yates, "but when you're finished, I hope I can understand it."

Hecht named his producing unit Jenny's Corporation after his two-year-old daughter and immediately began gathering a crew and casting the roles. Lee Garmes was brought in to do the cinematography and some direction, Ernst Fegte to design the sets, and George Antheil to write an original score rather than use Carl Maria von Weber's "Invitation to the Dance," which Fokine had adopted for his *Le Spectre de la rose* that Nijinsky made famous in 1911. All three men were tops in their fields, too expensive for a studio like Republic, but Hecht hired them anyway since he planned to shoot the entire film in three weeks rather than three months, meaning he could afford them after all on his minuscule budget. For his cast, Hecht hired old-timers Judith Anderson, Michael Chekhov, and Lionel Stander, but for the two principal roles chose unknowns, a former Olympic swimmer, Ivan Kirov, and a ballerina, Viola Essen. "I wanted a girl who was a first rate dancer, who could act, and who didn't look actressy." When Miss Essen came to audition, wearing a suit and shoes that were too small, Hecht signed her up. "She was all bulges and nervousness and even had a twitch but the moment I saw her I knew she was the girl I was looking for. There's something in a face you can see at first glance, and if it isn't there all the direction and pancake make-up in the world won't put it there. I didn't even have to give Viola a screen test."

The principals had to be able to dance, since Hecht's picture incorporated *Le Spectre de la rose,* which has as its source the Théophile Gautier poem of the same name. A young man—portraying the ghost of a dying rose—dances with a young lady who has worn it earlier that evening to a ball. At the end of his dance, the young man playing the rose kisses the young girl, then leaps out of her bedroom window, happy with his fate.

Hecht's script told of a brilliant young dancer, André Sanine, who is obsessed by *Le Spectre de la rose.* He goes through periods when he is completely normal, then begins to have severe headaches, hearing the music from the ballet play over and over, a "mania that had come to roost like a vulture in his head and to feed upon him, to devour his charm, his talent, and his bright smile." Before the film begins, in one of his fits of madness, Sanine has brutally beaten his beautiful young wife, a ballerina, on the opening night of *Le Spectre de la rose*. She has a weak heart and dies during the performance. When he was assaulting her in their dressing room, Madame La Sylph, a ballet teacher and former ballerina—"the remains of a pirouette"—had walked in and saved the girl's life, only to see her die onstage. Madame La Sylph doesn't inform the police of the real facts, so the girl's death is put down to natural causes.

The film, *Specter of the Rose*, begins when producer Max Poliakoff (Michael Chekhov) wants to produce a ballet starring Sanine but discovers he has been catatonic since his wife's death, cared for by Haidi (Viola Essen), one of La Sylph's young pupils, who is in love with him. Poliakoff manages to scrape together enough money to mount the ballet, Sanine is roused from his torpor, and falls in love with Haidi. A poet, Lionel Gans (Lionel Stander), warns Haidi that Sanine is a madman and brings detective Specs MacFarlan around to question him since he has been telling people he killed his wife. There is no evidence to go on, though, since both Sanine and La Sylph deny it. But—déjà vu with a vengeance—the pattern begins to repeat itself: Sanine marries Haidi during rehearsals for the new ballet and, as opening night draws near, he begins to be tormented once again by the *Spectre* music. On opening night, Sanine and Haidi disappear and the ballet has to be cancelled. In a tiny hotel room forty floors above street level, they've hidden themselves away, Sanine fighting his madness and Haidi taking care of him. Late one night, Sanine in his rose costume, sitting beside the sleeping Haidi, reaches out to kill her, his madness come completely to the surface. At that moment, he hears the *Spectre* music and begins to dance, but the room is so small that his movements are cramped. As the music grows in intensity, Sanine begins crashing into the walls, then, when the climactic strains of the rose's dance are heard, he hurls himself through the hotel window. "He was falling straight as an arrow, his arms lowered, his hands folded in front of him and his feet were making entrechats. His head was tilted gracefully to one side. He was dancing as he fell."

For the shot of the suicidal leap, Lee Garmes had a camera lowered from the top of a downtown Los Angeles building. Rather than use the footage when Sanine makes the leap, the film was reversed to show the ascent to the hotel room, giving the viewer a feeling of the height he was to jump from. For the last scene, in which Haidi falls asleep exhausted from her vigil, knowing Sanine will try to kill her, Hecht kept Miss Essen awake for three days and nights. When they shot the sequence, she collapsed and fell asleep on the bed as Kirov did the final dance.

Hecht took the name Sanine from the novel of the same name by Mikhail Artzybashev, written in 1907, a book that left a lasting impression on Hecht. A post–Yellow Decade novel, it created a sensation in its time since its neo-Dostoyevskian hero was a cynical, sadistic young man who believed that "first and foremost it is necessary to gratify one's natural desires." At the graveside of a friend, called upon to speak, Sanine only remarks, "One fool less in the world, that's all"—reflecting a sensibility that appealed to the youthful Hecht.[11] Hecht's alter ego in the picture, though, was Maxwell Bodenheim, in thin disguise as Lionel Gans—Ganz being Count Bruga's real name—played by Lionel Stander, who had previously portrayed Bodenheim in *The Scoundrel*. Hecht had Stander carry a battered sheaf of poems with him in every scene. In *PM* in 1941, Hecht had written of Bodenheim, "He carries a much scuffed briefcase over his frayed pocket, and although I haven't seen this bulging bit of impedimenta for 15 years, I know what is inside it. Poems." Hecht again put lines from Bodenheim's poetry as well as several lines of his own from the *Chicago Literary Times* into his character's mouth and even had Stander repeat lines he'd spoken in *The Scoundrel*.

Completely inessential to the plot, Gans nevertheless provides the film with its wit and humor. When someone begins philosophizing bombastically about Tolstoy's concern for the masses, Gans remarks, "When the eagle grows weary of flying he dreams of retiring to the chicken coop." When the detective threatens to arrest everybody except Gans, Stander quips, "If you arrested everybody I didn't like the world would become a pensive vacuum." He calls Poliakoff "a withered carnation in the Broadway buttonhole," and when Poliakoff and Madame La Sylph get angry with him for butting into their affairs, Gans replies, "The indignation of fools is my favorite crown" (a retort of Bodenheim's).

Specter of the Rose was completed in December 1945, received a great deal of advance publicity, and opened to good reviews in June of the following year. (During the *Specter* period, David Selznick called Hecht in several times to help with script problems on his *Gone-With-the-Wind-of-the-West*, *Duel in the Sun*, since he was rewriting virtually every scene King Vidor shot, frequently changing scenes while they were in progress. Selznick took script credit and Hecht took money.)

With *Specter* out of the way, Hecht and MacArthur took a sophisticated whodunit about the mysterious murder of several concert pianists called *Crescendo*, rewrote and polished it, and presciently retitled it *Swan Song*. The original play, written by Harriet Hinsdale and Ramon Romero with music by Sigmund Romberg, had been killed before it made it to Broadway. Rewritten by Hecht and MacArthur and staged by Joseph Pevney, it opened at the Booth Theatre on May 15th, 1946, to disastrous reviews. It was "corny," "an unmitigated bore," and "too old-fashioned." Robert Garland in the *Journal-American* remarked that "the rewrite goes on." Hecht and MacArthur made an effort to save the play—going on radio shows several times a week during the play's run to publicize it, as well as papering the house—but it closed after twenty-two performances. (At the same time, Hecht was negotiating with British producer J. Arthur Rank to write a film based on the life of Lord Byron to star Laurence Olivier, but nothing ever came of it.)

By the end of the war, convinced that the only chance the Jews had of surviving was to have a nation of their own, Hecht entered the last phase of his propaganda writing: he began working for the League for a Free Palestine, a group headed by Peter Bergson struggling to free Palestine from the British.

In 1922, England had accepted a mandate from the League of Nations to turn Palestine into a Jewish homeland, but had neglected their commitment since they were more concerned with maintaining good relations with the Arabs because of their oil, at the expense of the Jews. Britain's *White Paper of 1939: Palestine: Statement of Policy* forbade all further immigration of Jews into Palestine and stripped Jews already living there of the right to buy land. Winston Churchill, in the House of Commons, May 24th, 1939, protested that the White Paper was a shameful document and a crime against all European Jews.

"I had no interest in Palestine ever becoming a homeland for the Jews," Hecht said, "but now I had, suddenly, interest in little else." The League for a Free Palestine that Hecht had joined was the American fund-raising and propaganda arm of the Irgun Zvai Leumi, a small group of dedicated men and women who had given up all hope of negotiating with the British and had turned to armed rebellion to force them out. Ironically, the Irgun also had to contend with what they branded Jewish traitors, since most of the world's Zionist organizations and all the Jewish leaders in Palestine were cooperating with the British: they had ordered Jews to turn in all members of the Irgun to the British, who frequently hanged them. "The best thing a Jew can do," Hecht wrote, "is forget that there is any Jewish cause—and stick to causes that he can back up under a flag—and with a gun."

To gain support for a free Jewish state and to raise money for the Irgun and for Jews living in displaced-persons camps in Europe, Hecht wrote a theatrical pageant called *A Flag Is Born*. Hecht and Will Rogers, Jr., cochairman of the League, had gone to the American people to ask for money to buy ships to transport European Jews to Palestine (despite British refusal to allow them in), but without much success. So Hecht turned back to the theatre to write a story of an old couple on their way to Palestine who stop to rest in a graveyard on the eve of the Sabbath. While the old man is praying, he sees a vision of Solomon, who asks him who the enemy of the Jew is. The whole world, the old man answers. Then challenge the world, Solomon tells him. At the end of the play, the old couple discover a young Jewish boy hiding in the cemetery who, on the verge of suicide, has a vision of armed men and women. Join the fight for Palestine, they urge him, join the Irgun, join the Stern group (an organization similar to the Irgun, named after Abraham Stern, who was killed by the British). The boy takes the old man's prayer shawl, converts it into a flag, then as the curtain falls joins the ranks of marching men and women.

Kurt Weill wrote the score for the show, Luther Adler directed it, and Marc Connelly, Sidney Lumet, Quentin Reynolds, Louis Bromfield, Paul Muni, and Marlon Brando played the principal parts. The play went into rehearsal in August and opened September 5th, 1946,[12] at the Alvin Theatre, sponsored by Eleanor Roosevelt, Maxwell Anderson, and New York City mayor William O'Dwyer. Despite cries of "Propaganda!" from the audience on opening night and poor reviews from *The New York Times* and *The New Yorker*, the show was a success. It ran 120 performances, then went on tour and turned a large enough profit to buy a ship, a captured German yacht! The SS *Ben Hecht*, however, was seized by the British, who sent the Jewish refugees to detention camps on Cyprus.

On September 9th, Hecht left for Los Angeles to replenish his bank account. He told Gene Fowler he was going there for a rest. "You can believe it or not, but the tranquilities of the Strip, the subdued fistfighting at Chasen's and the little stabbings at the better cocktail parties around Beverly Hills assume a serenity in comparison to Broadway that is positively pastoral." Hecht tried unsuccessfully to interest a studio in filming *A Flag Is Born*, then retired to his Oceanside house (which he'd bought in 1943) to work on seven films over the next seven months. With Charlie Lederer he wrote *Kiss of Death* for Henry Hathaway from an unpublished short story by a New York City assistant DA. Alone he adapted a Dorothy B. Hughes novel, *Ride the Pink Horse*, for Robert Montgomery, who directed as well as starred in it. An original story, *Her Husband's Affairs*, went to producer Raphael Hakim. Hecht also adapted an old Edward Sheldon and Margaret Ayer Barnes play, *Dishonored Lady*, wrote an original for Otto Preminger, which was never produced, and script-doctored David Selznick and Alfred Hitchcock's *The Paradine Case* for ten thousand dollars and a guarantee that he would not receive credit since he felt the script had insoluble problems. (Hecht had to interrupt work on *The Paradine Case* because of a more pressing script commitment, and when he went back to work on it he couldn't remember the plot.) Since he had also signed to adapt a best-seller, *The Miracle of the Bells*, Hecht phoned Quentin Reynolds to ask if he wanted to do the script with him. When Reynolds agreed, Hecht told him, "Your first assignment will be to read the novel. I just can't. It's a hunk of junk."

For Paul Muni Hecht began a script based on the life of Alfred Nobel but had to give it up after doing fifty-five pages because of the plethora of prior commitments. "Ben owned a house at Oceanside where he had a script-writing factory," Henry Hathaway recalled. "I know he was writing *Kiss of Death* and he had Charlie Lederer down there and some other guys and they were all writing different things and pooling it. It was awful hard to get to Ben at that time."

David Selznick wrote Rose Hecht that he had warned Ben that most of what "he was making . . . at that script factory in Oceanside . . . would go for taxes and that he was simply digging himself into a deeper hole, but I couldn't seem to penetrate. Such is genius, I suppose, that one can't be a lord of language and at the same time have even an elementary recognition of the awful inevitability of taxes!" Yet with more than $500,000 banked from this film work, Hecht plunged back into ad writing and proselytizing for the Irgun, which had successfully put the eighty thousand British troops in Palestine on the defensive. The Haganah, the official Zionist military group, attacked Hecht in full-page ads of their own:

> There are new playboys in America; they play with Jewish blood. The thrills of Hollywood are no longer sharp

enough. They need lustier excitement, bolder show-
manship . . . they egg on the mad children of the Irgun;
the distant whiff of bombs is headier than a cocktail. . . .

On May 15th, 1947, Hecht published a full-page piece in fifteen
major American dailies which soon smeared him across newspapers all
over the world.

LETTER TO THE TERRORISTS OF PALESTINE

My brave friends,

You may not believe what I write you, for there is a lot
of fertilizer in the air at the moment.

But, on my word as an old reporter, what I write is true.

The Jews of America are for you. You are the feathers
in their hats.

In the past fifteen hundred years every nation of
Europe has taken a crack at the Jews. This time the British
are at bat.

You are the first answer that makes sense to the New
World.

Every time you blow up a British arsenal, or wreck a
British jail, or send a British railroad train sky high, or rob
a British bank, or let go with your bombs and guns at the
British betrayers and invaders of your homeland, the Jews
of America make a little holiday in their hearts. . . .

For weeks Hecht was attacked by the British press. Lord Beaver-
brook's *Evening Standard* called him a "penthouse warrior" and accused
him of "gross chauvinism, distortion of history, indoctrination of children, preference of solutions through violence, race pride, the stoking up
of hatred between nations, indifference to the sanctity of human life."
Lord Rothermere's *Daily Mail* labeled him a "vitriolic Zionist volcano
with a touch of the carnival huckster" and reprinted an article from the
Palestine Post that accused Hecht of "creating a criminal insanity that is
killing Jews as well as Britons." The *Standard* devoted its entire "Letters to
the Editor" section one day to Hecht, one correspondent calling Hecht a
"Nazi at heart" and nine others suggesting his films be banned.

Hecht was not only reviled in imperialist British newspapers and by
his Haganah foes, but by many of the very people he considered himself
a spokesman for: American Jews. Meyer Levin, in his autobiography *In
Search*, wrote:

The Haganah and Palmach were resistance groups; the Irgun and Stern were terrorist groups, yet terrorist and resistance actions were sometimes difficult to distinguish from each other. . . . And more complicating was the powerful propaganda carried on by the terrorist groups, particularly in the United States—propaganda so powerful as to give their activities an importance altogether out of relationship to reality. . . . In America, the noise-making Irgun Tsvai Leumi was permitted to give the impression that it alone opposed the British in Palestine. . . . Peter Bergson showed me a copy of a first manifesto, to be published as a full-page advertisement. This was the initiation of an attention-getting device which was in the coming years to prove costly, wasteful, sometimes harmful, and effective chiefly for Bergson, Ben Hecht, and their notoriety-loving friends. . . . Their [American Jews] activity was mobilized, vast funds were collected from them in the ensuing years, ostensibly for paying for "medical aid to Hebrew fighters," and they thought they were very wise in assuming that their funds were really paying for explosives; apparently their funds were paying for more full-page advertisements in which Ben Hecht could exercise his love for bellicose phrase-making. . . . And in the end, the Bergson-Hecht propaganda provided the greatest catch phrase toward anti-Semitism since Hitler . . . for it was in one of those full-page ads . . . that Ben Hecht wrote that with every bombing and shooting of British soldiers, "the Jews of America make a little holiday in their hearts."

I don't believe that any single phrase was ever more harmful to the Jewish people. Hecht published the statement with the flourish of the prophet speaking for his people; he must have realized that the British would accept this phrase as the slogan of the Jewish people: he wanted it so. And in this sense the phrase amounted to race-slander with murderous results.

How could he permit himself to speak for our people? I had read a book of his called A Guide for the Bedevilled, supposedly dealing with the Jews' problems. There is no need to discuss this pretentious hodge-podge of muddled and incomplete thoughts: one remark in it was sufficiently illustrative. Through all of his early life, and through his years in Chicago as a newspaperman, Hecht stated, he had never personally encountered anti-Semitism.

I first knew Ben Hecht in his newspaper days, and followed him on the *Chicago Daily News*. It is utterly inconceivable to me that a Chicago newspaperman with a name like Ben Hecht could have been unaware that anti-Semitism existed in America. . . . To make such a statement in a book that was supposed to be a guide for other Jews revealed, to me, more than anything else in the volume, Hecht's capacity for attitudinizing and self-deception.

Earlier, veteran correspondent Dorothy Thompson (one of Sinclair Lewis's wives) had written, on November 3rd, 1946, "I am greatly perturbed about the behaviour and propaganda of some Zionists, or self-appointed leaders or spokesmen for the Zionist movement, specifically the Bergson and Ben Hecht group. These people are the worst contributors to anti-Semitism in America to my mind."

Hecht's reaction to accusations of fostering anti-Semitism, a result of his support of "terrorists," was another catchphrase: "There are only two Jewish parties left in the field: the terrorists and the terrified."

In the midst of this controversy and plans to write a movie to be produced in France to raise money for the Irgun, Hecht was hospitalized in New York. In June 1947 his gall bladder was removed, incapacitating him for months. Gene Fowler wrote him, "It must have been a novelty to have had the knife in your front instead of your back for a change." In August he was well enough to narrate a radio version of *Specter of the Rose* on the *Inner Sanctum* radio show, quipping that radio "is a wonderful way to make money—almost as good as train announcing." For two nights in September, another propaganda play, *The Terrorist*, was presented by the American League for a Free Palestine at Carnegie Hall, starring Ruth Chatterton. The winter was spent recuperating in Nyack, where he wrote a children's book for Jenny, *The Cat That Jumped out of the Story*. The end of December saw him back in Hollywood, riding high in the studios' esteem because of rave reviews for *Kiss of Death* and good ones for *Dishonored Lady* and *Ride the Pink Horse*. There, he wrote the never-produced *Angel's Flight* for MGM producer Sam Zimbalist (now married to Mimsi Taylor), and did a first draft of *Cry of the City* for Darryl Zanuck and a quick rewrite of *Roseanna McCoy* for Sam Goldwyn.

He also continued his Irgun fund-raising with the help of Jewish racketeer Mickey Cohen, although this time the money that was raised aided no Jews in Palestine. As gangster Jimmy Fratianno revealed,

Mickey Cohen throws a copy of *The Herald* across his desk and says, "Jimmy, my God, what do you think of this?" His finger's pointing to this article about a ship loaded with guns and ammunition that sunk at sea. He's tapping his finger against the newspaper and looking at me with his hound-dog eyes, not a fucking expression on his face, and he keeps repeating, "Oh, terrible, terrible. What a tragedy." The story mentions no names. It don't say why it sank, the name of the ship, nothing. Just that a ship loaded with arms sunk somewhere in the fucking ocean. He says, "Jimmy, the boat carrying the guns and ammunition for the Jews has sunk. A million fucking dollars had gone to the bottom of the ocean." I think to myself, "You cocksucker, I know your game." The way I see it, Mickey made up a story about buying guns and ammunition for the Jews with the million raised at the benefits and then said the boat sank. A few unknown people died, some were saved, and it gets printed in the press. I says, "Mickey, congratulations. You've just pulled off the biggest, cleanest fucking score I've ever seen made." And he looks at me, just squinting, you know, and for a split second there's this big shit-eating grin on his face.[13]

In November of 1947 the Jewish War of Independence had begun in earnest. The Irgun, the Stern group, and the Haganah were now united to fight the British and—when they finally pulled out—the Arabs. Money that Hecht had raised in 1946 and 1947—which Mickey Cohen hadn't got his hands on—was used to buy a ship and weapons for the Irgun. The ship, the *Altalena* (with Menachem Begin aboard), arrived in Tel Aviv harbor on the 25th of June, 1948, during a United Nations–imposed truce, causing a power struggle within the newly formed nation. The Irgun commander on the *Altalena* insisted that part of the matériel be distributed to the Irgun, the rest to be divided equally by the other fighting forces. Ben-Gurion insisted it was one army, one nation, so everything should be divided equally. The Irgun refused and set up machine guns on the beach. Ben Gurion, claiming to be afraid of a divisive civil war, sent troops to take the ship by force—which began a civil war. Almost one hundred men and women were killed in the ensuing battle and the world was shocked to read of Jews killing Jews on the beaches of Tel Aviv. Ben-Gurion had hundreds of Irgun soldiers arrested and announced to the press, "Praise to the gun that sank the unsur-rendered ship!" One of the Irgun members killed on the *Altalena* was

Abrasha Stavsky, who had been smuggling Jews into Palestine since the end of the war. When the Haganah opened fire on the ship, he turned his back on Israel in shame and was shot in the back. "I turned my back on Israel," Hecht wrote, "the same time Abrasha Stavsky did."

Hecht had only contempt for Ben-Gurion since he was a Zionist leader, which to Hecht meant a reactionary and an apologist for the British maltreatment of the Palestinian Jews, a man who got involved in the fight against the British only after the Irgun, through their "terrorism," forced a showdown. After others had fought the fight to free Palestine, Hecht believed, Ben-Gurion and the Haganah took the credit and assumed the leadership of the new state.

Over the next dozen years Hecht's growing discontent with what he saw happening in Israel would prompt him to write *Perfidy*, a book ostensibly about the Kastner trial, which had begun in Israel in 1954. Kastner, a high government official who had collaborated with the Nazis, was the club Hecht would use to attack the Israeli government headed by Ben-Gurion: unbeknownst to the people of Israel, Hecht contended, their government was composed of who knew how many Nazi collaborators protected by Ben-Gurion and his cabinet, who had also known about the Nazi genocide during the war and had done nothing to stop it. Ben-Gurion retaliated by denying Hecht permission to be buried in holy ground in Israel.

13

CHILD OF THE CENTURY

Whether or not you believe, as has sometimes been suggested, that it was really Ben Hecht who authored the book of the Apocalypse, not to mention certain of the more astringent passages of the Old Testament, the fact remains that there is something definitely prophetic about the man as of one who had found the tablets of stone in the desert.

—THEODORE STRAUSS
The New York Times

CHILD OF THE CENTURY

Done with political activism for good, Hecht fired a last sally at the British in September of 1948 when United Nations mediator Count Folke Bernadotte was reported to have been murdered by the Stern gang. Said Hecht to the *New York Post*, it was the British who had him assassinated to further their interests in the Middle East (Bernadotte was trying to reduce the size of the Jewish state): "The assassination was that of an ass who wasn't worthy of so fine a death. He was a professional cat's paw hired to pull chestnuts out of the fire for the British. Jewish terrorists didn't kill this tool of the British." (Israel Eldad, one of the leaders of Lehi, a splinter group of the Irgun, has gone on record with the information that he, Yalin-Mor, and Itzhak Shamir—all Lehi commanders—made the decision jointly to have Bernadotte slain and it was Shamir who planned the operation.) The British government struck back—through the Cinematograph Exhibitors' Association[1]—by imposing a two-and-a-half-year ban on all Hecht films in the United Kingdom. In the book Hecht had just begun, he commented, "The literary Dane, Georg Brandes, wrote with a sigh one day, 'He who writes in Danish writes on water.' I had come to feel that propaganda writing was even less than water writing. It was writing traced on the air with a finger."

Hecht's decade of politics left him more disillusioned than ever, a direct result of the perfidy of Franklin Roosevelt and the leaders of the new Jewish state. If what he was looking for was simply another cause, Hecht could have allied himself with the screenwriters blacklisted the year before for their communist proselytizing. ("Lardner, Lawson, Bessie, Ornitz, etc.," Communist Party member Bodenheim wrote Hecht, "hid like agitated children behind glass window panes. . . . They were desperately attempting to protect fat jobs and bankrolls against the bogie-man, public condemnation.") But Hecht held no brief for communism, nor for Senator McCarthy and his "power-hungry bulldozing."

Hecht—other than for his Irgun involvement—had always kept clear of partisan politics. However, his cynically antipolitical superiority—above the ideological fray, smiling down contemptuously—resulted in the most diverse, even ludicrous, misinterpretations. In 1937, Mary McCarthy wrote, in her review of *To Quito and Back*, "Hecht, it would appear, has been converted, or frightened by intellectual fashion into giving lip-service to radicalism." George Jean Nathan went even further, maintaining that Hecht had incorporated "into his play a defence of Communism." Lawrence Langner concurred, calling *To Quito and Back* an offering that "glibly and artfully spread a communist gospel." These simple-minded evaluations got Hecht included in a list of "Hollywood Reds and Pinks" in Myron C. Fagan's *Documentation of the Red Stars in Hollywood*, published in the early fifties. Yet, *New York Times* film critic Otis Ferguson opined that "Hecht has always tasted bile at the thought of the Comrades."

Balance these antithetical points of view with that of film historians Arthur Mayer and Richard Griffith, in *The Movies* (1957): "Most message pictures were frankly New Dealistic, but a few, such as *Soak the Rich*, derided or deplored the rising tide of liberalism and radicalism. In an ad for this film which pained the more sober-sided radicals, Hecht and MacArthur were depicted singing 'We're the guys who wrote the yarn/ And here's what it's about / Class ideas don't mean a thing / When love kicks them out.'" Raymond Durgnat, in his 1970 book *The Crazy Mirror*, further reduced Hecht's political philosophy, espoused in *Soak the Rich*, to "an uncompromisingly Republican attitude."

The "Republican" *Soak the Rich* and the "communist" *To Quito and Back* were, on the contrary, works infused with a contempt for politics, the common man, the little man. *Soak the Rich* had been for Hecht a platform from which to knock the leftism that the Hollywood intelligentsia had become infatuated with. Hecht saw through this leftism as faddism, the faddism of the wealthy who weren't about to give up their money and comforts no matter how many protest meetings they attended, no matter how great their sympathy for the proletariat. Most of what Hecht was witness to in Hollywood in the early and mid-thirties was rhetoric—words without results—Beverly Hills party members leading the gullible, the impressionable, to support positions they would abandon for the next vogue: rejection of hard-line communism and the Soviet Union once Stalin signed the Nonaggression Pact with Hitler.

Where *Soak the Rich* was bemusedly skeptical, *To Quito and Back* was a vicious attack directed at the masses, which in Hecht's view was a group of "blood-thirsty morons." Supporting a left-wing revolution, in the words of a character in the play, "was like trying to love a woman with a harelip," in other words, a fanciful romantic attachment to the ugly and difficult of expression. Hecht wasn't pushing communism, he was bombinating over the superiority of the few over the Great Unwashed— and he was one of the elect, a result of his intelligence, talent, and above all his ability to see Life clearly, from above. He was not one of the ants blindly, unthinkingly, going through the motions of meaningless existence. He told Gene Fowler, in 1931, "The democratic theory that fools are entitled not only to opinions but to the expression thereof, that imbeciles be permitted to sit in judgement on their betters has always amazed me."

Hecht's politics—if indeed he had any—were elitist, neither right-wing nor left-wing. If there had been an Iconoclast Party, he would have been a card-carrying member.

John Howard Lawson, one of the blacklisted Hollywood Ten, said of the McCarthy years that "the cold war blew like an icy wind across the country to the Pacific Coast." Hecht, however, could choose not to feel it, since with one exception he had never joined any of the political groups that had burgeoned in California and New York during the thirties. Although he had harassed many a studio boss with his Irgun fund-raising, he'd sung Jews, not communists. Hecht was acquainted with many of the movie and book people listed in *Red Channels*, an index of alleged communists—Lionel Stander, Karen Morley, Edward G. Robinson, Margo, Dashiell Hammett, José Ferrer, Dorothy Parker, Marc Connelly, et al.—but prior to the fifties he personally had never appeared on any list. As disenchanted with politics as he had been when he was a reporter in Chicago, Hecht just wanted to return to writing for the sake of writing. "I was going nowhere that I knew of," he said, "and never again might have anything as interesting to utter as I had uttered about Jews. But having said my say, it was my nature to wander off, hoping for other topics."

The topic he chose, which would take the next five years to complete, was his autobiography, *A Child of the Century*, a title deriving from Alfred de Musset's *La Confession d'un enfant du siècle*, which he had read in his teens. In 1929 he had announced a novel to be called *A Child of the Century*, a companion volume to *A Hill of Skulls*, the two of which became *A Jew in Love*. He had also announced a sequel to *A*

Guide for the Bedevilled with the same title in 1947, but by 1948, at loose ends, he turned back to his own life as a source and embarked on an autobiography. He had toyed with the idea for years but, taken up with other projects, had lacked the time.

Needing money to support the writing of *A Child of the Century*, Hecht returned to Oceanside in October of 1948 to knock out as many scripts as possible, as quickly as possible, for as much money as possible. An adaptation of Gerald du Maurier's *Trilby* was followed by an adaptation of a Gogol play, *The Inspector General*. On the heels of that came MGM's *Big Jack*, which Hecht collaborated on with Gene Fowler and Robert Thoeren. At the same time, Gene Fowler had convinced L. B. Mayer to resurrect *Farike the Guest Artist*, an old script of his and Hecht's written in 1933 for W. C. Fields. But Wallace Beery, who was to star, died before shooting began. (The script had been shelved originally because the studio had wanted a vehicle for Marie Dressler, but what MGM got, said Hecht, was "a starrer for Bill Fields with Marie Dressler playing his stooge.") Hecht also continued to develop *Diamonds in the Pavement* for Harpo Marx, who introduced him to Frank Tashlin, a young gag writer who had worked on the Marx Brothers' *A Night in Casablanca*. Hecht hired him to do the gags for his story.

"We always had breakfast around a big table," Tashlin recalled, "then Ben and I would go down to his writing room beneath the house, at beach level, in Oceanside. It was a charming room with a little ceramic stove which Ben kept fired up. I used to write on the floor and he sat by the window with his writing board in his lap—on this board he had carved the titles of everything he'd ever written, *Count Bruga*, *Twentieth Century*, and so on. When he was sitting there thinking, he would rub crayon in all the carvings so the whole thing had a sort of Persian mosaic look. He would sit there with pads of yellow paper and an electric pencil sharpener looking out the window at the sea and the sandpipers, and he would sharpen fifty or sixty pencils, which was a slow process. This was the thinking process before he attacked the paper. Finally, with the pencils lined up beside him, it would start. He'd pick one up, put 'number one' on the top page of the pad, and the papers would fly off onto the floor like leaves. He'd say, 'Frank, I just did a thing here, now we need a joke. I left Harpo here, maybe you could work in a sequence.' So I'd make a note of that and we'd keep on going until one o'clock. We would work for four hours then go upstairs for lunch. Charlie Lederer was there but he wasn't working with us. Harpo would come down sometimes and Ben and I and whoever else was there would go out on the beach and play horseshoes. While we were having lunch, Ben's secretary was typing the stuff we'd written in the morning. She would arrive around noon and pick up Ben's pages off the floor, then at four-thirty or five o'clock in came the 'stuff all typed. We would sit around and Ben, who was a marvelous reader, would read it aloud. He'd laugh and say, 'Here's where your part goes in, Frank, let me read that.' Then he'd read my part and he'd be just as appreciative of it as if he'd written it himself. That would be the day's work. Then would come dinner. There were always people there. The evenings were spent playing with model railroads. In front of the fireplace there was an enormous table on which was the most intricate railroad setup, it was like Long Island City. There would be teams—say Ben and Lederer, and Harpo and I—and the idea was to set up several cars. But there were other cars in the way so you with your engine had just so much time to get in there and get your car and put it in the proper sequence. There was such screaming and yelling and this would go on until midnight, this kids' game which became more than a kids' game. Then Ben would read in bed until four o'clock and he was up early in the morning. It was a marvelous experience."

The result of all this camaraderie and high spirits never ended up on the screen. As Tashlin explains,

> *Diamonds in the Pavement*—which was renamed *Love Happy*—never came out the way it was planned, though, because of a dreadful producer by the name of Lester Cowan who botched it up. He was afraid of making a picture with Harpo. *Love Happy* was an original story by Ben for Harpo, but that story was never made. Mac Benoff was put on by the producer, he's the one who put in all the Groucho stuff. I don't know how Harpo let it happen other than he might have been fearful of appearing alone. [United Artists wouldn't back the project unless all three of the brothers appeared.] At that time, Groucho had become hot again with his *You Bet Your Life* show, so they dragged him in and the movie turned out to be a piece of crap. It could have been a classic film, the traditional pantomime film. David Miller, the director, didn't know what to do with it. [At one point, it was rumored René Clair would direct.] He should never do comedy. Even so, *Life* magazine came out with Harpo's picture on the cover and called it the best chase picture in thirty years. I saw it and thought it was just terrible. Ben loved Harpo though, and the thing he did was a labor of love. You had to love Harpo, he was the last gentleman in the world.

Harpo later wrote Hecht on February 17th, 1949, "I am an old, broken-down pantomimist, but time will heal. That is, time away from Cowan. . . . I started to vomit, not from food but from sheer delight realizing I was through with the picture and knowing that I won't see Cowan any more. . . . Groucho has constantly called him a thief and a liar and has refused to even talk to him."

In December, 1948, Hecht won third prize in an *Ellery Queen* mystery-story contest and the British ban began to sting: he was stripped of screen credit for *Love Happy* and *The Inspector General*. "The movie moguls, most of them Jews for whose pockets I had netted over a hundred million dollars in profits with my scenarios, were even nervous answering my hellos, let alone of hiring me," Hecht wrote. Otto Preminger, however— whose second directing job had been *The Front Page*, at the Max Reinhardt Theatre in Vienna—was not intimidated by the Hollywood brass and asked Hecht to write the scripts for *Where the Sidewalk Ends* and *Whirlpool*. (When released in England, the first would be credited to Rex Connor, the second to Hecht's chauffeur, Lester Barstow.) Hecht then returned to New York intending to produce a low-budget film of *Hedda Gabler* with Geraldine Fitzgerald; but with no financing forthcoming, he was back in Los Angeles early in 1949 to work with Howard Hawks on his first and last science-fiction script.

When Hawks was in Germany making *I Was a Male War Bride*, he had bought the rights (for nine hundred dollars) to "Who Goes There," a short-story he thought would make an interesting picture.

"How about doing a science-fiction story?" he asked Hecht. Hecht said no.

"But what if we call it *The Thing from Another World* and tell the story of a guy from another planet who's a vegetable that lives on human blood?"

"In that case, okay," Hecht agreed, seeing an opportunity to lampoon the neurotic fear of communism rife in the United States during the fifties: the "thing" (played by James Arness) was just Joe McCarthy dressed up as a blood-sucking vegetable. With Charlie Lederer, Hecht and Hawks wrote the script at Hawks's home in Bel Air. Hawks let his editor Christian Nyby actually direct but he supervised production, Nyby receiving directorial credit with Hawks billed as producer. Lederer received the sole writing credit.

Hawks then rehired Hecht and Lederer to do an extensive rewrite of an I. A. L. Diamond original, *Monkey Business*. "That was a case where we picked up a story that had been worked on and completely changed it," Hawks said. "Anyway, my script was mainly Ben and Lederer. I thought it was a pretty bad picture and oddly enough the French think it's one of the great pictures they've seen. I don't know why it appeals to them." "You only have to watch *Monkey Business*," wrote French director and critic Jacques Rivette, "to know that it is a brilliant film. Some people refuse to admit this however; they refuse to be satisfied by proof."

In October of 1951, with independent financing, Hecht wrote and directed *Actors and Sin*, a two-part picture derived from his short stories "Actor's Blood" and "Concerning a Woman of Sin." He blocked out a script in a week, cast the picture in three days, then with Lee Garmes, George Antheil, and Ernst Fegte went to the Motion Picture Center in Los Angeles and shot it in eight days. The first story, starring Edward G. Robinson, was reminiscent of *The Scoundrel*, the action switched from the publishing world to the New York theatre. The second starred Jenny Hecht as a nine-year-old girl who submits a screenplay titled "Woman of Sin" to a Hollywood agent (based on Leland Hayward), who sells it to a studio boss (L. B. Mayer) before discovering the author's age and identity.

When the film was completed, Hecht turned it over to George Schaefer, now a producer's representative, who arranged for it to be distributed by United Artists. Since Preminger was shooting a picture for United Artists, Hecht asked him if *Actors and Sin* could be second-billed with his *The Moon Is Blue*. Preminger didn't mind, but L. B. Mayer, furious because he thought—with reason—that Hecht's film made him out as an idiot, pressured theatre owners around the country to refuse to exhibit it. Hecht and United Artists sued the ABC Theater Corporation for strangling the film, but to little avail, since it got few bookings.

After working uncredited on the script of *Roman Holiday*, from a story by Ian McLellan Hunter, Hecht returned to New York for the October 29th premiere of *Black Velvet*, a play he and MacArthur had adapted for producer John Golden. Roasted by the critics, it closed at the end of the week. Hecht then wanted to make another movie at the Motion Picture Center based on his short story "Swindler's Luck," published in the *Saturday Evening Post* in January of 1952, but once again failed to get backing and had to cancel the production (he later sold the script, retitled *The Sunset Kid*, to Henry Hathaway, who failed to shoot it). Back in California by January, he turned down the opportunity to write *Topsy and Eva* for Betty Hutton and Ginger Rogers in order to lend Preminger a hand on the script of *Angel Face.*

In New York, Hecht wrote the book for *Hazel Flagg*, a Jule Styne musical based on *Nothing Sacred*, to star Thomas Mitchell; then he and Hugh Gray (translator of André Bazin's seminal volumes of critical essays on the cinema, *Qu'est-ce que le cinéma?*) did a script of *Ulysses*, a Kirk Douglas epic to be filmed in Italy. The original script had been written years before by German director G. W. Pabst, who had been unable to find backing for his portrait of Ulysses as a peace-maker. Eventually Pabst sold his script to Dino De Laurentiis and was hired to direct. Then when Kirk Douglas was cast by De Laurentiis, Paramount came in on the deal with sinews of war in exchange for distribution rights and script approval. Pabst's scenario wasn't acceptable to Hollywood since it only concerned itself with the last ten days of Homer's *Odyssey*, thus Pabst was ousted, replaced by Mario Camerini, an important prewar director who in the fifties was reduced to filming unexceptional commercial projects. Hecht and Hugh Gray were brought in to do a professional Hollywood script. "It was a most agreeable experience to work with Ben Hecht," Gray recalled. "I lived at his house in Nyack and what we did, the way we worked, was that we would meet in the morning, talk a little, then each would go to a room, he to his writing room and me to a room that was provided for me, and I would write a few scenes and he would write a few scenes and then we would swap. The division of labor was that I would be concerned with the scenes where it was imperative that one should have some sense of the historical or literary flavor and he was concerned with what one might call the human aspect.

"He enjoyed himself in a strange kind of way, he was a mixture of cynicism and humor and hardboiledness. He was a mysterious character to me. He was always writing. I'm an early riser, I get up and go to the kitchen and look for a cup of coffee, but no matter what time I woke up Ben was always sitting there in his dressing gown reading something or writing.

"I don't think Ben gave a damn once he got rid of a script. He didn't take the whole thing seriously. I don't know what he could have been had he not been a screenwriter. He was obviously in the good old tough style, the old Chicago newspaperman. He had a marvelous storytelling ability and was incredibly bright. I felt that what he made of himself was a hack, a hack of genius. I have always described him as a hack of genius."

In November of 1952 Hecht signed with CBS to script seven

half-hour dramas for a television series of his own, *Tales of the City*. In May, Willys Motors bought the show and the first was aired on July 2nd, 1953. Two of the stories were originals, but the rest were reworkings of plots Hecht had used before. The first was adapted from a *Collier's* story, "Cinderella from Cedar Rapids," which concerned a confused young couple in New York who are helped out by "the big heart of Broadway." "We had to make the first one very sentimental," Hecht admitted, "because we used it to sell the sponsor." The third derived from "Actor's Blood," the fifth was *Miracle in the Rain*, the sixth was taken from *Count Bruga*, and the seventh was about a crook Hecht had known in Chicago in the teens.

Between the airing of the second and the third shows, Hecht completed his 950-page manuscript of *A Child of the Century*, the longest book he was ever to write. Hardly an autobiography, it was more a collection of memories written in the form of short stories and, like *A Book of Miracles*, was interspersed with lengthy philosophical asides. Only 50 out of 633 published pages dealt with Hollywood, and only half of those with his movie scripting. The book's lengthiest section—355 pages—dwelt on his relatives, his friends, and the Chicago years, which remained the wellspring of his life even though he had left Chicago thirty years before; 118 pages were devoted to his decade of politics, leaving only 160 to cover the rest of his life, the New York and Hollywood years. Charlie Samuels's son Bob felt that "you can't really go by many of the things Ben wrote in *A Child of the Century*, because so much of it was pure fantasy, for example his saying that my father had a girl with two vaginas. ["Charlie Samuels had traveled and been touched by the wonders of life, which included a Southern lady with two vaginas. 'I would have married her,' said Samuels, 'but I figured I could never trust her.'"] My father didn't mind, though. Ben read all of these things to him before the book was published and was absolutely delighted when he could think up any expressive, outlandish way of describing one of his friends. I remember I was in the sixth grade in Nyack at the time of the book's publication. My teacher walked up to my desk and asked, 'Is this man really your father?'"

In March of 1954 *A Child of the Century* was published by Simon & Schuster. Most of the reviews were excellent, Saul Bellow opining, "Among the pussy cats who write of social issues today Hecht roars like an old fashioned lion"; Harry Hansen commented in the *Saturday Review* that sections of the book "touched universality," and *The New York Times* called it "excessively massive and solid as the Great Pyramid." Hecht came in for a drubbing from the Hollywood establishment, though: George Murphy remarked that he was "running out of patience with these people who take the best Hollywood has to offer and then find fault with it." A *Variety* editorial illiterately pontificated, "*A Child of the Century* doesn't stack up with any more substance than the words from a sick, soiled mind on a lavatory wall," the same criticism leveled at Hecht's first book, *Erik Dorn*.

F. Hugh Herbert—for whom, four years before, Hecht had introduced the published version of his play *The Moon Is Blue*, calling him "one of the few witty writers for the American stage"—publicly stated that it was "unbecoming of Hecht to make disparaging comments of an industry from which he derived a substantial income." (Shortly thereafter, Hecht received a letter from Herbert—"Some months ago in Hollywood, under pressure, I was called upon to issue a rather stuffy statement about the 'attack' you had made on the Motion Picture Industry. I hadn't read [A] *Child of the Century* at that time. . . . Meanwhile, I have read and thoroughly enjoyed [A] *Child of the Century* and these lines are by way of apology and congratulations. Recalling gratefully as I do the charming Preface you wrote to my book, I should have had the courage and integrity when I was importuned, to make some sort of a statement as President of the Screen Writers' Guild to tell all and sundry to go fry an egg." Rose Hecht thought Herbert "a prime example of one who attacks in public and asks favors and gives thanks in private.")

Hecht wrote with the dramatist's sense of enclosedness and completeness of action (i.e., he created stories with buildups and definitive endings), recycling and restructuring stories he'd heard, read, or reported; making up tales about his friends as well as himself for his and their delectation. *A Child of the Century* opened the floodgates, Hecht's past—Chicago and New York in the teens and twenties—becoming the major source of inspiration during his remaining ten years, inspiring him to fictionalize his life in three more volumes of memoirs and on his own TV talk show.

14

THE LAST DECADE

Three events occurred in 1953 and early 1954 that signaled to Hecht that his world was fast receding into the past. First was the death of Herman Mankiewicz, friend of thirty years; another, the publication of Margaret Anderson's *Little Review Anthology*, in which she included "The American Family." If the *Anthology* reminded Hecht nostalgically of the teens and twenties in Chicago, he was reminded more forcibly that those favorite years were long gone when, on February 7th, 1954, Maxwell Bodenheim and his third wife were murdered in a Bowery flophouse.

An alcoholic for two decades, Bodenheim had continued to write poetry, plays, and short stories in the face of penury and poor health. All but forgotten by the reading public, he still managed to publish a poem now and again—*The New York Times* ran two shortly before he was killed. His last book, *Selected Poems 1914–1944*, had been issued in 1946, and at the time of his death at the age of sixty he was working on a collection of autobiographical essays about life in Greenwich Village as he had known it, for publisher Sam Roth (who had pirated James Joyce's *Ulysses* in the twenties). The death of Bodenheim's second wife, Grace, a few years earlier had plunged him into despair; while she was living they had barely managed to scrape by, living in Brooklyn for many years and supported by Hecht, but with her death Bodenheim gave up their low-rent apartment and began moving from one cheap hotel to another. In 1953, at a bar in the Village, he met thirty-three-year-old Ruth Fagan, who had a history of mental illness, having set fire to her parents' house when she was a child. They were married two days after they met. Carousing in one of Bodenheim's haunts in November, they encountered Harold Weinberg, who, like Bodenheim, had been dishonorably discharged from the U.S. Army and who, like Ruth, had spent part of his youth in a mental institution. Mad Max—as he was called around the Village—and Ruth saw Weinberg from time to time over the next few months. Bodenheim was contemptuous of him, but when on the night of

February 6th they had no money for a place to sleep, they accepted Weinberg's offer to share his Bowery hotel room, Weinberg's generosity a result of sexual attraction to Ruth.

The following afternoon Bodenheim was found shot in the heart, the bullet having penetrated the paperback copy of Rachel Carson's *The Sea Around Us* he was carrying in an inside coat pocket. Ruth had been beaten, then stabbed to death. Weinberg was located and arrested a few days later. At first he claimed Bodenheim had murdered Ruth, then he admitted that he and Ruth were making love when Bodenheim awoke and there was nothing else to do but kill both of them. When arraigned, Weinberg sang "The Star-Spangled Banner" and proclaimed, "I just killed two Communist rats. They ought to give me a medal." He was committed to the Matteawan State Hospital for the insane. (Released in 1977, he was back behind bars the following year for attempted murder.)

At Bodenheim's funeral, his old friend Alfred Kreymborg eulogized, "We need not worry about the future, he will be read." Contrary to Kreymborg's prediction, Bodenheim's novels and volumes of poetry were all out of print at the time of his death, and thirty years later remain so. Hecht continued to write about him, though, as had been his wont since the twenties, keeping Bodenheim's memory alive in his autobiography, in a *Playboy* article, in a collection he would write in the early sixties, *Gaily, Gaily,* in the posthumously published *Letters from Bohemia,* and in *Winkelburg,* a play that was a pastiche of events from both Bodenheim's and Hecht's lives, with lines and scenes excerpted from *Fantazius Mallare, Count Bruga, 1001 Afternoons in New York, Lily of the Valley, Cutie,* and Bodenheim's poetry. Hardly a new work, *Winkelburg* was more a romanticized biography in dialogue form than a piece of theatre but the anecdotes and witty repartee, new to many although Hecht had drawn on them frequently over the years, made it a minor success— despite a taxi strike and a snowstorm—when it opened in Greenwich Village in January of 1958 (directed by Lee Falk, with Sinclair Lewis's son and Ring Lardner, Jr.'s wife in the cast).

Two years after Bodenheim's death, Hecht would perform the painful task of preserving Charlie MacArthur's memory in print, as well, in *Charlie: The Improbable Life and Times of Charles MacArthur.*

The Hechts—Ben, Rose, and Jenny—had spent the fall of 1955 in London, where Hecht worked uncredited on the script of *Trapeze* with Wolf Mankowitz. Then, at the beginning of the new year, they had settled in Paris so Hecht could adapt *The Hunchback of Notre Dame* for the Hakim brothers. (Hecht made a pilgrimage to the church of Saint-Sulpice to visit the bizarre bell-tower eyrie Huysmans had written of in *Là-Bas*, but was amused to discover there was none. Huysmans had made it up.) On their return to New York in April, they found Charlie seriously ill at New York Hospital, where on the morning of the twenty-first he died from severe anemia and nephritis, a result of a lifetime of hard drinking.

Despite the well-publicized legend of Hecht and MacArthur—most renowned team ever to turn out movie scripts and plays in twentieth-century America—the truth lay elsewhere. The legend holds for their early days—a few brief years in New York and Hollywood when they wrote *The Front Page* and their first movies. But after that, the friendship became increasingly strained and sad, although it continued till Charlie's death. Hecht had been disconcerted by Charlie's defection to Irving Thalberg and the Hollywood social elite in the thirties, but the deterioration of their relations began in the twenties—with MacArthur's courting of and marriage to Helen Hayes. Where Rose, a writer herself, encouraged the Hecht-MacArthur liaison, Helen didn't, restrained by strict upbringing and a narrow morality.

Hecht was Charlie's best friend but Helen was his wife and, to Hecht's displeasure, MacArthur more and more took Helen's road. As early as 1931—prior to the MacArthur-Thalberg connection—Hecht was registering his regret to Gene Fowler, accusing MacArthur of having his tongue up Helen's ass. During the hiatus in the completion of *Twentieth Century*—a result of MacArthur's refusal to return east to work on it—Hecht complained to Fowler (as quoted by Fowler's son, Will): "Angus McCheesecake, my collaborator . . . reveals as a last vestige of a dwindling talent an admiration for your compositions. We have not yet started on our Third Act owing to Madam McCheesecake continuing to exercise her charms over the semi impotent Angus—what the Hell goes on I can't imagine. The sonofobitch has turned into so timorous a time clock puncher, so god damn incredible and hump backed a masochist, shrew tickler, marital stooge, been bewitched into such spinelessness, so deflowered of his ego that I am speechless and appalled—not personally but as before some major phenomena. . . . Who was it wandered with a silk thread snarling his genitalia?"

They were to continue to work together, off and on, for many years, but the breach was never repaired. In 1937, when MacArthur was an MGM producer (Thalberg's influence), Hecht confided to Fowler that MacArthur had been promoted from writer to non-producing producer, a lucky break for him because of his drinking problem. At the time of their last collaboration—in 1949, on *Black Velvet*—Will Fowler recalled Hecht writing Gene, "I wrote a new play with MacArthur or rather, without him—for he is gone, poor boy—moaning low outside of life and nothing will ever whistle him back to the bonfire. He worked three weeks before hitting the skids—around Xmas. Liquor is only his surface problem. I can't blame him for staying drunk all the time. He looks on a lost world when he sobers. Not only Mary [his and Helen's daughter, who had died earlier that year, aged nineteen, of infantile paralysis], but chiefly himself, is gone. His mind is full of whimper and a ghost of righteousness and his will is decayed. At present he is shopping for some disease which might give him stature—blood clots, tuberculosis, etc. The medicos keep pronouncing him 'sound,' however, and he writhes at such libel."

Hecht devotedly made no mention of these feeling in *Charlie* and had only praise to speak in his eulogy: "Our lustiest and most high-hearted friend is dead, but the legend of Charles MacArthur will begin to grow now around his fine name. For Charlie was more than a man of talent. He was himself a great piece of writing. People scampered toward him as if pulled by a magnet. Alec Woollcott, who loved him, said to me once, 'What a perfect world this would be if it were peopled by MacArthurs.'"

After the service, MacArthur was buried in Nyack's Oak Hill Cemetery.

In 1960, Hecht would lose his closest friend, Gene Fowler, a result of a heart attack in Los Angeles.

Other than his informal biographies of MacArthur and Bodenheim, Hecht produced two other biographies during his seventh and last decade, both jobs of work, neither of which would see print in his lifetime. In January of 1954, he signed with Doubleday to ghost the "autobiography" of a new Hollywood star named Marilyn Monroe (which *Ladies' Home Journal* was to publish in a condensed version). Hecht went to San Francisco not long before she married Joe DiMaggio there and spent five days listening to her recount the story of her life. He returned to Oceanside and, in two months, turned out a 160-page manuscript. When he read it aloud to her at the Beverly Hills Hotel, Rose Hecht recalled, "Marilyn laughed and cried and expressed herself 'thrilled.' She said she never imagined so wonderful a story could be written about her and that Benny had captured every phase of her life."

Without Hecht's knowledge or permission, his agent at the time, Jacques Chambrun, sold the book for fifty thousand dollars to the *Empire News*, a British newspaper located in Manchester, perhaps reasoning that no one would be the wiser if the book was serialized in a tabloid in northern England. It wasn't long, however, before the thirteen-part serialization came to the attention of everyone concerned. Hecht wired Chambrun immediately: "Your sale of the copy is a violation of the arrangement I made with Miss Monroe on which I phoned you and telegraphed you a dozen times. The first knowledge I had of the sale of this copy was a telephone call from Miss Monroe's lawyer. I denied to him that such a sale had been made because I couldn't imagine it being done without my knowledge or consent. I also denied to Miss Louella Parsons [who broke the story] that the copy in the English papers was mine. I am making all these statements because your action has put me personally into the sort of hole I have never been in before. That of breaking my word." Marilyn Monroe brought suit against Hecht, which she later dropped. Rose Hecht said, "Doubleday wanted to put Chambrun in jail after what he had done but he came to Ben and me and Ken McCormack [the Doubleday editor who had commissioned Hecht to write the book] and cried a river of tears. And he was forgiven. But we had him agree—and he put it in writing—that he would not have anything more to do with the Marilyn Monroe book. Ben never saw a penny of the money Chambrun received either."

Although Doubleday and *Ladies' Home Journal* were displeased about the book's appearance in England, they still wanted to publish it. Marilyn Monroe, however, who hadn't signed a final contract, refused— at DiMaggio's insistence—to let it go to press. (It finally saw print twenty years later, brought out by Stein and Day. Milton Greene, the photographer who for a short time was Marilyn Monroe's business partner, sold the manuscript to Stein and Day, telling them Marilyn had written it and had given it to him because he would "do the right thing with it." Except for the addition of a few lines foreshadowing her death, the book was Hecht's manuscript, as Greene well knew. Frank Delaney, Greene and Monroe's lawyer at that time, has gone on record stating Greene was aware Hecht had written the book since in April of 1955 Greene wanted Marilyn to give Doubleday the go-ahead to publish it. Greene, however, has denied all knowledge of Hecht's authorship. Rose Hecht chose not to sue any of the parties involved in the theft: "Benny is dead," she explained, "I am an old woman, I am defenseless, and I've had my fill of lawyers and their exorbitant fees.")

The other biography, never to be completed, was of Jewish hoodlum

Mickey Cohen. "The first story Ben ever told me," Frank Tashlin recalled, "when we were writing *Love Happy* at his Oceanside castle, was about the call he received from Mickey Cohen, who was the top mobster in Los Angeles in those days. It was during the time Ben was gathering money for Israel. Shortly afterwards, Cohen appeared at Ben's house in a bulletproof limousine. Mickey never took his hat off and he had two big henchmen with him who also never took their hats off. Ben said, 'They acted like people I made up.' They had come to see whether Ben was serious about raising money for the Jews, and then Mickey donated. From it developed an association between Ben and Mickey Cohen."

Hecht had run into Cohen from time to time since 1947, when Cohen had pulled his "Jewish scam." (Hecht had taken Otto Preminger to meet him in 1955 to get firsthand information about underworld operations for *The Man with the Golden Arm*.) In 1957 Cohen showed Hecht a very rough draft of an autobiography. "I found it exciting and unusual," Hecht said. "It was frank and startling and I thought it might be the basis for a good book." Hecht made a deal with Cohen to write his biography on a fifty-fifty basis, stipulating that all financial matters be handled by lawyers. Then in January of 1958, Hecht signed with Holt to write *The Soul of a Gunman* for fall publication.

"I interviewed Cohen for a month, in cars, cafés, bars, anyplace I could get him alone." But there was always a phone around and someone was always calling, so in June, Hecht and Cohen traveled down to La Paz, Mexico, where they could talk uninterrupted. Hecht had approached Selznick, Zanuck, Harry Cohn, and Buddy Adler about filming the book, but none of them were interested. Nick Schenck's nephew wanted to produce, though, and went along on the Mexican junket to discuss the movie rights. But the project collapsed in September since, unbeknownst to Hecht, Cohen had given a long interview to a journalist who used the material for the basis of "The Private Life of a Hood," a profile of Cohen that the *Saturday Evening Post* ran in September. In addition, Hecht learned that Cohen was selling shares in the book. "I couldn't believe that anyone would be stupid enough to buy into a nonexistent property," Hecht commented. When Hecht asked him whether it was true, "Cohen didn't admit it or deny it but I understood what the silence meant." Hecht abandoned the book. (The completed sections were published in 1970 in a short-lived magazine, *Scanlon's Monthly*.)

* * *

Composing *A Child of the Century* had inspired Hecht's film writing—
The Thing and *Monkey Business* for Howard Hawks, *Whirlpool* and
Where the Sidewalk Ends for Otto Preminger—but his involvement with
the movies in his later years came down mainly to script doctoring and a
few independent productions he failed to find backing for. He and
Charlie Lederer rewrote the Pitcairn Island sequences in *Mutiny on the
Bounty* for Marlon Brando and Lewis Milestone, and adapted Charles
Finney's thirties novel *The Circus of Dr. Lao* (released as *The Seven Faces
of Dr. Lao*). For Henry Hathaway, Hecht cowrote two John Wayne
vehicles, *Legend of the Lost* and *Circus World*, and from producer
Samuel Bronston he received fifty thousand dollars for a polish and
rewrite of a Jesse Lasky, Jr., script, *John Paul Jones*. (Bronston wanted
Glenn Ford to star but figured the only way to get him to read the script
was if it had a "big name" like Hecht's on it. Lasky maintained that
"nobody was happy with the new script, even Ben Hecht, so Sam and I
put back most of the original, keeping a few good bits Ben had added
himself. By that time Ford was already working on another picture." It
was finally shot two years after Hecht had worked on it, directed by John
Farrow, starring Robert Stack.)

For Otto Preminger, Hecht doctored the scripts of Nelson Algren's
novels *The Man with the Golden Arm* and *Walk on the Wild Side*. Then,
the night before Preminger was to start directing *The Court-Martial of
Billy Mitchell*, he phoned Hecht and asked him to look at his script since
he wasn't happy with what he had. "He told me he'd rewrite the script by
the next morning," Preminger recalled, "but only if I got him some
Demerol. Ben had had an operation [the removal of his gall bladder in
1947] and he took Demerol ever after as a sleeping potion, but he wasn't
addicted. So I started calling doctors. The funny part is that whoever I
called said, 'I know, for Ben Hecht.' I couldn't get any but Milton
Sperling [who had coauthored the screenplay] got him some." Hecht
worked through the night and had the script rewritten by morning as
promised so Preminger could keep to his starting schedule.

Then in 1956 Hecht was serendipitously presented the opportunity to
effect a gleeful revenge on Ernest Hemingway, an old target Hecht had
been sniping at for decades with little result. Hecht had first met
Hemingway in Chicago during the winter of 1920, when Hemingway was
writing ad copy for the Co-operative Society of America. Veteran
newsman Lionel Moise had introduced them, Moise and Hemingway
having both recently worked for the *Kansas City Star*. Hecht also
encountered Hemingway several times with Sherwood Anderson, since

Anderson and Hemingway were friends, Hemingway living near Anderson in a rooming house on East Chicago Street. "Hemingway was too much concerned with his own *art*," Hecht felt. "I invited him once to have lunch with the boys but he never showed up. We weren't his kind of people, I guess. He was an artist, we were newspaper bums. The only one of us he ever bothered with was Swatty [Sherwood Anderson]. He waved whenever I saw him but that was it. It seemed to me as if he couldn't wait to get the hell out of Chicago."[1]

Hecht's antipathy toward Hemingway intensified over the years as Hemingway became what Hecht never would: the great American novelist. A character in *A Jew in Love*, in 1931, "talked in syrupy tones of his mother, Picasso, Hemingway, his meeting with Bernard Shaw, his dead wife and the fine work the Salvation Army was doing"; in 1934, in *Twentieth Century*, Oscar Jaffe refers to someone holed up "in a hotel under the name Hemingway to hide his grief"; and in his autobiography Hecht considered that "Sherwood Anderson, unlike Hemingway et al., did not grandly play the poet while busily wooing the box office." In the sixties, Hecht fired two parting shots: one in *Gaily, Gaily*, where he referred to "a hard-muscled pretty boy named Ernest Hemingway"; and one from the grave, in the posthumously published *Letters from Bohemia*, where he denigrated "the he-man Hemingway rushing his tourist information into print."

Thus, in 1956, when David Selznick asked Hecht to adapt *A Farewell to Arms*, he readily agreed. After some preliminary work in Hollywood during August, Hecht did a treatment on his return to New York in September, then in January flew to London to collaborate with John Huston, whom Selznick had hired to direct. Eight weeks later they had completed a full shooting script. In March, the Hechts rented a villa outside Rome, at Vejo, so Hecht could do rewrites during production.

Huston, on his arrival in Rome, was presented with another script Selznick had had prepared secretly by Italian director Pier Paolo Pasolini and with one of Selznick's famous memos, in which he instructed Huston how he wanted the picture directed. Already piqued by changes Hecht and Selznick had made in the novel—Huston's interest lay in interpreting Hemingway for the screen rather than making a love story for Mrs. Selznick (Jennifer Jones)—Huston began to object vociferously to Selznick. Selznick responded that he and Hecht both felt it was worse to approach the script "seemingly as though . . . the sole measure of whether the scenes were good or bad was whether they were Hemingway." In other words, there was to be no "Papa-worshipping groveling on this picture." Huston packed his bags and decamped. Said Hecht, "It was a case of two Caesars and one Alp."

Released in December of 1957, *A Farewell to Arms* was mauled by the critics but Hecht had finally hit his mark. Hemingway walked out of the theatre after seeing only the first half hour of the picture, complaining, "You write a book you're fond of and then you see that happen to it. It's like pissing in your father's beer."

Around the time he was slicing up Hemingway, Hecht saw his own work butchered when he screened the final cut of *The Iron Petticoat*, a comedy he'd scripted for Katharine Hepburn, with Bob Hope playing her leading man. Buying a full page in the *Hollywood Reporter*, Hecht announced his disaffiliation with the picture in an open letter to Hope—retaining his twenty-four-percent financial interest, however.

> My dear partner Bob Hope:
> This is to notify you that I have removed my name as author from our mutilated venture, *The Iron Petticoat*.
> Unfortunately your other partner, Katharine Hepburn, can't shy out of the fractured picture with me.
> Although her magnificent comic performance has been blow-torched out of the film, there is enough left of the Hepburn footage to identify her for sharp-shooters.
> I am assured by my hopeful predators that *The Iron Petticoat* will go over big with people "who can't get enough of Bob Hope."
> Let us hope this swooning contingent is not confined to yourself and your euphoric agent, Louis Shurr.
> —Ben Hecht

Hope responded with a full page of his own.

> My dear Ex-Partner Ben:
> The first thing I did on hearing of your withdrawal from *The Iron Petticoat* was to seek out my other fan, Dr. Shurr.
> I went down to the tank and handed him your ad. He read it under water and came up with this comment: "The billing is strengthened."
> I am most understanding. The way things are going you simply can't afford to be associated with a hit.
> As for Kate Hepburn, I don't think she was as depressed with the preview audience rave about her performance.

Let's do all our correspondence this way in print. It lifts
The Iron Petticoat.

Bob (Blow-Torch) Hope

Hecht spilled further bile over John Woolf, one of the heads of the British production company. "Your sabotaging of *The Iron Petticoat* is one of the most imbecile deeds in movie history. The picture was highly liked in Long Island before you put your stupid stamp on it. I am not going to remain silent while my hard and good work is ruined by a fool like you. I am broadcasting the fact that your sabotage is part of your aversion to me expressed in the London newspapers and that you are the type of English Jew who has never been off his hands and knees since he saw his first Duke." (A few years later, Woolf was knighted by the Queen.)

Although his contribution to the art of the American film was minimal during the fifties and sixties, the screen activity that did give him pleasure and the opportunity to exercise some creativity was *The Ben Hecht Show*. One of the earliest TV talk shows, it first aired on September 15th, 1958, on a local New York station, WABC, running thirty minutes Monday through Friday. Hecht's first guest was Robert Forman of Batten, Barton, Durstine and Osborn, the New York advertising agency that handled U.S. Steel, General Electric, and the Republican National Committee. The topic was TV commercials. After a brief introduction—during which Hecht looked at Forman and remarked, "We are the fearful fifties waiting for the sinister sixties, the best I can do is not add to the sense of panic"—the grilling began.

HECHT: Let's begin with one of your own commercials.

FORMAN: I . . .

HECHT: Can you tell me if Wildroot is an aphrodisiac?

FORMAN: It's the first choice of men because . . .

HECHT: Well then tell me what men do about Vitalis. For that matter, why does a commercial have to be ungrammatical?

FORMAN: Well, it just seemed . . .

HECHT: And if you can't tell me that, let me explain that the Chinese psychology is . . .

FORMAN: I'm afraid I don't . . .

HECHT: . . . the psychology you need. When I was a young reporter in Chicago . . .

FORMAN: I'm afraid you're way ahead of me. I . . .

HECHT: That's a shocking kind of statement to make. In that case, what about the noise in commercials? Do you know what Harun al-Rashid said about noise? Couldn't you sell your products with one commercial instead of three?

FORMAN: What we're trying to do is . . .

HECHT: I've never once used the word "yum-yum" yet in my own writing.

FORMAN: Maybe if . . .

HECHT: Is there any record of the number of suicides among viewers? I've heard eight hundred thousand by hanging alone.

FORMAN: I've never heard that. I . . .

HECHT: The thing that excites me the most is soap. Let me say . . .

FORMAN: But we never . . .

HECHT: Let me tell you that I find soap to be saponiferous in the manner of a Faubus debasing a Voltaire. . . .

The next evening Hecht began the show, "It seems I kept interrupting my guest last night. *Mea culpa*," then introduced well-known attorney Emile Zola Berman. Hecht, who disliked lawyers almost as much as advertising, let Berman speak without interruption, then, when informed that they had run out of time, smiled and remarked, "Delighted."

For two weeks the show ran smoothly, viewers more intrigued than outraged by Hecht's comments. With a wider scope than a show-business-oriented talk show, Hecht chatted with a girlie-magazine editor about "erotic magazines," with John Ciardi about poetry, with Weegee about the bizarre murders, suicides, and executions they had witnessed (which brought a deluge of protesting phone calls), with Gloria Swanson about Hollywood, with the *New York Post*'s drama critic about contemporary theatre, with William Zeckendorf about real estate, and with his old friend Dick Maney about press agentry. Then, on October 2nd, the station cancelled Hecht's scheduled guest, Alger Hiss (the topic was to be the United Nations Charter, which Hiss had written), allegedly because of a policy forbidding ex-convicts on the air. In reality, the station didn't want Hecht discussing communism with someone they considered so controversial that their ratings might take a dive.

Hecht spent one show telling stories about Teddy Roosevelt, another talking with Jack Kerouac about the new bohemianism. Westbrook Pegler, Drew Pearson, S. J. Perelman, and Grace Metalious were guests, as was a Catholic priest—who contended that Broadway did more for man's spiritual life than the church—and French singer Lilo, who thought that all men who were faithful to their wives were fools (Hecht smiled). On a program devoted to Hollywood, Hecht told old stories, reiterated old gripes about studio bosses, and attacked Louella Parsons (who a few months previous had criticized Hecht for his atheism, remarking that there was no room in Hollywood for nonbelievers): "Louella used to be a reporter with me in Chicago. She was the worst reporter the town ever knew. She's positively one of the most sad things in Hollywood. She makes it seem like a town full of boss-lovers—which it is. She bows when the boss is not there, just his shadow."

For his November 7th show, Hecht had scheduled eight Bowery derelicts to do a *This Is Your Life*-style show called "Obit to a Nobody." Hecht had rehearsed the group for several hours before the broadcast and had warned them about the kind of language they could and couldn't use but, nevertheless, ten minutes before air time, the station cancelled the show, alleging that the men might use shocking language over the air. In addition, the station contended they were drunk, but novelist-to-be Jacqueline Susann, who did commercials for the show, reported, "They were all sitting there so gentlemanly. They got up when I entered the room and each one of them came up to shake hands with me. They were sitting as well behaved as if they were in church. Of course they looked dreadful but that was the point of the whole show." *The Nation*, in an editorial, suggested that the station's reasons for cancelling went deeper than it was willing to admit: "It is a rule in American advertising that all women are young and beautiful and all men virile, and life is just one long sequence of joyful activity. No one in an ad is ever seen without a smile on his face unless he is falling off a ladder for an insurance company. Mr. Hecht was suggesting that there is also failure, despair, poverty and death. He broke a cardinal rule, he was condignly punished, and we hope has learned his lesson. Who does he think he is—Maxim Gorky?"

A few days later Norman Mailer was to appear, but he too was cancelled by the station's program manager. Hecht and Mailer intended to discuss Mailer's recently published essay "The White Negro," which, once again, scared the station because of its "controversial" subject matter—race relations, beatniks, and sex. This time the only reason given was that Hecht's show appealed to a "limited intellectual group" and that they wanted his program to "blast out of the theatrical and literary area."

The show ran without incident for three months, the guest list broadened, at the station's insistence, to include such celebrities as Steve Allen, Sheilah Graham (discussing Hollywood and F. Scott Fitzgerald), Stella Adler, a former lord mayor of Dublin, Harrison Salisbury (then only a *New York Times* reporter, there to talk about juvenile delinquency), Jimmy Durante, and Igor Cassini, the then current Cholly Knickerbocker. No matter the guest, Hecht was able to stir up controversy. Because of some "anti-British" remarks he made while interviewing Archbishop Makarios of Cyprus, a group of theatre owners in England tried unsuccessfully to reimpose the ban on his films in that country. Mickey Cohen created a furor when he revealed that he'd never murdered anyone who didn't deserve it.

On January 3rd, Hecht staged *3 Echoes on a Cloud*, a dialogue between Helen of Troy, Napoleon's Josephine, and Joseph Stalin. Hecht himself portrayed Stalin, for which *Time* magazine dubbed him "Ben Stalin" since there was more than a slight physical resemblance between the two men. Another night he listed and commented on his fifty favorite books, which drew more than nine thousand requests for copies of the list.

Then, on February 5th, 1959, with Senator Joe McCarthy's lawyer, Roy Cohn, scheduled to appear, the station cancelled not only Cohn but the entire show.[2] "During the twenty weeks the show has been on the air," WABC's program director told the media, "it has been given every opportunity to build audience appeal and provide viewers with stimulating programing. It has been found that despite this, the program has failed to attract either a substantial audience or a sufficient degree of advertiser interest to justify keeping it on."

"I was getting more mail than anybody," Hecht retorted, "including Pat Boone, but the station executives said it was the wrong kind of mail. It was too literate. 'These are not the kind of people who buy things advertised on TV,' they told me. It seems the paper must have lines on it and words must be misspelled. The station was very noble about it though. It was being attacked by nearly every group. There was the

Anti-Defamation League, the Catholics, the Arabs—and I believe the FCC was becoming restive. If the show had lasted much longer I would have had no admirers left." Hecht also informed the press that he was looking for a new sponsor to continue his show. There would be no commercials for a month, then Hecht himself would deliver one commercial. "If within the next two days the sponsor doesn't sell 10,000 of the advertised items I don't want any pay. If he does, I should get double our established figure. And I don't care if it's a Volkswagen or toilet seats." There were no takers.

Three days after his show was cancelled, "The Third Coming"—a TV play he'd written the year before for NBC's *Kaleidoscope* series—was broadcast. Jack Smight directed and Arthur Kennedy starred as a gag writer for a well-known comedian; the writer becomes a fake faith healer, but when his conscience begins to bother him he confesses the truth to a crowd that has come to be healed; they savagely attack him. NBC, aware of the reasons ABC had cancelled Hecht's interview show, was convinced the play was extremely controversial and would swamp their switchboard with protests, which had occurred the week before when Chet Huntley broadcast an editorial sympathetic to the NAACP. Extra switchboard operators were brought in to handle the deluge, but only fifteen calls were received.

With the deaths of his closest friends contributing to his dissociation from the fifties and early sixties, Hecht began retracting opinions held for a lifetime. He had played the iconoclast all his life, but now began attacking a new generation of American writers for using the same shock techniques he had used to draw attention to himself when he was young. If he couldn't join them, he was going to beat them. The year before he died, in a long interview in *Counterpoint,* he railed against the times.

> I don't like books with dirty words. [In the thirties he had had several copies of *A Jew in Love* specially printed with the word "shit" in the text for presentation to male friends.] I don't like books with unrestrained physiological attitudes toward the heroine. [*Fantazius Mallare* had been seized by the government because it was considered sexually obscene.] . . . I hear things in the theatre in New York that literally shock me and I'm not easy to shock . . . the new playwrights are so busy with dirty words you'd think they discovered a new plot. [Hecht had driven an opening-

night audience out of the theatre with a "dirty" first line decades before.] . . . The theatre and fiction have gotten wild and dirty. . . . I don't think today's writers know what guts are. They think it's a string of dirty words, I guess. . . . The deviates expose their problems with considerable gusto. Baldwin, Rechy, all their tiresome breed. This isn't guts or even gusto, really—it's like getting sick in public. And not even cleaning up the mess they make. . . . Males today haven't changed into females, but there isn't much difference between a male and a female. The women are standing at your side, working in the same profession, drinking your drinks, telling your dirty stories. . . . Women today are a bit masculinized—even those malnutrition cases in fashion magazines look like boys. All this may have something to do with a lack of gusto. The sexes have lost their mystery for each other. The double standard is practically gone. The double standard made you full of gusto—you had to lie all the time, you had to be a lively hypocrite.

Having attacked Hollywood for almost forty years, Hecht was now only too willing to laud the old studio system. Once the most acid critic of Hollywood moviemaking, Hecht began boosting the very moguls he had once scorned and publicly humiliated. In 1956 he told *Variety* that "Harry Cohn, Louis B. Mayer, Goldwyn and Zanuck in their heyday didn't talk, they yelled, they didn't think but they could feel, and they were shrewd showmen. It was the writer's job only to get to first base and then have the boss take over. The boss knew which way a script should be turned. He knew what 30 million people wanted to see . . . the boss was right." In the *Saturday Review* in 1962 he wrote, "When Hollywood is dead and gone as a maker of movies, it will be remembered by me at least as one of the nation's revolutionary centers of truth and sanity—off the screen."

Publicly revealing the off-the-screen truth behind an infamous episode in the history of what he now considered a "revolutionary" center of sanity, Hecht embroiled himself in a last scandal, which prompted an investigation by the Los Angeles district attorney. "Paul Bern," Hecht wrote in "Hollywood Danse Macabre" (*Playboy*, 1960),

remembered for having committed suicide as the impotent bridegroom of Jean Harlow, the great cinema sexpot, did no such thing. His suicide note, hinting that he was sexually incompetent and had therefore "ended the comedy," was a forgery. Studio officials decided, sitting in a conference around his dead body, that it was better to have Paul dead as a suicide than as the murder victim of another woman. It would be less a black eye for their biggest movie-making heroine, La Belle Harlow. It might crimp her box-office allure to have her blazoned as a wife who couldn't hold her husband. It was a delicate point of the sort that is clear only to the front office theologians of a great studio. The weird details of this "suicide whitewash" are in the keeping today of director Henry Hathaway, who was Paul Bern's protégé.

Bern, wed to Harlow for only two months, was found shot to death on September 5th, 1932, in his Beverly Hills house, a revolver in one hand. A note was found that read, "Dearest Dear—Unfortunately this is the only way to make good the frightful wrong I have done you and to wipe out my abject humiliation. I love you, Paul. You understand that last night was only a comedy." LA District Attorney William McKesson told the press he would investigate Hecht's accusation, since "any time a writer of Hecht's prominence makes such charges, it bears investigating." He added, however, that "there's very little probability that it was murder." Hathaway, when questioned by McKesson, said, "I wasn't there, and I would never have had access to information. I'm in no position to add anything. I'd like to forget it—in the name of Paul Bern." McKesson once again closed the case.

In an interview with the author in 1972, Hathaway told a different story. "We sat one night and I started talking about the different early things in Hollywood and I told Ben about my connection with Paul Bern. I told him what I actually thought was the Paul Bern story and he printed the whole story of it in *Playboy* magazine and I goddamn near got arrested because a headline comes out that says HATHAWAY CONCEALS THE MURDERER IN THE PAUL BERN CASE. I know who shot Paul Bern. It was a girl he'd lived with but she committed suicide the next day. She jumped off a ferryboat in San Francisco harbor." (The girl was Dorothy Millette, Bern's common-law wife, whom Bern had been supporting for years. It is now commonly accepted that in all probability she murdered Bern.)

The flurry of reprints and revivals of Hecht's work that had begun in 1942 came to an end in the late fifties, underscoring Hecht's feeling that the times were passing him by. During those years, *The Front Page* was republished, *I Hate Actors!* was reprinted as *Hollywood Mystery* and issued in France as *Mort aux acteurs*, and the screenplay of *Wuthering Heights* was included in *20 Best Film Plays* (the first collection of sound-film scenarios published in English); two paperback editions of selected stories came out under the title *Concerning a Woman of Sin and Other Stories*; *Miracle in the Rain* was reprinted in England, as was *The Collected Stories*; *Cutie, A Warm Mamma* was reissued with an Introduction by Bodenheim; and both *The Collected Stories* and *A Guide for the Bedevilled* were reprinted in the United States. *The Front Page* was performed on radio, television, and the stage, *Twentieth Century* on radio and the stage, and *Miracle in the Rain* on television. As well, Hecht stories were included in *Bachelor's Companion: A Smart Set Collection* (edited by Burton Rascoe); *Stories for Men*; *Box Office*; *Rogues' Gallery*; *Bedside Tales*; *Half-a-Hundred*; *America Is West*; *North South East West*; *Two-Fisted Stories for Men*; *The Bathroom Reader*; *To the Queen's Taste*; *A Treasury of Doctors' Stories*; *33 Sardonics I Can't Forget*; *The Art of the Mystery Story*; *The World's Greatest Stories*; *Man into Beast*; *A Caravan of Music Stories*; *Questing Spirit*; etc. (Many of the stories included in these anthologies were reprinted without Hecht's knowledge, the profits dropping into Jacques Chambrun's pockets. When, in 1961, Hecht was presented with incontrovertible proof of Chambrun's skulduggery, he severed all relations.)

In his sixties, no longer a force in the changing film industry, Hecht was not given much heed as a playwright or book writer either. A last novel, *The Sensualists*, was brought out by the same small New York company that had published *Perfidy*, and told the old story of a man, his wife, and his mistress but was tarted up with murder, lesbianism, suburban wife-swapping, and the de rigueur sex psychologizing. It was not a success. The reviews read like those for *Erik Dorn*, or any of his novels—John Wain, in *The New Republic*, wrote of "Mr. Hecht's dream people, they of the brittle epigrams and the eternally tired souls."

However, the "old fashioned lion" did write one last book that displayed his talents at their richest and most inventive. In the late fifties he had begun writing a series of stories that dealt with his early life in Chicago. Throughout 1962 and 1963 he published six of these pieces of alleged memorablia in *Playboy*, one in *Argosy*, and another in *Theatre Arts* (owned by Charlie MacArthur's brother); these were then collected and published under the title *Gaily, Gaily*[3] by Doubleday in August of 1963.

Hecht had spent his career ceaselessly reworking the same material, but *A Child of the Century* had marked the start of an intensive recapitulation of his past novelized into a string of neat stories rather than recounted in chronological, realistic form. "Lying is creation and fine editing," he wrote in *The Sensualists*. "When you tell truths you're sort of limited as an entertainer." In *Gaily, Gaily* dozens of oft-told stories reappeared. For example, the tale of the man who murdered his wife and made her skull into a tobacco jar—which Hecht heard when a reporter in Chicago—first appeared in *Count Bruga* in 1926, then showed up in *1001 Afternoons in New York*, in *A Child of the Century*, and in a book by Gene Fowler, who had been told the story by Hecht. The most amazing recombination occurred in "The Bum," for which Hecht interwove four short sketches written for *The Little Review* in 1915, part of another sketch from 1918, and a story he had recounted in his autobiography, in order to create still another tale from the assembled parts. The stories spanned his first five years in Chicago but were hardly autobiographical (as early as 1926 Hecht had written, "I find an increasing tendency when writing of myself to tell pleasant lies"). Hecht had reworked material before but never so successfully as in *Gaily, Gaily*, in which well-worn plots were amazingly transformed into vital new stories. *Gaily, Gaily* was the best fiction Hecht had written since *A Child of the Century*, or would ever write again.

Since the wellspring of his creativity from 1950 till his death was the reliving of his past in four books and one play (*A Child of the Century; Charlie; Gaily, Gaily; Letters from Bohemia*; and *Winkelburg*), one would have thought Hecht pleased to see his first novel, *Erik Dorn*, republished by the University of Chicago as part of its Chicago Renaissance series. Hecht, however, refused to attend the publication party given by the university press, wiring the editors, "I have no hankering to pose in your local festivities as a literary patsy." He also objected stringently to Nelson Algren's Introduction, which he had not been shown before publication. "I have never read his works," Hecht maintained, although he had rewritten scripts of two of Algren's novels for the movies. "I don't have the faintest idea what he writes like but in this case he stinks." The Introduction was generally laudatory (" 'What is literature?' Jean-Paul Sartre once inquired; one might reply—*Erik Dorn*"), but it was Algren's conclusion that upset Hecht, perhaps because it approached too near what he felt was the truth: "It wasn't splendor that was lacking in Hecht, it wasn't gas he ran out of, and it surely wasn't brass. It was belief. For he came, too young, to a time when, like Dorn, he had to ask himself, 'What the hell am I talking about?' And heard no answer at all."

In 1963, Hecht signed with CBS to script twenty-nine half-hour TV dramas and also began looking for angels to bankroll a picture he wanted to direct in New York, *The Empty Coffin*, and a musical version of *Underworld*. (In addition, he and Frank Loesser had been trying for some time to turn *Specter of the Rose* into a musical.) Early in 1964, he began two new books, *Shylock My Brother* (an attempt to historically document that Shakespeare was a Jew), and a history of the American theatre. He updated Fritz Lang's German classic *M* for Henry Hathaway (retitled *The Praying Mantis*) and was called in by Charlie Feldman to adapt *Casino Royale*, the rights to which Feldman had inherited from Gregory Ratoff, who had died owing him a small fortune. Hecht sold the screen rights to *Gaily, Gaily* to Walter Wanger for the token price of one dollar since Wanger, after the disastrous production of *Cleopatra*, needed a property to develop. In March, Jenny Hecht starred in a play in the Village, *The Bitch of Waverly Place*,[4] and on April 11th Hecht appeared on a TV show devoted to former New York mayor Jimmy Walker.

At seven-thirty on the morning of April 18th, 1964, a Saturday, Hecht suffered a heart attack. Rose entered the dressing room of their West Sixty-seventh Street apartment to find him slumped forward, his head pressed into a pillow, his glasses and e. e. cummings's *The Enormous Room* beside him. "I talked to him while I tipped him backward," Rose remembered, "his head on the floor, his birthday pajama top of soft dark silk around his still warm body. I talked while getting him smelling salts and while beginning to work on his chest with respiratory rhythm. I only stopped talking to force my tongue into his mouth still sweeter than wine to me and then I breathed into him while keeping on with the artificial respiration. I tried not to realize that his face was bleached of color where he had leaned upon the bed. When he was dead and the cops carried him to our bed for me and laid him on the ruffled pillow case, I went into the room and knelt beside him and spoke to him tender words in Yiddish; afterwards, when the room downstairs began to fill with friends, I sat with them, and with Jenny when she came, and every once in a while I went back to the room where he lay in our great bed and I kept on talking to him and telling him how dear he was, still in broken Yiddish. Except for a lullaby I used to sing to Jenny I had never spoken of love in the mother tongue. I felt these words would reach his soul. I guess that is what it means to be a Jew."

Rose intended to burn the Nyack house to the ground but was persuaded by Charlie Samuels that her gesture would only cause problems she wouldn't want to deal with at that moment.

Funeral services were held at Temple Rodeph Sholom on West Eighty-third Street, where eulogies were spoken by Menachem Begin (whom Hecht had known since the forties, when Begin commanded the Irgun), Peter Bergson, Luther Adler, and George Jessel. Hecht was buried on the eighth anniversary of MacArthur's death in Nyack's Oak Hill Cemetery, a few feet from Charlie's grave.

His last book, *Letters from Bohemia* (a collection of correspondence from MacArthur, Bodenheim, Fowler, Sherwood Anderson, H. L. Mencken, George Grosz, and George Antheil), would be published several months after his death. The last page of *The Preying Mantis* was in his typewriter the day he died, but Henry Hathaway never made the picture (although he announced it in 1974, to star Telly Savalas). Production rights to *Chicago*, the musical version of *Underworld*, were sold to scenic designer Sean Kenny and publicist Judd Bernard shortly before Hecht's death; Peter Brook was to direct, but it was never produced. *Circus World*, which he'd rewritten for Henry Hathaway in 1963, was released in June to generally favorable reviews. *The Sensualists* and *Gaily, Gaily* were reprinted in England, as were two collections of his short stories, *In the Midst of Death* and *Concerning a Woman of Sin*. All four were reprinted over the next few years, but ten years after his death, the University of Chicago's *Erik Dorn* was Hecht's only work in print.

> *There's never been anybody like me. When I die they'll say I was a shooting star. The whole world will watch me passing. I'll leave books behind that'll yell after me.*
> —Humpty Dumpty (1924)

> *The sad thing about writing fiction is that unless one writes classics one writes in a closet. Nothing can disappear like a book. The characters I made up are still alive . . . but in the closet always. Like all writers who have tried hard, I dream sometimes that the closet door will open.*
> —A Child of the Century (1954)

> *The world liked me and gave me all the money I wanted. I always had a lovely time.*
> —to Mike Wallace,
> February 1958

CHAPTER NOTES

CHAPTER 2

1. At the same time that Hecht was hobnobbing with the cream of Chicago's newsmen—Richard Henry Little, George Wharton, and critic Ashton Stevens—he was interviewing millionaires, priests, educators, actors, and writers (e.g., Arnold Bennett, John Masefield, Hugh Walpole, John Cowper Powys, Maurice Maeterlinck, Vicente Blasco Ibáñez, and, most important to Hecht at that time, Theodore Dreiser). After watching the sixty-seven-year-old "divine" Sarah Bernhardt play a seventeen-year-old boy on stage, he interviewed the orange-haired, one-legged first lady of the theatre. Also, he showed up with dozens of his confreres at Jack Johnson's wedding reception to witness the champ's white bride stroke his testicles to calm his nerves.

When William Jennings Bryan was in town on a fundamentalist crusade, Hecht turned his nose up in print at Bryan's Bible-thumping. In the middle of an interview that renowned evangelist Billy Sunday was holding in his home for reporters from all the dailies, Sunday jumped up and called out, "Mother, I almost forgot to tend to the furnace." Hecht covertly followed Sunday down a hallway and saw him enter the kitchen and bang two pots together to simulate the noise of stoking the furnace. The next day the *Journal* revealed the preacher's ruse for the delectation of its readers.

CHAPTER 3

1. From a wealthy Columbus, Indiana, family, Anderson had dropped out of college after three years to go to work for *Continent*, a religious magazine located in Chicago; she also wrote occasional book reviews for Floyd Dell and worked in *The Dial*'s bookshop.

2. Shortly after Bodenheim arrived in Chicago, he befriended a young Polish sculptor, Stanislaus Szukalski, who had been in town only since the beginning of

the year himself. With his long flowing hair, velvet suits, and iconoclastic ideas about art, Szukalski brought an air of Paris ateliers to the "hog butcher" by the lake. (Hecht described him as "a feline Madonna . . . with the careful cruelty of an obsolete Jesuit.") Together, Bodenheim, Hecht, and Szukalski formed The Questioners early in 1915, which met on Friday nights in one of the tin-roofed Fifty-seventh Street studios. There, on a small stage (surrounded by a semicircle of chairs for the invited guests, with a space behind for the general public that Hecht called "the slum circle," composed mainly of newspapermen and students from the University), they debated the advanced ideas of the day—Imagism and anarchy, free love and *vers libre*, the French decadents and Nietzsche. Russian political exile and littérateur Sacha Kaun showed up regularly as did Fedya Ramsay, a poetry-writing waitress Bodenheim was infatuated with. Sherwood Anderson turned up whenever he was looking for a new girl.

3. In 1914, Hecht had covered the public ceremonies held in Chicago for the nineteen men killed in the siege of Vera Cruz, City Hall politicians using their deaths as an excuse for a political rally since it was near election time. Unable to publish the true story at the time, Hecht stored the information away until two years later, when he wrote the play, moving the setting from Chicago to a small Indiana town where a local boy, a soldier, is going to be buried after being killed heroically in the battle of Santa María. The mayor tries to use the boy's death as an opportunity to climb higher up the political ladder, while the boy's father is attempting to use his death to force the government to give him a pension. When the boy shows up alive and sees what's going on he blackmails his father into splitting the pension money with him.

CHAPTER 4

1. "The Unlovely Sin" reflected the same cynical attitude toward American life held by Mencken. It tells of members of a family waiting for the great-grandmother to die since they despise her. The father, a failed writer turned businessman, and his son (the narrator) speak a literary language the rest of the family doesn't understand:

> "I'll go before her, mark my words. You don't know her as I do. She'll live forever," the grandmother says.
> The father responds, "Zola."
> "No, Anatole France," I answered.
> He was thoughtful for a moment. It was a way we have of giving our opinions to each other when not alone.
> "The early Huysman," my father said at last.
> "Wedekind," I objected.
> He laughed.
> My grandmother looked at me suspiciously.
> "What are you talking about?" she asked.

One of the few works of fiction Hecht ever wrote with a father figure, it is the only one in which the father is a sympathetic character.

2. As usual, the stories were based on actual experience or observations. "Decay" was a portrait of the desolate life of an immigrant family, "Nocturne" a picture of Chicago's Loop and its four A.M. denizens. "Broken Necks" was based on an actual hanging Hecht had witnessed where the condemned man spat on a priest's crucifix. "The Yellow Goat" told of an experience he had had one night with a prostitute when he and Sherwood Anderson were carousing in a gin mill; he rewrote this story as "The Eternal Fugitive" for *Smart Set*.

3. He would also parody it in his novel *Gargoyles*, in which Sandburg turned up as a minor character. See p. 65.

4. During this period Hecht also covered most of the big news stories that were breaking in Chicago, by far the most interesting being the IWW trial held in 1918. The government was claiming that the Wobblies were interfering with the war effort by calling strikes, thereby discouraging conscription, which the Wobblies denied, claiming they had no intention of battling the government, only corporations. A protracted trial was held, lasting from April to September, with Hecht's coverage carried on the front page of the *News*. Later, in the *Chicago Literary Times*, Hecht wrote about meeting Big Bill Haywood during the trial:

> The only American red with an intelligent understanding of American newspapers I ever met was Big Bill Haywood whose trial I covered before Judge Landis. During a recess a number of radicals gathered around the reporters whom they knew and proceeded to curse out the "prostitute press" and denounce the newspapers for being filled with lies against them. When they had run out of breath, Haywood spoke up. "You boys strike me as being kind of dumb," he smiled at the men on trial with him. "The press is ten times fairer toward us than the radical papers are toward the capitalists. Did you read the stories of yesterday's session? None of you could have written a more impartial and even sympathetic account than appeared in the *News* or even in the *Tribune*. Don't waste your wind blowing down the press. The newspaper is as fair as the reporter it happens to have on the case. As for its policies it's just a big wind bag floating around blindly. If you want to stand in with the papers, all you got to do is learn how to handle the reporters."

5. Jones opened his "social club" on the second floor of a carriage house as a meeting place for radicals, but also to avoid police harassment. Frequently pulled in whenever the authorities rounded up anarchists and Wobblies, Jones reasoned that a club which exerted some influence, however small, would be protected by the neighborhood wardheelers, ever conscious of all the mechanisms that influenced voters. In a short time, the Dill Pickle proved so successful Jones moved it to Tooker Alley, then an exclusive residential area off State Street.

CHAPTER 5

1. The only change Putnam's had insisted on in *Erik Dorn* was the deletion of the final *s* from *breasts* in a scene where Rachel was carried from the bathroom to the bedroom.

2. The Morals Commission led a citywide investigation into the influence of low wages on working girls' morality, and in a ludicrous series of public hearings concluded that a girl must take home at least eight dollars a week to keep from turning to prostitution.

3. From R. K. R. Thornton's introduction to *Poetry of the Nineties*, Penguin Books, Harmondsworth, England, 1970.

4. Kreymborg was considered one of the better young poets of the day, publishing in both *Poetry* and *The Little Review*, plus having one-act plays put on by the Provincetown Players. He had tried to raise financing for a magazine, *The American Quarterly*, since 1908 but without success. Early in 1913 he had been given a printing press from the shop his friend Man Ray was working at, but it had fallen off the truck that was transporting it and had been irreparably damaged. Later that year he had convinced Albert and Charles Boni, owners of the Washington Square Bookshop, to finance another magazine, *Glebe*. The first issue came out in July of that year, but *Glebe* lasted only ten issues because of a conflict between the Bonis—who wanted to publish European poetry exclusively—and Kreymborg, who wanted to publish new American poets. Although short-lived, *Glebe* made literary history, a result of the Imagist issue with work by Ezra Pound, James Joyce, H. D., Ford Madox Ford, and William Carlos Williams. For a short time these poets were grouped together under the banner of Imagism before it was abandoned for Vorticism, which in turn was abandoned for Polyphonism, all of which Hecht called Syntaxism. Bodenheim responded to the changing isms by announcing the Monotheme School of Poetry, in which only one subject would be written about by all poets.

5. Smith, in a chapter titled "The Star," drew a portrait of Hecht: "He's the kind of fellow who appears to have out-grown, or cast aside, practically all the known precepts of normal living, and doesn't give a copper for anybody or anything . . . declares that he doesn't believe in religion or even in ethics. He takes pleasure in repudiating most of the ten commandments, the Golden Rule, and a large part of the Sermon on the Mount. . . . Most heartily he scoffs at success. He does not demean himself to ridicule such things as riches or fashion, but he does talk venomously about success. . . . This young man strolls through the world with a queerly bitter greeting for it, yet with an engaging smile. He asserts he hates the world, hates the human race, spurns its contrivances for being peaceable and joyous, and has no hope for it. He says he does not believe in marriage or in honesty. But he is married and lives true to his wife. And he never stole anything. . . . Of course, you understand that he is rather run after by foolish women,

literature-mad girls who want to learn the secret of writing, and others who are plain crazy. But just let Mrs. Hecht come in sight, and he shakes off the insects in petticoats and waves them good-bye. . . . Look at the wall alongside his desk . . . he's pasted up a few pictures. . . . As for the poster advertising a Griffith movie, I suppose he put it up as a joke on himself, a piece of irony." *Deadlines: Being the Quaint, the Amusing, the Tragic Memoirs of a News-Room*, Covici-McGee, Chicago, 1923.

6. Although Covici was publishing the paper, he took his name off the masthead after the sixth issue in order to dissociate himself from it, a result of the trouble he was in with the government for publishing *Fantazius Mallare*. The issue that came out immediately before the hearing was renamed *Ben Hecht's Chicago Literary Times: A Modern Sardonic Journal* to further stress that it was a product of Hecht's entirely. Three issues later the logo reverted to the *Chicago Literary Times*.

7. Early in May, Hecht and Covici sold their interest in the *Chicago Literary Times* to a lawyer named Blonder. Issues 6 and 7 of volume 2 were published by Blonder in a smaller format, and it was in number 6 that Hecht wrote that Liveright had almost been persuaded to take over the *Chicago Times*, a part of the cover-up Hecht affected with Blonder, who was informed only when he got the copy for issue 7 that Hecht was leaving shortly for New York. Blonder put out the final issue with Hecht's name misspelled as Hect.

CHAPTER 6

1. Mankiewicz was born in New York City in 1897 and graduated from Columbia University at the age of nineteen. After serving with the Allied Expeditionary Forces during World War I he became director of the Red Cross News Service in Paris, then worked briefly in the *Chicago Tribune*'s Berlin office, returning to the United States in 1922 as publicity man for Isadora Duncan. Shortly afterwards, he was hired by the *New York World*, where many of the members of the Round Table worked. Consequently he began moving in the city's literary circles. In 1923, he joined the *New York Times*' drama department as backup man for George S. Kaufman.

2. McEvoy's background was a mystery to his friends in Chicago. "Nobody could figure out what his origins were," Harry Hansen recalled, "because he was a foundling. Some of us thought he was a Yugoslav but he had this Irish name which didn't belong to him. He was a very jovial fellow though, very friendly and always full of little quips." Born in New York City in 1894, he attended Notre Dame for two years before going to work for the *Chicago Record-Herald* and the *Tribune*.

3. Marie had telephoned Hecht in a panic to tell him that Teddy, who was spending the summer with Marie's mother in Cleveland, had been injured and

might lose an eye. Hecht rushed to Cleveland, as did Marie, only to discover that the injury was not serious. Hecht went on to Chicago, where he visited family and friends, and attended a party for Sinclair Lewis given by Dr. Morris Fishbein, editor of the *Journal of the American Medical Association* and a former employer of Rose's. Lloyd Lewis recalled that there was a lot of kidding about how Sinclair Lewis had allegedly been offered a baronetcy in England, so Hecht dubbed him "Sir Red."

4. While Hecht and MacArthur were writing their play, Rose—when she wasn't cooking for the almost omnipresent guests—would slip away to the nearby woods to work on the novel she had begun in Chicago. Where Hecht's books had been imitations of other writers' styles and current literary trends, Rose's novel was an imitation of Hecht's imitations. *Woman on the Balcony* told the story of Rose's meeting with Hecht, their affair, and the breakup of his marriage, the same material Hecht had based two novels and a play on.

5. Bruga's first name is Hippolyt, which Hecht took from an anarchist waiter named Hippolyte Havel, who had worked with Emma Goldman and who was despised by Bodenheim because they were so much alike. Bruga's given name in the novel is Jules Ganz, echoing Jay Gatz, the real name of the title character in *The Great Gatsby*, published earlier that year. Hecht referred to Bruga as "the ideal caricature," having called Bodenheim "the ideal lunatic" in the *Chicago Literary Times*. That phrase, as well as "the kaleidoscopic mountebank," were his working titles for the book.

6. A newsman from the age of sixteen, Johnson worked for *The New York Times* and the *Herald* during the twenties, joining the staff of *The New Yorker* in 1932. He won a Pulitzer Prize for journalism and, according to *New York Tribune* editor Stanley Walker, was considered by many of his contemporaries to be "the best all-round reporter in the country."

7. When it was discovered that Al Woods was planning to produce *Mannequin*, a French play with a similar plot, *Riviera* was dropped.

CHAPTER 7

1. Sadakichi Hartmann's euphemism for Hollywood.

2. Rose got a job in Hollywood as well, but one that won her no screen credit, since all she did was a quick rewrite of *Ritzy*, an Elinor Glyn story that Miss Glyn had adapted for the screen.

3. Myron's success would be virtually immediate. *Two Arabian Knights* would win Milestone an Oscar for Best Comedy Direction, and *The Racket*, Caddo's second production, would be nominated for Best Production.

4. Howey had arrived in Chicago in 1903 and gone to the *News* office looking for a job. Henry Justin Smith told him he needed a first-rate reporter familiar with the city, asking Howey how well he knew Chicago. "Like a book," Howey replied. "How long would you allow to get from here to the intersection of Jackson and Washington Boulevards?" Smith asked him. "About ten minutes," said Howey. Since the two boulevards run parallel, Howey didn't get the job.

New York Tribune editor Stanley Walker recalled that MacArthur and Howey "used to go out together after work, drink all night and throw canteloupes at strange people until eight A.M. Back at the office, Howey, feeling that he might be getting too intimate with his staff, would abuse MacArthur and rewrite all his copy." *City Editor,* Stanley Walker, Introduction by Alexander Woollcott, Frederick A. Stokes Company, New York, 1934.

5. Hildy's girlfriend's mother was based on Helen Hayes's mother.

6. During the scripting Hecht knocked out an outline for a newspaper comedy, *The Headliner,* which he sold to First National. It was made quickly and cheaply as *The Big Noise,* directed by Allan Dwan, and released before *The Front Page* was finished. (Credit for screenplay and adaptation went to Tom Geraghty, who had originated the plot of *The New Klondike.*)

7. Cormack went to Hollywood to adapt it for Milestone and Thomas Meighan; shortly afterward Hecht got Herman Mankiewicz to write the titles for Caddo's third project, a film version of Rex Beach's novel *The Mating Call.*

8. "The first published version of an American play to sell in any appreciable quantity."—Donald Friede.

9. Also, then well-known artist Hidalgo made statuettes of Hecht, Eugene O'Neill, Theodore Dreiser, Sherwood Anderson, Anita Loos, Lester Cohen, and Hendrik Willem Van Loon, which were photographed and published in *The Independent* under the heading "Liverwriters."

10. In November, Hecht composed another play, *Christmas Eve,* which Covici—now in partnership in New York with another of Liveright's former vice presidents, Donald Friede—published in a limited edition of 111 copies, to be given out by the Hechts as Christmas presents. Subtitled *A Morality Play,* it concerned two couples—one married, the other engaged—who swap partners the evening the play takes place. Later, the devil appears to the four of them and engages them in conversation, but grows fainter as the evening wears on, finally disappearing altogether, a result of their skepticism.

11. On February 7th, 1929, Marie Hecht married a Russian artist named Essipov, and on February 23rd and March 2nd *The Front Page* was slapped with lawsuits. The first was brought by a Chicago minister, who, as head of the Illinois Vigilance Association, wanted twenty-four members of the Chicago cast of the play arrested for "63 blasphemies." The case was thrown out of court, but what surprised many

Chicagoans was that the municipal government didn't interfere with the play's run, since it questioned the honesty and competence of many City Hall politicians still in office. The other suit was brought by the Shuberts, who claimed Jed Harris had agreed that all the play's road companies would play Shubert theatres exclusively, but had failed to live up to the agreement. After three weeks of deliberation, the judge ruled in Harris's favor, delighting Hecht, since it had been the Shuberts who had tried to bilk him and McEvoy out of money due them for *The Yellow Mask* in 1923.

12. In December, Hecht and Herman Mankiewicz went over to the Paramount studios in Astoria, Queens, and, while Walter Wanger looked the other way, made a short comic film, *More Soup*, which they cowrote and both acted in. They presented it along with the production costs to Adolph Zukor, Paramount's president, for Christmas.

CHAPTER 8

1. "Armitage Trail was lucky to have four dollars in his pocket at any given time," W. R. Burnett remembered. "He got $25,000 for *Scarface* because Hughes wanted to use the title and some of the material. The book was an awful piece of crap. Armitage Trail never drew another sober breath, and in about two years he died of a heart attack in Grauman's Chinese Theatre."

2. René Clair was "struck" by this image—"With one blast Scarface mows down a row of billiard cues standing up against a wall. This good visual idea, as I later learned from the screenplay writers, Ben Hecht and Charles MacArthur, figured explicitly in their script. Who is the author? The men who conceived that image or the man who got it down on film?" Howard Hawks also claims credit for the idea.

3. The day before it opened, a musical comedy adapted from the German by Marie Armstrong Hecht Essipov opened; both plays closed on the same day in mid-June 1931.

4. At the end of 1930, Hecht and MacArthur bought the managerial rights to a play about a prison break, *Road Out of Hell*, by Albert Bein, for $5,000. In their agreement they were required to produce the play no later than September 12th, 1931, or forfeit their rights. Instead, they turned it into a screenplay and sold it to Paramount. Since MacArthur did most of the work of transposing the play to a scenario, he received $6,750, Hecht $2,250, and Bein $5,000. Then they sold seventy-five percent of their stage rights for $1,000 to Arthur Hopkins, who had produced MacArthur's play *Salvation*. Hopkins didn't produce the play either, but sold his rights to Henry Hammond, who produced it in 1933. Directed by Joseph Losey, the drama only lasted twelve performances.

CHAPTER 9

1. *The Champion from Far Away*—not illustrated by Arno—did include six *Chicago Literary Times* articles plus two old *Liberty* stories from 1925 and 1926 ("Lindro the Great" and "The Shadow"), "The Rival Dummy" (the source for the movie *The Great Gabbo*), the two *Saturday Evening Post* stories published the year before, "The Bull That Won" from *Physical Culture*, and the long story about Charles Ort and the Florida land boom, "An American Kangaroo."

2. Although soft-spoken and gentle—contrary to the stereotypically crude and boorish studio boss—Thalberg nevertheless did not let friendship get in the way of moviemaking. As Bernie Hyman remarked of him, "He's a sweet guy but he pisses ice water."

3. On November 25th, 1932, a week prior to its Broadway opening, Covici published the play with full-color illustrations of the sets designed by Herman Rosse, who had illustrated *1001 Afternoons in Chicago.*

4. Another reporter Hecht knew in Chicago, Dan MacGregor, had been killed during the battle of Chihuahua.

5. Sam Marx, *Mayer and Thalberg: The Make-Believe Saints*, Random House, New York, 1975.

6. "The thing that interested me and Ben," Hawks said, "was that after a battle a Mexican woman would pretend that the dead man she had been living with was alive and put a cigarette in one hand and a drink in the other and for that evening pretend that he was alive. But we couldn't figure out how to use it. One night at about two o'clock I woke Ben up and said, 'Ben, when we introduce Villa and he comes in and there are six bodies hanging from a scaffold, he'll say, "Cut 'em down. The six bodies are the jury and they're trying the mayor of the town." 'Okay, okay,' Ben said. 'Never mind any more.' And when I arrived at breakfast the next morning, the whole sequence was written."

CHAPTER 10

1. AUTHOR'S NOTE: I first saw *Once in a Blue Moon* in London at the National Film Theatre's Hecht-MacArthur retrospective, held in 1974. Expecting the worst, I was surprised to find the dialogue completely comprehensible. Since then, I have seen the picture at the Zukor Theatre in the old Astoria studios and once again had no difficulty with the dialogue. I also find it curious that the film was so reviled in its time, since it is a charming if small fairy tale in which Jimmy Savo plays his part with wistful sadness rather than imitation Chaplin antics.

2. November 4th, 1935, letter to Sherwood Anderson:

". . . Thank you for your letter. I'm glad you remembered my mother because she always talked of you as the best of my younger days.

Regards and Memories,
Ben Hecht"

October 13th, 1935, letter from Sherwood Anderson to his mother:

". . . had a long talk with Ben Hecht today. You know we were once great friends in Chicago. His old mother was killed in an automobile accident in Los Angeles, and the last thing she said to him before dying was that he should have stuck to me and gone with me on my road."

Letter from Carl Sandburg to Charles Harcourt, 1935:

". . . when I mentioned Ben Hecht as though I still like him, Sherwood said, 'He has a child's mind.'"

CHAPTER 11

1. "I happened to see in manuscript the play Mr. Hecht wrote. It was infinitely more interesting, more playable, and even commercially more valuable than the play the Guild produced. . . . Mr. Hecht gave the Guild a play that was in essence autobiographical, a play about an articulate, clever man who talked himself to a standstill. But the producers, apparently still under the spell of the old superstition that a play cannot be 'talky,' proceeded to excise almost all of the hero's connected conversation and to substitute scenes of action and love interest. What talk of a semi-intellectual nature was left the hero they camouflaged as best they could."—Mary McCarthy, *Partisan Review*, December 1937.

Why did Hecht allow this? Or wasn't he allowed a choice? In that social realist era, were his Raskolnikovian superiority and scorn for the masses found unacceptable fare by the Guild? Or did Paramount, which was bankrolling the Guild, insist on the old formulas—action and romance—to secure a popular success?

2. Hawks took cast and crew to Arizona to start filming, but when Howard Hughes, who was producing, saw the first rushes, he wired Hawks to delay further shooting since there were no cloud formations in the backgrounds. Hawks told Hughes to direct the picture himself, then quit. Hecht's story was then changed by Furthman and Hughes to such an extent that it was no longer his, although many of the elements he and Hawks had devised were retained. (Shot mostly in 1941, *The Outlaw* was not released nationally until five years later in a highly censored version with directorial credit going to Hughes himself. It had made Jane Russell a notorious sex symbol long before audiences got a chance to see her.)

CHAPTER 12

1. John Cogley, *Report on Blacklisting*, vol. 1, *Movies*, The Fund for the Republic, 1956.

2. On October 12th, 1941, *The New York Times Magazine* reprinted the play's introductory speech, "What Is America?" Also in October, an abridged wartime edition of *Count Bruga* was published and on November 23rd Hecht's short story "The Mystery of the Fabulous Laundryman" was broadcast on NBC. A selection of his *PM* columns was brought out by *PM*, and a special signed edition of one column, "The Bewitched Tailor," was issued with a drawing by George Grosz, who had illustrated the hardbound Viking edition of eighty-six of Hecht's *PM* columns, *1001 Afternoons in New York*, also issued that October.

3. *The View from the Sixties: Memories of a Spent Life*, David McKay Co., New York, 1966.

4. When Szukalski's father was killed in an automobile accident in the teens, Szukalski sold his body to a hospital to pay the burial expenses, but made the hospital agree to one condition: he must be allowed to be present for his father's dissection. Afterwards, Szukalski proudly boasted that he learned anatomy from his father. Hecht related the tale in *Humpty Dumpty* in 1924 without changing Szukalski's name, retold it in his *PM* piece, and in 1954 would tell it once again in *A Child of the Century*. Marie Hecht also used the story in her book *My First Husband*, and Bodenheim changed Szukalski's name to Feodor Stanovitch and used it in *Duke Herring*.

5. Charles Higham, in his earlier book *The Films of Orson Welles*, knew no better: "For much authentic dialogue closely modeled on the novel, Welles (with Joseph Cotten's aid) added a number of striking inventions."

6. When he was in Germany in 1919, Hecht had also prophesied that Germany would be involved in another world war within twenty years.

7. Hecht also polished the other stories and wrote the continuity. Although six tales were filmed, one starring W. C. Fields was deleted after preview audience reaction made it evident that its comedy clashed with the dramatic tone of the other five stories.

8. The story has been widely reprinted, appearing in both volumes of Hecht's collected stories, in an anthology, *Rogues' Gallery*, and as late as 1962 in *Ellery Queen's Mystery Magazine*.

9. Hecht's title was a reference to the twelfth-century Jewish philosopher Maimonides's *Guide for the Perplexed*.
   "I wanted to publish the *Guide* the moment I saw it," Scribner's editor Max

Perkins wrote Hecht, "just on principle, and then very much more after I had read it for its fire and power as literature."

10. Earlier that year, Hecht edited a volume of his collected stories for Crown, for which he asked Gene Fowler to write a Preface. Fowler's Introduction concentrated on *Erik Dorn*, published twenty-four years earlier, so Hecht penned his own Introduction. The book was dedicated "For David Lebenson [one of Rose's relatives] who was killed fighting the Germans."

11. Sanine's real name is Paul Dixon, one of the characters from *The Scoundrel*; a poster painter is named Kropotkin; Specs MacFarlan was the name of a Homicide Bureau detective Hecht had known in Chicago; and a minor character was called Jack Jones after the ex-Wobbly who ran the Dill Pickle Club.

12. The day before *A Flag Is Born* opened, *The Front Page* was revived on Broadway by Hunt Stromberg, Jr., staged by MacArthur. It ran a total of seventy-nine performances, closing on November 9th.

13. Ovid Demaris, *The Last Mafioso*, Times Books, New York, 1981.

CHAPTER 13

1. This was not Hecht's first run-in with the CEA, which in the thirties had recommended that the already heavily censored *Scarface* be returned to the censor for "further consideration because of its morbidity and bloodshed."

CHAPTER 14

1. Jay Robert Nash, *The Innovators*, Regnery Gateway, Chicago, 1982.

2. Unfortunately, *The Ben Hecht Show* is gone forever, no kinescopes having been kept.

3. From Bliss Carman's "In the House of Idiedaily": "Oh, but life went gaily, gaily. . . ."

4. In 1951, when Hecht was looking for a young actress to star in his film *Actors and Sin*, Rose secretly taught eight-year-old Jenny the lines. "I figured that to have Rose and Jenny both around a picture would be sure death to it," Hecht remarked, but after listening to "dozens of miniature Mae Wests going through elocutions," he gave in when Rose and Jenny "walked in and demanded the part."

In his review in *The New York Times*, Bosley Crowther found Jenny "vastly bizarre . . . with the air of a middle-aged gnome." (Jenny had curly, blond Harpo Marx hair and her mother's intense, rather bulging eyes.) Jenny next appeared in Viña Delmar's play *Mid-Summer*. This time, Jenny's notices were very good, Brooks Atkinson writing that she was "frequently hilarious as the precocious daughter," the *Post* opining that she was "more terrifying than the child monster in *The Children's Hour*." Some members of the cast, though, felt Jenny's performance more inspired by life than art. (Most people saw her as a "spoiled brat" constantly deferred to by Rose.) During a scene between Mark Stevens and Geraldine Page, Jenny, seated at a table, loudly riffled a deck of cards. Or she would sneeze or wink at the audience. Stevens was irked, said Hecht, because Jenny was such "an uninhibited little wench." Next, Jenny thumbed her nose at one of the actress's maids. The Hechts parried: "Miss Vicki Cummings kicked a hole in Jenny's dress while she was in it" and "hurled Jenny against the scenery." More charges were leveled by Stevens and Cummings—Jenny had screamed at Stevens, burped in his face, Rose had made "terrible" scenes backstage. Geraldine Page thought it all "nonsense," but Actors' Equity was brought in to investigate. Had Jenny kicked Stevens? Said she, "I have never kicked any actor—onstage or offstage—and I never lie." Then, in Boston, Jenny struck one of the other youngsters in the play. "What a fuss they made over two little children in a squall," Rose said. "When I tried to explain that this was the way with children all over the world, the Equity representative walked away." The Hechts told the press they were considering suing Stevens. "I knew him in Hollywood," Hecht told reporters. "He screamed and raved on the stage and called people names. He was known out there as a surly fellow." Equity judged that it would drop all charges if Jenny quit the play. She did and the Hechts didn't sue Stevens. (The following summer, Jenny was back on the boards for *Mid-Summer*'s Chicago run.)

Rose wrote a play for her, *Lentil*, but no backers could be found. Jenny then played with Billie Burke in *Mother Was a Bachelor*, in Palm Beach, and in *Mrs. McThing* with Helen Hayes. In 1958 she played in *The Helen Hayes Story* on television, then the following year, when she was sixteen, she starred in *The Diary of Anne Frank* at the Nyack Playhouse. Edward Schreiber, who had starred her in a twenty-minute short, *Katie's Lot*, wrote a feature film for her, but no money could be raised.

Next, Hecht slated her for Broadway. "Bertolt Brecht and Lion Feuchtwanger collaborated on a play called *Simone*," Hecht wrote. "It was Brecht's last dramatic work. After Brecht died, Feuchtwanger had the final say in his hands. He did one final thing. He selected Jenny Hecht to play the part of Simone, and then he died. After Jenny received Feuchtwanger's go-ahead I went to work adapting the play. . . . When Jenny Hecht plays its Joan of Arc heroine in New York, it will be the first time Brecht's world-famous name will appear as a drama author on a Broadway marquee." The play was presented at the Cleveland Playhouse from January 31st through February 24th, 1962, and was later rewritten by Hecht for a New York debut, but once again the necessary backing couldn't be found. (Needless to say, Hecht's adaptation was sold to Hollywood—to Sam Goldwyn, who never produced it.)

Chapter Notes

Brought up to believe she was a prodigy, unfamiliar with discipline or criticism, Jenny at age twenty was in adolescent rebellion against her parents. No longer wanting to become a Broadway or Hollywood actress and rejecting any assistance from Ben and Rose, she began ushering in the early 1960s for the Living Theater in New York. When the Internal Revenue Service padlocked the Becks' theatre for nonpayment of taxes, Jenny helped them give an illegal performance, for which she and the cast were arrested. Hecht sent his lawyer, Mark Lane, to the jail to spring her but Jenny refused, saying, "I do not want to be separated from the group, from these wonderful people I love. I'm not going to be defended separately by my father's lawyer. If I'm hungry, somebody in the group buys me food. If they're hungry, I buy them food. We're so close."

When the Living Theater left America for a six-year stay in Europe, Jenny went along as a member of the cast.

In 1971, Jenny Hecht was found dead in a Los Angeles hotel room. She was twenty-eight years old, an apparent suicide or possibly the victim of a drug overdose.

BEN HECHT

FILMOGRAPHY

FILMS

Since Hecht was for the most part concerned only with the writing of a script, extensive credits have not been given, except for the seven pictures he directed as well as wrote.

1915

Double Trouble   Triangle/Fine Arts
Director: D. W. Griffith
From the novel by Herbert Quick
Adaptation: W. Christy Cabanne
Screenplay: D. W. Griffith (Anita Loos and Ben Hecht, uncredited)

"Sometimes the idea for a film would come from an outside source, such as one that was mailed in by a young reporter Doug Fairbanks had encountered in Chicago. His name was Ben Hecht, and his plot was flippantly scrawled on the back of a used envelope. It concerned a young man who had been rejected by his sweetheart and was bent on suicide. Being too cowardly to do the job himself, the hero hired a mob of gangsters to shoot him by surprise from ambush. No sooner was the deal made than the sweetheart relented and agreed to marry the hero, from which point it was up to me to concoct his frantic endeavors to track down the leader and cancel the deal. The movie was a huge success." —Anita Loos, *A Girl Like I.*

AUTHOR'S NOTE: I have never been able to substantiate this claim of Anita Loos's, and tend to think her memory faulty, first of all since Hecht was just making his fledgling attempts at literary writing in 1915, and also because Loos credits Hecht as the source of the plot when in fact it was adapted from a novel.

1926

The New Klondike   Paramount
Director: Lewis Milestone
Story: J. P. McEvoy
Screenplay: Tom Geraghty and J. Clarkson Miller (Ben Hecht and Ring Lardner, uncredited)

1927

Underworld   Paramount
Director: Josef von Sternberg
Original story: Ben Hecht
Adaptation: Charles Furthman
Screenplay: Robert N. Lee
British title: *Paying the Penalty*
French title: *Les Nuits de Chicago*
Academy Award: Best Original Story (Ben Hecht)

American Beauty   First National
Director: Richard Wallace
Original story: Ben Hecht and Michael Arlen, uncredited
Story: Wallace Irwin
Screenplay: Carey Wilson
Produced by Carey Wilson

1928

The Big Noise   Robert Kane/First National
Director: Allan Dwan
Original story: Ben Hecht
Screenplay and adaptation: Tom Geraghty (Allan Dwan, uncredited)
Titles: George Marion, Jr.

1929

The Unholy Night   MGM
Director: Lionel Barrymore
From the unpublished short story "The Green Ghost," by Ben Hecht
Adaptation: Dorothy Farnum
Screenplay: Edwin Justus Mayer
Titles: Joe Farnum
Original title: *The Doomed Regiment*
See: *Le Spectre Vert* (1930)

The Great Gabbo   Sono-Art-Worldwide
Director: James Cruze (Erich von Stroheim, uncredited)
From the short story "The Rival Dummy," by Ben Hecht
Dialogue and continuity: F. Hugh Herbert

"The use of Gabbo's dummy, Otto, as an outlet for the feelings the ventriloquist dares not express makes *The Great Gabbo* a direct ancestor of the most memorable passage of the acclaimed British film *Dead of Night* (1945), or Richard Attenborough's *Magic* (1978), and an Alfred Hitchcock television episode, "The Glass Eye." . . . The stage production sequences were shot in Multicolor, a process which tendered the screen garish in a film of generally subdued visual effect."—Michael Price and George Turner, "Talkie Trouble: *The Great Gabbo*," *American Cinematographer*, March 1985

"The worst color sequences I have ever seen."—Paul Rotha

More Soup   Paramount
Silent short written, directed, and acted by Ben Hecht and Herman Mankiewicz as a Christmas present for Adolph Zukor.

1930

Roadhouse Nights   Paramount
Director: Hobart Henley
Original story: Ben Hecht, loosely adapted from Dashiell Hammett's novel *Red Harvest*
Screenplay, dialogue, and continuity: Garrett Fort
Produced by Walter Wanger
Original title: *The River Inn*

The reporter in the picture is named Hansen after Hecht's friend and fellow journalist from Chicago Harry Hansen.

Le Spectre Vert   MGM
Director: Jacques Feyder
Screenplay and dialogue: Yves Mirande

Foreign-language version of *The Unholy Night* (1929).

Scarface   Caddo/Atlantic Pictures (Howard Hughes)
Director: Howard Hawks
From the novel by Armitage Trail (pseudonym of Maurice Coons)
Story and screenplay: Ben Hecht
Additional dialogue: John Lee Mahin, Seton I. Miller, and W. R. Burnett
Additional contributions to the story: Fred Pasley, uncredited (Pasley was a Chicago reporter and Al Capone's biographer)
Produced by Howard Hawks and Howard Hughes
Other titles: *Shame of a Nation* and *Racketeers*
Cameos: Howard Hawks (a patient in a hospital bed) and John Lee Mahin (as MacArthur of the *Tribune*)
See: *Scarface* (1983)
Not released until 1932 because of Howard Hughes's legal battles with state censorship boards

"*Scarface* with Paul Muni was recently barred from Germany when it was discovered that there was an uncommonly close resemblance between some of the gangsters in the picture and certain high Nazi officials." —*Filmfront*, vol. 1, no. 3 (January 28, 1935)

Early in 1933, Howard Hughes announced a sequel to *Scarface*, but he changed his mind because of flagging interest in gangster pictures at the box office.

Street of Chance   Paramount
Director: John Cromwell
Original scenario: Ben Hecht and Charles MacArthur, uncredited
Screenplay: Howard Estabrook and Lenore Coffee
Dialogue: Lenore Coffee
Academy Award nomination: Best Writing Achievement
Original title: *The Big Shot*

Hecht's and MacArthur's script was written in 1928 and derived in all probability from the outline for the play they wrote for Jed Harris, who rejected it in favor of *Twentieth Century*.

1931

The Front Page   Caddo
Director: Lewis Milestone
From the play by Ben Hecht and Charles MacArthur
Adaptation and additional dialogue: Bartlett Cormack (and Charles Lederer, uncredited)
See: *There Goes My Girl* (1937), *His Girl Friday* (1940), *The Front Page* (1974), and *Switching Channels* (1988).

Monkey Business   Paramount
Director: Norman Z. McLeod
Story: Ben Hecht, uncredited
Screenplay: S. J. Perelman, Will D. Johnstone, and Arthur Sheekman
Produced by Herman Mankiewicz

The Unholy Garden   Goldwyn
Director: George Fitzmaurice
Story and screenplay: Ben Hecht and Charles MacArthur
Produced by Sam Goldwyn
French title: *L'Oasis de la terreur*

The Homicide Squad   Universal
Directors: George Melford and Edward Cahn
From the novel *The Mob* by Henry Cossitt
Screenplay: John Thomas Neville and Tom Reed (Ben Hecht and Charles MacArthur, uncredited)

The Sin of Madelon Claudet   MGM
Director: Edgar Selwyn

From the play *The Lullaby* by Edward Knoblock
Screenplay: Charles MacArthur (Ben Hecht, uncredited)
British title: *The Lullaby*
Academy Award: Best Actress (Helen Hayes [MacArthur])

Quick Millions   Fox
Director: Rowland Brown
Screenplay: Rowland Brown and Courtenay "Brick" Terrett (Ben Hecht and
        Charles MacArthur, uncredited)
Additional dialogue: John Wray

One of the characters in the picture is named "Bugs" Raymond after Charles
MacArthur—"Bugs" was one of Hecht's familiar nicknames for him—and
another was dubbed "Nails" Markey after fellow Chicago journalist Gene
Markey.

1932

Back Street   Universal
Director: John Stahl
From the novel by Fannie Hurst
Screenplay: Gladys Lehman and Lynn Starling (Ben Hecht and Gene Fowler,
        uncredited)

Beast of the City   MGM
Director: Charles Brabin
Story: W. R. Burnett
Screenplay: John Lee Mahin (Ben Hecht, uncredited)

Million Dollar Legs   Paramount
Director: Edward Cline
Screenplay: Joseph Mankiewicz, Henry Myers, and Nick Barrows (Ben Hecht,
        uncredited)
Produced by Herman Mankiewicz

What Price Hollywood?   RKO
Director: George Cukor
Story: Adela Rogers St. John
Screenplay: Jane Murfin, Ben Markson, Rowland Brown, and Gene Fowler (Ben
        Hecht, uncredited)
Produced by Pandro S. Berman
Academy Award nomination: Best Original Story (Adela Rogers St. John)

1933

Queen Christina   MGM
Director: Rouben Mamoulian
Original story: Salka Viertel and Margaret Levino

Screenplay: Salka Viertel and H. M. Harwood (uncredited rewrite by Ben Hecht
    and Gene Fowler)
Dialogue: S. N. Behrman
Produced by Walter Wanger
French title: *La reine Christine*

Rasputin and the Empress   MGM
Director: Richard Boleslawski
Screenplay: Charles MacArthur (Ben Hecht, uncredited; additional scenes by
    Robert Sherwood, uncredited)
Producer: Irving Thalberg
British title: *Rasputin the Mad Monk*
French title: *Raspoutine*
Academy Award nomination: Best Original Story (Charles MacArthur)

Hallelujah, I'm a Bum!   Feature Productions (Lewis Milestone)
Director: Lewis Milestone
Original story: Ben Hecht
Screenplay: S. N. Behrman
Music and lyrics: Richard Rodgers and Lorenz Hart
Presented by Joseph Schenck
British titles: *Hallelujah I'm a Tramp* and *Lazy Bones* (the British version was cut
    and redubbed)
Reissued in the United States in an edited version, retitled *The Heart of New York*

Topaze   RKO
Director: Harry D'Arrast
From the play by Marcel Pagnol
Adaptation: Benn W. Levy (Ben Hecht and Charles MacArthur, uncredited)
Produced by David O. Selznick

Turn Back the Clock   MGM
Director: Edgar Selwyn
Screenplay: Ben Hecht and Edgar Selwyn

Design for Living   Paramount
Director: Ernst Lubitsch
From the plays *Design for Living*, *The Vortex*, and *Hay Fever* by Noël Coward
Screenplay: Ben Hecht
Produced by Ernst Lubitsch
French title: *Sérénade à trois*

1934

Upperworld   Warner Brothers/Vitaphone
Director: Roy Del Ruth

Original story: Ben Hecht (Charles MacArthur and Eugene Walter, uncredited)
Screenplay: Ben Markson

Viva Villa!   MGM
Directors: Howard Hawks and Jack Conway
Suggested by *Viva Villa: A Recovery of the Real Pancho Villa—Peon . . . Bandit . . . Soldier . . . Patriot* by Edgcumb Pinchon and O. B. Stade
Screenplay: Ben Hecht
Produced by David O. Selznick
Academy Award nominations: Best Adaptation (Ben Hecht), Best Picture

Twentieth Century   Columbia
Director: Howard Hawks
From the play of the same name by Ben Hecht and Charles MacArthur, based on an unproduced play, *Napoleon of Broadway*, by Charles Milholland
Screenplay: Ben Hecht and Charles MacArthur (Gene Fowler and Preston Sturges, uncredited)
French title: *Train de luxe*

George Bernard Shaw's favorite film was *Twentieth Century*.

Shoot the Works   Paramount
Director: Wesley Ruggles
From the play *The Great Magoo* by Ben Hecht and Gene Fowler, uncredited
Screenplay: Claude Binyon
Dialogue: Howard J. Green
Presented by Adolphe Zukor
See: *Some Like It Hot* (1939)

Riptide   MGM
Director: Edmund Goulding
From the novel *The Green Hat* by Michael Arlen, uncredited
Screenplay: Charles MacArthur and Edmund Goulding (Ben Hecht, uncredited)
Produced by Irving Thalberg

The President Vanishes   Paramount
Director: William Wellman
From the novel by Anonymous (Rex Stout)
Adaptation and screenplay: Lynn Starling (Ben Hecht and Charles MacArthur, uncredited)
Produced by Walter Wanger
British title: *Strange Conspiracy*

Crime Without Passion   Hecht-MacArthur Productions/Paramount
Directors: Ben Hecht and Charles MacArthur
Associate director: Lee Garmes
From the short story "Caballero of the Law" by Ben Hecht
Screenplay: Ben Hecht and Charles MacArthur

Produced by Ben Hecht and Charles MacArthur
Photographed by Lee Garmes
Special effects: Slavko Vorkapitch
Musical score: Frank Tours
General manager: Arthur Rosson
Scenery: Albert Johnson
Film editor: Arthur Ellis
Recorded by Joseph Kane

Cast:

Lee Gentry	Claude Rains
Carmen Brown	Margo
Katy Costello	Whitney Bourne
Eddie White	Stanley Ridges
State's Attorney O'Brien	Leslie Adams
Della	Greta Granstedt
Miss Keeley	Esther Dale

Cameos: Ben Hecht, Charles MacArthur, Helen Hayes, Fanny Brice, and Gertrude Lawrence

1935

Once in a Blue Moon   Hecht-MacArthur Productions/Paramount
Directors: Ben Hecht and Charles MacArthur
Associate director: Lee Garmes
Story: Rose Caylor (Hecht), uncredited
Screenplay: Ben Hecht and Charles MacArthur
Produced by Ben Hecht and Charles MacArthur
Photographed by Lee Garmes
Musical score: George Antheil
Original titles: *Laugh, Little Clown* and *Tower of Babel*

Cast:

Gabbo the Great	Jimmy Savo
General Onyegin	Nikita Balieff
Duchess	Cecilia Loftus
Nina	Whitney Bourne
Princess Ilena	Edwina Armstrong (Hecht)
Ivan	Sandor Szabo
Captain	J. Charles Gilbert
Count Bulba	Hans Steinke
Kolia	George Andre
"The General"	Jackie Borene
Nikita	Michael Dalmatoff

Also in the cast, as extras, were a former governor-general of Siberia, a grandson of Leo Tolstoy, and Lucius Henderson, a moviemaking pioneer, who managed the Majestic Film Company before D. W. Griffith took over.

Released in 1936

Ben Hecht Filmography

The Scoundrel   Hecht-MacArthur Productions/Paramount
Directors: Ben Hecht and Charles MacArthur
Associate director: Lee Garmes
From the play, *The Scoundrel* (aka *All He Ever Loved*), by Ben Hecht and Rose Caylor (Hecht)
Story: Ben Hecht and Charles MacArthur
Screenplay: Ben Hecht and Charles MacArthur
Produced by Ben Hecht and Charles MacArthur
Photographed by Lee Garmes
Musical director: Frank Tours
General manager: Arthur Rosson
Settings: Albert Johnson
Art director: Walter Keller
Assistant director: Harold Godsoe
Film editor: Arthur Ellis
Recorded by Joseph Kane

Cast:

Anthony Mallare	Noël Coward
Cora Moore	Julie Haydon
Paul Decker	Stanley Ridges
Julia Vivian	Martha Sleeper
Carlotta	Rosita Moreno
Maggie	Hope Williams
Jimmy Clay	Ernest Cossart
Mildred Langwiler	Everley Gregg
Maurice Stern	Eduardo Ciannelli
Mrs. Rollinson	Helen Strickland
Howard Gillette	Richard Bond
Rothenstein	Lionel Stander
Massey	Frank Conlan
Calhoun	O. Z. Whitehead
Felix Abrams	Raymond Bramley
Slezack	Harry Davenport

Cameos: Ben Hecht, Charles MacArthur, Alexander Woollcott, and Alice Duer Miller
Academy Award: Best Original Story (Ben Hecht and Charles MacArthur)

The Florentine Dagger   Warner Bros./Vitaphone
Director: Robert Florey
From the novel by Ben Hecht
Screenplay: Tom Reed
Additional dialogue: Brown Holmes

Spring Tonic   Fox
Director: Clyde Bruckman
From the play *Man-Eating Tiger* by Ben Hecht and Rose Caylor (Hecht)
Adaptation: Howard I. Young

Screenplay: H. W. Hanemann and Patterson McNutt
Comedy sequences by Frank Griffin

Barbary Coast   Goldwyn
Director: Howard Hawks
From *The Barbary Coast: An Informal History of the San Francisco Underworld* by
    Herbert Asbury
Story and screenplay: Ben Hecht and Charles MacArthur (Stephen Longstreet,
    uncredited; Longstreet did two weeks' work on the script when he labored
    briefly for Hecht as one of his script-factory writers)
French title: *Ville sans loi*

"The wit, vigor and *panache* of Mr. Ben Hecht and Mr. MacArthur have raised
nearly to international halma form (in Mr. Aldous Huxley's phrase) a conven-
tional film story. . . . *Sous les toits de Paris* contained a sequence in which
Préjean was surrounded by a gang with drawn razors in the darkness of a railway
viaduct—the smoke blew continually across, and the dialogue was drowned in the
din of shunting trucks. The steamy obscurity, the whispers, the uproar overhead
combined to make the scene vividly sinister. There is a moment in *Barbary Coast*
that takes its place with Clair's when the Big Shot's gunman, on his way to
commit another murder . . . feels the pistols of the vigilantes against his ribs.
They walk him out to the edge of the acetylene-lighted town along streets
ankle-deep in mud, holding a mock trial with counsel and witnesses as they go;
the low voices, the slosh of mud round their boots, the rhythmic stride are
terrifying because they have been exactly imagined, with the ear as well as the
eye." —Graham Greene, *The Spectator*

1936

Soak the Rich   Hecht-MacArthur Productions/Paramount
Directors: Ben Hecht and Charles MacArthur
Story and screenplay: Ben Hecht and Charles MacArthur
Produced by Ben Hecht and Charles MacArthur
Photographed by Leon Shamroy
Production manager: John Ojerholm
Assistant director: Harold Godsoe
Cameraman: Charles Harten
Art director: Walter Keller
Film editor: Leo Zochling
Recorded by Joseph Kane

Cast:

Humphrey Craig	Walter Connolly
Belinda Craig	Mary (Mimsi) Taylor
Buzz Jones	John Howard
Joe Muglia	Lionel Stander
Tulio	Francis Compton

Captain Pettijohn	Joseph Sweeney
Sandwich Sign	John W. Call
Black Eye	Edwin Phillips, Jr.
Tommy	Robert Wallsten
Rockwell	George Watts
Dean Phillpotts	Ed Garvey
The butler	Con MacSunday
Jenny	Isabelle Foster

Cameos: Ben Hecht, Charles MacArthur, Ilka Chase, and Alice Duer Miller

1937

Hurricane   Goldwyn
Director: John Ford
From the novel by James Norman Hall and Charles Nordhoff
Adaptation: Oliver H. P. Garrett
Screenplay: Dudley Nichols (uncredited rewrite by Ben Hecht)
Produced by Sam Goldwyn

The Prisoner of Zenda   Selznick
Director: John Cromwell
From the novel by Anthony Hope
Adaptation: Wells Root
Screenplay: John L. Balderston (Ben Hecht, uncredited)
Additional dialogue: Donald Ogden Stewart
Produced by David O. Selznick
French title: *Prisonnier de Zenda*

Nothing Sacred   Selznick
Director: William Wellman
From the short story "Letter to the Editor" by James Street
Screenplay: Ben Hecht (final sequences by Ring Lardner, Jr., and Budd
            Schulberg, uncredited)
Produced by David O. Selznick
French title: *La joyeuse suicidée*

King of Gamblers   Paramount
Director: Robert Florey
Story: Tiffany Thayer
Screenplay: Doris Anderson (Ben Hecht and Charles MacArthur, uncredited)
British title: *Czar of the Slot Machines*

A Star Is Born   Selznick
Director: William Wellman
Story: Robert Carson and William Wellman
Screenplay: Robert Carson, Dorothy Parker, and Alan Campbell (Ben Hecht and
            Gene Fowler, uncredited)

Produced by David O. Selznick
Academy Award: Best Original Story
Academy Award nominations: Best Picture, Best Director, Best Screenplay, Best
    Actor, Best Actress
French title: *Une Étoile est née*

There Goes My Girl   RKO
Director: Ben Holmes
Story: George Beck
Screenplay: Harry Segall

An uncredited loose remake of *The Front Page*.
See: *The Front Page* (1931), *His Girl Friday* (1940), *The Front Page* (1974), and
    Switching Channels (1988).

1938

The Goldwyn Follies   Goldwyn
Director: George Marshall
Story and screenplay: Ben Hecht
Specialties and songs for the Ritz Brothers by Sid Kuller and Ray Golden
Additional comedy sequences: Sam Perrin and Arthur Philips
Songs by George Gershwin. Lyrics by Ira Gershwin, and additional music by
    Vernon Duke.

"In 1932, shortly after the death of his friend Florenz Ziegfeld, Samuel Goldwyn announced that henceforth he would carry on tradition by producing an annual Follies considerably more lavish than any ever offered by the pioneer Ziegfeld. This announcement was repeated in 1934 and 1935. In 1936, the film press recorded that the story, reputedly centering around George Jean Nathan, was being written by a New York newspaperman under the pen name of Harry Selby. Later in the year, Harry J. Green was assigned to the screen treatment. Shortly thereafter, Alice Duer Miller was reportedly working on the script with the team of Kalmar and Ruby. Still later, Harry J. Green was re-signed to collaborate with Kalmar and Ruby. At some period, Dorothy Parker and her husband, Alan Campbell, and Anita Loos and her husband, John Emerson, made contributions to the manuscript. As production was about to start early in 1937, the script was discarded in favor of a new one which Ben Hecht (hitherto unconnected with the production) wrote for Mr. Goldwyn in two weeks.

"A further look at the evidence suggests that the *Follies* project attracted Mr. Goldwyn in idea, but the closer it came to realization the less certain he was of what he wanted it to be. Continued revisions of the picture after it was in release support this, and almost proof positive is Mr. Goldwyn's last-minute summoning of Ben Hecht, which is his good custom whenever he is in doubt or in trouble."
    —Richard Griffith, *Samuel Goldwyn: The Producer and His Films*

Angels with Dirty Faces   Warner Bros.
Director: Michael Curtiz

Story by Rowland Brown (and Ben Hecht and Charles MacArthur, uncredited)
Screenplay: John Wexley and Warren Duff
Academy Award nominations: Best Original Story, Best Director
French title: *Les Anges aux figures sales*

1939

Gunga Din   RKO
Director: George Stevens
From the poem by Rudyard Kipling
Story and adaptation: Ben Hecht and Charles MacArthur
Screenplay: Ben Hecht, Charles MacArthur, Joel Sayre, and Fred Guiol
Produced by George Stevens
See: *Sergeants 3* (1962)

Stagecoach   Walter Wanger Productions
Director: John Ford
From the short story "Stage to Lordsburg" by Ernest Haycox
Screenplay: Dudley Nichols (Ben Hecht, uncredited)
Produced by Walter Wanger and John Ford
Academy Award nomination: Best Picture, Best Director
French title: *La Chevauchée fantastique*

Let Freedom Ring   MGM
Director: Jack Conway
Story and screenplay: Ben Hecht (suggested by Grace Lumpkin's novel *To Make My Bread*, uncredited)
Produced by Harry Rapf

Wuthering Heights   Goldwyn
Director: William Wyler
From the novel by Emily Brontë
Screenplay: Ben Hecht and Charles MacArthur (John Huston, uncredited, for a quick polish at Sam Goldwyn's request)
Produced by Sam Goldwyn
Academy Award nominations: Best Screenplay (Ben Hecht and Charles MacArthur), Best Director, Best Picture
French title: *Les Hauts de Hurlevent*

"Most startled group in the industry who are observing the enthusiastic audience reception of the film must be the story and scenario staffs of the Hollywood studios . . . *Wuthering Heights* in theme, characters, plot and setting possesses not one familiar attribute for which studio scenario departments search zealously through thousands of manuscripts, plays, novels, and synopses. It violates all the accepted rules of successful film stories. Its leading characters are something less than sympathetic—they are psychopathic exhibits. And the ending is stark, dire, tragic, an uncompromising finale which utterly disregards all popular theories of screen entertainment."—*Variety*, April 19, 1939

It's a Wonderful World   Frank Davis Productions/MGM
Director: W. S. Van Dyke
Story: Ben Hecht and Herman Mankiewicz
Screenplay: Ben Hecht
Original titles: *Life Is a Wonderful Thing* and *The Lady Protests*
French title: *Ce Monde est merveilleux*

Some Like It Hot   William C. Thomas Productions/Paramount
Director: George Archainbaud
From the play *The Great Magoo*, by Ben Hecht and Gene Fowler
Screenplay: Lewis R. Foster and Wilkie C. Mahoney
See: *Shoot the Works* (1934)

Retitled *Rhythm Romance* when Billy Wilder's *Some Like It Hot* was released.

In November of 1938, Paramount announced that Leo McCarey was to direct a second screen version of BH and Gene Fowler's play *The Great Magoo* (Paramount retained the rights to the play from the 1934 film *Shoot the Works*). The picture was to star Miriam Hopkins, Alison Skipworth, and Jack Oakie. Instead, the play was turned into a musical farce for Bob Hope and Gene Krupa, directed by George Archainbaud and entitled *Some Like It Hot*. Almost nothing of the original play survived in this second and last screen version. *Some Like It Hot*, *Variety* assessed, "presents opportunity for profitable exploitation to attract the jivesters and can be tied up easily with contests among local alligators and ickies. Krupa puts out some hot stuff for the rug-cutters."

Lady of the Tropics   MGM
Director: Jack Conway
Story and screenplay: Ben Hecht
Produced by Sam Zimbalist
Original titles: *Passport to Heaven* and *Passport to Paradise*

At the Circus   MGM
Director: Edward Buzzell
Treatment and original story: Ben Hecht, uncredited
Screenplay: Irving Brecher
Produced by Mervyn LeRoy
Other title: *The Marx Brothers at the Circus*
French title: *Un Jour au cirque*

The protagonist is named Philip Marlowe. *The Big Sleep* had just been published.

Gone With the Wind   Selznick
Director: Victor Fleming
From the novel by Margaret Mitchell

Ben Hecht Filmography

Screenplay: Sidney Howard (Ben Hecht, Jo Swerling, Oliver H. P. Garrett, and Barbara Keon, uncredited)
Produced by David O. Selznick
Academy Awards: Best Picture, Best Screenplay
French title: *Autant en emporte le vent*

1940

His Girl Friday   Columbia
Director: Howard Hawks
From the play *The Front Page* by Ben Hecht and Charles MacArthur
Screenplay: Charles Lederer (Ben Hecht, uncredited)
Produced by Howard Hawks
French title: *La Dame du Vendredi*
See: *The Front Page* (1931), *There Goes My Girl* (1937), *The Front Page* (1974), and *Switching Channels* (1988).

"The French love for Howard Hawks became, through constant screenings at the Cinémathèque, almost unconditional. Almost, I say, because there was a night in the 1967 Hawks retrospective when Henri Langlois showed a brand-new print of *His Girl Friday*. The print had no subtitles, and one must remember that this is perhaps the fastest-talking film in the history of the American cinema. The audience was very excited before the performance, and even into the first reel or two. But even those with a fair knowledge of English were not able to keep up with the constant stream of wisecracks, and the mood of the audience grew restless, almost mutinous. . . . The audience knew they were missing something—especially because some English or American people in the audience were laughing constantly."—Richard Roud, *A Passion for Film: Henri Langlois and the Cinémathèque Française*

I Take This Woman   MGM
Director: W. S. Van Dyke
Story: Charles MacArthur (Ben Hecht, uncredited; 49-page synopsis written by Hecht, dated January 31, 1938)
Screenplay: James Kevin McGuinness
Produced by Louis B. Mayer
Original titles: *A New York Cinderella*, *Second Chance*, and *Unto Thee Only*

The Shop Around the Corner   MGM
Director: Ernst Lubitsch
From the play *Illatszertar*, aka *Parfumerie*, by Nikolaus Laszlo
Screenplay: Samson Raphaelson (Ben Hecht, uncredited)
Produced by Ernst Lubitsch

Foreign Correspondent   Walter Wanger Productions
Director: Alfred Hitchcock

From the autobiography *Personal History* by Vincent Sheean
Screenplay: Charles Bennett and Joan Harrison (Ben Hecht, John Howard Lawson, Bu
    Schulberg, and Harold Clurman, uncredited)
Additional dialogue: Robert Benchley and James Hilton
Produced by Walter Wanger
Academy Award nominations: Best Picture, Best Screenplay
French title: *Correspondant 17*

Angels Over Broadway   Columbia
Directors: Ben Hecht and Lee Garmes
From the short story "Don Quixote and His Last Windmill" by Ben Hecht
Screenplay: Ben Hecht
Produced by Ben Hecht
Associate producer: Douglas Fairbanks, Jr.
Photographed by Lee Garmes
Film editor: Gene Havlick
Art director: Lionel Banks
Music: George Antheil
Sound: Lodge Cunningham
Gowns: Kalloch
Costumes: Ray Howell

Cast:

Bill O'Brien	Douglas Fairbanks, Jr.
Nina	Rita Hayworth
Gene Gibbons	Thomas Mitchell
Charles Engle	John Qualen
Hopper	George Watts
Dutch Enright	Ralph Theodore
Louis Artene	Eddie Foster
Eddie Burns	Jack Roper
Sylvia Marbe	Constance Worth
Sylvia's escort	Richard Bond
Joe	Frank Conlan
Rennick	Walter Baldwin
Tony	Jack Carr
Jack	Al Seymour
Miss Karpin	Catherine Courtney
Head Waiter	Edward Earle
Pawn Shop Owner	Jimmy Conlin
Cigarette Girl	Ethelreda Leopold
Doorman	Billy Lally
Gamblers	Al Rhein
	Jerry Jerome
	Roger Gray
	Harry Strong

Cameo: Ben Hecht

Original title: *Before I Die*
Academy Award nomination: Best Original Screenplay (Ben Hecht)

Comrade X   King Vidor Productions/MGM
Director: King Vidor
Story: Walter Reisch (coauthor of *Ninotchka)*
Screenplay: Ben Hecht and Charles Lederer (Herman Mankiewicz, uncredited)
Produced by Gottfried Reinhardt
Academy Award nomination: Best Original Story

1941

The Mad Doctor   Paramount
Director: Tim Whelan
Original screenplay: Ben Hecht and Charles MacArthur, uncredited
Screenplay: Howard Green
Original titles: *Destiny* and *The Monster*
British title: *A Date with Destiny*

When Hecht and MacArthur were producing films at Astoria, they wrote a script for John Barrymore, which they sold to Paramount for $50,000. Titled *The Monster*—Barrymore's nickname among his close friends—it was rejected by the studio, so Hecht and MacArthur retailored it for Noël Coward, changing the title to *Destiny*. Paramount wasn't interested in the alcoholic Barrymore as a lead or in Coward after *The Scoundrel*. Instead it was turned into a grade-B horror film.

The Outlaw   Howard Hughes Productions
Director: Howard Hughes; begun by Howard Hawks, uncredited
Story: Ben Hecht and Howard Hawks, uncredited
Screenplay: Jules Furthman
French title: *Le Banni*

Lydia   Alexander Korda
Director: Julien Duvivier
Remake of *Un Carnet de bal*, directed by Julien Duvivier
Story: Julien Duvivier and Lazlo Bus-Fekete
Screenplay: Ben Hecht and Samuel Hoffenstein
Produced by Lee Garmes

Early in 1941 French director Julien Duvivier escaped occupied France for New York, where he was introduced to Hecht by Lee Garmes, both Duvivier and Garmes having recently worked for Alexander Korda in England. Duvivier had contracted with Korda to do an English-language film and hired Hecht to write the script. Hecht enlisted Samuel Hoffenstein—a friend from Hollywood staying at Nyack—to collaborate with him. The project Duvivier, Hecht, and Hoffenstein decided on was a remake of Duvivier's 1937 picture *Un Carnet de Bal*. They worked together at Hecht's house in Nyack through February and by the first of

March had a completed script, which at first was titled *Forbidden City* but later changed to *Lydia*.

Second Chorus   Paramount
Director: H. C. Potter
Story: Frank Cavett
Screenplay: Ian McLellan Hunter and Elaine Ryan (Ben Hecht, uncredited)
Produced by Boris Morros

1942

Roxie Hart   20th Century–Fox
Director: William Wellman
From the play *Chicago* by Maurine Watkins
Screenplay: Nunnally Johnson (Ben Hecht, uncredited)
Produced by Nunnally Johnson

The newspaper reporter is named Walter Howard after Walter Howey, the legendary editor who also served as the inspiration for Walter Burns in *The Front Page*.

Ten Gentlemen from West Point   20th Century–Fox
Director: Henry Hathaway
Story: Malvin Wald
Screenplay: Richard Maibaum (Ben Hecht and Darryl Zanuck, uncredited)
Additional dialogue: George Seaton

Gene Fowler's son-in-law played a small role in the picture.

Tales of Manhattan   20th Century–Fox
Director: Julien Duvivier
A portmanteau picture for which Ben Hecht wrote the continuity and two of the stories, as well as polishing the other stories by Ferenc Molnár, Donald Ogden Stewart, Samuel Hoffenstein, Alan Campbell, Ladislas Fodor, L. Vadnai, L. Gorog, Lamar Trotti, and Henry Blankfort
Produced by Boris Morros and S. P. Eagle [Sam Spiegel]
French title: *Six destins*

Tales of Manhattan was the first picture to open in Paris after it was liberated by the Allies.

China Girl   20th Century–Fox
Director: Henry Hathaway
Story: Melville Crossman (a Darryl Zanuck pseudonym)
Screenplay: Ben Hecht
Produced by: Ben Hecht
French title: *La Pagode en flammes*

Hecht named one of his characters Bull Weed after the protagonist of *Under-world*.

The Black Swan   20th Century–Fox
Director: Henry King
From the novel by Rafael Sabatini
Adaptation: Seton I. Miller
Screenplay: Ben Hecht and Seton I. Miller
French title: *Le Cygne noir*

Journey into Fear   Mercury/RKO
Director: Orson Welles
From the novel of the same name by Eric Ambler
Screenplay: Joseph Cotten (and Ben Hecht, Richard Collins, and Ellis St. Joseph, uncredited)
Produced by Orson Welles
French title: *Voyage au pays de la peur*

1944

Lifeboat   20th Century–Fox
Director: Alfred Hitchcock
Story: John Steinbeck
Screenplay: Jo Swerling (Ben Hecht, uncredited; Hitchcock called Hecht in to read the final
     script and to rewrite the ending)
Academy Award nominations: Best Director, Best Original Story

The Very Thought of You   Warner Bros.
Director: Delmer Daves
Story: Lionel Wiggam (Ben Hecht, uncredited)
Screenplay: Alvah Bessie and Delmer Daves
Produced by Jerry Wald

1945

Spellbound   Vanguard Films/Selznick
Director: Alfred Hitchcock
From the novel *The House of Dr. Edwardes* by Francis Beeding
Adaptation: Angus MacPhail
Screenplay: Ben Hecht
Produced by David O. Selznick
Academy Award nominations: Best Picture, Best Director
French title: *La maison du docteur Edwardes*

Watchtower of Tomorrow   MGM
Director: Alfred Hitchcock

Story and screenplay: Ben Hecht
Original title: *The World of Tomorrow*
A short film for the State Department about the United Nations.

Cornered   RKO
Director: Edward Dmytryk
Original story: Ben Hecht, uncredited
Story and adaptation: John Wexley
Screenplay: John Paxton
Produced by Adrian Scott

"William Dozier had become the new story head at RKO. Either because he considered it a good property, or because he wanted to make his presence immediately felt (Adrian Scott assumed the latter), he had purchased a twenty-page treatment of a tough suspense mystery written by Ben Hecht. Or was it? It was such poor stuff that we were inclined to guess that Hecht had simply put his name to someone else's material and shared in the payoff, which was a fat $50,000."—Edward Dmytryk, *It's a Hell of a Life But Not a Bad Living: A Hollywood Memoir*

1946

Specter of the Rose   Republic
Director: Ben Hecht
From the short story by Ben Hecht
Screenplay: Ben Hecht
Produced by Ben Hecht
Associate producer: Lee Garmes
Photographed by Lee Garmes
Musical score: George Antheil
Production designer: Ernst Fegte.
Choreography: Tamara Geva
Musical director: Morton Scott
Film editor: Harry Keller
Assistant director: Harold Godsoe
Dialogue director: Serene Kassapian
Sound: Ferrol Redd
Costumes: Adele Palmer
Sets: John McCarthy, Jr., and Otto Siegel
Makeup: Bob Mark
Hair Stylist: Peggy Grey

Cast:

Madame La Sylph	Judith Anderson
Max Polikoff	Michael Chekhov
André Sanine	Ivan Kirov
Haidi	Viola Essen

Lionel Gans	Lionel Stander
Specs McFarlan	Charles "Red" Marshall
Kropotkin	George Shdanoff
Jack Jones	Billy Gray
Jibby	Juan Panalle
Mr. Lyons	Lew Hearn
Mamochka	Ferike Boros
Alexis	Constantine Hassaleuris
Luigi	Ferdinand Pollina
Olga	Polly Rose
Jimmy	Jim Moran

Modern dancers: Freda Flier, Miriam Schiller
Classical dancers: Miriam Golden, Alice Cavers, Arleen Claire, Grace Mann, Nina Haven, Celene Radding, Allan Cooke, John Stanley

Gilda   Columbia
Director: Charles Vidor
Story: E. A. Ellington
Adaptation: Jo Eisinger
Screenplay: Marion Parsonnet (Ben Hecht, uncredited)
Produced by Virginia Van Upp

Notorious   RKO
Director: Alfred Hitchcock
Story and screenplay: Ben Hecht
Produced by Alfred Hitchcock
Academy Award nomination: Best Original Screenplay (Ben Hecht)
French title: *Les enchaînés*

Duel in the Sun   Vanguard Films/Selznick
Director: King Vidor (William Dieterle, Josef von Sternberg, Sidney Franklin, and Otto Brower, uncredited)
From the novel of the same name by Niven Busch
Adaptation: Oliver H. P. Garrett
Screenplay: David O. Selznick (Ben Hecht, uncredited).
French title: *Duel au soleil*

1947

Dishonored Lady   Hunt Stromberg Productions/Mars Films
Director: Robert Stevenson
From the play by Margaret Ayer Barnes and Edward Sheldon
Screenplay: Edmund North (Ben Hecht, uncredited)

Kiss of Death   20th Century–Fox
Director: Henry Hathaway

From an unpublished story by Eleazer Lipsky
Screenplay: Ben Hecht and Charles Lederer
Academy Award nomination: Best Original Story (Eleazer Lipsky)
French title: *Le Carrefour de la mort*

"One day Ben Hecht gave the *policier* the finishing touch, producing, from a tenth-rate novel by Eleazer Lipsky, an admirable script which was a supreme example of all the features of the detective story genre combined."—Claude Chabrol, "Evolution du film policier," *Cahiers du cinéma*, no. 54 (Christmas 1955)

Her Husband's Affairs   Columbia
Director: S. Sylvan Simon
Story and screenplay: Ben Hecht and Charles Lederer
Produced by Raphael Hakim
Original title: *My Awful Wife*

Ride the Pink Horse   Universal-International
Director: Robert Montgomery
From the novel by Dorothy B. Hughes (remade in 1964 by Don Siegel as *The Hanged Man*)
Screenplay: Ben Hecht and Charles Lederer
Produced by Joan Harrison
French title: *Et tournent les chevaux de bois*

The Paradine Case   Vanguard Films/Selznick
Director: Alfred Hitchcock
From the novel by Robert Hichens
Treatment: James Bridie
Adaptation: Alma Reville and James Bridie
Screenplay: David O. Selznick (Ben Hecht, uncredited)
French title: *Le procès Paradine*

1948

Rope   Transatlantic/Warner Bros.
Director: Alfred Hitchcock
From the play by Patrick Hamilton
Adaptation by Hume Cronyn
Screenplay: Arthur Laurents (Ben Hecht, uncredited, for revising and tightening final scene)
Produced by Alfred Hitchcock and Sidney Bernstein
French title: *La Corde*

The Miracle of the Bells   Jesse Lasky Productions/RKO
Director: Irving Pichel

From the novel by Russell Janney
Screenplay: Ben Hecht and Quentin Reynolds
Produced by Jesse Lasky
French title: *Le miracle des cloches*

Cry of the City   20th Century–Fox
Director: Robert Siodmak
From the novel *The Chair for Martin Rome* by Henry Edward Helseth
Screenplay: Richard Murphy (Ben Hecht, uncredited)
Produced by Sol Siegel
Original title: *The Law and Martin Rome*
French title: *La Proie*

Portrait of Jennie   Selznick
Director: William Dieterle
From the novel by Robert Nathan
Adaptation: Leonardo Bercovici
Screenplay: Paul Osborn and Peter Berneis (Ben Hecht and David Selznick,
     uncredited; at Selznick's request, Hecht composed the Foreword for
     the picture)
Produced by David O. Selznick
French title: *Le Portrait de Jennie*

1949

Love Happy   Artists Alliance/United Artists
Director: David Miller
Story: Harpo Marx
Screenplay: Frank Tashlin (Ben Hecht, uncredited)
Additional scenes: Mac Benoff
Produced by Mary Pickford and Lester Cowan
French title: *La Pêche au trésor*

Roseanna McCoy   Goldwyn
Director: Irving Reis
From the novel by Alberta Hannum
Screenplay: John Collier (Ben Hecht, uncredited)

The Inspector General   Warner Bros.
Director: Henry Koster
From the play *The Inspector General* by Nikolai Gogol
Screenplay: Philip Rapp and Harry Kurnitz (Ben Hecht, uncredited)
Original title: *Happy Times*
Produced by Jerry Wald
French title: *Vive Monsieur le Maire!*

Whirlpool   20th Century–Fox
Director: Otto Preminger
From the novel by Guy Endore
Screenplay: Ben Hecht and Andrew Solt (Because of the British ban on his
            pictures, Hecht used his chauffeur's name—Lester Barstow—on the
            film credits in England)
Produced by Otto Preminger
French title: *Le mystérieux docteur Corvo*

Big Jack   MGM
Director: Richard Thorpe
Story: Robert Thoeren
Screenplay: Marvin Borowsky, Otto van Eyss, and Gene Fowler (Ben Hecht,
            uncredited)

1950

Perfect Strangers   Warner Bros.
Director: Bretaigne Windust
From the play *Ladies and Gentlemen* by Ben Hecht and Charles MacArthur,
            based on *Twelve in a Box* by Ladislas Bus-Fekete
Adaptation: George Oppenheimer
Screenplay: Edith Sommer
Produced by Jerry Wald
British title: *Too Dangerous to Love*

In 1939, Hecht and MacArthur adapted a Hungarian play, *Twelve in a Box*, by
Ladislas Bus-Fekete, which they retitled *Ladies and Gentlemen*. It starred Helen
Hayes and was staged by MacArthur. The reviews were crushing. Brooks
Atkinson, in *The New York Times*, wrote, "It is a little number that Charles
MacArthur and Ben Hecht have run up from a pattern by L. Bus-Fekete, the
Hungarian hack." In 1948, Hecht and MacArthur offered the film rights to
Warner Bros. George Oppenheimer was assigned the adaptation. "I was at
Warners' working for Jerry Wald," Oppenheimer recalled, "and I finished an
assignment and he said to me, 'How would you like to do *Ladies and Gentlemen?*'
I said, 'Jesus, God, no. It's a terrible play!' I went home and then I discovered that
they had not bought the play. And suddenly I thought, 'My God, what a fine
friend I am!' I went back to the studio the next day and said, 'Jerry, I
misunderstood completely. I got the wrong play.' I lied like a trouper and said, 'I'd
love to work on that play. It's a fine play.' They paid them each $25,000. It was an
old play and not worth a hell of a lot. I did the screenplay kicking myself all over
the lot. With the money, Charlie bought a speedboat, but didn't even have the
decency to call it 'Oppenheimer.' " In the late fifties, the Hakim Brothers took an
option on the play for $10,000, thinking to make a second film version. It was
never produced.

Where the Sidewalk Ends   20th Century–Fox
Director: Otto Preminger
From the novel *Night Cry* by William L. Stuart
Adaptation: Victor Trivas, Frank P. Rosenberg, and Robert E. Kent
Screenplay: Ben Hecht (Because of the British ban on his pictures, Hecht used
      the pseudonym Rex Connor on the film credits in England)
Produced by Otto Preminger
French title: *Mark Dixon, détective*

Edge of Doom   Goldwyn/RKO
Director: Mark Robson
From the novel by Leo Brady
Screenplay: Philip Yordan (Ben Hecht, uncredited, for a complete rewrite of the
      script in August of 1950 after a disastrous preview)
British title: *Stronger than Fear*
French title: *La Marche à l'enfer*

1951

The Thing   Winchester Pictures/RKO
Director: Christian Nyby (Howard Hawks, uncredited)
From the short story "Who Goes There?" by John W. Campbell, Jr.
Screenplay: Charles Lederer (Ben Hecht, uncredited)
Produced by Howard Hawks
British title: *The Thing from Another World*
French titles: *La chose* and *La chose d'un autre monde*

Strangers on a Train   Warner Bros.
Director: Alfred Hitchcock
From the novel by Patricia Highsmith
Adaptation: Whitfield Cook
Screenplay: Raymond Chandler and Czenzi Ormonde (Ben Hecht, uncredited;
      Czenzi Ormonde, once Hecht's assistant, wrote the final script with
      help from Hecht)
Produced by Alfred Hitchcock
French title: *L'inconnu du Nord-Express*

The Secret of Convict Lake   20th Century–Fox
Director: Michael Gordon
Story: Anna Hunger and Jack Pollexfen
Adaptation: Victor Trivas
Screenplay: Oscar Saul (Ben Hecht, uncredited)

September Affair   Paramount
Director: William Dieterle
Story: Fritz Rotter and Robert Thoeren (Ben Hecht, uncredited)

Screenplay: Robert Thoeren (Andrew Solt, uncredited)
Produced by Hal B. Wallis

Hecht's story derived from a sequence in his film *The Scoundrel*: Anthony Mallare—on his way to a tryst with a lady pianist—is killed in an air crash. In *September Affair*, the male lead and a lady pianist enjoy a brief affair during the several days they are presumed dead in a plane crash.

1952

Actors and Sin   Sid Kuller Productions
Director: Ben Hecht
From two stories, "Actor's Blood" and "Concerning a Woman of Sin," by Ben Hecht
Screenplay: Ben Hecht
Produced by Ben Hecht
Executive producer: Sid Kuller
Photographed by Lee Garmes
Music: George Antheil
Sound: Victor Appel and Mac Dalgleish
Voice-over by Ben Hecht

Cast: *Actor's Blood*

Maurice Tillayou	Edward G. Robinson
Marcia Tillayou	Marsha Hunt
Alfred O'Shea	Dan O'Herlihy
Otto Lachsley	Rudolph Anders
Tommy	Alice Key
Clyde Veering	Rick Roman
Mr. Herbert	Peter Brocco
Mrs. Herbert	Elizabeth Root
George Murry	Joe Mell
Mrs. Murry	Irene Martin
Emile	Herb Bernard
Thomas Hayne	Bob Carson

Cast: *Woman of Sin*

Orlando Higgens	Eddie Albert
Daisy Marcher	Jenny Hecht
J. B. Cobb	Alan Reed
Miss Flannigan	Tracey Roberts
Mr. Blue	Paul Guilfoyle
Mr. Devlin	Doug Evans
Mrs. Egelhofer	Jody Gilbert
Mr. Brown	George Baxter
Producer	George Keymas
Movie Star	Toni Carroll

Ben Hecht Filmography

Movie Hero	John Crawford
Miss Wright	Kathleen Mulqueen
Moriarity	Alan Mendez
Joseph Danello	Sam Rosen

Original title: *Duet*

"A depressing double bill."—Lindsay Anderson

O. Henry's Full House   20th Century–Fox
Directors: Howard Hawks, Henry Hathaway, Henry King, Henry Koster, and
    Jean Negulesco
Screenplay for Howard Hawks episode ("The Ransom of Red Chief"): Nunnally
    Johnson (and Ben Hecht and Charles Lederer, uncredited)
Other screenplays: Richard Breen, Walter Bullock, Ivan Goff, Ben Roberts, and
    Lamar Trotti
Produced by André Hakim
British title: *Full House*
French title: *La Sarabande des pantins*

The Wild Heart   RKO/Selznick
Directors: Michael Powell and Emeric Pressburger
From the novel *Gone to Earth* by Mary Webb
Screenplay: Michael Powell and Emeric Pressburger (Ben Hecht, uncredited)
British title: *Gone to Earth*
Other title: *Gypsy Blood*

Monkey Business   20th Century–Fox
Director: Howard Hawks
Story: Harry Segall
Screenplay: Ben Hecht, Charles Lederer, and I. A. L. Diamond
Produced by Sol Siegel
French title: *Chérie, je me sens rajeunir*

Monkey Business is the story of a scientist who discovers a drug that restores a
person's psychological youth, a plot device similar to the one Hecht had toyed
with in *Her Husband's Affairs*, in which a scientist develops a formula to give
flowers perpetual life.

Angel Face   RKO
Director: Otto Preminger
Story: Chester Erskine
Screenplay: Frank Nugent and Oscar Millard (Ben Hecht, uncredited)
Produced by Otto Preminger
French title: *Un si doux visage*

Hans Christian Andersen   Goldwyn/RKO
Director: Charles Vidor

Story: Myles Connolly
Screenplay: Moss Hart (and Ben Hecht, uncredited; in the spring of 1942 Hecht
        went to Los Angeles to write a treatment of *Hans Christian Andersen*
        for Sam Goldwyn, who delayed the production for ten years, then
        hired Hecht's friend Moss Hart to do the script)
Produced by Sam Goldwyn
Original title: *The Life and Stories of Hans Christian Andersen*

1953

Roman Holiday   Paramount
Director: William Wyler
Story: Ian McLellan Hunter
Screenplay: Ian McLellan Hunter and John Dighton (Ben Hecht, uncredited)
Produced by William Wyler
Academy Award: Best Motion Picture Story (Ian McLellan Hunter)
Academy Award nominations: Best Screenplay, Best Picture, Best Director
French title: *Vacances romaines*

1954

Living It Up   York Pictures/Paramount
Director: Norman Taurog
From *Nothing Sacred*, screenplay by Ben Hecht, and Hecht's book for *Hazel
    Flagg* (the musical version of *Nothing Sacred*)
Screenplay: Jack Rose and Melville Shavelson
French title: *C'est pas une vie, Jerry!*

Indiscretion of an American Wife   Columbia
Director: Vittorio De Sica
From the short story "Stazioni Termini" by Cesare Zavattini
Screenplay: Cesare Zavattini, Luigi Chiarini, Giorgio Prosperi, and Truman
        Capote (Alberto Moravia, Carson McCullers, and Paul Gallico,
        uncredited)
Opening title written by Ben Hecht
Italian title: *Stazioni termini*
Other title: *Terminal Station Indiscretion*

1955

Ulysses   Lux Films/Ponti–De Laurentiis/Paramount
Director: Mario Camerini
Uncredited adaptation of Homer's *Odyssey* by G. W. Pabst
Screenplay: Ben Hecht, Hugh Gray, Irwin Shaw, Franco Brusati, Ennio de
    Concini, Ivo Perilli, and Mario Camerini

Italian title: *Ulisse*
French title: *Ulysse*

The Court-Martial of Billy Mitchell   United States Pictures/Warner Bros.
Director: Otto Preminger
Story and screenplay: Milton Sperling and Emmet Lavery (Ben Hecht, uncredited)
Produced by Milton Sperling
British title: *One Man Mutiny*
Academy Award nomination: Best Story and Screenplay
French title: *Condamné au silence*

The Indian Fighter   Bryna Productions
Director: André de Toth
Story: Ben Kadish
Screenplay: Ben Hecht and Frank Davis
French title: *Rivière de nos amours*

The Man with the Golden Arm   Carlyle Productions/United Artists
Director: Otto Preminger
From the novel by Nelson Algren
Screenplay: Walter Newman and Lewis Meltzer (Ben Hecht, uncredited)

Guys and Dolls   Goldwyn/MGM
Director: Joseph Mankiewicz
Screenplay: Joseph Mankiewicz (Ben Hecht, uncredited)
From the book of the musical by Abe Burrows and Jo Swerling
Suggested by two short stories of Damon Runyon

1956

Miracle in the Rain   Warner Bros.
Director: Rudolph Maté
From the novella by Ben Hecht
Screenplay: Ben Hecht

Trapeze   Joanna Productions/Susan Productions/United Artists/Hecht-Lancaster
Director: Carol Reed
From the novel *The Killing Frost* by Max Catto
Adaptation: Liam O'Brien
Screenplay: James Webb (Ben Hecht and Wolf Mankowitz, uncredited)
Produced by James Hill
French title: *Trapèze*

The Iron Petticoat   Hope Records/Benhar Productions/Remus Films/Harry Saltzman

Director: Ralph Thomas
Story and screenplay: Ben Hecht
Produced by Betty E. Box
British title: *Not for Money*

1957

The Hunchback of Notre Dame   Paris Films/Panitalia/Allied Artists
Director: Jean Delannoy
From the novel by Victor Hugo
Screenplay: Jacques Prévert and Jean Aurenche (Ben Hecht, uncredited)
Produced by Robert and Raymond Hakim
French title: *Notre-Dame de Paris*

A Farewell to Arms   20th Century–Fox
Director: Charles Vidor
From the novel by Ernest Hemingway and the play, based on the novel, by
    Laurence Stallings
Screenplay: Ben Hecht
Produced by David O. Selznick

Legend of the Lost   Batjac/Dear Films (Robert Haggiag)
Director: Henry Hathaway
Story and screenplay: Ben Hecht and Robert Presnell, Jr.
Produced by Henry Hathaway
Original title: *Legend of Timbuctoo*
French title: *La Cité disparue*

Henry Hathaway gave Robert Presnell's script to Charlie Feldman (Hathaway's as
well as Hecht's agent), who liked it but felt it had to be rewritten. Hecht
completely redid the Presnell scenario, in particular the dialogue, over three
weeks at Nyack.

1958

The Fiend Who Walked the West   20th Century–Fox
Director: Gordon Douglas
Remake of *Kiss of Death* (1947) as a Western
Screenplay: Harry Brown and Philip Yordan
Produced by Herbert Bayard Swope, Jr.

The Gun Runners   Seven Arts/United Artists
Director: Don Siegel
From the novel *To Have and Have Not* by Ernest Hemingway
Screenplay: Daniel Mainwaring and Paul Monash (Ben Hecht, uncredited)
Alternative titles: *Rub My Back* and *One Trip Across*

According to Frank M. Laurence, in *Hemingway and the Movies*, Siegel hired Mainwaring "to write the screenplay after Ben Hecht and Paul Monash had drafted unacceptable versions."

Queen of Outer Space   Allied Artists
Director: Edward Bernds
Story: Ben Hecht
Screenplay: Charles Beaumont
Original title: *Queen of the Universe*

Walter Wanger, after the debacle of *Cleopatra*, asked Hecht if he could use his name to sell a story to a studio, to which Hecht generously agreed, digging out an unproduced script he had written in 1951. The *Variety* reviewer remarked that the women in the picture "looked like they'd be more at home on a Minsky runway than the Cape Canaveral launchpad."

1959

John Paul Jones   John P. Jones Productions/Warner Bros./Samuel Bronston
Director: John Farrow
Story and screenplay: John Farrow and Jesse Lasky, Jr. (Ben Hecht, uncredited)
French title: *Le Maître des mers*

1960

North to Alaska   20th Century–Fox
Director: Henry Hathaway
From the play *Birthday Gift* by Ladislas Fodor
Screenplay: John Lee Mahin, Claude Binyon, and Martin Rackin (Ben Hecht, uncredited)
Produced by Henry Hathaway
French title: *Le grand Sam*

Hathaway says that almost nothing of Hecht's was used in the final script.

1962

Walk on the Wild Side   Famous Artists/Columbia
Director: Edward Dmytryk
From the novel by Nelson Algren
Screenplay: John Fante and Edmund Morris (Ben Hecht, uncredited)
Produced by Charles Feldman (Famous Artists Agency)

"Charlie Feldman hired Ben Hecht to polish the script, and for two weeks I 'lived in' at his home in Nyack, New York, while he conscientiously and meticulously reworked the dialogue from page one to the final fadeout. Ben was perhaps the most 'organized' writer I have ever worked with . . . though Feldman criticized Hecht's work as not sexy enough. . . . As might be expected, most of the leads were Feldman clients. This helped establish a new guide rule in Hollywood—one could either be a producer or an agent, not both."—Edward Dmytryk, *It's a Hell of a Life But Not a Bad Living: A Hollywood Memoir*

Billy Rose's Jumbo   Euterpe/MGM
Director: Charles Walters
Second unit director: Busby Berkeley
From the musical play *Jumbo* by Ben Hecht and Charles MacArthur (music and
    lyrics by Richard Rodgers and Lorenz Hart)
Screenplay: Sidney Sheldon
Produced by Joe Pasternak
Other title: *Jumbo*

Mutiny on the Bounty   Arcola/MGM
Director: Lewis Milestone (Carol Reed, uncredited)
From the trilogy by Charles Nordhoff and James Hall
Screenplay: Charles Lederer (Ben Hecht, uncredited)
French title: *Les Révoltés du Bounty*

When Marlon Brando and producer Aaron Rosenberg agreed that the ending they had filmed was "no good," they called in Hecht at the suggestion of their screenwriter Charlie Lederer, who had also suggested that Lewis Milestone be brought in to direct when Carol Reed quit. Hecht rewrote Lederer's Pitcairn Island sequence—eleven drafts had already been done—which Milestone then refused to shoot because of violent disagreements with Brando over how the picture should be acted and directed. Milestone shut himself up in his dressing room for two weeks while Brando directed Hecht's ending.

Sergeants 3   Essex-Claude/United Artists
Director: John Sturges
Uncredited remake of *Gunga Din* (1939), adapted by Ben Hecht and Charles
    MacArthur
Story and screenplay: W. R. Burnett
Produced by Frank Sinatra

Cleopatra   20th Century–Fox
Director: Joseph L. Mankiewicz
Screenplay: Joseph L. Mankiewicz, Ranald MacDougall, and Sidney Buchman
    (Ben Hecht, uncredited)
Produced by Walter Wanger
Academy Award nomination: Best Picture

1964

The 7 Faces of Dr. Lao   Galaxy Productions/Scarus/MGM
Director: George Pal

From the novel *The Circus of Dr. Lao* by Charles Finney
Screenplay: Charles Beaumont (Ben Hecht and Charles Lederer, uncredited)

Circus World   Samuel Bronston/Midway Productions/Paramount
Director: Henry Hathaway
Original story: Nicholas Ray and Philip Yordan
Screenplay: Ben Hecht, Julian Halevy, and James Edward Grant
British title: *The Magnificent Showman*

Shortly after the publication of *Gaily, Gaily*, Henry Hathaway asked Hecht to fly to Spain to work on the picture but Hecht was too involved in the promotion for *Gaily, Gaily*. Instead, Hathaway returned to the United States, to Nyack, where he and Hecht wrote most of the script from an original idea of Nick Ray's. Once finished with the promotion for his book, Hecht flew to Spain to complete the scenario.

Seventh Dawn   United Artists
Director: Lewis Gilbert
From the novel *The Durian Tree* by Michael Koen
Screenplay: Karl Tunberg (Ben Hecht, uncredited, for restructuring the ending)

1967

Casino Royale   Famous Artists/Columbia
Directors: John Huston, Ken Hughes, Val Guest, Robert Parrish, Joe McGrath
From the novel by Ian Fleming
Screenplay: Wolf Mankowitz, John Law, and Michael Sayers (Ben Hecht,
          uncredited)
Produced by Charles Feldman

Not long before his death in 1964, Hecht wrote a 130-page version of the script at the request of Charlie Feldman; apparently none of his material was used by the time the picture was finally made.

1968

The Brotherhood   Paramount
Director: Martin Ritt
Screenplay: Lewis John Carlino (Ben Hecht, uncredited)

Hecht worked on an early draft of the script, *Brotherhood of Evil*, for Paramount in 1959, collaborating in Nyack for several days with Robert Parrish, who was to direct. According to Parrish, the picture was called off when its star, James Mason, became ill.

1969

Gaily, Gaily   Mirisch/Cartier/United Artists
Director: Norman Jewison
From Hecht's alleged memoir
Screenplay: Abram S. Ginnes
Associate Producer: Hal Ashby
British title: *Chicago, Chicago*

"Jewison never understood the Chicago mystique, that rambunctious, fuckin' crazy, melodramatic, comedic, really ballsy kind of time that was. He never understood until we got to Chicago to meet with Mayor [Richard J.] Daley. Jewison hadn't really finally committed himself on the budget to the picture. He raised a question as to whether it would be possible to shoot in Chicago because Daley was notoriously difficult to deal with in terms of getting locations. Jewison kept saying to me, 'Chicago couldn't really have been like that, you've exaggerated.' So with a great deal of effort he arranged for a meeting with Daley. He was going to fly in from the Coast with his art director and his production manager, and I was to fly in from New York, and we were all to meet with Daley on a particular day. Our appointment with Daley was for ten o'clock in the morning, so we arrived at city hall at about two minutes to ten and went up to Daley's office. There were two marvelous Chicago cops standing with their jackets off, big sweat patches under their arms, and their holsters out at the receptionist's desk. And Jewison walked in with his entourage and said, 'We have an appointment with Mayor Daley.' One of the cops says, 'He ain't here.' Jewison says, 'This was arranged, we flew in from the Coast, the writer flew in from New York.' The cop says, 'He ain't here, so what d'ya want us to do?' Jewison was terribly upset and practically ready to drop the project at that point. I asked the cops, 'Where is he?' The two cops said, 'He's in Florida, bonefishin'.' That rang a note with me but it didn't mean anything to Jewison, so I asked the cops, 'Is the mayor's assistant here?' So after a great deal of hestitation they brought up Daley's assistant, who was the typical ex–newspaper man with a tic. He said, 'Well, the mayor's sorry but he had to leave town.' We said, 'The cops said he was bonefishing in Florida, why the hell didn't you notify us!' We made certain kinds of threatening noises, we'll give a statement to the press . . . Anyway, he said, 'Go back to your hotel room, we'll see what we can do.' We went back to the hotel, sat there waiting, Jewison was ready to take a plane. I kept saying to him, 'Norman, I have a funny feeling you're about to learn about Chicago à la Ben Hecht because this smells like typical Chicago stuff.' He said, "I don't know what you're talking about, that's too melodramatic.' At that point, the bellhop is slipping the afternoon papers under the door. The headline says, SCANDAL IN COOK COUNTY JAIL—MAYOR FLEES CITY. Some citizens' report came out the day before and the mayor just took off. The same fuckin' thing that had been happening in Chicago for the last fifty years. Jewison just sat there. He was staggered. He said, 'You arranged it, you son of a bitch, you're trying to teach me about Chicago!' "—Abram S. Ginnes

"*Gaily, Gaily* should be wonderful. . . . A good subject, a charming plot, and not too bad a script have been lost along the way in this overproduced period re-creation that is only moderately entertaining. The director, Norman Jewison, tries hard, but he just doesn't have the feeling for Hecht's Chicago. . . . Ben Hecht—a fast, unpretentious realist—was the greatest American screenwriter. Jewison so consistently puts the camera in the ornately wrong place that the whole picture begins to be decorative and 'artistic'—just what Hecht hated most in movies. When Jewison opens a scene through jewelled droplets on a window, one can almost hear Hecht roaring obscenities."—Pauline Kael, *The New Yorker*

1974

The Front Page   Universal
Director: Billy Wilder
From the play by Ben Hecht and Charles MacArthur
Screenplay: I. A. L. Diamond and Billy Wilder
French title: *Spéciale première*
See: *The Front Page* (1931), *There Goes My Girl* (1937), *His Girl Friday* (1940), and *Switching Channels* (1988).

1983

Scarface   Universal
Director: Brian De Palma
Uncredited remake of *Scarface* (1930; released 1932) story and screenplay by Ben Hecht
Screenplay: Oliver Stone

Previous to *Scarface* De Palma had acquired a reputation for stealing other directors' work, notably that of Alfred Hitchcock, but with *Scarface* his theft reached even greater proportions. His film credits neither Hecht, Hawks, nor Armitage Trail as sources. (The novelization of the film credits no one but Oliver Stone!) De Palma's only recognition of Hecht and Hawks is a one-line dedication to them that flashes onscreen after the picture is over. At a private, industry screening in New York City, the audience—aware of the Hecht/Hawks original—booed the film when the dedication appeared.

"De Palma's voluminously vulgar *Scarface* carries a tag dedicating itself, in the most specious gesture in film history, to Ben Hecht and Howard Hawks."—Karen Jaehne, *Cineaste*, Nov. 3, 1984

1986

Je Hais les Acteurs (I Hate Actors!)   Gaumont/Septembre Films/Films A2
Director: Gerard Krawczyk
From Hecht's novel *I Hate Actors!*
Screenplay: Gerard Krawczyk

"Gerard Krawczyk . . . flunks the test of a first theatrical feature film in this awkward adaptation. Even Hecht admirers are cool about this rather dour satire of Hollywood. . . . Krawczyk remains faithful to the book, but his 1940s Hollywood is a meek French Riviera stand-in peopled by an all-Gallic troupe who neither correspond to any models or legends nor pass auditions of dramatic plausibility."—*Variety*, Oct. 29, 1986

1988

Switching Channels   Tri-Star
Director: Ted Kotcheff
From the play *The Front Page* by Ben Hecht and Charles MacArthur
Screenplay: Jonathan Reynolds
Produced by Martin Ransohoff

"Sixty years ago the talents of Ben Hecht and Charles MacArthur combined to create something special. It was called *The Front Page*. It was an occasion that introduced new possibilities for romantic comedy and served as an inspiration for a generation of future talent. These men gave a reason to rejoice to everyone who shared that special affection for farce. Everyone involved in the production of *Switching Channels* wishes to thank Messrs. Hecht and MacArthur for making laughter an event."—Full-page ad for *Switching Channels* in *The New York Times*, November 8, 1987.
See: *The Front Page* (1931), *There Goes My Girl* (1937), *His Girl Friday* (1940), and *The Front Page* (1974).

TELEVISION

1946

The Bum   (ABC) Broadcast on Christmas Eve. Hecht wrote the teleplay and played the protagonist.

1948

Dr. Pygmalion   Hecht and Lee Garmes made a half-hour pilot for a series about a plastic surgeon, to star Karen Steele (Huntington Hartford's wife—Hartford financed the pilot), but were unable to interest a sponsor. In 1958, Hecht tried to revive the project but met with no success.

1949

The Front Page   (CBS) Series that ran from September 29th, 1949, to January 26th, 1950, based on Hecht's and MacArthur's play *The Front Page*. Walter Burns was portrayed by John Daly and Hildy Johnson by Mark Roberts. The newspaper they worked for was called the *Center City Examiner*. "We have come to know that newspapermen are literate, well-mannered, and business-like members of our society. Hildy and his boss do not ring true today."—*TV Guide* (1949)

1950

The Play's the Thing   Based on Hecht's short story "The Pink Hussar."

Twentieth Century   (*Ford Theatre*, CBS) Hecht and MacArthur's play, starring Fredric March and Lilli Palmer.

1953

Tales of the City   (*Willys Theatre*, CBS) Directed by Robert Stevens. Teleplays by Ben Hecht. Narrated by Hecht. Seven episodes broadcast live every other week from June 25th to September 17th.

The World's Our Oyster   (*Ford Theatre*, CBS) Script by Ben Hecht, Everett Rhodes, and Donald Henderson Clarke. Aired November 3rd.

1954

The Mask   (ABC) Story and teleplay by Ben Hecht. Broadcast live on February 7th.

Light's Diamond Jubilee   (CBS) Directed by King Vidor, William Wellman, and Norman Taurog. Teleplay by Ben Hecht, Robert Benchley, Arthur Gordon, Irwin Shaw, Max Shulman, John Steinbeck, Mark Twain, and G. K. Chesterton. Two-hour special produced by David O. Selznick to commemorate the seventy-fifth anniversary of Edison's discovery of the incandescent light. Broadcast October 24th, 9 P.M. to 11 P.M. The show had the largest audience in the history of television, up until that time.

1956

Up, Down, and Across   (CBS) A television version of Hecht's play about Maxwell Bodenheim, *Winkelberg*, starring Marlene Dietrich and Robert Newton.

Twentieth Century   (*Ford Star Jubilee*, CBS) Hecht's and MacArthur's play, starring Orson Welles, Betty Grable, and Keenan Wynn. In color, ninety minutes.

Death of a Nobody   Directed by Hal Roach, December 31st.

1958

The Quality of Mercy   (CBS) Directed by Hal Roach. Originally a film script adapted for Kirk Douglas from Robert Carson's novel; Douglas rejected Hecht's script in favor of *The Indian Fighter.*

1958–1959

The Ben Hecht Show   Late-night talk show broadcast on a local New York station (WABC), September 15th through February.

1959

The Unexpected: The Voice of Tut Ankh-Amen.

The Third Commandment   (Channel 4, New York City) Teleplay by Ben Hecht. One-hour drama in the *Kaleidoscope* series, hosted by Charles Van Doren, starring Arthur Kennedy, Anne Francis, Fay Spain, and Regis Toomey. Aired February 8th.

Hello, Charlie   (*Goodyear Theater*, NBC) Directed by Sidney Lanfield. A thirty-minute drama based on an incident from *Charlie: The Improbable Life and Times of Charles MacArthur*, with Tony Randall, John Dehner, Joe E. Ross, and Walter Burke. Aired September 28th.

1961

Some Troubles with the Cave Man   (CBS)

Upside Down Hero   (CBS)

Valentine for a Gunman   (CBS)

1970

The Front Page   Produced by the Plumstead Playhouse Company, starring Robert Ryan as Walter Burns and George Grizzard as Hildy Johnson; introduction by Helen Hayes.

UNREALIZED PROJECTS (DATED)

Queer People   (1931)
Farike the Guest Artist   (1934) Script by Hecht and Gene Fowler, written for W. C. Fields and Marie Dressler, who died before the picture could be made. Later adapted for Wallace Beery, 1946. Aka *Frankie as Guest.*

Sarah Bernhardt   (1940) A Selznick production aimed for Ingrid Bergman but when she refused to play it, the project was cancelled. In 1963, Selznick tried to interest Samuel Bronston in the project, to no avail.

The Phantom Killer   (1942) Screenplay.

Joan of Arc   (mid-1940s) Uncompleted script for David Selznick; Selznick wanted Ingrid Bergman to star, but when she refused, he cancelled the project.

The Captain Fled   (1945) Script with Charles Lederer.

Lord Byron   (1946) Hecht was to write and direct for J. Arthur Rank. Laurence Olivier was to star.

Angel's Flight   (dated March 8th, 1948) Script for producer Sam Zimbalist, MGM.

Trilby   (1948) Script by Hecht and MacArthur for Jesse Lasky.

Europa and the Bull   (scripts dated January 19th and February 7th, 1950) Script by Hecht, Ladislas Fodor, and Jerry Davis. A satirical drama for Dore Schary; Louis B. Mayer thought the story too intellectual, so cancelled production.

Star Sapphire (1950) Script by Hecht and Charles Lederer for Howard Hughes. Aka *Blue Sapphire*.

The Big Lie   (1951) Script for Otto Preminger.

Moll   (script dated November 4th, 1952) Story by Hecht and Gene Fowler for Howard Hawks.

Orpheus in the Underworld   (1953) Musical for Billy Rose.

Evening Lady   (dated March 2nd, 1954) Script by Hecht and Charles Lederer.

War and Peace   (1954) Hecht announced he was doing a script.

The Old Army Game   (September 29th, 1955) 67-page treatment by Hecht and Charles Lederer for producer Edwin Knopf. Original title: *Operation Home*.

The Life and Death of Al Capone   (1955) Script by Hecht, Gene Fowler, and Westbrook Pegler.

Aphrodite   (1958) From the novel by Pierre Louÿs, to be produced by Robert Haggiag's Dear Films (which had coproduced *Legend of the Lost*). Hecht was to adapt the novel and direct the picture in Italy in an English and an Italian version.

Granada   (1959) Mario Lanza script, incomplete. (Lanza died before the picture could be made.)

My Testament   (1959) Typescript.

The Actress   (1960) Teleplay, 25 pp.

Winkelberg   (1960) Hecht and director Robert Parrish formed Rex Productions to produce a film of Hecht's play *Winkelberg* about Maxwell Bodenheim. It was to be shot in actual Greenwich Village locations, but they were unable to raise the money. Shooting was announced to begin August 23rd, 1960. Edward Schreiber—who had starred Jenny Hecht in a 20-minute color short called *Katie's Lot*—then bought the film rights but also failed to raise the money.

Scarlett O'Hara.   (early 1960s) Musical version of *Gone With the Wind*. Hecht was to write the lyrics for a stage production.

The Lost Soul   (early 1960s) Hecht had formed a company called 38 Inc. to produce his script.

A Midsummer Night's Dream   (early 1960s) Hecht worked with Don Costa and Burgess Meredith on a musical version of the Shakespeare play.

The Promoters   (early 1960s) Hecht was hired to write a script for producer William Coates.

Mary Todd Lincoln   (early 1960s) Film script, complete.

Bring Me Joe Feeney   (1964) Film script, to star Sammy Davis, Jr.

The Preying Mantis   (1964) A remake of Fritz Lang's *M*, for director Henry Hathaway, which Hecht was adapting when he died in 1964. Hathaway announced the project in 1974, to star Telly Savalas as a pimp, to be shot in the red-light district of Amsterdam, script by Arnold and Lois Peyser.

UNREALIZED PROJECTS (UNDATED)

Ballerina   For Gregory Ratoff. 134 pp.

Billion Dollor Baby   Outline. (*Million Dollar Legs?*)

The Breaking Point

Cyrano de Bergerac   To be directed first by Orson Welles in 1947, then later by Harry D'Arrast, for Alexander Korda. Written in 1939–40.

In 1948, when Korda was once again contemplating a production, he claimed he owned the Hecht script, but Hecht denied Korda's ownership, maintaining he'd signed no contract nor been paid for his work.

The Eternal Husband   Script by Hecht and Charles Lederer, from a story by Dostoyevsky, for Marcello Mastroianni, to be directed by John Huston.

Evil

Fanny of the Follies   Treatment about the life of Fanny Brice. Bought by Ray Stark.

Fargo

A Gay Life   First draft.

Hello Harriet

Impassioned

Larry

Love Is a Long Goodbye   From Hecht's short story "Swindler's Luck," published in the *Saturday Evening Post*. Rights to the story purchased by Henry Hathaway. Aka *The Sunset Kid*.

Marco's Millions

Mary Magdalene   For David Selznick.

The Mating Call

Packy Hudson   Complete script.

Sidewalks of New York

Skid Row

Squatter's Rights   Script by Ben Hecht and Rose Caylor (Hecht) for MGM.

Star of Scotland   For Henry Hathaway.

Toast of all Paree

Trio   For Henry Hathaway, to be produced by Charlie Feldman.

Unfinished Crime.   Outline.

BEN HECHT

BIBLIOGRAPHY

Dated publications are arranged chronologically at the beginning of each year; undated books and periodicals are arranged alphabetically after the dated material. Newspaper reportage has not been included.

1914

Mother Earth, magazine edited by Emma Goldman, contains several short contributions by BH.

1915

"The Sermon in the Depths," *The Little Review,* vol. 2, no. 3, May.
"Slobberdom, Sneerdom, and Boredom," *The Little Review,* vol. 2, no. 4, June/July.
"Sick Idealism," *The Little Review,* vol. 2. no. 4, June/July.
"The American Family," *The Little Review,* vol. 2, no. 5, August.
"Moods; Sorrow, Humoresque, Rain; An Invitation to Cheat Posterity; My Island," *The Little Review,* vol. 2, no. 6, September.
"Songs and Sketches: Night; Sleep Song; Autumn Song; Death Song; The Synagogue; In the Sun; On the Beach," *The Little Review,* vol. 2, no. 7, October.
"Dregs; Life; Depths; Gratitude," *The Little Review,* vol. 2, no. 8, November.

1916

"Three Flesh Tints: The Incense Burner; The Goldfish in a Bowl; A Nude," *The Little Review,* vol. 3, no. 3, May.
"The Poet Sings to the World," *The Little Review,* vol. 3, no. 5, August.
The Best Short Stories of 1915, ed. by Edward O'Brien; Small, Maynard and Co., Boston, and Thomas Allen, Toronto. Includes "Life" by BH.

1917

"Stanislaus Szukalski, Chicago's Seismic Sculptor," *Vanity Fair*, June; uncredited.
"The Unlovely Sin," *Smart Set*, July.
"The Monster," *Smart Set*, August.
"Mrs. Margaret Calhoun: A One-Act Play," by Maxwell Bodenheim and BH, *Smart Set*, August.
"The Devil Slayer," *Smart Set*, September.
"A Sort of a Story," *All-Story*, September 22nd.
"Caricature," *Smart Set*, October.
"The Doting Burglar," *All-Story*, October 6th.
"The Movie Maniac," *Smart Set*, December.

1918

"The Policewoman's Daughter," *Smart Set*, January.
"Jazz," *Smart Set*, February.
"Snow Monotones," *Poetry: A Magazine of Verse*, February.
"A Humoresque in Ham," *Smart Set*, April.
"Fragments," *The Little Review*, vol. 4, no. 12, April.
"Nocturne," *The Little Review*, vol. 5, no. 1, May.
"The Man with One Wife," *Smart Set*, June.
"Lust," *The Little Review*, vol. 5, no. 2, June.
"The Sinister Sex," *Smart Set*, July.
"Broken Necks," *The Little Review*, vol. 5, no. 3, July.
"How's Chicago Now?" *Forum*, vol. 60, August.
"Infatuation," *Smart Set*, September.
"Decay," *The Little Review*, vol. 5, no. 5, September.
"Happiness," *Smart Set*, October.
"Shanghaied," *Smart Set*, October.
"Nothing but Good of the Dead," *Smart Set*, November.
"Pounding Ezra (a conversation . . .)," *The Little Review*, vol. 5, no. 7, November.
"The Yellow Goat," *The Little Review*, vol. 5, no. 8, December.
Minna and Myself, poems by Maxwell Bodenheim and a play, *The Master Poisoner*, by Bodenheim and BH, intro. by Louis Untermeyer; Pagan Publishing Co., New York.

1919

"The Successor to Mr. Hennerby," *Smart Set*, January.
"The Eternal Fugitive," *Smart Set*, February.
"Dog Eat Dog," *The Little Review*, vol. 5, no. 12, April.
"Tempo De Pantaloon," *Smart Set*, May.
"Rouge," *The Little Review*, vol. 6, no. 5, September.

1920

"Black Umbrellas," *The Little Review*, vol. 7, no. 2, July/August.
The Hero of Santa Maria, a play by Kenneth Sawyer Goodman and BH; Stage Guild Plays, No. 1, Chicago.
The Hero of Santa Maria, F. Shay, New York.
The Wonder Hat, a play by Kenneth Sawyer Goodman and BH; Stage Guild Plays, No. 3, Chicago.

1921

"Blue Sunday," a one-act play, *The Double Dealer*, vol. 1, no. 5, May.
Erik Dorn; G. P. Putnam's Sons, New York and London, September. The first printing of the first edition appeared in three states: (1) yellow lettering on purple cloth (front boards) (2) maroon on yellow (3) orange on green. Fourteen thousand copies sold in first four months.
"At the Feet of the Goddess," *Smart Set*, November.
Youth, magazine published by Sam Putnam; includes essays by BH.
Puberty, a parody of *Youth*, ed. by BH, November.

1922

"Winkelburg," *Smart Set*, March.
"The Bomb Thrower," *The Little Review*, vol. 8, no. 3, Autumn.
"Adventures of the Broken Mirror," *Harper's Bazaar*, September.
Fantazius Mallare: A Mysterious Oath, drawings by Wallace Smith; Covici-McGee, Chicago, September. "Limited edition for private circulation only." 2,025 numbered copies.
Gargoyles; Boni & Liveright, New York, September 15th.
"The Last Sorrow," play by BH and Maxwell Bodenheim; included in *The Wave*, ed. by Vincent Starrett.
Nonsenseorship; G. P. Putnam's Sons, New York and London. Includes "Literature and the Bastinado" by BH.
1001 Afternoons in Chicago, pref. by Henry Justin Smith, illus. by Herman Rosse; Covici-McGee, Chicago.
20 Contemporary One-Act Plays, ed. by Frank Shay; D. Appleton and Co., New York. Includes "The Hero of Santa Maria" by Kenneth Sawyer Goodman and BH.

1923

Chicago Literary Times, biweekly newspaper/magazine ed. by BH and Maxwell Bodenheim from March 1st, 1923, to June 1st, 1924.
The Florentine Dagger: A Novel For Amateur Detectives, drawings by Wallace Smith; Boni & Liveright, New York, July.

The Florentine Dagger, in *The Cleveland World*.
"The Code of Death," *Coloroto*, November.
The Best Short Stories of 1922: America, ed. by Edward O'Brien; Small, Maynard
    and Co., Boston, and Jonathan Cape, London. Includes "Winkelburg" by
    BH (originally published in *Smart Set*).
Gargoyles; Boni & Liveright, New York, reprint.
1001 Afternoons in Chicago; Grant Richards, London, first British edition.
Stanislaus Szukalski, intro. by BH; Covici-McGee, Chicago.
A Treasury of Plays for Men, ed. by Frank Shay; Little, Brown, Boston. Includes
    "The Hand of Siva" by Kenneth Sawyer Goodman and BH.
Under False Pretenses; Covici-McGee, Chicago.

1924

"The Sentimentalist," *The American Mercury*, October. Not a new story but a
    slightly expanded version of "The Nostalgia of Mishkin," a part of the
    abandoned novel *Moishe* that had been published in the *Chicago Literary
    Times* in June of 1923 and in Hecht's "1001 Afternoons" column in the
    Chicago Daily News in 1922.
Broken Necks, and Other Stories, ed. by E. Haldeman-Julius; Little Blue Book,
    No. 699, Girard, Kansas.
Cutie, A Warm Mamma, by BH and Maxwell Bodenheim; Hechtshaw Press,
    Chicago; limited to 200 copies.
The Dil Pickler, ed. by Jack Jones, 1924–25; reprints of articles by BH from
    Chicago Literary Times.
Erik Dorn, introd. by Burton Rascoe; The Modern Library, no. 29, Boni &
    Liveright, New York, reprint.
The Florentine Dagger; William Heinemann, London, first British edition.
Humpty Dumpty; Boni & Liveright, New York, 1st printing, October; 2nd
    printing, November; 3rd printing, December.
The Kingdom of Evil, illus. by Anthony Angarola; Pascal Covici, Chicago. "This
    edition is limited to 2,000 numbered copies of which 1,900 are offered for
    sale by subscription only."
Tales of Chicago Streets, ed. by E. Haldeman-Julius; Little Blue Book, No. 698,
    Girard, Kansas.

1925

"The Unfaithful Widow," *Redbook*, December.
The Low Down: A Magazine for Hypocrites, ed. by BH and Herman Mankiewicz;
    New York; 2 issues.
Cutie, A Warm Mamma; Hechtshaw Press, Chicago, reprint.
Humpty Dumpty; Boni & Liveright, New York, reprint.
The Wonder Hat and Other One-Act Plays, by Kenneth Sawyer Goodman and
    BH, pref. by Thomas Wood Stevens; D. Appleton and Co., New York.

1926

"The Shadow," *Liberty*, January 30th.

"9:55," *Redbook*, March.

"The Magic Pen," *Redbook*, May.

Count Bruga; Boni & Liveright, New York, 1st and 2nd printings, May; 3rd printing, June.

"Her Name Was Mary," *McClure's*, June.

"The Tardy Phantom," *Shrine*, June.

"The Covetous Male," *McClure's*, August.

Broken Necks; Pascal Covici, Chicago, 1st and 2nd printings, October; 3rd printing, November.

The Key Largo Breeze, a real estate promotional paper, written and edited by BH and J. P. McEvoy.

The Best Short Stories of 1925, ed. by Edward O'Brien; Small, Maynard and Co., Boston. Includes "Lindro the Great" by BH.

Humpty Dumpty; Boni & Liveright, New York, reprint.

1927

"The Lifer," *Redbook*, February.

"Phoney," *Redbook*, April.

"Don Juan's Rainy Day," *College Humor*, May.

"The Gestures Were Perfect," *Redbook*, May.

"The Little Blue Man," *Redbook*, May.

"Zalzala," *Redbook*, May.

All He Ever Loved and *Man Eating Tiger*, Rose Caylor (Hecht) and BH; Pascal Covici, Chicago. Announced but apparently never issued.

1001 Afternoons in Chicago; Pascal Covici, Chicago, reprint.

Broken Necks, Count Bruga, Humpty Dumpty, 1001 Afternoons in Chicago; Serge Dinamoff, USSR.

The Policewoman's Love-Hungry Daughter and Other Stories of Chicago Life, ed. by E. Haldeman-Julius; Little Blue Book, No. 1163, Girard, Kansas.

The Unlovely Sin and Other Stories of Desire's Pawns, ed. by E. Haldeman-Julius; Little Blue Book, No. 1164, Girard, Kansas.

Jazz, and Other Stories of Young Love, ed. by E. Haldeman-Julius; Little Blue Book, No. 1165, Girard, Kansas.

Infatuation and Other Stories of Love's Misfits, ed. by E. Haldeman-Julius; Little Blue Book, No. 1166, Girard, Kansas.

The Sinister Sex and Other Stories of Marriage, ed. by E. Haldeman-Julius; Little Blue Book, No. 1167, Girard, Kansas.

1928

The Front Page, by BH and Charles MacArthur, intro. by Jed Harris; Covici-Friede, New York; 1st printing, August; 2nd printing, September; 3rd and 4th printings, October.

Christmas Eve: A Morality Play, Covici-Friede, New York. Limited edition of 111
   signed and numbered copies.
Gargoyles, Boni & Liveright, New York, reprint.
Humpty Dumpty, Boni & Liveright, New York, reprint.

1929

"The Rights That Failed," *The Morning Telegraph*, January 19th.
"Farewell My Bluebell," *The Little Review*, vol. 12, no. 2, May (final issue).
"Ben Hecht Tells All," *Theatre*, June.
The Front Page; Grant Richards and Humphrey Toulmin, London.
The Front Page; Cayme Press, London.
The Best Plays of 1928–29; Small, Maynard, Boston. Includes "The Front Page"
   in story form, with extracts from the dialogue.

1930

"Baby Milly and the Pharaoh," *Saturday Evening Post*, July 12th.
"The Champion from Far Away," *Saturday Evening Post*, August 9th.
The Florentine Dagger; G. G. Harrap and Co., London, cheap edition reprint.

1931

A Jew in Love; Covici-Friede, New York. 150 signed and numbered copies on
   handmade paper.
A Jew in Love; Covici-Friede, New York, 1st, 2nd, and 3rd printings, January; 4th,
   5th, and 6th printings, February; 7th printing, January 1932.

Distinguishing the first state of the first edition is the 25th line of p. 306, which
reads: "As far as I'm concerned God is a pain in the ass." This was promptly
altered for all future printings and editions to read: "As far as I'm concerned God
gives me a pain."
   In the middle of p. 123, this exchange occurs:
   "I'd like to hear," said Mark. "Maybe I can answer your arguments."
   "You can answer ----," said Boshere.
   Several copies were printed for Hecht's friends to read: "You can answer
shit."

A Jew in Love; Triangle Books, New York.
"Henry Varnum Poor," *Creative Artist*, May.
"In the Midst of Death," *Liberty*.
"The Mystery of the Man with the Accordion," *Liberty*.
The Best American Mystery Stories of the Year, vol. 1; John Day Co., New York.
   Includes "The Ax" by BH.
The Champion from Far Away; Covici-Friede, New York.
Count Bruga; Liveright Fiction Reprints, New York.

The Devil's Dilemma; Covici-Friede, New York. One copy, spine and title page printed with title, otherwise blank.
1001 Afternoons in Chicago; Covici-Friede, New York, reprint.
The Wonder Hat, Magazine World; Columbus, Ohio, vol. 7, no. 2, reprint.

1932

"The Boy Pirate," *Liberty*, January.
"Mystery of the Fabulous Laundryman," *Liberty* (United States), *Grand* (Great Britain), January.
"Actor's Blood," *Saturday Evening Post*, February 20th.
"Ballad of the Talkies," *Contact*, vol. 1, no. 1, February.
"Mr. Fowler on the Spot," *The New York Times*, November 27th.
A Jew in Love; Grosset and Dunlap Book Club Edition, New York, reprint.

1933

Twentieth Century, by BH and Charles MacArthur; Covici-Friede, New York.
"Caballero of the Law," *Saturday Evening Post*, May 6th. The source for the Hecht and MacArthur film *Crime Without Passion*.
The Front Page; Covici-Friede, New York, reprint.
The Great Magoo, by BH and Gene Fowler, illus. by Herman Rosse; Covici-Friede, New York.
The Great Magoo; Van Rees Press, New York, reprint.

1934

"Hollywood's Obstacle Race: How to Win," *MS.: A Magazine for Writers*, April.
"Dog Eat Dog," *Scope*, a magazine of proletarian literature, ed. by Harold Lambert and Nathan Levine; Bayonne, New Jersey, September/October.
The Florentine Dagger; William Heinemann, London; reprint.
A Jew in Love; Fortune Press, London, first British edition.
1001 Afternoons in Chicago; Covici-Friede, New York, reprint.
The Smart Set Anthology, ed. by Burton Rascoe and G. Conklin; Reynal and Hitchcock, New York. Includes "A Humoresque in Ham" by BH.

1935

"Vagabondia," *Scholastic*, March 30th.

1936

Actor's Blood; Covici-Friede, New York.
Hecht's Prayer to His Bosses, illus. by Billy Brice; Stanley Rose's Bookshop, Los Angeles.

1937

Representative One-Act Plays, ed. by Margaret Mayorga; Little Brown and Co., Boston. Includes "The Wonder Hat" by Kenneth Sawyer Goodman and BH, October.
Stories for Men, ed. by Charles Grayson; Little, Brown and Co., Boston. Includes "Mystery of the Fabulous Laundryman" by BH.
To Quito and Back; Covici-Friede, New York.

1938

The Hero of Santa Maria, by Kenneth Sawyer Goodman and BH; Stage Guild, Chicago, reprint.
A Jew in Love; Blue Ribbon Books, New York, reprint.
Theme and Variation in the Short Story, ed. by H. Blaine and W. Dumble; Cordon Co., New York. Includes "The Pig" by BH.

1939

A Book of Miracles; Viking Press, New York, June.
A Jew in Love; Triangle Books, New York, 8th printing.
To Helen Hayes in "Ladies and Gentlemen." Limited edition of poem to Helen Hayes distributed on opening night of the Hecht and MacArthur play.

1940

The Bedside Esquire, ed. by Arnold Gingrich; Tudor, New York. Includes "Snowfall in Childhood" by BH.
A Book of Miracles; Nicholson and Watson, London, first British edition.
The Front Page; Covici, New York, reprint.
Ultime di Cronaca, intro. by Mario Beltramo, trans. by Enrico Cogliottini; Editioni del Secolo, Rome, first Italian edition of *The Front Page*.

1941

"What Is America?" by BH and Charles MacArthur; *The New York Times Magazine*, October 12th.
"Uncle Sam Stands Up," *PM*, December 8th.
Best One-Act Plays of 1941, ed. by Margaret Mayorga; Dodd, Mead and Co., New York. Includes "Fun to Be Free" by BH and Charles MacArthur.
A Book of Miracles; Sun Dial Press, Garden City, reprint.
Count Bruga; Illustrated Editions Co., London, cheap edition reprint.
Fun to Be Free: A Patriotic Pageant, by BH and Charles MacArthur, foreword by Wendell Willkie; Dramatists Play Service, New York.

Ladies and Gentlemen, by BH and Charles MacArthur, from a play, *Twelve in a Box*, by Ladislas Bus-Fekete; Samuel French, New York.

1001 Afternoons in New York, illus. by George Grosz; Viking Press, New York.

1001 Afternoons in New York: Selected Stories from the Pages of New York's Newest and Most Provocative Newspaper—PM; PM, New York.

The Bewitched Tailor; Viking Press, New York. Limited edition of 850 copies of one of Hecht's *PM* columns; signed by Hecht, with a drawing by George Grosz.

1942

"Uncle Sam Stands Up," *Scholastic*, January 5.

Lily of the Valley, typescript and promptbook; Windsor Theatre, January 26th.

"Sonnets to the Critics in Rebuttal," *PM*, January 28th.

"Snowstorm Reverie," *Reader's Digest*, January.

"Lament for the Living," *The New York Times*, February.

"Student and the Beggar," *Reader's Digest*, February.

"Crime Without Passion," *Ellery Queen's Mystery Magazine*, Spring.

"Imposter in Heaven," *Redbook*, August.

The Florentine Dagger, A Tower Mystery; World Publishing Co., September, reprint.

"A Champion in Chains," *Esquire*, October.

"Clinical Stage Notes," *American Mercury*.

Famous Fireside Plays, ed. by Charles Newton, New York; includes a radio adaptation of *The Front Page*.

Sixteen Famous American Plays, ed. by Bennett Cerf and Van Cartmell, intro. by Brooks Atkinson; Random House, Modern Library edition. Includes *The Front Page*.

1943

Count Bruga; Avon Books, New York.

"Miracle of the 15 Murderers," *Collier's*, January 16th.

"The Doughboy's Dream," *Collier's*, February 27th. Printed as a booklet and distributed to the U.S. Army.

"A Letter from Ben Hecht," *PM*, February 22nd.

"Remember Us!," *American Mercury*, February.

"Uncle Sam Stands Up," *Big Song Magazine*, February.

"Prayer," excerpt from *We Will Never Die*, PM, March.

"Concerning a Woman of Sin," *Collier's*, March 27th and April 3rd.

"Serenade to a Nickel," *Redbook*, March.

"Miracle in the Rain," *Saturday Evening Post*, April 3rd.

"Ballad of the Doomed" and "Almighty God," *The Answer*, April.

"God Is Good to a Jew," *Collier's*, July 21st.

"Café Sinister," *Collier's*, August 21st.

"Uncle Sam Stands Up," *Hit Parader*, August.

"Ballad of the Doomed Jews of Europe," *B'nai Brith Messenger*, September 24th.
"The Pink Hussar," *Collier's*, September 25th.
Ben Hecht—Selected Great Stories, Avon Modern Short Story Monthly, No. 11, New York. See: *Concerning a Woman of Sin*, 1969.
Box Office, ed. by M. Barrows and G. Eaton; Ziff-Davis, Chicago and New York. Includes "Crime Without Passion" by BH.
Miracle in the Rain, Alfred Knopf, New York.
20 Best Film Plays, ed. by Dudley Nichols and John Gassner; Crown, New York. Includes the scenario of *Wuthering Heights* by BH and Charles MacArthur.
We Will Never Die, The Committee for a Free Jewish Army and Free Palestine, New York.

1944

"The Common Man," *Rob Wagner's Script*, vol. 30, no. 673, February 19th.
"I Hate Actors," *Collier's* serial, March and April.
"The Most Unforgettable Character I've Ever Met," *Reader's Digest*, July.
The Bachelor's Companion, A Smart Set *Collection*, ed. by Burton Rascoe and G. Conklin; Grayson, New York. Includes "A Humoresque in Ham" by BH.
The Best One-Act Plays of 1943, ed. by Margaret Mayorga; Dodd, Mead and Co., New York. Includes "A Tribute to Gallantry" by BH.
Count Bruga, abr., illus. ed., no. 117; Royce Publishers, Chicago, reprint. "Meet the dilliest character ever created for your amusement."
A Guide for the Bedevilled; Charles Scribner's, New York. Serialized in the *New York Post*.
"A Guide for the Bedevilled," excerpts in *The Answer*, May 1st.
I Hate Actors! Crown, New York.
Stories for Men, ed. by Charles Grayson; Doubleday, Doran, Garden City, N.Y. Includes "The Mystery of the Fabulous Laundryman" by BH.
Uncle Sam Stands Up: A Patriotic Cantata, music by Ferde Grofé; Robbins Music Co., New York.

1945

"Rendezvous of Love," *Reader's Digest*, September.
"The Whistling Corpse," *Ellery Queen's Mystery Magazine*, September.
"Lucky Handkerchief," *Good Housekeeping*, November.
America Is West, ed. by J. Flanagan; University of Minnesota Press. Includes "The Auctioneer's Wife" by BH.
"Assignment in Hollywood," *Good Housekeeping*.
The Bedside Tales, intro. by Peter Arno; William Penn Publishing Co., New York. Includes "The Shadow" by BH.
Best Film Plays of 1945, ed. by Dudley Nichols and John Gassner; Crown, New York. Includes the screenplay of *Spellbound* by BH.

The Best One-Act Plays of 1944, ed. by Margaret Mayorga; Dodd, Mead and Co., New York. Includes "Miracle on the Pullman" by BH.

The Collected Stories of Ben Hecht; Crown, New York; Nicholson and Watson, London, first British edition; Grosset and Dunlap, New York, reprint.

Concerning a Woman of Sin and Other Stories, editions for the Armed Services, no. 921, Council on Books in Wartime, New York. (See: *Concerning a Woman of Sin*, 1969.)

Desert Island Decameron, sel. by H. Allen Smith; Doubleday, Doran, Garden City, N.Y. Includes "The Missing Idol" by BH.

A Guide for the Bedevilled; Scribner's, New York, reprint; Doubleday, Doran, Garden City, N.Y., reprint.

Half-a-Hundred, ed. by C. Grayson; Blakiston Co., Philadelphia. Includes "Crime Without Passion" by BH.

North, East, South, West, ed. by C. Lee; Howell, Soskin, New York. Includes "Man Hunt" by BH.

Rogue's Gallery, ed. by Ellery Queen; Little, Brown and Co., Boston. Includes "Miracle of the 15 Murderers" by BH.

Stories from 1001 Afternoons in New York, Avon Modern Short Story Monthly, No. 26, New York.

Two-Fisted Stories for Men. Includes "Crime Without Passion" by BH.

1946

"The Rival Dummy," *Ellery Queen's Mystery Magazine*, June.

"Samuel Hirshfeld, M.D.: Funeral Address Delivered by His Friend Ben Hecht," December 15, 1946, 8 pp., wrappers.

The Art of the Mystery Story; Simon & Schuster, New York. Includes "The Whistling Corpse" by BH.

The Bathroom Reader, intro. by Earl Wilson; William Penn Publishing Corp., New York. Includes "Mystery of the Fabulous Laundryman" by BH.

A Flag Is Born, American League for a Free Palestine, New York.

The Hero of Santa Maria, by Kenneth Sawyer Goodman and BH; Stage Guild, Chicago, reprint.

Hollywood Mystery, Bart House Mystery, No. 25; Bartholomew House, New York; retitled *I Hate Actors!*

Meurtres à Hollywood (Mort aux Acteurs), trans. by Michel Arnaud; Nuits Blanche, No. 6, La Nouvelle Edition, Paris; trans. of *I Hate Actors!*

Miracle in the Rain; Peter Huston, Sydney, Australia, first Australian edition.

33 Sardonics I Can't Forget, ed. by T. Thayer; Philosophical Library, New York. Includes "On a Day Like This" and "Ten-Cent Wedding Rings" by BH.

"Terrified Doctor," *Cosmopolitan*.

To the Queen's Taste, ed. by Ellery Queen; Little, Brown and Co., Boston. Includes "Crime Without Passion" by BH.

A Treasury of Doctors' Stories, ed. by N. Fabricant and H. Werner; Frederick Fell, New York. Includes "Movie Scenario" by BH.

1947

Caravan of Music Stories, ed. by N. Fabricant and H. Werner; Frederick Fell, New York. Includes "A Humoresque in Ham" by BH.

The Cat That Jumped Out of the Story, illus. by Peggy Bacon; John C. Winston Co., Philadelphia and Toronto.

The Collected Stories of Ben Hecht; José Janes, first Spanish edition.

Concerning a Woman of Sin and Other Stories, Avon Modern Short Story Monthly, New York. (See: *Concerning a Woman of Sin*, 1969.)

A Flag Is Born, Answer Book Service, New York.

Man Into Beast, ed. by A. Spectorsky; Doubleday, Doran, Garden City, N.Y. Includes "The Adventures of Professor Emmett" by BH.

Questing Spirit: Religion in the Literature of Our Time, ed. by H. Luccock and F. Brentano; Coward, McCann, New York. Includes "The Little Candle" by BH.

The World's Great Stories, ed. by H. Haydn and John Cournos; Crown, New York. Includes "Snowfall in Childhood" by BH.

1948

"Actor's Blood," *Ellery Queen's Mystery Magazine*, May.

1949

"Double Exposure," *Ellery Queen's Mystery Magazine*, August.

The Queen's Awards, ed. by Ellery Queen; Little, Brown and Co., Boston. Includes "Double Exposure" by BH.

A Treasury of Great Reporting, ed. by Louis Snyder and Richard Morris; Simon & Schuster, New York. Includes "Well, I Got Him, I Got Him Anyway," a story originally published in the *Chicago Daily News*, June 22nd, 1920, about murderer Carl Wanderer, for which Hecht received no byline.

25 Best Plays of Modern American Theater, ed. by John Gassner; Crown, New York. Includes *The Front Page* by BH and Charles MacArthur.

1950

Best Detective Stories of the Year; E. P. Dutton, New York. Includes "Double Exposure" by BH.

The Collected Stories of Ben Hecht; Hammond, London, reprint.

The Front Page; Samuel French, New York.

The Iron Gate of Jack & Charlie's "21," Jack Kriendler Memorial Fund, New York. Includes "To Jack" by BH:

This dizzy tavern is overrun
With muttering Fascists and camouflaged Reds,
All tying on an identical bun.
And Genius and Wizard are so many heads
Of Gothamite cattle at Twenty One. . . .

1951

"Wistfully Yours," *Theatre Arts*, July.
"Cinderella from Cedar Rapids," *Collier's*, November 3rd.
"Guilty," *Ellery Queen's Mystery Magazine*.
The Moon Is Blue, play by F. Hugh Herbert, intro. by BH; Random House, New York.

1952

"Swindler's Luck," *Saturday Evening Post*, January 12th.
"Romeo and Juliet," *Esquire*, June.
Cutie, A Warm Mamma, by BH and Maxwell Bodenheim, with a previously unpublished intro. by Bodenheim; Boar's Head Books (Samuel Roth), New York, reprint.
The World's Best Doctor Stories, ed. by N. Fabricant and H. Werner; Garden City Books, Garden City, N.Y. Includes "Miracle of the 15 Murderers" by BH.

1953

Hazel Flagg, book by BH, music by Jule Styne, lyrics by Bob Hilliard; Hart Stenographic Bureau; February 11th.
The Fabulous Fanny, Norman Katkov; Alfred A. Knopf, New York. Includes a chapter by Hecht on Fanny Brice.
The Little Review Anthology, ed. by Margaret Anderson; Hermitage House, New York. Includes "The American Family" and "Autumn Song" by BH.

1954

"Sex in Hollywood," *Esquire*, March.
"My Story," biography of Marilyn Monroe ghostwritten by BH; *The Empire News*, Manchester, England; serialized from April through August.
"Mystery of the Fabulous Laundryman," *Ellery Queen's Mystery Magazine*, June.
"The Tired Horse," *Esquire*, September.

"Gertie," *The Rotarian*, October. Excerpt from *A Child of the Century*.

"Sic Transit," *Esquire*, December.

A Child of the Century; Simon & Schuster, New York; Books Abridged, New York, 111 pp. Also included: *Mary Anne* by Daphne du Maurier; *Journey to the Far Amazon* by Alain Gheerbrant; *Forty Plus and Fancy Free* by Emily Kimbrough.

Manhattan: Stories from the Heart of a Great City, ed. by Seymour Krim; Bantam Books, New York. Includes "Mystery of the Fabulous Laundryman" by BH.

1955

"Rehearsal for Murder," *Ellery Queen's Mystery Magazine*, January. Reprint of "Guilty" from 1951.

A Child of the Century; Signet Books, New York, reprint.

The Empire City: A Treasury, ed. by Alexander Klein; Rinehart, New York. Includes "Don Juan in New York" by BH.

The Front Page; Samuel French, New York.

1956

"Eulogy for Charles MacArthur," April 23rd.

"The Tired Horse," *Ellery Queen's Mystery Magazine*, August.

Anthology of Best Short-Short Stories, vol. 7, ed. by R. Oberfirst; Oberfirst Publications, Ocean City, N.J. Includes "The Tired Horse" by BH.

1957

"Bosoms Away," *Esquire*, July.

Charlie: The Improbable Life and Times of Charles MacArthur, intro. by Helen Hayes (MacArthur); Harper & Bros., New York.

Great Stories About Show Business, ed. by J. D. Lewis; Coward-McCann, New York. Includes "Actor's Blood" by BH.

1958

"Chicago Night's Entertainment," *Ellery Queen's Mystery Magazine*, July. Originally published in the *Chicago Daily News* and in *1001 Afternoons in Chicago* as "Sgt. Kuzick's Waterloo."

"Chicago: Circa 1920," *Saturday Review*, November 15th.

"Wanted—a New God," *Esquire*, November.

"Hooray for the Bad Taste Kid," *Esquire*, December.

The Passionate Playgoer, ed. by George Oppenheimer. Includes "MacArthur" and "Trapdoor Billy."

1959

"No Room for Vice," *Playboy,* January.
"Some Slightly Crazy People," *Saturday Evening Post,* March 28th.
"Elegy for Wonderland," *Esquire,* March.
The Sensualists; Julian Messner, New York; Dell, New York, reprint.
A Treasury of Ben Hecht: Collected Stories and Other Writings; Crown, New York.
Treasury of Modern Jewish Stories. Includes "God Is Good to a Jew" by BH.

1960

"Ballad of Newspaper Critics," *Saturday Review,* June 18th.
"Hollywood Danse Macabre," *Playboy,* November.
Anthology of Ellery Queen's Mystery Magazine. Includes "Rehearsal for Murder" by BH.
A Child of the Century; New American Library, New York, reprint.
Concerning a Woman of Sin: Nine of the World's Great Writers Explore the Face of Hollywood, ed. by Daniel Talbot; Fawcett World Library, New York. Contains stories by BH, John O'Hara, William Faulkner, Christopher Isherwood, F. Scott Fitzgerald, William Saroyan, Irwin Shaw, Budd Schulberg, and Ring Lardner. (See: *Concerning a Woman of Sin,* 1969.)
The Sensualists; Anthony Blond, London, first British edition; Mondadori, Rome, first Italian edition.

1961

"Nose for Noose," *Saturday Review,* January 21st.
"A Jackpot of Corpses," *Playboy,* March.
"George S. Kaufman," *Saturday Review,* June.
"The Man Who Reported the Roar of the Roaring Twenties Sizes Up the TV Version," *TV Guide,* November 4th.
Concerning a Woman of Sin: Nine of the World's Great Writers Explore the Face of Hollywood, ed. by Daniel Talbot; A Consul Anthology, World Distributors, London; first British edition. (See: *Concerning a Woman of Sin,* 1969.)
Elegy in Manhattan, by George Jessel, intro. by BH; Holt, Rinehart and Winston, New York.
Perfidy; Julian Messner, New York; 1st and 2nd printings.
The Sensualists; Four Square Books, London, reprint; transl. into Portuguese by Luiz Carlos Branco; Sobraces, Saõ Paulo, first Brazilian edition; first Japanese edition.

1962

"Hollywood's Gift to America," *Saturday Review*, January.
"Clara," *Playboy*, March.
"Queen Dido," *Playboy*, May.
"The Bandit," *Playboy*, July.
"Miracle of the 15 Murderers," *Ellery Queen's Mystery Magazine*, September.
"The Fairy," *Playboy*, November.
The Front Page, Les Oeuvres libres, no. 191, Paris.
Spéciale Dernière, adap. by Jacques Deval, *L'Avant-Scène du théâtre*, no. 262, Paris; trans. of *The Front Page*.

1963

"The Bum," *Playboy*, May.
"Letitia," *Playboy*, July.
"The Noble Experiment," *Playboy*, December.
Ellery Queen Anthology. Includes "Actor's Blood" by BH.
Erik Dorn, intro. by Nelson Algren, *Chicago in Fiction* (Saul Bellow, advisory editor); University of Chicago Press, reprint, with a previously unpublished intro.
Gaily, Gaily; Doubleday, Garden City, N.Y.
"The Nymph Who Lost Her Head," *Argosy*.
"Ben Hecht on a Late Bohemian: Bodenheim Becomes 'Winkelberg'—Back Here at the Old Stand," interview with BH by John Wilcock, *The Village Voice Reader*; Grove Press, New York.

1964

"The Sunset Kid," *Ellery Queen's Mystery Magazine*, January. Includes reprint of "Swindler's Luck" by BH.
The Sensualists; Dell Publishing, New York, May, reprint.
The Counterpoint Anthology, interview with BH by Roy Newquist; Rand Mc-Nally, September.
The Counterpoint Anthology; Heinemann, London.
Letters from Bohemia, Doubleday, Garden City, N.Y.
Concerning a Woman of Sin; Mayflower Books, London. (See: *Concerning a Woman of Sin*, 1969.)
Gaily, Gaily; Elek Books, London, first British edition.
In the Midst of Death; Mayflower Books, London. (See: *Concerning a Woman of Sin*, 1969.)

1965

Gaily, Gaily; New American Library, New York, reprint.
Letters from Bohemia; Hammond, London, first British edition.

1966

The Sensualists; Four Square Books, London, November, reprint.
Gaily, Gaily; Four Square Books, London, reprint.
Masterpieces of Suspense; Hart Publishing Co., New York. Includes "Swindler's Luck" and "Miracle of the 15 Murderers" by BH.

1967

Ellery Queen Anthology. Includes "The Rival Dummy" by BH.

1968

The Last Bookman; Candlelight Press, Chicago. Collection of essays and reminiscences on Vincent Starrett; includes "Adventures of the Literate Ghost" by BH.

1969

Gaily, Gaily, movie edition (with 8 pp. of stills); New American Library, New York, September.
Concerning a Woman of Sin; Mayflower Books, London, reprint. *Avon Modern Short Story Monthly* published 2 vols. of BH stories—*Ben Hecht: Selected Great Stories* (1943) and *Concerning a Woman of Sin and Other Stories* (1947); although some of the same stories appeared in these vols. as in *The Collected Stories of Ben Hecht*, *The Collected Stories* was not the source. In 1945, Editions for the Armed Services issued *Concerning a Woman of Sin and Other Stories*, a paperback collection of ten stories plus the intro. from *The Collected Stories*, published the same year. Fawcett, in 1960, and World Distributors, in 1961, published *Concerning a Woman of Sin: Nine of the World's Great Writers Explore the Face of Hollywood*, which took its title from the BH story and included only that Hecht story. In 1964, Mayflower Books, issued 2 vols. of BH stories, also selected from *The Collected Stories—Concerning a Woman of Sin* and *In the Midst of Death*.
Ellery Queen's Minimysteries; World Books, New York. Includes "Crime Without Passion" by BH.
The Sensualists; Four Square Books, London, reprint.

1970

"The Incomplete Life of Mickey Cohen," *Scanlon's*, vol. 1, no. 1, March.
A *Child of the Century*; Ballantine Books, New York, reprint.
Ellery Queen Anthology. Includes "Mystery of the Fabulous Laundryman"
    by BH.

1971

Ellery Queen Anthology. Includes "Crime Without Passion" by BH.
The Movies: An American Idiom, Arthur McClure; Fairleigh Dickinson University Press, Rutherford, N.J. Includes "Elegy for Wonderland" by BH.

1972

Ellery Queen Anthology. Includes "Miracle of the 15 Murderers" by BH.

1973

"The Mystery of the Man with the Accordion," *Liberty*, vol. 1, no. 11, Winter;
    reprint of the BH story from 1931.
Scarface; *L'Avant-Scène du Cinéma*, no. 132, Paris.

1974

"Chicago's Greatest Newspaperman," *Onstage*, vol. 1, bk. 4, December; about
    Walter Howie.
My Story; Stein and Day, New York. Purportedly Marilyn Monroe's autobiography, actually ghosted by BH in 1954; published in two parts in *McCall's*, July
    and August.

1975

The Front Page, novelization by Ira Wallach; Warner Paperback Library.

1977

Best Film Plays 1945, ed. by Dudley Nichols and John Gassner; Garland
    Publishing, New York, reprint of the 1946 Crown edition. Includes the
    scenario of *Spellbound*.

1978

Fantazius Mallare; Harcourt Brace Jovanovich, New York, reprint.
The Kingdom of Evil; Harcourt Brace Jovanovich, New York, reprint.

1981

On the Twentieth Century, book and lyrics of the 1978 Broadway musical by Betty
Comden and Adolph Green, based on plays by Ben Hecht, Charles
MacArthur, and Bruce Millholland; Drama Book Specialists, New York.

1982

The Innovators: 16 Portraits of the Famous and the Infamous, by Jay Robert Nash;
Regnery Gateway, Chicago. Includes "Ben Hecht: A Writer for All Seasons,"
an interview with BH originally published in the *Chicago Literary Times*,
November 1962.

1985

A Child of the Century, intro. by Sidney Zion; Primus, Donald I. Fine, Inc., New
York. Reprint with a previously unpublished introduction; hardcover and
trade paperback editions published simultaneously.

INDEX

Index

Index

Index